Biography of a Mexican Crucifix

Biography of a Mexican Crucifix

Lived Religion and Local Faith from the Conquest to the Present

JENNIFER SCHEPER HUGHES

OXFORD
UNIVERSITY PRESS

2010

OXFORD
UNIVERSITY PRESS

Oxford University Press, Inc., publishes works that further
Oxford University's objective of excellence
in research, scholarship, and education.

Oxford   New York
Auckland   Cape Town   Dar es Salaam   Hong Kong   Karachi
Kuala Lumpur   Madrid   Melbourne   Mexico City   Nairobi
New Delhi   Shanghai   Taipei   Toronto

With offices in
Argentina   Austria   Brazil   Chile   Czech Republic   France   Greece
Guatemala   Hungary   Italy   Japan   Poland   Portugal   Singapore
South Korea   Switzerland   Thailand   Turkey   Ukraine   Vietnam

Published by Oxford University Press, Inc.
198 Madison Avenue, New York, New York 10016

www.oup.com

Oxford is a registered trademark of Oxford University Press

Library of Congress Cataloging-in-Publication Data
Hughes, Jennifer Scheper.
Biography of a Mexican crucifix : lived religion and local faith
from the conquest to the present / Jennifer Scheper Hughes.
   p. cm.
Includes bibliographical references and index.
ISBN 978-0-19-536706-5; 978-0-19-536707-2 (pbk.)
1. Mexico—Church history. 2. Catholic Church—Mexico—
History. 3. Mexico—Religious life and customs—History.
4. Crosses—Mexico—Morelos (State). 5. Jesus Christ—Crucifixion.
I.Title.
BX1428.3.H84 2010
282'.72—dc22   2009012196

Printed in the United States of America
on acid-free paper

To You, Señor, as promised,

and to my own sweet saints:

Santos, Santiago, Salvador, and Raphael Benedito

Preface

Behind the Curtain: A Manifesto for Popular Religion

The work that follows is an invitation to draw near to the Cristo
Aparecido, the "Christ Appeared," a sculpted image of the crucified
Christ on the cross that is almost five centuries old. And likewise,
through him, this study invites the reader to draw near to his loving
devotees, in particular to the devout of Totolapan, today a small
peasant community of indigenous and European origin, in the
northernmost corner of the Mexican state of Morelos. For them, the
Cristo Aparecido is not a statue but instead their beloved patron saint,
a manifestation of the divine, around which their collective spiritual
life is organized and finds its focus. Their faith in their Cristo is both
the starting point for and the locus of this study.

But how is it possible for a scholarly project to accompany a
people, even if only for a short while, on their journey of faith? Must
an academic work such as this one necessarily distance itself from
the faith of the people whom it takes as its object of study, lest the
authority of the scholarship be diminished by the association? These
questions are particularly poignant and pointed when local, popular,
or "folk" religiosities are at the center of inquiry, as these have been
subjected to many violences and violations, literal and figurative, of
the military, missiological, political, theological, and scholarly sort,
not least in Mexico. This is certainly the perception of the local
devotees of Totolapan, many of whom feel that their faith has been
vulnerable to offense and injury over the course of centuries, in the
present moment most of all.

Popular devotion to images seems in many instances to have made poor and marginal communities even more vulnerable to damaging outside interventions. Consider, for example, the eighteenth-century adolescent mystic of Chiapas, Mexico, María de la Candelaria.[1] Inspired by visions and speaking as the mouthpiece for a miraculous image of Mary called the Virgen del Rosario, the young *india* galvanized an indigenous rebellion. Neither the girl nor the image itself was ever actually seen by the many pilgrims who came to pay homage; a makeshift curtain, a *petate*, shielded them from view in the small hermitage where they made their home.

Fray Simón de Lara, parish priest and *doctrinero* of the pueblo, led the charge against the faith of his flock in 1712. Certain that it was in fact a "pagan idol" that occupied the dark space behind the curtain, Lara sought to expose María de la Candelaria as a diabolic fraud and a hoax. In the wake of the government troops who had cleared the way, Fray Simón de Lara picked his way among the recently massacred bodies of those who had assembled to protect the Virgin and her spokeswoman, and reached the front of the *ermita*. There he stopped to preach a triumphant sermon: "yes, in this very ermita, behind the petate, you placed your idol. And it is here that you approached to pay it homage, to sell your soul to the Devil. You spilled out holy oils upon its monstrous face. . . . Remember now that I warned you of the great deception of María de la Candelaria, but you did not want to listen."[2] With the ermita surrounded and the plaza of the pueblo overtaken, the soldiers inside pulled back the curtain to discover not María, who had fled, and not an "idol," but only an a "much-adorned altar upon which had been placed the Virgen del Rosario with the infant Jesus in her arms."[3] Government troops and the local priests conspired together to violently eradicate this local expression of Roman Catholicism.

In his astute reflections on the cult, Mexican historian Juan Pedro Viqueira Albán admires both the faith and the courageous rebellion of the people of San Juan Evangelista Cancuc; but he also grapples with his own disbelief about what is really "behind the petate."[4] Here the modern scholar's own doubts dimly echo the ultimately devastating apprehensions of Fray Simon de Lara. Inga Clendinnen was the first to caution the historian of colonial Latin America against treading the dangerous path of the missionary. As he attempted to isolate the native from the Christian practices of his neophyte charges, the colonial friar was "forced by the nature of his peculiar vocation to subject a lived faith to vivisection, carving it into transportable, stateable, teachable propositions: a disturbing, dispiriting, and finally effectively disabling business."[5] And indeed, it may be that the critical, questioning approach of the modern (and yes, even the postmodern) scholar, often puzzled before the faith of the poor, is exceeded in their skepticism only by that of the overly zealous cleric, himself plagued by doubts about the legitimacy of his flock's "religion."[6]

I have struggled here to avoid such an approach. Instead, assuming that their faith has an integrity of its own, I have tempered my own impulse to distance myself from that which the people of Totolapan have taken up as their dearest belief. It is my earnest hope that nothing I write here has the potential to weaken or challenge them in their devotion to the Cristo Aparecido. For them, I hope this work adds to the treasury of knowledge about their Cristo.

Two distinct intellectual movements in the last third of the twentieth century offer me a way forward: the work of subaltern historians and that of liberation theologians. As they forged their field, subaltern studies historians of India looked for ways to shape their work so as to reflect the agency of subordinate social groups "as makers of their own destiny."[7] Acknowledging this agency obliged these historians to "stretch the category of the political [beyond] the logic of secular-rational calculations inherent in the modern conception of the political," as Dipesh Chakrabarty so aptly puts it.[8] This was particularly true because "the peasant-but-modern political sphere was not bereft of the agency of gods, spirits, and other supernatural beings."[9] Boldly stated, taking seriously the agency of the subaltern may also require taking seriously the agency of the divine, as for the subaltern so often the actions of God and the spirit are coeval with the human.[10]

This sentiment finds a powerful parallel in the work of Latin American liberation theologians writing in the 1970s and 1980s. After largely overcoming an initial and nearly disastrous skepticism about popular religious practice (an ambivalence that I will discuss at some length in chapter 6), liberation theologians and their intellectual heirs, Latino theologians, came to see their task, in part, as articulating the *sensus fidelium*, the theological legitimacy of popular ways of knowing. In their insistence on a "preferential option for the poor," liberation theologians have asserted that the resources of the Church should be channeled into slums, shantytowns, and *favelas*. But they have also called scholars to reread history from the point of view of the "condemned of the earth": in this new approach, it was "the Indian, the peasant, the African slave, the exploited classes, [who] would be the hermeneutic starting point for history."[11]

Here, then, I intend to venture with all respect behind the curtain. Not to "lift the veil" in order to expose fallacy and fraud (as did the soldiers at María de la Candelaria's ermita, or Dorothy in the palace of the Wizard of Oz), but in order to take seriously a people's faith on their own terms and for its own sake. This is because, as I will explain later, for believers themselves the drape is there neither to create an illusion nor to obscure, but rather to highlight the presence of the sacred within.

And so I have allowed the commitments and concerns of devotees to guide and shape my focus here. For example, several Mexican scholars before me have taken up the study of Fray Antonio de Roa, the sixteenth-century Spanish Augustinian friar to whom the Cristo Aparecido first appeared. Roa has been the periodic object of scholarly-clerical interest and fascination from the close of the sixteenth century. Here, however, though Roa appears as a protagonist in the first and second chapters, he soon falls into the margins of the story, as he does for today's devotees. For one who accompanies them in their faith, the real protagonist of this narrative is the Cristo himself, and his journey over five centuries. So the invitation into his story will include, at times, asking the reader to avert their questioning, skeptical gaze, to pause for a moment as the devout humbly cast their own eyes downward in deference to the divine.

While I attempt to approximate the faith of the people of Totolapan in relation to their Cristo, this study is not confessional in nature. It does not represent a statement of my own faith and belief. Nor do I seek to represent solely the perspective of devotees. I offer here, to the best of my abilities, a synoptic narrative. That is, I labor to construct a comprehensive view of events pieced together from disparate and varied perspectives. I strive to allow multiple voices, including scholarly ones, to flesh out the story of the Cristo. However, I also try whenever possible to give the people of Totolapan the last word. The primacy of their relationship with the image makes them, as far as I am concerned, the ultimate authority on all matters pertaining to him. This is so not because in their spiritual practice they have access to a direct experience of the divine, unmediated by language, culture, and historical contingency. Rather it is this very contingency that makes theirs the privileged voice in this book.

This dual commitment to scholarly integrity and to the integrity of the Totolapans' faith and belief has shaped and defined the writing styles that I have employed. The writing, at times, is deliberately seductive; specifically intended to draw the reader in, to help him or her imagine, for example, what it might be like to join the friar on his knees before Christ, or to stand expectantly in the crowd among devotees as they wait for the procession of their Cristo to begin. But to those readers for whom such experiences remain inaccessible, I have offered other perspectives with which I hope they may be able to identify as an entry into this topic: the agnostics and skeptics that one occasionally encounters among the peasants of Totolapan, and the modern-minded priests and bishops that appear in the twentieth century. Some readers may find they identify most of all with the careful and respectful labors of the restorers and historians of the Instituto Nacional de Antropología e Historia, the Mexican governmental body dedicated to historical preservation of art, who collectively create an opening for the secular world's rapprochement with religious folk art and popular piety.

Acknowledgments

Many communities, scholarly and religious, helped this project to come to fruition. Without the generosity and trust of the people of Totolapan, this work would not have been possible. In particular, I acknowledge the assistance and support of the Flores family, especially Maricela Flores, director of culture for the municipality of Totolapan. Many offered of themselves, sharing personal recollections, providing on-the-spot explanations and clarifications, and granting me access to community records. Of these, I mention don Florentino Vergara by name: the shape of this book was revealed to me in the midst of a moving and illuminating conversation we shared that left us both with tears in our eyes. I hope that the profound respect that I have for the topic of this book is evident to the devotees of the Cristo Aparecido, and I offer my deepest apologies for anything that I have misrepresented or misunderstood.

In Tepoztlán, I was graced with many kindnesses. I thank Sarita and Shanti for their hospitality and Sebastian Belaustegui for his beautiful photographs. The women of the weekly prayer group to the Señor de Chalma, especially doña Clara, accepted my presence and even my stumbled prayers. I extend a particular note of thanks to Pamela Voekel and Bethany Moreton, for finding me in the first place and then supporting this project from beginning to its close. The community of scholars that they, with Elliot Young, unite annually at the Tepoztlán Institute for Transnational History of the Americas was a hospitable, helpful, and inspiring intellectual context in which to share the first drafted pages of this book.

At the Instituto Nacional de Antropología e Historia, Teresa Loera, Luis Miguel Morayta Mendoza, and José Nao generously offered their time and expertise, as did Padre Baltasar Lopez, minister of sacred art at the Diocese of Cuernavaca. Padre Angel Sánchez Campos, at the Paroquia de Yautepec, allowed me access to his extensive personal archive of materials from the episcopacy of don Sergio Méndez Arceo. Staff and librarians at the Archivo General de la Nación and the Bancroft Library were patient and obliging.

The Episcopal Church Foundation, the Doctoral Council of the Graduate Theological Union, and the Academic Senate of the University of California, Riverside, helped to fund this project. María Lupita Hernández Alamilla and Harold Morales provided research assistance, and Jessica Delgado interrupted her own research and writing to puzzle over colonial documents with me. Paul Ramírez shared with me his brilliant unpublished work on epidemic disease in Mexico City. The profound and priestly Sara Miles generously read and commented an early draft of the manuscript. I also thank supportive colleagues from Mt. Holyoke College and the University of California, Riverside, but especially Andrew Jacobs and Catherine Allgor, midwives in many ways. Without the affection and care graciously provided for my children by Mrs. Willa Davis and the teachers of the UCR Child Development Center, this book might not have come so soon to completion.

I conclude with an expression of deepest gratitude to those who were present at the inception of this project. William B. Taylor first drew my intention to the inquisition case that interrogated the Cristo's origins, and then received and responded to my long and enthusiastic missives from the field. The scholar-visionary, Rosemary Radford Ruether, has been a most excellent

supporter, colleague, and friend. Eduardo Fernández, S.J., allowed himself to
be persuaded to make the rigorous pilgrimage on foot from Tepoztlán to
Chalma in my stead. David Sweet has engaged with me in a twenty-year-long
conversation about the faith and struggles of the people of Latin America.

I also recognize Brother M. Thomas Shaw, beloved mentor and guide.
With regret he released me from other responsibilities so that I might finish
this book.

No small offer of thanksgiving is due to the poets, writers, observers, inter-
preters and artists of my extended family: to my parents, Nancy and Michael;
my siblings, Sarah and Nathanael; and to George Scheper and Diane Ganz,
Jeanne Scheper and Tiffany Willoughby-Herard, and David Scheper—not just
kin, but kindred spirits.

Whatever depth and accuracy this work possesses are largely due to those
that I have acknowledged here; its foibles are all my own.

Contents

Note on Translations

All translations from Spanish texts, colonial or modern, are my own unless otherwise noted. In many instances I provide the original Spanish in the corresponding notes. In my transcription of colonial materials, I have left original inconsistencies in spelling and grammar largely intact.

Biography of a Mexican Crucifix

I

Introduction

The Iconography of Suffering

The Mexican venerates a bleeding and humiliated Christ, a Christ
who has been beaten by the soldiers and condemned by the judges,
because he sees in him a transfigured image of his own identity. And
this brings to mind Cuauhtémoc, the young Aztec emperor who was
dethroned, tortured and murdered by Cortés.

—Octavio Paz, *Labyrinth of Solitude*

This book is a history of popular devotion to a single, carved
image of Christ crucified, known by his devotees as the Cristo
Aparecido, or the Christ Appeared, spanning five centuries of
Mexican history. The three-foot-tall crucifix, sculpted from
maguey, a plant native to the New World, depicts the bloody and
tortured Jesus at the very moment of his death. The missionary
friars who first discovered the image in the mid-sixteenth century
declared it to be the most poignantly beautiful and graphic
depiction of Christ's suffering on the cross they had ever seen. It
quickly became one of the most celebrated religious images in
New Spain, widely revered for its miraculous healings, and a
model, a prototype, for subsequent devotions to other miraculous
images of Christ on the cross. Today the Cristo Aparecido is, above
all, the beloved patron saint of the people of Totolapan (also
known as Totolapa, or Totolapam), a small, rural community of
some seven thousand mestizo peasants of indigenous Nahua and
Spanish origin, located in the *altos de Morelos*, the mountainous
northernmost corner of the state of Morelos. Because of its
documented early-colonial origins, in the twentieth century
the government declared the image to be part of the national
patrimony of Mexico. It is among the oldest extant New World
crucifixes, and it has been the object of uninterrupted,
continuous devotion since its origins (see figure 1.1).

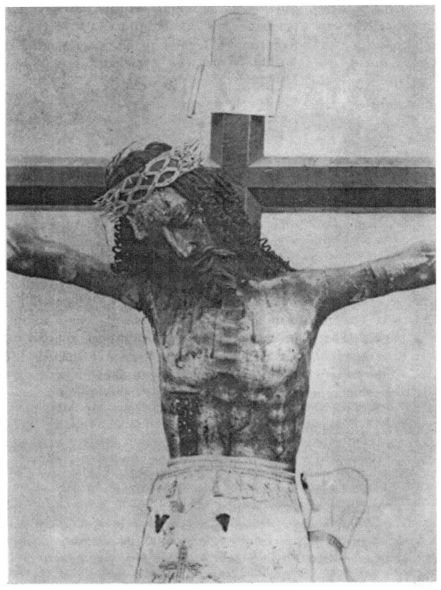

Un acercamiento de la milagrosa imagen del Cristo de Totolapan, para apreciar mejor su belleza.

FIGURE I.I. The *Cristo Aparecido*. Mexico, circa 1969. Photograph by Lauro López Beltrán. From *Fray Antonio de Roa, Taumaturgo penitente*, 2nd ed. Mexico City: Editorial Jus, 1969. Reproduced by permission of Editorial Jus.

Simultaneously a diachronic study of local religion, a work of cultural history, and a creative study of material culture, this history of the Totolapan Cristo is, most of all, a biography. The suggestion that the history of an image might be recounted as the story of a life highlights devotees' own relationship to their *santo*; they attribute to him *animus*—existence, being, and agency.[1] This biography, or object history if you prefer, is made possible by the miraculous, or exceptional, or at the very least unlikely survival of this material object through crisis and calamity as well as through more than four hundred and fifty years of active devotional use.

The story told here is a chronological but not exhaustive account of the life of the Cristo Aparecido. The constellation of events that constitute this loosely bound set of "recollections" has been determined as much by the sources available for recuperating the image's nearly five-hundred-year history as by the devotees' estimation of what events really mattered and, finally, by my own perception of what might be a rich vein of human experience for exploration. Perhaps for this reason, the narrative strays away from the orderliness and seamlessness suggested by the biographic form, offering in its place a rough assemblage of moments rife with meaning: pain, joy, loss, beauty, and danger. I guide the reader through several critical moments of the Cristo's history: its miraculous appearance to a community of newly converted indigenous Christians and their friars in the Indian pueblo of Totolapan in 1543;[2] the covert removal of the image to Mexico City in 1583; the conditions of the Cristo's celebrated return to its community of origin over two hundred and fifty years later, in 1863; and, in the twentieth century, its encounter with modernizing reforms coming from within the Roman Catholic Church, including efforts to reframe the Cristo's significance within the politically radical theology of liberation. Each instance is an opportunity to explore key motifs and problems in the religious history of Mexico. Thus, the biography of the Cristo becomes, to some degree, a microcosm of this varied and variegated religious landscape. Through him we observe the way in which national crises and global movements play upon local contexts and influence a diminutive object. In a complimentary fashion, history as refracted through the Cristo Aparecido reveals an almost prismatic local diversity, which makes any effort at generalization difficult if not impossible.

The Cristo of Totolapan has found its deepest resonance and most persistent devotion among indigenous and indigenous-descended communities. For this reason, underlying this entire book is the following proposition: at all points in history indigenous Christianity is complex, diverse, dynamic, contested, but generally of indigenous making and design; at once authentically indigenous and fully Christian. That is, in the cult to the Cristo Aparecido I find a profound local experience of Christian gospel. At the same time I regard the santo as a work of Native American sacred art and the religious complex that surrounds him as an expression of indigenous religion. These conclusions emerge precisely from the exercise of remaining "close" to devotees in my interpretation and analysis, as I describe in the preface to this book.

In making this set of claims, I am arguing against a variety of established conventions for viewing popular religiosity. Latin American Christianity is stunningly plastic. Perhaps owing to the very ambiguity of its colonial origins, it is characterized by an intense valuing of tradition and, simultaneously and paradoxically, by a tremendous capacity to absorb new ideas and practices. Although in theory Roman Catholicism is an exclusive religion (and the Christian god a jealous god) in practice and on the ground in Latin America and in other colonial settings it has proven to be surprisingly expansive, inclusive, and accommodating; not only able to encompass and absorb religious practices external to the tradition but also relatively pliant and available for religious innovation from within. There are many labels and metaphors that have been applied in the effort to describe this complex reality. The term "syncretism" is the one that has dominated; indeed, even many of the residents of Totolapan, where the Cristo today makes his home, understand theirs to be a "syncretic" religion (they use the technical term), derived from both indigenous and European religious traditions. The popular, "syncretic" faith of Latin America has been derided by critics from many camps: colonial priests saw in the "excesses" of popular religion a lingering idolatry and diabolism.[3] In the twentieth century, social scientists of a Marxist persuasion have labeled the corresponding worldview a politically paralyzing "false consciousness." Most recently, politicized indigenous communities asserting a pure indigeneity have renounced Indian Christian practice as nothing more than a necessary (and temporary) compromise with colonialism, bereft of authenticity. "Syncretic" religion is therefore a bastard religion; by all counts "an unholy mixture of paganism, peasant magic and half-baked Christian doctrine."[4] Recently, more sympathetic scholars, hoping to avoid the simplistic and reductionist interpretations that often accompanied use of this descriptor, have preferred the scientific label "hybridity" and the racial term *mestizaje* to describe the complexity of Latin American Christian practice and belief.

Though they might have willed it to be otherwise, the history of the Cristo Aparecido does not just involve the lay believers of Totolapan and other humble devotees of the region. That is, local religion never functions in a vacuum, independently of larger religious and secular institutions. The fate of the Cristo is also determined by, and connected to, bodies and individuals acting within the "institutional" Church: the Inquisition, the religious orders and their friars, bishops and parish priests. Throughout this history, many friars emerge as protagonists; these frequently worked to insure the preservation of the Cristo and his illustrious history, even as they have periodically been at odds with his community of local believers in Totolapan. The Cristo's fate is also wedded to the history of the various *conventos* and *iglesias* (monasteries and churches) where he has made his home. Consequently his biography also becomes a story about the rise and fall of the conventos and the religious orders in Mexico. Finally, in addition to these ecclesial institutions and actors, the history of the Cristo Aparecido is influenced by secular forces, most of all by the institutions of a revolutionary state that has long struggled to negotiate the meaning and place of the Church and its religious objects, like the Cristo Aparecido, within a nationalist and secular framework.

What I have to say in the pages that follow about the meaning and nature of Mexican devotion to the crucified Christ is in some ways utterly specific to the singular Cristo Aparecido. At the same time, though the focus of this study is on the life of one particular crucifix, it is also a story of his *cristos hermanos*. These "kindred christs" are the other crucifixes that devotees understand to be "siblings" of the Cristo Aparecido, either because they seem to bear a resemblance to theirs in history or appearance or because they are images from neighboring communities included in the same fiesta cycle. I have appropriated the term to include the entire panoply of Mexican cristos. Therefore, in some respects, my conclusions about this particular image and his devotees apply to crucifixes in active devotional use in other communities throughout Mexico and Latin America.

The Indigenous Body and the Body of Christ: Crucifixes as Narratives of Indigenous Suffering

> The tremendous power of Mexican christs is that they express the pain of an oppressed people.
>
> —Enrique Dussel, *Historia general de la Iglesia en América Latina*

Perhaps the single most salient feature of Mexican Christianity in the first three centuries of its history was the development of a deep and multifaceted relationship between the Indians of the New World and the religious images of the Christian pantheon, crucifixes most of all. This book explores the complexities, paradoxes, and poignancies of this relationship in detail and with specificity. The intimacy of the relationship between indigenous Mexicans and their many cristos has led modern observers to conclude that the crucified God was inevitably a potent religious symbol for the people of Mexico: an afflicted deity for a profoundly afflicted people. At some points in the history of Mexico, an interpretation based on the conflation of the indigenous body with the body of Christ has, indeed, emerged as meaningful in local engagement with crucifixion imagery. However, at least as frequently, this theological association has been of little consequence for local belief and practice.

Images of Christ crucified have been at the center of indigenous devotion in Latin America from the very beginnings of Christianity in the New World, achieving a lasting vibrancy within indigenous Christianity through the present. Shrines to various manifestations of Jesus' suffering flourished in larger percentage in the colonies than in Spain itself. This was by design: the Franciscan missionaries in particular, and the mendicant orders in general, intended that the New World would be the stage for a purer and truer Church, one grounded in a Christ-centered faith. Today, this continues to be the case, as local devotions to artistic images depicting the suffering of Jesus are more common and numerous than those honoring images of the Virgin Mary, including the Virgin of Guadalupe, in much of Mexico.[5]

Nevertheless, in the last decade, it is Guadalupe, the Mexican mother of God, who has captured the imagination and the affections, it would appear, of historians, anthropologists, and theologians. At least a dozen recent books and literally countless articles from many disciplines engage the topic.[6] Meanwhile, in spite of and utterly indifferent to this scholarly neglect, local devotions to images of Christ's suffering continue to rival (and often surpass) those to the Virgin Mary.[7] While Guadalupe herself has come to symbolize, among other things, the incorporation of an indigenous past into a secular, nationalist identity, crucifixes have proven largely resistant and inaccessible to a nationalist project. For the most part, the images themselves and the devotions surrounding them have been regarded with ambivalence (and sometimes outright suspicion) by secular and theological scholars alike. These have tended to give the subject wide berth, perhaps because they find the crucifixes embarrassingly baroque or even artless, or perhaps because they perceive the meanings of these crucifixes to be more obscure or more problematic than the less troubling—and since the eighteenth century politically momentous—Virgin of Guadalupe.

This is not to say that the overwhelming presence of crucifixes in the religious life of Mexico has not on occasion garnered the attention of artists and intellectuals. The unchallenged consensus explaining both the original reception of the images in the colonial period and the lasting vibrancy of these Christ devotions is the one summarized so jarringly by Octavio Paz in the epigraph that opens this introduction: that for the descendents of Nahua-speaking Indians, the symbol of the crucifix rehearses unceasingly the story of the conquest of Mexico. Enrique Dussel rephrases the same sentiment: the power and longevity of the crucifix in the Catholicism of mestizo Mexico has its origins in an immediate and unmediated indigenous identification with Christ's suffering in which they have seen mirrored their own. Appealing to a notion of psychological catharsis, art historian Pál Kelemen concludes that "the Indians, now degraded to the lowest caste in their own land, might well have found release for their emotional tension by embracing the realistic agonizing Christ."[8] This explanation for the theological and cultural significance of Mexican cristos is widely accepted and circulated today by outside observers.[9]

It is to the famed sixteenth-century "Protector of the Indians," the Dominican friar Bartolomé de las Casas, that we can attribute this original interpretation. Las Casas not only catalogued and decried the violent destruction of the indigenous people of the New World but he also argued tirelessly for the return of their political sovereignty. The Indians were fully human, Las Casas reasoned before the Spanish court, and authentic Christian conversion could not be achieved by conquest and violent imposition. There was "one way" to

FIGURE I.2. *Bartolomé de las Casas*, by Br. Robert Lentz, OFM. Icon, United States, 1992. By permission of Trinity Stores.

FIGURE 1.3. *Our Lord of Charitable Works.* Guaman Poma de Ayala. Adapted from a drawing dating from Peru, 1615, in the collection of the Royal Library of Denmark; used by permission.

convert the Indians of the New World, and that was that they must have political sovereignty and complete freedom to accept or reject the religion as a set of propositions and doctrines, without compulsion or coercion.[10] But this was not the reality of New Spain, the tireless advocate inveighed, where the Indians were so violated and abused that they had become themselves "scourged Christs": "For I leave in the Indies Jesus Christ, our God, scourged and afflicted and buffeted and crucified, not once but millions of times, on the part of all the Spaniards who ruin and destroy these people and deprive them of the space they require for their conversion and repentance, depriving them of life before their time."[11] The representation of Las Casas by the modern iconographer Robert Lentz captures this theme: the friar demands a halt to the oppression of the suffering Indians in the name of the suffering Christ (figure 1.2).

The Andean Indian chronicler Guaman Poma de Ayala most likely adopted this powerful association from Las Casas, who he much admired. His 1615 manuscript depicts a fiesta procession in honor of "Our Lord of Charitable Works" in which the profile of the crucified Christ is mirrored in the profile of the Indian who carries the processional image: sad, head bowed, defeated yet faithful still; the resemblance between the face of the Indian and the face of Christ is transparent (figure 1.3).[12]

Twentieth-century artists have echoed this colonial interpretation. The Mexican muralist José Clemente Orozco draws the analogy most starkly in his painting that adorns the walls of the National Preparatory School in Mexico. A subsequent lithograph based on the mural, "The Franciscan" (1929), shows a Spanish friar protectively and lovingly cradling the naked, wasted body of an Indian (figure 1.4). Clemente Orozco's image is, in essence, a pietà in which the friar stands in the place of the grieving Mary, and the Indian for the deceased body of Jesus, limp and lifeless in his mother's arms. The association of the suffering of Christ with the affliction of a colonized indigenous population also captured the artistic imagination of Mexican artist Francisco Goitia, as expressed in his provocatively titled painting "Tata Jesucristo" or "Papa Jesus Christ" (1927) (figure 1.5). In spite of the title, the familiar figure of Jesus himself is utterly absent from Goitia's rendering. Instead, the painting depicts two indigenous women in mourning; their bodies almost disappear into the dark and shadowed background of his canvas. Of one of his subjects all that is visible are her hands (which completely obscure her face), her feet, and the long, dark hair that shrouds her body. In an interview Goitia explained how he posed his models:

> I tried my models sitting this way and that, but no, I didn't feel it exactly right. At last I investigated everything I could about them. I then made them come and sit for me on the Day of the Dead, when of their own accord they would be dwelling on sorrow, and little by little I uncovered their sorrow and the revolution and their dead. And they writhed, and one turned her foot up in pain. Then I knew I had it! Those hands and feet gave their grief [its] genuine form. I would never have thought of it myself, but of course that is the way grief is, and so I was satisfied at last. They weep tears of our race, pain and tears our own and different from others. All the sorrow of Mexico is there.[13]

In Goitia's painting the suffering of Christ and the suffering of his indigenous models are collapsed together; it is the contorted, grieving Indian women who stand for Christ, and who carry the suffering of Mexico, much as Christ himself is said to bear the suffering of the world.

Beyond their passing acceptance of this centuries-long conflation of indigenous suffering with the suffering of Christ, modern scholars have been reluctant to offer sustained study and interpretation of the history, meaning, and significance of images of Christ for the faith of the Mexican people. For the most part, they have tended to concur that in the Latin American context

FIGURE I.4. *Franciscan* [San Francisco e indio]. Lithograph, Mexico, 1929. José Clemente Orozco. By permission of Fundación José Clemente Orozco.

FIGURE 1.5. *Tata Jesucristo.* Francisco Goitia. Oil on canvas, Mexico, 1926. By permission of Museo Nacional de Arte.

crucifixes are irretrievably linked to a narrative of suffering, violent subjugation, resignation, and passivity. Liberation theologians in particular have been
scathing in their criticism of the destructive power these images hold over
oppressed populations. However, these rhetorical statements are rarely backed
by substantive ethnographic, historical, or documentary evidence. This
unchallenged interpretation obscures a five-centuries-long process of contes-
tation and meaning-making in which clergy and Indians (and later mestizos)
alike struggled to shape and define the parameters of appropriate understanding of the crucifix.

Persuaded and intrigued by these artistic interpretations, I began research-
ing the topic of crucifix devotion in order to ground a broader inquiry into the
motif of suffering in Mesoamerican popular religion. I thought that a study
focusing on the meaning devotees made of these graphic representations of
human affliction would serve as a lens to understand indigenous efforts to negotiate, categorize, interpret, and survive their own experience of unprecedented suffering under conquest and colonial rule. Throughout the Cristo
Aparecido's biography the themes of suffering, violence, and vulnerability are
indeed rehearsed and reinvented. One of the salient dynamics that emerged in
my study is clerical preoccupation with the theme of the suffering of Jesus in

the face of alternate indigenous engagements. Throughout many centuries, including the most recent one, friars and priests have persisted in asserting an interpretation of the crucifix that dwells on torture, pain, the broken body, and death. More often than not, for the many friars, priests, and clerics to whom I will introduce the reader along the way, the Cristo Aparecido is embedded within a narrative of Christ's earthly passion, in light of which every inch, every surface, of the image can be understood, explained, and interpreted.

At the same time, there are many occasions on which these themes are muted or absent in devotion. In spite of the copious blood, torn skin, and exposed bones of the Cristo's gaunt and distorted corpse, the motif of suffering, whether human or divine, does not encompass all that his devotees have found meaningful, potent, or sacred within their image. For the believers of Totolapan today, for example, the narrative in which their Cristo comfortably rests is only very secondarily one of Christ's passion as remembered in the Gospels. Rather, the primary story they recount concerns how and where the image appeared, where it has traveled, what blessings it has poured out upon them, and what signs of life and *animus* it has shown. Today the theme of beauty often emerges more strongly in devotions than the theme of suffering, and affection for the Cristo is a more prevalent emotion then pity. Mexican cristos, in general, have often proven surprisingly resistant to an association with suffering both historically and in the present.

The theme of indigenous suffering is, in fact, one of the persistent undercurrents in the biography of the Cristo, but this is not because the Indians, generally speaking, have seen Christ's affliction as somehow analogous to their own. Rather, among many other meanings and uses, Christians images, including crucifixes, have been for the Indians a protection, buffer, and "shield of arms" against the most damaging consequences of colonization. That is, the process of colonization and its legacy left these communities, in some instances, utterly dependent on the efficacy of these same images for their health, well-being, and even survival. Indigenous devotees in the colonial period and the present have perceived that their collective fate and the fate of their cristos are profoundly linked.

Lived Religion and Local Faith

Inasmuch as this work is biographical in nature, it is just as importantly an exploration of collective engagement with the Cristo Aparecido over time, and of the negotiated interpretation of religious experience. That is, it is a spiritual history of the Cristo's devotees and of their religious practice and belief: namely, a study of "lived religion." Harvard Divinity School scholars Robert Orsi and David Hall were the first to identify and schematize the "lived religions" approach within the field of religious studies, intentionally adopting methods and interpretive paradigms from the discipline of anthropology. Orsi's most famous work, and the text that best exemplifies the methods and commitments of this approach, is *The Madonna of 115th Street*, which documents a faith community's relationship to an image of the Virgin Mary in Italian Harlem. The book recounts shifts in the collective celebration of the Madonna to trace the changing status of Italian-American Catholics in New York throughout the twentieth century.[14] Orsi's study is a project with obvious similarities to my own. Thomas Tweed's *Our Lady of the Exile*, about a Cuban shrine in Miami, and Timothy Matovina's *Guadalupe and Her Faithful* about Latino Catholics in San Antonio, Texas, are more recent works in this vein.

At the same time that some religious studies scholars have begun to engage religion as a cultural phenomenon, historians have recently made what I see as a parallel move in their growing interest in the study of "local religion." William Christian's highly praised book, *Local Religion in Sixteenth-century Spain*, in which he uncovers the faith and practice of ordinary Spanish Christians, is foundational for the field.[15] The emerging fields of "lived" and "local" religion represent a search for increasingly nuanced theoretical models and more satisfying interpretive frameworks for understanding what is traditionally termed, derided, and even disregarded as "popular religion"—the faith, beliefs, and practices of poor, colonized, and marginalized people.

I share this scholarly commitment, and thus the biography of the Cristo rests at the nexus of these two methodologies. I have given privileged place to the experiential, exploring what people feel in their encounter with the image, not in order to isolate some "unmediated" experience of the divine or to discern a set of types or archetypes, as religious studies scholars have traditionally been wont to do.[16] Rather, because the Cristo is a locus around which collective and individual interpretation has taken place for almost five centuries, he provides the opportunity for a phenomenological exploration of the variety of religious meanings that accrue to a specific local, cultural context over time. Over the broken body of the Cristo, sacred meanings are made, broken, and made again. Whereas scholars of religion have historically distanced themselves from the embodied faith and everyday religious practice of poor and marginalized people, the biography of the Cristo draws the reader close to local devotees and believers, offering an intimate portrait of their practices of faith.

A work of this broad historical scope must necessarily be interdisciplinary in nature. Thus I employ the methods of archival research, oral history, and ethnographic study to interpret the local significance of popular practices in order, ultimately, to explain the crucified Christ's enduring vitality for the faith of the Mexican people. A large part of this project involved many hours in libraries and archives, where I consulted and studied the colonial sources that allowed me to uncover the Cristo's origins and his history in the first four hundred years. My family and I also spent six months, in 2003–2004, engaged in field research in the pueblo of Totolapan. There I studied current devotion to the image, interviewing devotees and participating in the religious life of the people. I returned later in 2004 to attend the annual fiesta and have continued to be in touch with local government officials and lay leaders. In 2008, I engaged in a smaller-scale research project among migrants of Totolapan to the California coastal community and mission town San Juan Capistrano. And so my research was directed and sustained by both a forward and backward movement: beginning with the origins of the Cristo I have followed the image forward through history, just as I have sought to trace the faith of modern-day devotees backward through time.

The form that this book takes cannot be solely attributed to the theoretical twists and turns and shifting intellectual commitments of contemporary U.S. scholars. Its shape has also been necessarily influenced by the very colonial Latin American texts that I rely upon as sources. Only at the conclusion of the writing did I realize that in some respects I have perhaps unwittingly emulated the friar Alonso Ramos Gavilán's sweeping seventeenth-century history of the shrine of the Virgin of Copacabana in the Andes, *Historia de Nuestra Señora de Copacabana* (1621). In similar fashion, though I do not regard them uncritically, I must acknowledge the influence of the magisterial colonial *crónicas* and *historias* that painstakingly record the indigenous culture that the missionaries encountered in the New World at the same time that they celebrate the work of the religious orders in bringing about indigenous conversion to Christianity.[17] Like these authors, I grapple with finding a way to explain, understand, and even celebrate the complex phenomenon of indigenous Christianity. Native Indian efforts to categorize the same set of experiences have also shaped my understanding. The drawings of the indigenous Peruvian noble Guamán Poma de Ayala capture the vitality of indigenous Christianity in Latin America along with the abuses suffered by the Indians of Peru at the hands of priests and secular authorities alike. These sketches have left their indelible mark on my mind and no doubt a discernable imprint upon my interpretation.[18] Two contemporary works also bear mention here, as they strive, like mine, toward a comprehensive history and complex interpretation of a single Mexican image: David Brading's historical treatment of the cult of the Virgin of Guadalupe, *Mexican Phoenix: Our Lady of Guadalupe: Image and Tradition Across Five Centuries* (2003), and the interdisciplinary volume about a Mexican black Christ, edited by José Velasco Toro, *Santuario y región: Imágenes del Cristo Negro de Otatitlán* (1997).

On the surface, this book takes the form of an "object history," tracing the journey and survival of the physical image itself across time and space.[19] Each chapter is woven around a single, chronological moment in the encounter between believers and the image. The first two substantive chapters are concerned with the sixteenth century. Chapter 2 takes as its starting point the miraculous appearance of the Cristo to the community of newly converted indigenous Christians of Totolapan and their friars in 1543. It introduces the reader to the physicality of the Cristo as a material object and interrogates the image's origins, both mythological and art historical. Here I explore the coming together of indigenous artistic media and technologies with European iconography. Chapter 3 focuses on the ministry of the Spanish friar Antonio de Roa and his evangelizing efforts to inspire devotion to the Cristo among the recently converted Christians of Totolapan. During this period, the indigenous community came to see the Cristo Aparecido as their own, even as they resisted the friar Roa's efforts to associate the image with human sinfulness and suffering. In this chapter, the Cristo is a window onto the complex dialogic and missionary frontiers that defined the cultural and geographic landscape of early New Spain.

The middle two chapters span the 280 years that the Cristo resided in Mexico City. Chapter 4 begins with the covert removal of the image from the Indian pueblo of Totolapan to Mexico City in 1583, where he became part of the religious life of urban, baroque Mexico. The locals of Totolapan grieved the loss of their image. Nonetheless, it was among the Augustinian friars and Indian Christians of Mexico City that the Cristo Aparecido demonstrated the first recorded signs of animate life. Friars and Indians together witnessed the miracle, and the Cristo became, for a time, one of the most celebrated sacred images in New Spain. This chapter explores the phenomenon of living images and tells the story of the Cristo at the height of his power and influence, and of an emerging urban faith in the colonial center. Here, also, I treat the role of the Cristo Aparecido in defeating the typhus epidemic of 1736–1737. Scant research to date explores the impact that repeated waves of epidemic disease had upon the emerging Christian faith of Mexico; this chapter makes forays into this uncharted territory.

In chapter 5, the biography continues with the circumstances of the image's celebrated return from Mexico City to his community of origin in 1861. A wave of Bourbon-era reforms in the eighteenth century led to the Cristo's increasingly marginal status in the City of Mexico and paved the way for the process of increasing secularization, culminating in a critical period of state appropriation of church property in the second half of the nineteenth century. The result was a crisis for the religious orders that freed the Cristo to be returned, finally, to the people of Totolapan. Here the impact on the Cristo of the separation of church and state in Mexico emerges as salient. In 1861, the people of Totolapan welcomed the Cristo home with much local pomp and celebration. He had been away for almost 280 years, but he had not been forgotten. This chapter also serves as a bridge into the twentieth century during which, once again in his community of origin, devotion to the Cristo gains new vigor and becomes the central symbol of local collective identity.

The final three chapters are devoted to the twentieth century and are more ethnographic in nature. In chapter 6 the story of the Cristo Aparecido becomes intertwined with the life and ministry of the politically radical liberationist bishop of Cuernavaca, don Sergio Méndez Arceo. In this context, the Cristo's story is a means to investigate the local impact of Vatican II and the influence of liberation theology, in the 1970s and 1980s. In the liberation theology movement both intellectuals and parish priests sought to challenge traditional conceptions of Christ's affliction on the cross, interpreting the image as a metaphor for social suffering, structural injustice, and oppression. In particular, I look at how the faith in the Cristo Aparecido was influenced by this discourse and, even more important, how he weathered and survived the controversial efforts of the much-loved "red" bishop of Cuernavaca to strip the churches of Morelos (including the cathedral) of their baroque and "outdated" saints.

In some ways it is chapter 7 that is the culminating chapter of the book. Here I analyze an explosive conflict in Totolapan that erupted between the lay religious leadership (*mayordomos*) who were devotees of the Cristo Aparecido and the Franciscan friars who have served as the town's parish priests since 1993. At the height of the conflict, which occurred in 1998, the mayordomos held their priests hostage in the local church. Based on interviews with lay leaders on both sides of the conflict and with clergy, I use this critical moment as a window into the symbolic value this particular crucifix holds in the present for devotees, priests, and the government representatives who sought to mediate the conflict.

The final chapter, chapter 8, brings the reader to the annual celebration of the fiesta in honor of the Cristo Aparecido. Rather than penitential, the fiesta is aesthetic in nature as the pueblo innovates ever more beautiful ways to adorn their streets and *iglesia*. Tenderness and affection, rather than pity or sorrow, are the emotions with which devotees most commonly regard their santo Cristo. At the beginning of the twenty-first century, devotion to the Cristo Aparecido finds new expression in the exercise of transnational religion: migrants from Totolapan travel to and fro across the U.S.-Mexican border, sometimes settling in San Juan Capistrano. In this southern California locale, immigrants immerse themselves in the religious life of the local Catholic church at the same time that they continue to organize and participate in the annual fiesta in Totolapan.

Each instance in the life of the Cristo is an opportunity to introduce and explore the most salient religious issues in the history of Mexico. Not least among these are: the military conquest of the Indians of the New World and the concomitant process of Christian mission and evangelization; the birth of an indigenous, "syncretic" Christianity; the impact of epidemic disease on religious practice; the rise of a baroque spirituality and aesthetic; the sometimes violent process of secularization and nationalization; the utopian vision and practice of the politically radical theology of liberation and its institutional dismantling; the rise of charismatic Catholicism; and the impact of immigration on religious life and practice. Each of these is read, in turn, through the popular devotion to a crucifix that over the centuries has been an animate and participatory protagonist in shaping local and regional history and social self-identity.

Approaching the grand sweep of history from the perspective of our diminutive Cristo reveals other persistent themes, in addition to those I have already mentioned here. First among these is the Church's profoundly ambivalent relationship to popular piety. The institutional church was not at all times antagonistic, as many might believe. Rather, at one moment its clerics and bishops supported and fomented expressions of popular religion, and then maligned and undermined these in the next. Nevertheless, the reader will in some ways perceive that the popular faith of Mexico has been a faith "under siege" in every century. This is certainly the perception of contemporary devotees, as I explore in chapter 7. Nevertheless, efforts at religious "reform" did not in most cases have their intended effect; in some cases efforts at modernization and nationalization actually strengthened and underscored devotion to the colonial Cristo.

Additionally, history from the point of view of the Cristo leads me, at times, to defy traditional historical periodization of Mexico. Mexico's independence from Spain in 1821, for example, seems to have had very little discernable, immediate impact on popular devotion to the Cristo, or on the fate of the image itself. Similarly, the Mexican revolution does not loom large in the history of the Cristo. Further, the approach to history I employ here leads me to place some historical periods and processes into comparative focus, so that the reader may note resonances in the impact of the "spiritual conquest" of the sixteenth century, the eighteenth-century Bourbon reforms, the anti-clericalism and church-state conflicts of the nineteenth century, and even the modernizing impulse of liberation theology in the latter twentieth century. Finally, ownership of the Cristo is a salient theme throughout, as various communities seeking access to the symbolic capital lent by the Cristo have vied for control over the physical image itself as well as over its interpretation and meaning.

2

"Christ Appeared"

Material Religion and the Conquest of Mexico

This Christ, immortal as death itself, does not rise again. For to what purpose? Death alone was what he awaited. Down he flows, from his mouth half agape, black as the mystery indecipherable, to nothingness, and never arrives. . . . This Spanish Christ, which was never alive, black as the mantle of earth, lies like a level plain, horizontal, stretched out soulless and hopeless, its eyes shut against the sky that stings with rain and scorches the bread.
—Miguel de Unamuno, "El Cristo yacente de Santa Clara de Palencia"

Scene 1. The Friar on His Knees before Christ.
Convento San Guillermo de Totolapan, 1543

On the Friday in 1543 when the Cristo Aparecido first appeared to Fray Antonio de Roa, the fervent Spanish missionary had assumed his habitual posture of prayer. On his knees, disrobed to his waist, the friar sighed and wept before the altar in his austere monastic cell on the second floor of the Augustinian *convento* (or priory) in Totolapan. Perhaps he prayed for forgiveness for his meager life, wretched instrument that it was for bringing God's divine mercy to the Indians of the New World. Or perhaps, as Roa knelt weeping before his makeshift altar, he pleaded with God not only for his own sinful and wretched soul but also for the salvation of his neophyte Indian charges.

It was in this posture that Roa's young Indian assistant, Francisco de Tolentino, discovered the friar when he opened the door to the monastic cell and announced the arrival of an unknown Indian from Mexico City. In an Inquisition testimony given in 1583, as a man of seventy-eight and indio principal and *gobernador* of Totolapan, don Francisco recalled as if it were yesterday the arrival of the enigmatic visitor: "He was a young Indian man, dressed in white clothing, and with a beautiful face. He called at the door of the convento and he told us to summon the prior, saying that he had come from Mexico [City] and that he had brought a crucifix." Don Francisco vividly remembered as well how, upon hearing the news of the unfamiliar Indian's arrival, Fray Antonio rose to put on his habit and, little by little, gradually made his way down the stairs to the convento entrance. Roa's pace that day, as usual, was slow, hindered by the cumbersome chains that he wore cinched to his body and by the cruel cilice that scraped and clawed at the flesh under his habit. But eventually the pious friar arrived at the gate and bid the stranger welcome.

Then, beholding the cross and its wasted corpse for the first time, Fray Antonio fell again to his knees. And it is no wonder; the image that he encountered that day was such a gaunt, hungry form that one could hardly imagine that it resulted from only three hours on a cross (figure 2.1). The lifeless head, crowned with thorns, blood and matted hair, bowed slightly to the right. Sinew, muscle and veins were all visible in his emaciated arms. Chest sunken, ribs and even spine visibly protruding—the suffering written on this body must have seemed to reflect some prior extreme ascetic practice, resonating with Roa's own severe discipline of penitential self-mortification. Roa embraced the image and kissed Christ's feet before he rose.

"What do you wish me to give you? I will pay you very well, whatever you wish, and if you want twenty or thirty pesos, we will give them to you," Roa gratefully offered the stranger. But the mysterious messenger only responded, "Place it now where it should be and soon we will sort it out." Again, more cryptically, the stranger repeated, "Put it where it should be; that which you desire will come to be."

And so Roa and his assistant, Francisco, together bore the crucifix to Roa's cell, where they placed it on Roa's altar, and the friar lost himself in prayer before the image. He had often begged God for just such a crucifix, one to which he could devote his penitential exercises. Here, finally, as if out of nowhere, had appeared the answer to his prayers. When Roa roused from his reverie and descended from his cell, the mysterious Indian was nowhere to be found. Don Francisco, along with the doorman and several teachers from the school, searched the entire village and surrounding countryside. They spent all of that day and the next looking without avail. Defeated, they

FIGURE 2.1. Antonio Roa receives the Cristo. *Nuestro Señor Aparecido*. Francisco
Antonio Vallejo. Oil on Canvas, Mexico, circa 1760. By permission of the
Instituto Nacional de Antropología e Historia on behalf of the people of Mexico.

returned to Fray Roa and admitted, "Father, the Indian who brought the crucifix does not appear to be anywhere, and we have looked for him throughout the whole pueblo."

"Do not feel badly," Roa reassured them, "Does not it seem to you that God himself has left us this gift?" In this way it came to seem to everyone in the pueblo that God had sent the holy crucifix to Totolapan by way of a miracle.[1]

The Cristo Aparecido arrived at the door of the convento of Totolapan in the arms of an Indian stranger. Its cross painted green, color of life and vitality, the image was also carefully swaddled, bringing to mind simultaneously the infant Jesus in the manger and the "sacred bundle," the assembled sacra of indigenous America. It arrived, a cocooned power waiting to be freed.[2] With Roa's declaration of the image's divine origin, the biography of the Cristo Aparecido begins. It is a story that has been called myth, legend, truth, and miracle; recounted and retold over centuries in the sonorous intonations of the voice of faith. Yet Roa's conclusions about the Cristo have not gone uncontentested; twentieth-century art historians have also pondered the Cristo's origins, employing their own methods of discernment and applying their own categories of interpretation to make their own determinations. This chapter weaves together two seemingly irreconcilable origin myths, one art historical and the other the narrative of faith, in order to explain the circumstances in which the unknown Indian's arrival with the crucifix was understood to be extraordinary.

This exploration of the image's provenance is the means by which the reader makes the Cristo's physical aquaintance; we reach out as do the blind, in confidence yet searching, to trace the edges, contours, and outlines of his venerable form. I myself, who have never touched or held the image, serve as the intrepid guide, leading a pilgrimage past a boundary that no devotee would ever cross: questions about the material origins of the image hold little meaning or relevance for believers in the Cristo; in fact, they are anathema. At the close, the reader will be versed in its heft and texture, proportions and material content, and the techniques of its construction. Here, at the boundary between miracle and art history, begins the reader's relationship with the Cristo Aparecido of Totolapan.

It was not by chance that the Cristo first appeared to Roa while the friar was ensconced within the thick walls of the Totolapan convento. The sixteenth century in Mexico was an age of vast and imposing monastery fortresses and diminutive saints. These expressions of Christianity, wildly contrasting in scope and scale, were the two fundaments of an art historical universe that was meant to inspire, impose, foster, persuade, coax, and evoke a new faith for a New World. Grandeur and intimacy marked the baroque aesthetic that was to emerge with full force in the next century, in which sumptuously adorned churches and cathedrals seduced believers into ever more exhuberent emotional engagement with the sacred. But the roots of this paradoxical, potent religious aesthetic, at least in its New World expression, can be traced, in part, to sixteenth-century encounters like this one between Roa and the Cristo, in which the seemingly impenetrable and austere conventos provided the aesthetic context for intimate and familiar spiritual engagement with religious images. In the course of his life history, it becomes clear that the fate of the Cristo and the fate of the conventos that he has occupied over the course of his existence are utterly and resolutely bound together. Even more important, tracing the origins of the Señor Aparecido also brings focus to his cristos hermanos, the many other representations of Jesus' suffering, and, indeed, to the entire plurality of Christian religious images that came to populate the New World by the end of the sixteenth century.

The dearth of images prior to 1543 had left Roa longing and praying for a simple crucifix; but some forty years later, at the Third Mexican Council, priests were already noting the "multitude" of images of Christ that the Indians themselves then possessed. The arrival of the Cristo in Totolapan thus marked the beginning of an astonishing "population explosion" of crucifix images in New Spain within the span of less than half a century. From the mid-sixteenth century, the appearance of sculpted christs and other Christian saints became a frequent, though never mundane, New World miracle. Secular modern art historians are in unusual accord with Roa and his Augustinian contemporaries, both parties concluding that the Cristo could not be the product of Indian artistic agency. Nevertheless, there is significant evidence that many of these miraculous images, the Cristo Aparecido not least among them, were the result of early collaboration between Spanish and indigenous artisans. It is arguable that the Cristo himself was, on the contrary, an artistic expression of nascent indigenous Christian faith.

Of Missionaries and Monasteries, Friars and Fortresses

This chapter follows Fray Antonio Roa from his promising arrival in New Spain, through his troubled and painful sojourn to Totolapan, to his faith-saving encounter with the Cristo. His spiritual journey traces the contours of the religious and spiritual geography of New Spain. The story of how Roa's life became intertwined with the Cristo, like all such histories, is rough-hewn, much like the coarsely woven habit Roa himself wore. The available sources regarding the life and ministry of Antonio de Roa are hagiographic, the work of Spanish companions in religious life who not only shared his theological convictions but wished to make of Roa a saint for the Augustinian order.[3] Nevertheless, these sources provide rich details about the religious life of this devoted monastic and missionary.

Born as Fernando Álvarez de la Puebla López in 1491 to noble Spanish parents, Roa was identified at an early age as a person of profound faith, capable of fervent devotion and almost ceaseless prayer.[4] After taking the Augustinian habit in 1528, the young friar spent many long hours in the Augustinian convento in Burgos kneeling before the crucifix there, his face nearly always streaming with tears.[5] Roa was the crème de la crème of Spanish religious, precisely the kind of person his superiors believed suited to the rigors and challenges of the New World missionary frontier. In this regard Roa shared much in common with his peers. Missionaries to the New World were hand-selected; the best and the brightest of their orders, they arrived eager and fresh-faced and filled with the certainty and enthusiasm of youth.

The arrival of a group of twelve Franciscan missionaries in newly conquered Mexico City in 1524 had marked the symbolic beginning of Christian mission in the New World. Like Roa, these young men were on fire with faith, hope, and fervor. Seeing themselves as laboring in the spirit and examples of the twelve disciples of Christ, they dreamt of a new Christendom: an Indian-Franciscan millennial kingdom that was free of the excesses of European religious practice.[6] European Christianity was bankrupt, they felt, and the Indians, from what they had heard, uniquely and naturally inclined toward those religious qualities they themselves most admired and pursued: simplicity, humility, poverty, and obedience. Hernán Cortés himself famously welcomed them upon their arrival: the terrible, rough conqueror knelt to kiss the delicate, pure hands of the friars. Cortés offered this dramatic and impressive gesture of humility before the recently conquered lords and holy men of the Aztec city of Tenochtitlán; and so the military subjugation of the people of Mexico paved the way for their so-called spiritual conquest.

The first Augustinians arrived in Mexico City in 1533, some ten years after the twelve, and thus were relative latecomers to New Spain. By this time, the Franciscans and Dominicans were already well established in the colonial center, and the Crown worried that there was not room for the Augustinians in the city. It was almost a decade after their arrival before the Augustinians received approval to establish a convento of their own in Mexico City. The Crown initially forbade it, on the grounds that the Franciscans and Dominicans were already established there, and that the local native communities upon whose labor the orders drew for their sustenance would be overburdened by the demands of maintaining a third order.[7]

In their first decades in the New World, the Augustinians were also less admired than their Franciscan and Dominican counterparts. A letter dating from this period is a case in point: "As you are already aware, the order of San Agustín is not as esteemed (temida) as those of St. Dominic and Saint Francis."[8] The Dominicans had their prominent priests: the irascible defenders of human rights and protectors of the Indians, Antonio de Montesinos and Bartolomé de las Casas, who for better or for worse assured the order a special place in history.

And unforgettable, of course, were the beloved Franciscan personalities whose utopianism, devotion, and mildness made them the favored priests of the Indians, at least according to Franciscan-authored histories of the spiritual conquest. Of these, perhaps the most tenderly regarded was Toríbio de Benavente, who earned the name Motolinía, the Nahua word for "poor," for the devotion he showed to his vows of poverty and humility.[9]

Mexico City was clearly the domain of the Franciscans, who were by now legend, and thus the Augustinians were thrust to the margins of the colony. The Augustinians, therefore, worked hard to prove their mettle on the missionary frontier, in the wild, contested backlands where Spanish influence was thin and Indian resistance ongoing. As an order, they took on the responsibility for mission in territories in which indigenous populations were dispersed and the languages varied. The Sierra Alta was the key mission field for the Augustinians of the province. They worked primarily along the northern border of central Mexico, among "wild" and resistant Indians, the so-called Chichimecas, who had yet to be brought into the forced settlements known as *reducciones*. The rigorous physical and spiritual geography of the region tested these eager young men. They often worked alone or in pairs, walking the rugged terrain from community to community, sleeping outdoors, and passing significant periods in relative isolation. Even though they were also immersed in indigenous communities, one can imagine that these friars must have experienced their cultural and linguistic separation from the Indians as a kind of spiritual solitude.

This was certainly the case for Roa, who, traveling from Spain with the second group of Augustinians in February of 1535, sought out the "solitude" and spiritual challenges of the missionary frontier.[10] Removed as he was from his monastery, without any shelter, the Sierra Alta became Roa's *desierto*, his spiritual wilderness.[11] Roa, partnered with Fray Juan de Sevilla, was assigned to the area of Molango, the site of the first Augustinian *doctrina*, in the present-day state of Hidalgo.[12] There, Roa encountered both Huaxtecan- and Nahuatl-speaking Indians, and also perhaps a few who spoke Otomí.[13] With no knowledge of these languages, he traversed the hills in search of "idolatrous" Indians that he could bring to Christ. Roa, more and more despondent, wandered in a troubled landscape. Struggling with what in today's terms can only be understood as culture shock, Roa's early missionary strategy consisted, in part, of tying a rope around his waist and diving into caves in pursuit of Indians who, clearly harassed by his evangelizing efforts, sought out their own solitude and escape in these dark grottos. Further disheartened when these same people laughed at his tears of frustration, Roa decided to return to Spain, his missionary endeavor an utter failure.

The friar then traveled to the convento of Totolapan, where he awaited passage to Spain. He did not arrive in Totolapan triumphantly or full of evangelical zeal and fervor, but rather plaqued by doubt and in a spirit of defeat. Probably he was not only questioning his vocation as a missionary but also struggling with the meaning and implications of his own Christian faith. To pass the time while he waited, Roa began to study Nahuatl with a local youth and became acquainted with the people of Totolapan.[14] The meaningful hours he spent discussing the nuances of Christian moral doctrine with the Indian neophyte Christians there was the stimulus by which Roa underwent a profound experience of reconversion. Their nascent but deep faith restored his confidence and hope in the ability of Indians to adopt Christianity. The Totolapan Christians' passion for the new religion thus rescued Roa's beleaguered vocation as a missionary.

With his own faith renewed and buoyed up by theirs, and with his newly aquired language skills, Roa decided to return not to Spain but to the un-Christianized Indians of the wild Sierra, the location of his prior missionary defeat. Roa's ministry encompassed almost thirty leagues of territory, about ninety to a hundred miles, all of which he traversed entirely on foot. Much of his career as a missionary, which spanned more than three decades, was spent as prior of the convento in Molango. From 1542 until about two years later, Roa served as prior of the convento of Totolapan and *doctrinero* to the indigenous Christians there. Though his formal tenure in the pueblo was brief, Totolapan remained a spiritual touchstone for the friar for the rest of his life: he frequently returned to visit the community, including Totolapan in his rounds of the region.

Jorge de Ávila, the first Augustinian to arrive in Totolapan, began construction of the convento there in 1534. Named San Guillermo, it was the second that the order built in Morelos. The convento in nearby Ocuituco, established in 1533, was the Augustinians' first both in Morelos and in the New World. Monasteries such as these were key features, punctuating and commanding the physical and spiritual and cartography of early New Spain. The great stone edifices were not so much literal military fortresses as spiritual ones.[15] The Convento de San Guillermo in Totolapan certainly functioned as such for Roa; recall how the relatively new monastery provided a much-needed spiritual refuge where the friar could recover from his initial missionary failures.

In size and scale, the conventos were intended to rival the monolithic and monumental architecture of the Aztec state, especially the great temple pyramids of Tenochtitlán, the megacity that, in 1519, awed and inspired Cortés and his pieced-together, scraggily band of Spanish conquerors.[16] The Aztec Templo Mayor was the ritual center of the city and the geographic navel of the universe: the axis mundi of the Nahua-speaking people of Mexico, where space and time and earth and sky met.[17] The Christian conventos, also enormous in size and scale, were intended similarly to impress, as Grijalva explains: "That which most elucidated the [majesty of the] kingdom, and which most demonstrated the greatness and generosity of its souls, was the construction of the temples and conventos, testaments to the posterity and opulence of the Reign."[18]

As the location for the education and indoctrination of newly converted indigenous Christians, monastery complexes were the centers for Christian evangelization in the New World. Their *capillas abiertas*, giant open-air chapels, could accommodate hundreds, if not thousands, of eager listeners. In the massive, walled atrial courtyards that encompassed church and priory, friars offered not only sacraments but also instruction and catechism. The missiological purpose and function of the conventos is represented especially well in Fray Diego Valadés's 1579 sketch of an idealized *atrio* courtyard. At the center of the monastery compound appear the Twelve Franciscans symbolically bearing the New World church on their shoulders, while around them friars gather with small groups of attentive Indians to offer instruction on the basic tenets of Christianity, and perform baptisms, confessions, and marriages.[19] Here, cloistered within thick walls, buffered from paradox and shielded from contradiction, friars played out their fantasy of a "millennial kingdom," of a new utopian Indian Christendom that would usher in the last age.

The Augustinian order, in particular, seems to have been committed to creating ever more impressive architectural expressions of the power and permanence of Christendom in the Americas. Robert Ricard's groundbreaking comprehensive study of sixteenth-century evangelization is suggestive. Though Augustinian achievements in the spiritual conquest hardly loom large in Ricard's text, he does suggest that the order may have been particularly devoted to the spiritual and architectural ordering of Indian religious life: "The Franciscans, indeed, seem to me to have been especially interested in ethnographic and linguistic studies, and more concerned with training a native clergy; the Dominicans, more scrupulously attached to orthodoxy and less optimistic about the Indians' religious capacities; the Augustinians, more competent in organizing native communities, more given to building vast monasteries, and more interested in giving their neophytes a higher and more advanced spiritual training."[20]

The example of the convento in Yecapixtla, just a few miles from Totolapan, stands as a case in point. The Franciscans, the first to arrive in the community, established a modest chapel there in 1525. But some ten years later, again under the direction of the tireless Jorge de Ávila, the Augustinians replaced this humble chapel with an imposing convent-fortress. Similarly, once the Augustinians finally received royal authorization for their Mexico City monastery complex, the structure they built was more impressive than those of other orders. They launched the project in August of 1541, with the generous patronage of doña Isabel Moctezuma de Cano, daughter of the famed Aztec emperor.[21] An observer in 1554 described the monument as "a truly magnificent work, of such merit and fame, that in all fairness, it could be classed as the eighth wonder of the world, in addition to the seven already acclaimed by historians and poets."[22]

Construction of these spiritual fortresses may have been the special strength of the Augustinians, but it was not uniquely their endeavor. Each of the religious orders saw to the fabrication of these imposing and ponderous stone buildings, which were more often than not built by the forced labor of Indian neophyte Christians. As such they have at times served as a fitting metaphor for the violent imposition of Christian faith upon a subjugated population: one can almost feel the sheer weight of the effort and human cost that was required, and sense the compulsion necessary, for their construction. But these icons of monumental faith, not utterly dissimilar from their Aztec counterparts, bear the imprint of an Indian hand that seems to lighten their heavy, intolerant, and resistant disposition.[23] In these churches and conventos, the delicate frescos that grace their interior walls are also more often than not of Indian design. Vivid floral motifs dance strangely against somber surfaces.

Colonial and modern sources have also pondered how "idols" of pre-Columbian deities were hidden away, presumably by Indian laborers, within the walls of Christian churches during construction, or subsequently buried beneath or behind their altars. These "idols-behind-altars" became a key interpretive lens for understanding the process of religious syncretism in Mexico, in which, according to some schools of thought, Christianity was simply a thin veneer upon an enduring and resistant native spirituality.[24] Indigenous Christianity in Latin America is a varied and complex faith, one that requires multiple metaphors to grasp.

As impressive and commanding as it was, the architecture of the monastery-fortresses was not, on its own, enough to convert the people of Mexico: Christianity could not win souls by awe and imposition alone. Unlike the Aztec Triple Alliance conquest of the region in the fifteenth century, which simply incorporated surrounding territories and their existing religious traditions into an ever-expanding religio-political empire, the process of Christian evangelization meant a dramatic break with the religious past, "a radical cognitive disjuncture such as Augustine had described in his Confessions," requiring that new subjects actually think and feel differently in their reoriented religious practice.[25] Images of Christian saints, including especially crucifixes, were assembled and deployed to immerse these new Christians in an emotional, "passional," and moral world.[26] While monastery buildings might evoke awe and humility among Indian populations, the sculpted saints that came to populate them played upon a broader, subtler, and more complex emotional range. In devotion to these saints, the quality of the individual believer's relationship with the divine was emphasized, especially the requisite emotional intensity and the intimacy of that relationship.

Yet in Mexico in the first half of the sixteenth century, three-dimensional images of almost any sort, either small ones for use in personal devotion or larger ones meant to grace church buildings, were in short supply. Monasteries and churches, including Totolapan's own convento and iglesia of San Guillermo, stood empty in anticipation, ready to receive them.

The Cristo and Its Hermanos: Genealogy of a Crucifix

A key aspect of the miracle of the Cristo Aparecido was the impossibility of its very existence in the early colonial period. After news of the miraculous image spread, religious authorities unsuccessfully tried to determine whether the Cristo Aparecido had been "made in Castile or whether in these lands." Several colonial sources explain that, at the moment of the Cristo's appearance, there was no artist skilled enough in New Spain to create an image of such beauty and craftsmanship. Neither did it seem plausible to sixteenth-century observers that the image was sent from Spain, as space was at a premium in the frequent but smallish ships that arrived from Europe. In spite of the fact that an Indian brought the Cristo to the convento, the possibility of indigenous authorship during this early period was never considered. Their inability to discern an earthly, artistic origin for the image led both priests and lay believers alike to attribute the Cristo's existence to the hand of God.[27] Though the image's divine provenance has been questioned at least since the end of the sixteenth century, when an Inquisition hearing scrutinized the Cristo's beginnings, this continues to be the view of believers in Totolapan today, who bristle at questions about the Cristo's material origins.

The scarcity of religious images in his day explains, in part, Roa's dramatic emotional response upon beholding the Cristo for the first time. When I first encountered the Cristo Aparecido, resting in his *nicho* in the back of the iglesia de Totolapan, I had trouble accepting that it was the image that I had read so much about. Far from the magnificent and arresting image that evoked Roa's tears, what I beheld seemed at first utterly mundane and unremarkable. Tucked away in the recesses of the nave, behind the altar, he seemed almost unassuming; his presence there inspired no response or placed no demand upon the beholder. In comparison, the image of Christ at the Column (also of colonial origin), that resides today at the front entrance of the Totolapan sanctuary, had a more immediately commanding presence, though an almost ghoulish and frightening one, by the locals' own admission.

In his path-breaking study of the reception of religious images, David Freedberg describes the experience of a colleague that was in some ways similar to mine before the Cristo. Motivated by scholarly interest and curiosity more than by faith, she made a rigorous sojourn to visit the Virgin of Rocamadour, in southwestern France. But ultimately she experienced disappointment upon finally beholding the Virgin: "I could not believe it. . . after so long a journey, all I saw was a small ugly Madonna, with a supercilious look on her face."[28] For my part, I felt none of the antagonism or frustration that Freedberg's colleague described, but I did feel some incredulity, and wondered if I wasn't missing something.

Later, I came to understand that the beauty, the majesty, of the Cristo Aparecido is lost at such a distance. In size he is diminutive, the *corpus* itself less than
three feet in length. Though the image is too large to have been originally intended for use at a home altar, at the same time its ability to move, shake, and
inspire observers is dependent upon a more intimate relationship than that allowed by his current remote and inaccessible position behind the altar at the
rear of the nave.[29] Images of the Cristo's size and stature were meant to be engaged from up close and not to impress and impose from a distance. But more
to the point, my experience of being unaffected and untouched in my initial
encounter with the image stemmed in large part from the subsequent proliferation of crucifix images in Mexico: by the twentieth century they were commonplace, even ordinary; only the trained eye of the devotee or the art historian
is able to distinguish one cristo from the next.

For the missionaries, Christianizing the New World began with extirpation, the deliberate destruction of the material objects of indigenous religious
culture. Through this violent and devastating process of erasure, friars eradicated text, temple, and image from the spiritual landscape in an attempt to
wipe clean the slate of indigenous religious imagination.[30] They aimed to create a tabula rasa, a clean slate, upon which they could build a new Indian Christendom. In the beginning they worked haphazardly if enthusiastically, but
within the century Christian iconoclasm became formalized and systematized
in the institution of the auto de fé. Among the most famous of the self-
proclaimed extirpators was the Franciscan Diego de Landa, whose auto de fé in
the Yucatan in 1562 consigned some five thousand Mayan "idols" to flames and
similarly destroyed twenty-seven sacred texts. At the same time that he worked
this mass-scale deicide, Landa oversaw the torture of almost as many Indians,
subjecting 4,500 Mayans to violent interrogation. The use of torture and terror
in his renegade (and ultimately illegal) "Inquisition" caused the deaths of
approximately two hundred Mayans over the course of three months.[31]

Alonso Ramos Gavilán, an Augustinian friar and missionary to the Indians
in Peru in the first decades of the seventeenth century, was another self-
declared destroyer of Indian idols. Also in the Andes, the Jesuit Francisco de
Ávila pioneered a system of *denuncias* and *visitas de idolatrías* that culminated in
mass-scale destruction in his infamous auto de fé that took place in Lima in
December of 1609.[32] At this terrifying public event Ávila proudly displayed the
many discovered "idols," offered a sermon in Quechua inveighing against idolatry, and then put to flame the ancestral mummies, *huacas*, and other sacred
objects. One local Indian religious leader (exposed by Ávila himself) was tied
and bound, forced to witness the destruction of these objects, publicly whipped,
and then exiled to the Jesuit house in Chile.[33] For historian Pierre Duviols, the
denuncias and visitas of Ávila inaugurated the systematic extirpation of idolatry
in Peru. Beyond this, for some historians Ávila single-handedly launched the
Jesuits as the most committed and effective extirpators in the Americas.[34]

In this way, the process of Christian evangelization began with and continued alongside the almost unprecedented destruction of religious art and artifacts as friars, priests, and bishops worked a veritable art historical "holocaust."
Upon this stripped and denuded art historical landscape, they labored tirelessly
to fashion a new religio-visual universe both for themselves and their Indian
neophyte charges. This they accomplished in part with the construction of conventos and the fabrication of simple wooden cruciforms. The first Christian
images created in New Spain date from the time of the conquest. These were
the crudest of crosses, without representation of the body of Jesus, often made
by newly conquered Indians at the command of conquistadors. After conquering a village or town, Hernán Cortés ordered the local Indians to make a cross
out of large pieces of wood in the presence of their priests and lords, and
charged them all to care for it with great reverence.[35] He and other conquistadors often erected similar rough-hewn wooden crosses to mark the locations of
their military victories.[36] In an ironic twist on the idols-behind-altars theme, the
conqueror Francisco de Alarcón left behind a cross in each place through which
he passed, burying at its feet a bottle containing the date and details of his
military victory there, as if to provide a hidden transcript interpreting the significance of the cruciform.[37] One can imagine that the pious person who
stopped briefly to acknowledge the presence of the cross did not realize that
they were in fact paying homage to their own military defeat. Or maybe they
did. In the context of colonial Yucatan, as elsewhere, there is much evidence
that for the Indians the cross quickly became inextricably connected to Spanish
domination: "the association between the arrival of the Spanish, their physical
presence in Yucatan and their claim on the place, and the cruciform was rein-
forced by the Spanish themselves, and appears to have been established in the
consciousness of Maya authors also."[38] Nonetheless, at no point did imperial
domination ever constitute the total and exclusive meaning of the cross for
indigenous Christians.

Echoing the techniques of these military conquerors, who were largely responsible for Christian evangelization during the initial period, the first missionaries also employed humble—some have said "artless"—wooden crosses
in their parallel spiritual conquest of the New World. One can imagine the
haste and simplicity with which these images must have been crafted, as every
toppled idol was perforce replaced by an image of the cross.[39] In one such instance, friars ordered the felling of a sacred tree that had been much adored as
a deity, compelling the Indians to use it in the construction of a cross.[40] During
the first few years of evangelization, plain wooden crosses literally came to litter
the Mexican landscape as friars ordered the Indians to raise them at crossroads,
mountaintops, and rocky cliffs in order to "liberate" the terrain from the influences of demons and devils.[41]

A pressing need remained for more sophisticated and evocative Christian
representations, both to fill the material cultural void wrought by iconoclastic

destruction and also because the "discovery" of the peoples of the New World and the missionary project of their evangelization gave birth to a vast market for the full inventory of Christian religious art, in all its varied forms and media. In the decades immediately following the conquest, the increasingly urgent demand for crucifixes and other religious images by churches, convents, chapels, and for private devotion (not least among Spanish colonials) far surpassed the available supply. The market for such images may have also been amplified by the counter-Reformation generally and by the Council of Trent specifically, after the middle of the sixteenth century. Countering the Protestant Reformation's iconoclasm, which included both theological tracts against Catholic devotion to images of saints as well as the physical destruction of such images, sometimes by angry mobs, the Council of Trent explicitly reaffirmed the importance of saints' images to Christian faith.[42]

This increased demand soon necessitated a system of importation from Europe and, even more important, a system for local production and distribution. There is little readily available data on the importation of religious images from Europe to the New World, but a complete, life-sized image was both burdensome and costly to transport, more often than not prohibitively so. Even so, some images did arrive from Spain. For example, occasionally the disembodied sculpted heads, hands, and feet of images were shipped from Europe across the Atlantic. The torsos and limbs of these saints were then completed in Mexico, sometimes employing indigenous techniques, where the bodies were finally assembled: a stunningly innovative system of transnational artistic production. This century also saw the arrival of crucifixes from Asia, adding to the complexity of the art historical moment.[43]

Yet importation alone was not sufficient to meet the demand for Christian images. The very existence of the Cristo Aparecido and its cristos hermanos in this early period is evidence of some more or less formal system of apprenticeship, or even possibly for at least a small number of artisan workshops.[44] In all likelihood by the early 1540s Spanish religious artists began to journey to New Spain, drawn by the emergence of the potentially lucrative market. Andrés Estrada Jasso, who has researched the early production of religious images in Mexico, believes that the existence of the Cristo Aparecido of Totolapan points to the arrival in Mexico of a skilled and prominent Spanish sculptor in the late 1530s. He attributes the Cristo Aparecido and others to the hand or direct influence of Matias de la Cerda, an early Anadalusian immigrant.[45] Though the assertion of Cerda's authorship is speculative, the Cristo Aparecido clearly bears the imprint of a skilled European artistic hand: at the point in history in question, even the most gifted and committed Indian artist would have required considerable training in European iconography to produce the image. Stylistically and iconographically the Cristo is utterly European: in facial features and skin tone, in the starkness of the representation of the human form, and in the exaggerated "realism" of the suffering of Christ he closely resembles crucifixes of Spanish and European origin dating to this period.

Yet, due to the nature of its material construction, it is certain that the Cristo is of New World and not European provenance. Modern day restorers and researchers from the Instituto Nacional de Antropología e Historia in Morelos have determined that the image is carved from the wooden shaft of the maguey, a plant native to Mexico. Commonly known in the United States as the century plant, its wooden spikes and clusters of yellow flowers appear only rarely, about once in twenty-five years, after which it dies. The Spanish Jesuit and naturalist José de Acosta called the maguey, ". . . a tree of miracles, innumerable are the uses of this plant."[46] Indeed, in precolonial Mexico it had both commercial and religious uses. Light, fibrous, and easily carved, the rare, wooden material that grows from the center of the plant was commonly used for the creation of pre-Columbian art works.[47] Its course fibers were woven into paper used for sacred codices, and its sharp thorns were used to pierce delicate flesh in Aztec ritual bloodletting. In Mexico to this day, the sap of the maguey is used to make the native fermented drinks pulque and mescal. Nectar from the plant is also boiled into agave syrup, a sugar substitute that health-conscious Californians ladle by sweet spoonfuls into steaming mugs of herbal tea.

Though the Cristo's form is European, his *alma* (internal structure, or "soul"), is thus native to Mexico, dramatic evidence that some degree of collaboration was necessary for its fabrication. One can imagine the Indian artist showing the European how to first identify and harvest, and then chisel and sculpt, the unlikely, slender, soft fiber. The European sculptor in turn demonstrated how the aching arms and the sad, thin face of Christ emerged from the generous and giving material, both artists lovingly and skillfully working the form. Perhaps the Cristo was, already at its beginnings, an instrument of catechesis as, while they worked side by side, the Spanish artist narrated the emerging image, recounting to the Indian the pain that Jesus experienced as the Roman soldiers lashed and bound the Savior, then roughly hammered nails at hands and feet.

The suggestion that the Cristo Aparecido is an early instance of artistic cooperation between European and Indian artisans is plausible, in part, because the intriguing and much-studied *cristos de caña*, which also likely have their origins in this period, must have required an even greater degree of collaboration for their creation. These images are the most famous New World cristos, much admired, then as now, for their artistic innovation. Appropriating a local Tarascan medium unique to Michoacán, these images were not carved but rather molded from corn pith paste and a combination of discarded papers, fabric, and wood. Though they were essentially hollow, vaguely analogous to the ubiquitous children's piñata, most often they were modeled around an internal supporting structure. Because the technology was more complex and detailed than simple carving, these cristos clearly not only necessitated a closer artistic collaboration between European and Indian but also reflect a heavier indigenous hand and influence. So intriguing was the technology for Europeans that the cristos de caña soon arrived in Spain as curiosities from the New World. They continue to hold tremendous interest for art historians, particularly in their efforts to understand and interpret the union of European and native technologies. For historian William B. Taylor, these cristos also serve as an apt metaphor for emerging indigenous Christianity, which he regards as an authentically Indian construction, assembled, as pastiche, from adopted European symbols and meanings.[48]

Santeros and Saints: Artists as Miracle-Workers

In spite of the evidence, art historians have for the most part argued against indigenous authorship and probably exaggerated the role of the Spanish in the construction of the first generations of Mexican crucifixes.[49] Certainly the involvement of Indian artists in the creation of European-style Christian images was a relatively recent phenomenon during the first half of the sixteenth century. Yet there is evidence that during this period there were Indians who became, against significant odds, skilled craftsmen in their own right, even possibly practicing their art with varying degrees of independence from Spanish systems of production. These were the first generation of Mexican *santeros*, folk artists responsible for the fabrication, preservation, and repair of Christian images for local devotional use. As such, they were also agents of Christianization and vehicles for the Christian miraculous.

Bartolomé de las Casas, in his *Apologética historia*, observed in the 1550s that there were Indians who were "admirably skilled carvers of wood who produce works worthy of the highest praise and, above all, the most perfectly devout crucifixes to win Christians to great devotion."[50] Another colonial observer, Torquemada, writing several decades later, mentions an Indian sculptor named Miguel Mauricio, from the town of Santiago, whose skill rivaled that of the best Spanish artisans.[51] Guaman Poma depicts an Indian santero at work on a crucifix in his early seventeenth-century chronicle (figure 2.2) By the end of the sixteenth century, Indian artists even came to pose a significant threat to Spanish ones. A 1589 regulation, issued by the viceroy with the intention of protecting Spanish workshops, declared that Indian artisans were allowed to create religious images for their own consumption but were prohibited from contracting with Spaniards for the production of religious images for formal installation in churches.[52]

Nevertheless, what impressed Spanish and indigenous observers alike in this period was not primarily the artistry of Indians but rather the divine authorship that was frequently evident in the earliest Mexican crucifixes, as was

PINTOR
LOSARTIFICIOSPĨTOR

escultor en tallador bordador seruicio de dios y dela s. yglecia—

agun naper sona cristiano pue da tocar ni nguna y
gen ni bo uala porq uien de aq llo no cren los infie
ho yazen caso enel año de 1613 bordador dela y glia mã
uas enel puello de s p de uarochiri pintado pecado sacae
por ello las mugeres de cen tonta ui edo gran dici mo q̃

FIGURE 2.2. *Indian Santero.* Guaman Poma de Ayala. Adapted from a drawing dating from Peru, 1615, in the collection of the Royal Library of Denmark; used by permission.

observed of the Cristo Aparecido. In the extraordinary flourishing of New World Christian forms, colonial observers saw the hand of God as, time and time again, artist and image were joined by a miracle. Colonial chroniclers record, for example, how Indians discovered branches of trees that already showed the shape of the crucifix. In some instances a branch that was being used as firewood was retrieved from flames when it was recognized as following the form of the crucifix or when it refused to burn.[53] An Indian artist then completed the miracle, employing his skill to free the rest of the figure from the rescued branch. Following the natural contours of the limb, the figure of Jesus and the cross were both carved from a single piece of wood. Also understood to be cristos aparecidos, these miraculous images were thus spared the fate of so many sacred indigenous "idols" consigned irretrievably to flames by Spanish friars, as those who had venerated them stood by watching, powerless to deliver them.

In this way indigenous artistry and divine authorship were woven together into the fabric of colonial miracle stories recounting the origins of exceptional images. One account describes the likeness of Christ captured in woven textiles by women artisans, so skillfully rendered that it could not have been solely of human origin: "This year a woman offered a cloth of this kind with a crucifix woven on both sides. Although the one seemed to be more the right side than the other, the cloth was so well made that all who saw it, the friars as well as the lay Spaniards, admired it, saying that whoever wove it would also be able to weave a tapestry."[54] This was also the case, for example, of the Cristo del Noviciato, which, around the same period as the appearance of the Totolapan Cristo, was brought to the Dominican convento by mysterious Indian men claiming to be the sculptors of the image. Their admission of authorship did nothing to lessen the Dominican's sense that the image was of divine origin, a perception that was confirmed when the Indians mysteriously disappeared, leaving the Cristo behind.[55]

The struggles and difficulties native sculptors inevitably faced in asserting their authority and skill to create Christian images also constituted part of the hagiographies of some images. In the context of sixteenth-century Peru (in what is now Ecuador), for example, Ramos Gavilán recounts the history of the Indian sculptor Francisco Tito Yupanqui who created the image of the Virgin of Copacabana in 1582. Though Ramos Gavilán affirms the Christian spirit of prayerfulness and sense of the sacred with which Yupanqui carved the image, he also describes how Yupanqui was mocked, taunted, and humiliated by the Spanish for his lack of skill. In a letter attributed to the artist and preserved by his brother, Yupanqui himself poignantly recalls the painful experience:

> I left there saying, "Jesus, Saint Mary; may God and the virgin, His holy mother, help me," For they told me that the image was not well made, and that it looked like a man with a beard or what appeared to be whiskers. They found much fault in it, much that was not good,

and they told me I should not carry on making it. And once his
lordship had seen the image, everyone laughed a lot, ridiculing [me]
the painter. Each Spaniard who took it in his hands laughed upon
seeing it, and they told me that native Andeans cannot paint images
of the virgin, nor make statues. I ended up feeling weak, appalled,
and vexed. I went to church to ask for Our Lord's mercy and that I
might somehow manage to get the image of Our Lady painted, and
all the rest. I asked in my prayer for license to do this work, that He
would grant me the hand to make sculpted images and to be a
skillful painter.[56]

Yupanqui's original efforts to create the image actually failed, and he was compelled to construct a second that met Spanish standards. In the official history
of the shrine, this artist's persistence in the face of ridicule, and the subsequent Spanish recognition of the beauty of the image he eventually created,
are indications of divine involvement in the artistic creation of the Virgin of
Copacabana.[57]

In another example, the Cristo Negro de Otatitlán, Mexico, the story of
mysterious artistic origins is again rehearsed with the creation of the image
from the intertwining of divine and human agency and action. As the story
goes, two well-dressed visitors arrived at the house of an Indian man. The Indian had a cedar log and had been searching for a skilled sculptor to create an
image of the Virgin. When the Indian communicated this wish to the strangers
at his door, the elegant men offered themselves as sculptors. The next day when
the Indian went to visit them he discovered, "by the prodigious grace of the all-
powerful God, that the ordinary piece of wood had been transformed into a
prodigious effigy of Christ Crucified." The angels had disappeared, without
payment, but had also left money and food behind. Here, yet again, the artists
are angels in disguise. It is noteworthy that in spite of the Indian's explicit
request for a Virgin, the angels deemed the crucifix a more fitting gift.[58]

Miracle stories that bind artist and image are not limited to Indian protagonists. A young local girl recounted the origin legend of another Andean image
of Christ crucified, the Cristo de la Soledad of Huaraz, to anthropologist Barbara
Bode: "Long ago three priests were living together. One asked to be left alone to
carve a crucifix. When the other two returned in about a week to bring food to
their companion, they found he had disappeared. There was only a beautiful
crucifix, and they concluded that the priest-sculptor himself was the Christ on
the cross."[59] In this instance the identification between image and artist is complete: the sculptor, priest, crucifix, and Christ are all one and the same.

These accounts have in common with the Cristo Aparecido of Totolapan
that the act of artistic creation itself is perceived as miraculous. In the case of
the Aparecido, the absence of a clear author/owner led to the conclusion that
the image was of heavenly origin: fashioned and molded by God, the divine

artist, much as He had sculpted and shaped the first human form, Adam himself, worked from clay. The mysterious Indian was not author of the Cristo but
a mere porter, bearer of God's gift into the world. For modern-day devotees
there is no other reasonable explanation for how a seemingly ordinary Indian
would come to have come to have possession of a rare object of such obvious
material value. Likewise, there was no other explanation for why the messenger
refused remuneration and then disappeared.

After the very existence of these extraordinary images was clarified, some
explanation was also required for how they arrived in far-flung, seemingly inaccessible territories. Origin legends also therefore engage the problem of distribution of images once they have been created, a topic addressed in the story of
the Cristo Aparecido's genesis. Along with theme of artistic production, then,
the distribution of crosses, crucifixes, and saints' images is a minor theme
in the colonial histories of the spiritual conquest written by Motolinía, Mendieta, and Torquemada. In these accounts, Indians are not only posited as agents
of artistic production of miraculous Christian images but also as the agents of
their distribution. As was true for the Aparecido, Indians, often in the form of
angels, were literally the bearers of Christ into Indian pueblos and into Spanish
churches and monasteries.

Indians were certainly agents of the distribution of Christian imagery in
the New World: Spanish sources record how they erected "with great enthusiasm" crosses at summits and in the mountains, at every crossroads, and in
front of every home.[60] A few of these Indian-erected crosses were recognized to
be miraculous: one piously twisted and bent to gesticulate the sign of the cross
and another was miraculously fragrant and odiferous.[61] Later, Indians were
also involved in the distribution of the more artistically complex crucifixes. Indian angels also delivered the Cristo del Noviciato, much like the Aparecido.
In his chronicle of the Dominican order in Mexico, Juan Bautista Méndez
pieces together the legend of the appearance of the Noviciato Cristo to the
famed sixteenth-century friar Domingo de Betanzos. The two cristos have so
much in common that Méndez is careful to clarify that theirs is fact distinct
from the Cristo of Totolapan, with which it is often confused. Because of its
similarities to the Totolapan narrative, I reproduce it here in full:

> In those years one did not easily come across images, as the land had
> only recently been conquered. . . . And one day, a padre was in his cell
> and two Indians arrived at the door in search of him. . . . The Indians
> asked them if they wanted to buy the image, and that was when [the
> friars] discovered an admirable [representation] of the holy crucifix . . .
> with all perfection as could have been done by the most excellent
> sculptor, very devoutly and well made, such as that which the most
> fervent spirit might desire. Fr. Domingo and the *portero* admired that
> the Indians, who had not yet had mastered the art form, had produced

one so well made. And so they told them that it had been made as a copy of one that the Marqués del Valle [Cortés] had in his oratorio.

Fr. Domingo, that servant of God, content at having seen his greatest desire fulfilled, wrapped the holy crucifix in his arms and he entered the convento to arrange it and pay the officials, and the Indians entered behind him. The portero then closed the door and remained inside. The padre arrived at the stairs embracing [the image of] his Lord, just as his heart was also embraced in the love of God, until he arrived [at the stairs] and discovered that the Indians were no longer following him. He went back and looked from one side to the other and could not find them. And deciding that they had stayed at the door, he went back in search of his benefactors. He asked the portero if they had departed and he replied that no. They looked for them throughout the whole convento . . . but even up until today nothing more is known of those *indios*. . . . And that which those first padres piously discussed is that for, for the good of the souls and the consolation of his servant, Fr. Domingo, God had sent Angels in the form of Indians. [62]

For both Betanzos' Cristo and the Totolapan image, angels in the form of Indian messengers are the vehicles for the arrival of miraculous crucifixes.

Méndez goes on to discuss several other images of Christ left by Indians. In the community of women religious of the order of the Immaculate Conception in Mexico City, a life-sized image of Christ on the cross was offered as a gift by mysterious Indian men dressed in white. These angels did not leave the image with one of the sisters, as one might expect, but rather gifted it to an Indian woman working for them as a servant. Another image, a Christ at the Column, was left by Indians at the parish church of Santa Catarina Mártir, also in Mexico City, and yet another, an Ecce Homo painting, at the convent of Santa Catalina de Sena.[63] In each case, the Indian bearers of the images inexplicably disappear, asking and receiving no payment and offering no explanation for their actions.

Another subset of cristos aparecidos appeared by way of miraculous "substitution," replacing indigenous images. According to these stories, a cristo inexplicably appears in the place of an indigenous deity or image. This is the case for the Señor de Chalma, today the most powerful and famous of the Mexican cristos. His shrine is the second-most visited pilgrimage site in all of Mexico, after Tepeyac, the sanctuary of the Virgin of Guadalupe. According to a devotional history of the image written in the eighteenth century, the Señor originally appeared by a miracle in one of the local caves, where the local indigenous communities had continued to worship their traditional deities, despite constant warnings, admonitions, and threats on the part of their diligent friars. The Augustinians Nicolás de Perea and Sebastián de Tolentino discovered the image by chance one morning. Entering the cave one morning, the friars saw the displaced "idols" lying broken on the ground, and the triumphant, glowing crucifix standing in their place.[64]

Art historians, not persuaded by the colonial accounts of Indian angels, have posed their own answers to the question of how images of Christian saints, often quite large, made their way into the Mexican hinterland at a time in history when such journeys were made by foot. For the Cristo of Totolapan and the cristos de caña, lightness was a key attribute of the technology used in their construction. Maguey, the material out of which the Cristo Aparecido was sculpted, and the hollow caña technology both produce seemingly weightless images. In precolonial religious practice, the technology of creating light images was probably innovated to facilitate their processional use. The new Christian religion also included processions of religious objects in its practice, and so it is logical that the pre-Columbian technology would have been appropriated for the creation of light, easily carried Christian processional images.[65] Modern-day priests responsible for carrying the Cristo Aparecido on long processions often observe that "no pesa nada," he weighs nothing. Of the cristos de caña, Motolinía notes that, "sometimes the [Indians] make the crucifix in such a way that, although it be the size of a man, a child could lift it from the ground with one hand."[66] Their characteristic lightness would have clearly facilitated transportability and distribution. In this way, these images are an unexpected fulfillment of Jesus' own biblical promise to his followers: "For my yoke is easy and my burden is light" (Matthew 11:30). For art historians, lightness serves as one explanation for how the unknown Indian man managed to carry the Cristo Aparecido from Mexico City, a fairly rigorous one-day journey by foot under the best of circumstances, and a journey that would have been made much more grueling had he been carrying a weighty crucifix.[67]

Skeptical modern-day observers, not persuaded that Indian angels played a central role in the distribution of crucifixes throughout the colony, tend to assert that it was the missionary friars themselves who carried these images with them as they sought to evangelize more remote communities. Art historian Estrada Jasso does not accept the substitution "miracle" for the Cristo de Chalma, for obvious reasons; but neither does he imagine that Indians (angels or otherwise) were agents of distribution. Rather, he is of the opinion that missionaries themselves were the bearers of images: "it cannot be explained how else fray Nicolas de Perea, elderly and a little blind, was able to walk through the mountains of Chalma with a Christ on his back, on a path unknown by the Indians, if it were not light; and in this period light meant 'de Caña.'"[68] Others agree that the friars themselves engineered the miraculous appearance of the cristos. One priest who had served as prior of Totolapan in the 1980s explained to me: "These images were made to appear by the friars." As he spoke he smiled at me knowingly, suggesting that the massive introduction of these images was part of a deliberate and elaborate deception on the part of the Spanish missionaries who contrived the miracles.

The many images discussed here are the Señor Aparecido's cristos hermanos, kindred christs who share with the Aparecido similar origins: origins that blur the boundary between miracle and artistic creation. Whether they were borne into more remote communities in the arms of Indian angels, as devotees hold, or carried by the Spanish friars themselves, as secular observers believe, the images themselves were powerful instruments for Christian mission. As one art historian suggests, "these images were the first to arrive in the most faraway places in the advance of the faith: they are the evangelizers of Mexico, the ones that remained behind when the missionary continued on his journey."[69] The process by which the Cristo Aparecido and its hermanos became agents of indigenous evangelization is the primary subject of the subsequent chapter.

A Meditation on Suffering

Roa and the other Augustinian friars of Totolapan were surprised by the Cristo's unlikely arrival at the remote convento, but even more than this, they were stunned by the skill and deliberateness with which the author had created a meditation on divine suffering. The most salient physical feature, for the friars, was that the image was an unprecedented and uniquely graphic engagement with the theme of Jesus' affliction on the cross. In this way, the very early Cristo Aparecido may have anticipated the exaggerated hyperrealism of the subsequent generations of crucifixes that have come to be seen as paradigmatic of Mexican piety.

In the first few centuries after the death of Jesus, early Christian artists abstained from depicting Jesus on the cross. The memory of Jesus' death was still raw and recent, and the cross too stark a reminder and too transparently a symbol of capital punishment. Possibly the earliest depiction of Christ on the cross is a fifth-century Roman image carved into a panel of an ivory casket. The panel depiction is of the resurrected, living Christ: eyes open, his limbs and body full of vigor, this is the Christ who has triumphed over death. It was not until almost five hundred years later, as the millennium drew to a close, that crucifixes more deliberately engaged the theme of Christ's affliction, and more routinely came to show Jesus as wounded and even dead on the cross.

Arguably the most paradigmatic of the tormented Crucifixion images is the one represented by the German painter Matthias Grünewald, in his Isenheim altarpiece. The work was completed early in the sixteenth century for St. Anthony's monastery located in the Alsace region of northeastern France. This is an image that has garnered the attention of theologians, writers, and philosophers for centuries.[70] The tortured and afflicted Christ is reduced, in Grünewald's rendering, to something less than human, at once dead and wracked with pain. Perhaps it is the hands and feet of this dead, even decomposing, Christ that are the most shocking: gnarled and contorted with the spasms of death, the nails are a grey-black and the hands monstrous and claw-like. His flesh is marked with blisters, wounds, and oozing pus, some say because the monks of St. Anthony's ministered to people with skin afflictions. More than four centuries later, in 1954, the surrealist artist Salvador Dalí created his famous Crucifixion painting, *Corpus Hypercubus*, in response to Grünewald. Dalí explained that his intention was to create a crucifix image "containing the most beauty and joy of anything anyone has painted up to the present day. I want to paint the Christ who will be the absolute antithesis of the materialist and savagely anti-mystical Christ of Grünewald."

For the most part, the first sixteenth-century Mexican representations of Christ were not preoccupied with the theme of physical affliction. The indigenous artistic media commonly employed did not lend themselves particularly to the theme of suffering. For example, a genre of crosses and crucifixes created using Indian techniques of turquoise inlay, featherwork, and adorned with precious metals and stones, are clearly designed to be things of beauty without obvious reference to suffering. The crucifixes carved by Indian artisans from cross-shaped branches are for the most part small, simple images, not suitable for the painfully detailed depictions of blood, torn skin, and open wounds that so often characterize those explicitly tormented christs that have come to be seen as paradigmatic of Mexican piety. The great stone atrial crosses that also represent early indigenous-Christian artistry may be the first examples of Mexican Christian sculpture.[71] In these monumental crosses, the theme of Christ's suffering is referenced only abstractly, represented symbolically with the presence of the instruments of Jesus torture (the lash, the crown of thorns, the nails); and these are embedded, almost hidden, within the highly stylized indigenous design. The churchyard cross of Atzacoalco, "in a very curious way, becomes equivalent to Christ: the blood flows from it, and it is crowned with thorns. It seems to be turning into an idol, with the mask of Christ notably larger and more plastic, and the fluted finials about to become hands."[72] Solid and imposing, the Indian-sculpted atrial crosses communicate strength, power and presence, not affliction and pain.

Neither do the cristos de caña readily lend themselves to the graphic representation of suffering. The technology is not a delicate one, and even the limbs of these images take on an almost impressionistic rather than cadaveric quality. Absent from the majority of these are the veins, sinew, and strained and taut muscles that characterize later sculpted cristos. At the extraordinary Museo de Arte Virreinal in Tepoztlán there is a "Cristo de Pasta de Caña" that is in exceptionally fine condition. Dating from the seventeenth century, the corpus is perhaps two and a half feet in length. Rather than gaunt and drawn, the figure on the cross is almost thick-wasted, with a slightly rounded belly reminiscent of Jesus as recalled by many Byzantine icons. Layered upon him, as if upon a palimpsest, one observes the representation of two kinds of blood. The first is clearly an older, prior, original layer: a series of almost geometric, abstract, parallel lines that are meant to represent lashings.[73] These run nearly horizontally across the body, faint and dark grey-blue, like so many faded tattoos. Upon these there have been added, in some subsequent century, darker red rivulets, channels, and fingers of blood running lengthwise, down the corpus. The single wound on his body is where the soldier's lance pierced his side—a fairly deep gash on his left side from which blood runs. The nails that fix his hands and feet are large, oversized, and disproportional to the rest of the body. Blood runs from these wounds, as well. But the face of this Christ is tranquil, eyes ever so slightly open, and at peace.

Some observers have described the facial expressions of the sixteenth-century Mexican christs as containing an element of calm and even serenity in comparison with those of subsequent centuries: "All traces of physical torment and cruel wounds are contained and, in some cases, only hinted at" in these early representations.[74] Art historian Nelly Sigaut suggests that the later concern for the gritty details of physical affliction is also absent in many early colonial two-dimensional painted works. In some instances, blood was added in later centuries to early colonial paintings of Christ's passion and Crucifixion as later sensibilities found these prior images wanting in this regard.[75] The addition of blood was a common practice with sculpted and modeled images, as well, as is evident on the caña cristo in the Museo de Arte Virreinal, as succeeding generations of santeros sought to make earlier images more realistic and "lifelike." Perhaps the decline of caña technology sometime in the late seventeenth century (according to key sources) was due in part to its inefficacy as a tool for the communication of suffering, which began to take center stage in the artistic imagination of Christian artists at around this time.[76] Yet in one interesting respect the cristos de caña may have functioned as poignant expressions of suffering. One historical memory holds that Indians inserted letters narrating their suffering under conquest and Spanish rule inside caña images that were sent to Spain.[77]

Though it would be around a century before copious blood became commonplace in artistic representations of Christ's passion and Crucifixion, this is not to say that these were absent in the first half of the sixteenth century. The Cristo Aparecido is a case in point. However, the fact that explicitly suffering images of Christ were exceptional among those designed by indigenous artists challenges the current scholarly consensus that the Indians themselves were most taken with the doloroso (or pained) aspect of the crucifix. In retrospect, the Roa crucifix may in fact prefigure the subsequent shift in aesthetic and spiritual sensibilities.

Conclusions

Here I have viewed the military and spiritual conquest of Mexico through the lens of material religion and visual culture. This approach reveals the collaborative indigenous-Spanish authorship for the Cristo Aparecido and many of its cristos hermanos. Indeed, in the sixteenth century, Indian santeros were among the most effective agents of Christian evangelization: creating works of Christian imagery and and then distributing these into the conventos and capillas of New Spain. I have also suggested that the first generations of Mexican crosses and crucifixes worked by Indian hands were not primarily expressions of a theology of suffering, but rather were designed as objects of beauty and power. Though indigenous-authored crucifix images do not seem to emphasize graphic depictions of pain or suffering through most of the sixteenth century, we cannot therefore presume that suffering was not part of their symbolic content. This content was, in fact, an interpretive layer that the friars sought to communicate to the Indians. This process is the primary subject of the following chapter, in which I treat Antonio de Roa's ministry to the pueblo of Totolapan.

Neither the art historical nor mythological explanations of the Cristo's origins currently acknowledge the destruction wrought by the military and spiritual conquest. However, this dual conquest had a tragic human and artistic cost; and so the story of indigneous persecution and death are deliberately part of the account I have offered. One of the persistant themes that emerges in the biography of the Cristo Aparecido is that the fate of the Indians and the fate of their images are linked. Perhaps the first example of this was Diego de Landa's violent auto de fe in in 1562, in which the Franciscan friar oversaw the destruction of almost five thousand Mayan images and, simultaneously, directed the torture of almost as many Mayans themselves. In this chapter the reader has also encountered a tragic and painful inverse correlation: as the decline of the indigenous populations accelerated apocalyptically, the population of Christian santos surged. The priest Lauro López Beltrán, one of the Totolapan's twentieth-century pastors, distressingly observed of the origins of the Cristo Aparecido that, "as the Indian disappeared, Christ appeared and multiplied." I do not believe that López Beltrán intended to suggest either a causal or casual connection between the two events. Nonetheless, it does seem significant (with respect to the emergence of new religious practices and spiritual sensibilities) that the rather sudden proliferation of saints' images, a function of the progress of Christian evangelization generally, proceeded in the face of demographic collapse, wrought by violent subjugation and the spread of infectious diseases. The Cristo Aparecido arrived, to lend his power, protection and *consuelo* to the people of Totolapan on the eve of the most destructive epidemic ever suffered in central Mexico. Between 1545 and 1548, typhus took between 60 and 90 percent of population.[78]

3

Performance and Penance

The Cristo and Christian Evangelization in New Spain

The face of the crucified Christ was dark and gaunt, like that of the Indian servant. . . . Blackened, suffering, the Christ maintained a silence that did not set one at ease. He made one suffer; in such a vast cathedral, in the midst of the candle flames and the daylight that filtered down dimly, the countenance of the Christ caused suffering, extending it to the walls, to the arches and columns, from which I expected to see tears flow.

—José María Arguedas

Scene 2. The Blood of a Saint Shed for You. Pueblo de Totolapan, 1543

The monastery, the atrial gardens, and the streets of Totolapan have become once again the stage upon which friar Antonio de Roa enacts his Calvary. The friar rehearses for the hundredth time Jesus' painful journey along the road to Golgatha, the gloomy mount where the Savior was crucified. Both director of and lead actor in this impromtu street theater, Roa carries a heavy wooden cross through the pueblo. Walking barefoot over burning coals, he stumbles under the tremendous weight. Indian youths, trained to assist Roa, have been cast as Roman soldiers, flogging the friar's bare shoulders with all their might. The commotion soon draws a crowd of onlookers to the now familiar scene. Women, children, and men gather tightly around the spectacle. Blood that has been drawn gathers in large pools on the earth. One soldier shouts insults and spits upon the saint. A second recoils and, distressed at the scene as it unfolds, draws back, wringing his hands. Yet a third,

weeping, turns the lash upon his own flesh, offering himself in
place of Roa, whose already battered and subjugated body, it
seems, could hardly bear more punishment.

Upon receiving the image of the Cristo Aparecido, the friar-missionary
Antonio de Roa claimed it as his own, as God's answer to his prayers. Recall
how he had the image carried immediately to his own monastic cell, where it
probably remained until the conclusion of his relatively brief tenure as prior of
Totolapan, sometime in 1544. Even so, the Cristo was never exclusively the
object of Roa's private devotion. If that had been the case, the biography of the
Cristo might have ended as soon as it had begun. Instead, the image quickly
became the primary referent of Roa's public rituals. Above all, the Cristo was
a catechetical tool for the indoctrination of the newly converted indigenous
Christians of Totolapan, the instrument of their evangelization and hoped-for
salvation.

By the middle decades of the sixteenth century, the most pressing concern
for the monastic orders was not persuading Indians to accept the faith; the initial "conversion" of Mexico was, for the most part, swiftly and facilely accomplished. Rather, the urgent need in Roa's day was for the more arduous work of
Christian catechesis, the ongoing education and formation of Christian neophytes. Though they celebrated that the Indians had, for the most part, accepted Christianity in principal, the friars worried that this acceptance was only
superficial, that the Christian ethos had not yet penetrated the indigenous
heart, soul, and imagination. This led to Spanish fears about Indian "back-
sliding": that the new converts might return, in short order, to their more
deeply rooted traditional beliefs and practices. Furthermore, the Spanish had
apprehensions that Indians' understanding of Christianity was plagued by
misconceptions because their reception of the new religion was filtered
through indigenous cultural categories and conceptions. Most distressing for
the friars was the possibility that indigenous engagement with Christian
imagery might be tainted by the prior practice of "pagan idolatry," and that
their understanding of Christ's suffering and death would be miscompre-
hended through the lens of the Aztec practice of human sacrifice.

Driven by these concerns, the friars not only labored to instruct the Indians
in a set of beliefs and doctrines, as one might expect, but also worked to instill
in them a Christian sentiment, a Christian-informed aesthetic experience; to
communicate to them the shape, smell, and feel of devotion to the Christian
god. Conversion, then, was not a one-time event, marked, for example, by
Christian baptism, but an ongoing process of deepening and internalization.
On the one hand, the Indians needed to comprehend the basic tenets of the
faith, but on the other hand, they also needed to know what it *felt* like to be a
Christian. With this as his motivation, the friar Roa immediately went about
the business of encouraging local devotion to Christ by sharing his own awe

El V. Siervo de Dios, y Apostol de la Cierra alta, Fr. ANTONIO de ROA. Prior que fue de este Convento de Totolapam, Fue tan Penitente, que de un Convento à otro lo llebaban tirando de una Soga à la garganta, hasta hazerle caer muchas vezes en llegando à una de las muchas Cruzes, que por todos los Caminos havia, arrodillado la besava con tiernos suspiros, y lagrimas; y hazia le escupieran el Rostro, le dieran muchas vofetadas, y de azotes en cada una de ellas. Empleava el dia en Predicar, y administrar à los Indios de aquel Pueblo, para seguir otro, otro dia del proprio modo. En llegando la noche, llegava la Disiplina general (en la qual tambien los Indios le azotaban) Saliendo despues desnudo de medio Cuerpo arriba, Cargando una pesada Cruz à el hombro, por las Calles publicas, que ya estaban sembradas de vivo fuego, el que iva pisando con sus desnudos pies, y apagando con su viva Sangre. Por ultimo lo curaban, bañando su llagado Cuerpo con una Caldera de agua hirviendo. Sino era con recina que de Ocotes encendidos, desllaban por todo su Cuerpo, abrazandole de pies à Cabeza.

FIGURE 3.1. Roa's Penance, *Fray Antonio de Roa*. Francisco Antonio Vallejo. Oil on canvas, circa 1760s. By permission from the Instituto Nacional de Antropología e Historia on behalf of the people of Mexico.

and reverence for the Cristo Aparecido to the Totolapans. From his first encounter, when he fell on his knees before the image in full view of his Indian assistants, Roa's public penance provided the interpretive framework for indigenous reception of the Cristo, the theological narrative within which the image was to be embedded.

Toward this end, Fray Antonio emulated the suffering of Christ on the cross through the public, ritual infliction of pain on his own body, and through an ascetic discipline in which he deprived himself of food, sleep, and all forms of comfort. In the context of the missionary frontier, this christo-mimesis, or imitation of Christ, was not simply an expression of Roa's personal devotion but also served a heuristic purpose. Roa acted out a multilayered pantomime in order to bring to life for the Nahua-speaking Indians of Totolapan the gospel story of Jesus' arrest and torture at the hands of Roman soldiers and his painful road to Calvary, pointing, ultimately, to Jesus' Crucifixion and death. Thus the missionary Roa transformed himself into a sort of living crucifix. The friar became a work of art, a *retablo vivo del dolor*, or a living image of pain, in which his desecrated body also modeled Christian penitence and penance.[1] Roa's practice of physical self-discipline was a tableau vivant through which he sought to animate the Cristo Aparecido for Indian observers.[2] Employing these very public penitential practices to narrate the story of the suffering and death of Jesus, Roa's dramatic passion plays were designed to communicate to the Indians the complicated mixture of contrition, compassion, remorse, pity, sorrow, fear, love, and even affection that a Christian is meant to feel before an image of the crucified Christ. In this way, perhaps, the Indians might learn how to weep before an image of Christ, or be moved "spontaneously" to cause pain to themselves.

Recruiting Indians to participate in his penitential exercises was essential to the catechetical process through which Roa labored to make the passion of Christ real to them. A select group of local Indian youths became Roa's "reluctant torturers," sometimes bitterly resisting Roa and other times drawn by him to participate whole-heartedly in his passion plays. For the indigenous community, it must have been difficult to separate completely Roa's suffering from the suffering of Christ, as Roa's body and the afflicted and tortured body of Christ were symbolically conflated. As he demanded and inspired the participation of the Indians, Roa's own body became a dialogic frontier, a theological hinterland where intended European meanings and indigenous interpretations merged and diverged.

In the sixteenth century, the Cristo himself occupied this murky contact zone, and therefore is a lens to explore the complex and sometimes painful processes by which the indigenous people of Mexico came to see themselves as Christians. Roa and the Indian community of Totolapan struggled in relationship to define the meaning and significance of the Cristo and, more broadly, of Christian belief and practice. The negotiation of religious meaning between

Roa and the Totolapans, as it was most everywhere in the New World, was marked by a deep intimacy between indigenous people, the Christian god, and His emissaries, the familiar and all-too-human European friars. The latter were occasionally inspiring heroes, saints, and martyrs, but perhaps even more often they were frustrating and disappointing ministers—limited products of their culture, time, and place. In the sometimes painful give-and-take that characterized the intimacy and familiarity of this relationship, the Indians worked their own conversion and began to define the content and parameters of indigenous Christianity.

The story of Roa and the original devotees of the Cristo Aparecido serves as evidence that, while the forceful introduction of Christianity brought the motif of suffering to the theological center stage in a way previously foreign to the New World, the Indians' devotion to images of Christ crucified and the cross did not emerge from a "natural" identification of Christ's suffering with their own, as is widely held by modern scholars. Rather, their complex and multifaceted relationship to the Christian crucifix grew out of, and in response to, a persistent, encompassing, and exhaustive missionary effort on the part of Spanish friars in which they attempted to use crucifix devotion to inculcate in the Indians a phenomenology, epistemology, and theological aesthetics of suffering along Christian lines and in Christian symbols. At no point did Christian missionaries encourage an association between the suffering of Christ and the suffering of indigenous Mexicans. If anything, Roa's performances negated the reality of indigenous suffering: he was the sufferer, *Christ* was the sufferer, not they. Thus the story of their military conquest and death by epidemic disease is absent from the historical record treating the origins of the Cristo.

In a final section I explore the question of iconographic commensurability between the equally rich and abundant Aztec and Christian visual religion. I argue that the Mesoamerican pantheon did not provide the interpretive framework for the reception of Christian images. Rather, it was the affective and emotional aspects of their prior religious practice that the Indians brought with them into their newly adopted religion.

Mimetic Saints and Articulate Images: Roa and Spanish Missionary Methods and Meanings

Fray Antonio de Roa's extreme penitential disciplines preceded the miraculous arrival of the Cristo Aparecido in Totolapan. However, before 1543 Roa's physical self-disciplines were actions without a referent, cast as if by random before an abstract and invisible god. Recall how desperately and persistently Roa had begged and pleaded to God for a crucifix that could receive his devotions. After its miraculous arrival, the Cristo became not only the object of Roa's piety but also the referent for his penitential performances, that to which his passion plays pointed. To Roa, it must have seemed that the diminutive Cristo Aparecido, with his sorrowful, delicate features and open arms spread wide, could encompass the friar's own battered body, the fragile, nascent faith of the Totolapans, and, indeed, the entire Christian narrative within his generous embrace. It is no wonder, then, that the friar wept when he first beheld the image.

At the time of the Cristo's appearance in 1543, the community of Totolapan had felt the impact of Spanish conquest and colonization for two decades. However, the process of methodical Christian evangelization and education had barely begun. The Totolapans were already Christians, to be sure: that is, they had been baptized and were probably familiar with the key personages of the Christian narrative: Jesus, Mary, and God the Father. They attended mass and received sacraments when a priest was available, and may have even been able to recite the Lord's Prayer. Yet their knowledge and experience of Christianity was almost certainly limited to these broad brushstrokes, and so Roa's role as *doctrinero* of the parish was to give content, substance, and form to their neophyte faith.

It may be that most friars saw themselves less as *misioneros* seeking the conversion of souls than as doctrineros whose task was to catechize the Indians in the nuances of the faith. In the interpretation of historian and linguist James Lockhart, both the Nahua and the Spanish friars assumed a de facto conversion to Christianity based on the military conquest.[3] This was the fundamental premise of the Requerimiento, the formal statement of sovereignty and declaration of war that was read as a matter of policy by conquistadors to the indigenous communities they encountered. The Requerimiento demanded that these communities willingly submit to the authority of the Roman Catholic Church and its representatives in the New World, the Spanish king and queen, or be forced into submission "to the yoke and obedience of the Church and of their Highnesses" through kidnapping, enslavement, and warfare. In either case, Christianization was inevitable, assured, and ultimately assumed: a collective conversion, rather than a matter of individual persuasion. The military defeat of the people of Mexico thus became the ritual enactment of their conversion: a literal "baptism by fire."

Roa and other Spanish missionaries to the Americas engaged the full panoply of methods for evangelization and catechesis available at their disposal. Some of these they brought with them from Spain and others were improvised in the colony and later formalized and institutionalized. Among these were forceful, even violent, techniques including extirpation, forced baptisms, obligatory participation in Christian liturgical life under threat and coercion, the disruption of community and culture by the compulsory settlements known as *reducciones*, a range of physical disciplines, and other punishments. Not surprisingly, subtler strategies were by far more persuasive and compelling to indigenous peoples.

Christian art and images, in particular, were among the most effective and successful tools for Christian catechesis.[4] This Roa and other friars clearly recognized. However, the potency of religious images was, at least initially, utterly dependent upon the friars, who not only brokered indigenous engagement with Christian visual culture but who were themselves, as extraordinary personalities, powerful agents of Christian conversion. In their own time, these giants of history were sometimes for the Indians inspiring personages whose methods of modeling and persuasion included visible expressions of intense religious fervor and devotion, extremes of monastic austerity, and dramatic acts of penitence. By the second half of the sixteenth century, the labors and accomplishments of the Spanish mendicant friars had taken on legendary proportions, not least among their monastic peers. Roa was certainly numbered among these, as one twentieth-century reflection declares that Roa, along with his fellow Augustinian monastics, were "the cornerstone on which the magnificent work of the Augustinian order was built."[5]

In his discussion of sixteenth-century *venerables*, or saintlike Spanish friars, historian Serge Gruzinski writes that these holy men were, in they eyes of the indigenous people, *curanderos* of sorts: miracle workers and healers who controlled the elements. Though for the most part Roa and the other friars never intended to make of themselves objects of indigenous veneration, these holy men and their relics did, according to Gruzinski, in some instances, become for the Indians "the immediate, physical, palpable, tangible expression of another reality, the one evoked much more distantly by the Christian images and more abstractly by the sermons."[6] In this way they contributed to the emergence of a "subjective experience of the Christian miraculous."

Roa was not alone in his appeal to visual culture for the edification of the Indians. In fact, religious images and other artifacts of material religion were at the very heart of the Christian conversion of the New World. When and where religious art came to the fore of methods for evangelization, friar and image were often mutually interdependent for their efficacy, as each signified the other. In the previous chapter, I explored how friars were both bearers and recipients of miraculous images. In the most pointed case, the signification was total: the Cristo de la Soledad of Huaraz came into being when the local priest miraculously metamorphosed into a sculpted crucifix. Here I argue for a similar conflation between Roa's disciplined body and the tortured body of Christ as represented in the Cristo Aparecido. In the epigraph that opens this chapter, Andean novelist José María Arguedas seems to shudder at his memory of the silent Christ, mute and menacing, that hangs in the Cuzco cathedral. In stark contrast, colonial images were meant to speak to the Indians. Roa's performances were intended to "awaken" the Indians to the voice of Christ speaking to them from the image of the crucifix, and to instill this voice with a specific content. Thus the intention of the missionary, or doctrinero, was to awaken image and devotee to one another.

The subject of Jesus' passion dominated the missionaries' sermons, though pedantic methods sometimes failed to inspire Indians, and even frequently lulled audiences to sleep. The frontispiece of the 1585 edition of Mendieta's *Historia eclesiástica Indiana* depicts just such a catechetical lesson. In the black-and-white line drawing, a friar speaks from a raised pulpit to a large group of seated Indians who are listening with varying degrees of attentiveness (figure 3.2). Indicating with a long pointer to a series of images from the life of Christ, the friar gestures in particular to an illustration of Christ on the road to Calvary burdened under the cross. He dutifully explains the details of Christ's persecution in a lecture format. The Indians are, for the most part, attentive, though finally passive, students. A second friar dozes behind the pulpit. A drawing by Guaman Poma similarly depicts a disinterested Indian audience, some listeners even dozing during a priest's sermon.

A contrasting image, shown in figure 3.3, opens the fourth book of Mendieta's text. Here a friar indicates with a similar pointer to Christ hanging on the cross. In this second representation, however, the skilled preacher has succeeded in transporting his audience to the actual historical moment of the Crucifixion. The Indians gather near the foot of the cross to receive the lesson, physically present at the moment of Christ's agony. The missionary has succeeded in literally animating the passion story for his students, transporting them spiritually to the moment of Christ's death. Here, the Indians respond physically to the friar's instruction: their eyes are fixed on their instructor (notably not on Christ himself) but they kneel, fold their arms across their chest in a sign of devotion, and clasp their hands in prayer.

These illustrations are evidence of the crucial role visual images played in the missionary endeavor, in particular artistic depictions of Christ's agony on the cross. The contrast between Mendieta's two depictions, one a mundane lesson and the other a transformative encounter with the divine, reveals that at least initially it was the skill, techniques, and the person of the friar that served to instill religious images with meaning and emotive power for indigenous audiences. By all accounts, Roa was uniquely gifted in this regard.

Roa's self-mortification, through which he sought to bring Christ's suffering to life, is the primary focus of the diverse sources through which we can reconstruct the friar's life and ministry.[7] Most notably, Roa's self-flagellation emerges as the primary topic of concern for indigenous witnesses from Totolapan in an Inquisition case from 1583. Although the stated purpose of the hearings was to discern whether the Cristo Aparecido was of miraculous origin, the line of questioning, and consequently the content of the testimonies, quickly turned toward Roa's violent and brutal penitential practices.

Roa's penance was considered extreme, even in a period when the practice of self-discipline was common among the religious orders and laity alike. Juan de Grijalva's colonial history of the Augustinian order notes the shock and even horror that characterized people's responses to hearing of Roa: "the life of the

Spus Dñi supme: Euangelizare paupib' misitme Esa.61

FIGURE 3.2. Friar sleeps during his colleague's pedantic sermon. Gerónimo de Mendieta. Print, Mexico, 1596. *Historia eclesiástica Indiana*. Mexico City: Antigua Librería, 1870. Frontispiece, Book I.

Non iudicaui me ſcire aliquid inter vos
niſi Jeſum Chriſtum, & hunc crucifixum. 1.
cor.z

FIGURE 3.3. Vivid and emotive sermon transports Indian parishioners to the moment of
the crucifixion. Gerónimo de Mendieta. Print, Mexico, 1596. *Historia eclesiástica Indiana.*
Mexico City: Antigua Librería, 1870. Frontispiece, Book II.

blessed Fr. Antonio de Roa is so admirable, and so great were his penitences . . . that he terrified these nations."[8] Because penance was considered excessive by the standards of his order, his provincial commanded Roa to moderate these disciplines. The friar skillfully negotiated his way out of obeying his superior without creating offense.[9]

Roa's disciplines were considered a *raro modo*, a strange method, but colonial observers themselves recognized that, perhaps owing to their exaggerated, even extreme, nature, these practices were an effective means of evangelization and catechesis. The first missionaries to the New World often compared themselves to the original disciples of Jesus, who first labored to build up the Christian church. The disciples' power to work healing miracles and other wonders facilitated the rapid spread of Christianity throughout the Roman Empire and the Middle East, even into Africa. The Spanish missionaries to Mexico often wondered why God had not similarly blessed them, and even suggested that extreme bodily disciplines might be an acceptable substitute for more traditional miracles: "If the Indians were witnesses to the austerity and purity of the life of their preachers, what need did they have of miracles?"[10]

Roa contrived a variety of ways to have pain inflicted on his body. He trod barefoot in the mountains over sharp rocks; he had himself whipped in front of the crosses that were planted all over the sierra; he walked through flames or had boiling water spilled on his bare body—all of these on a nearly daily basis. The majority of these exercises, it would seem, were staged in public spaces, either on the church patio, in the open air in the sierra, or at various predetermined spaces throughout the village. Totolapan thus became the *teatro*, the theater, of Roa's physical disciplines.[11]

These disciplines either preceded or followed a sermon about the theological doctrine that Roa was intending to communicate. After preaching about the pains of hell, Roa walked on live flames. Exhorting his followers to understand that the body is a slave, he ordered hot resin to be poured on his bare chest. When he commanded others to whip him in front of the crosses scattered throughout the sierra, he followed with a sermon arguing that this was what God had suffered for all sinners.[12] After whipping himself in front of a cross, Roa would pray out loud, "I am the sinful one, God, I deserve these punishments, not you, who is innocence itself."[13] Roa's penitential practices were thus designed to demonstrate with his body the doctrines that he preached.

In the 1583 Inquisition case that scrutinized the origins of the Cristo Aparecido, Indian men in their sixties and seventies testified about their experience of Roa over forty years earlier.[14] These testimonies are firsthand recollections of the arrival of the crucifix, the disappearance of the anonymous Indian messenger, and of Roa's penitential practices. Juan de Santa María had, at the age of just sixteen, served as one of Roa's assistants. As the first Indian witness, he recalled how Roa commanded him to insult and verbally abuse him, describing how Roa would remove his habit and put his head between his legs and ask each of the assistants to give him ten lashings and three blows. We did "exactly as Roa ordered," Santa María explained: "We martyred him until we ourselves were exhausted." Under the friar's direction, Santa María together with the other assistants also held Roa down and poured smoldering *copal* (incense) on his bare flesh. They then dragged him by the feet from the altar to the church door, "which injured him so badly that the floor was nothing else than a lake of blood." The subsequent witnesses, each in turn, described in graphic detail a similar routine of abuse.

For Roa himself, these disciplines must have had multiple meanings and significations. Certainly they comprised part of an ascetic, monastic discipline that he brought with him from Spain. Grijalva explains that upon taking the Augustinian habit Roa had already begun to incorporate *las asperezas del cuerpo*, the harsh punishment of the body, into his spiritual practice.[15] But while Roa's ascetic disciplines preceded his contact with the indigenous people of the New World, they garnered additional significance in the new setting. I have argued that here they became, for Roa, deliberate tools for catechesis and evangelization, to be imitated and, ultimately, adopted by the Indians themselves. Additionally, as the personal continuation of a prior practice, they connected him ritually to the Augustinian brothers he left behind in Europe and to other friars laboring, like himself, much alone on the fringes of the colony. That is, they must have provided a much needed continuity and consistency for the friar himself.

Most notably, Roa's own understanding of Christian penance seems to have taken on an additional valence in relation to the "poverty" of the routine practices of the native people he encountered. Osorio de San Román, author of the earliest printed source that includes details of Roa's life, describes how, "Seeing that the Indians were barefoot, he took off his shoes; and seeing that they walked around without clothing and slept on the floor, he covered himself with a simple sack and used a plank to sleep upon; seeing how they ate roots lived with a rare simplicity, he deprived himself of all luxuries in his meals; for many years he did not wish to eat even bread, or wine, or meat. In this way he made himself equal to them, in order to win them all to God."[16]

The meaning of the traditional monastic discipline of the mendicant orders was thus transformed in the missionary setting. On the one hand, imitation of carefully and deliberately selected indigenous habits was an effective means of gaining the Indians' interest, trust and respect and therefore considered efficacious as a missionary strategy. But even more interesting, Christian asceticism seems to have been partially redefined in relation to the cultural practices of the indigenous population. Historian Louise Burkhart describes Nahua cultural codes for moderation, modesty, and restraint, particularly around the consumption of food.[17] The friars avidly documented and even admired these practices and, at least at an early stage of evangelization, through these observations came to recognize the Indians as naturally inclined toward the practice of Christianity, perhaps even naturally "Christlike" in the austerity, simplicity, and humility of the routine practice of their daily life. San Roman's observation that Roa imitated or emulated these practices to deepen his own penance suggests the possibility that making oneself like the Indians was simultaneously a form of christo-mimesis, making oneself like Christ.

The inverse was simultaneously true. Other colonial sources attribute the increased intensity of Roa's penances in the New World setting not to imitation but rather to the inherent moral weakness and spiritual incapacity of the Indians. Alonso Fernández, author of a 1611 hagiographic casting of Roa's life, argues that the penitential friar's public displays of self-punishment were a response to the his perception that the Indians of his doctrina were insufficiently sincere or thorough in their own penance: "Considering that the Indians naturally paid little attention to sin, spilling few tears over their guilt, [Roa] decided to preach to them about the mystery and wisdom of the cross . . . to move them to penitence and to instill in them the fear of God. [For these reasons] the saint offered his own flesh in sacrifice to God for the well being of his flock."[18] Juan de Grijalva's subsequent and definitive history of the order records that as Roa preached he had himself scourged publicly, as the Indians "give little weight to words without deeds."[19]

Roa's public self-mortifications were thus multivalent but, most important for this discussion, they were deliberately intended to model appropriate devotion to representations of the cross, and to the crucifix more specifically. Osorio de San Román explains how when Roa encountered any cross at all, he would remove his shirt and receive many powerful blows. He would ask the Indians to spit in his face and insult him, and then explain that this is what God suffered at the hands of sinners. All of this was designed to "teach his children the respect that is owed to the cross and the reason why it is paid reverence."[20]

Roa's example is illustrative of a strategy employed, to varying degrees, by other missionaries. Though they do not treat Antonio de Roa specifically, colonial histories of the spiritual conquest by the sixteenth-century Franciscan chroniclers Juan de Torquemada, Gerónimo de Mendieta, and Toribio de Benavente Motolinía serve to place Roa's missionary effort within the broader context of colonial strategies for stimulating crucifix devotion and for communicating a Christian theology of suffering and contrition. These texts make it clear that Roa was not alone in using his own body to provoke an emotional response from the Indians in front of the crucifix. Cortés himself was possibly the first to demonstrate reverence to the crucifix for the benefit of the Indians. After compelling Moctezuma (who agreed but not without "great sighs") to allow him to erect a crucifix inside the Aztec Templo Mayor, the conqueror was the first to adore the image, kneeling in front of it and "shedding many tears of devotion."[21]

European friars frequently engaged in such displays specifically intended for the edification of the Indians. For example, in one of the Franciscan missionary schools there were nearly a thousand children under the friars' care and supervision. In the place where the children gathered for instruction, the friars set up an image of Christ before which they knelt, prostrated themselves, or held their arms outstretched to represent the cross. In so doing, they hoped that "the children might see by example the devotion and reverence with which God is sought." The friars also scourged themselves in front of the students, prayed, cried, and *se ponían en cruz*, assumed the posture of the cross, so that the children might come to be "branches in the tree of Christ."[22]

Thus, Roa's "antics" were not merely an isolated extreme but rather must be understood to form part of a larger missiological method and project. The drama, pain, and horror of the Crucifixion were an essential part of the colonists' faith that the friars sought to relay to the Indians. It was precisely the interior life of their Christian neophyte Indian charges that Fray Roa and other Spanish friars sought to affect. Torquemada explains that the "origins of the great reverence and devotion that the Indians had for the Holy Cross . . . was the continuous preaching and doctrine that the first masters gave them . . . in the wood of the cross and the example *por obra* [in deed] that they gave in their life . . . *que toda era cruz y penitencia* [that all was cross and penance]."[23] In what can readily be interpreted as elaborately orchestrated dramas, the friars attempted to solicit, seduce, and compel Indians into an emotional engagement with the crucifix, mediated by penitential practice. In this way they worked to embed the crucifix within a Christian interpretative framework and to define the parameters of Christian emotional engagement.

Roa's public penance was intended, in part, to weave a theological narrative about the suffering of Christ around the Cristo Aparecido, and to make the Cristo speak so that this narrative might be "audible" to the people of Totolapan, to stimulate a dialogue of sorts between image and devotee. The late sixteenth-century Augustinian reflection on the nature of images of Christ's suffering written by the Augustinian Osorio de San Román is telling in this regard. San Román explains that "An image of Christ in the Garden at Gethsemane, a Christ at the Column, an Ecce Homo; all of these images work miracles in the hearts of people. Who has not heard their voices and seen their tears, or contemplated the blood represented on an image of Christ? What secrets does a Christ at the column tell?"[24] Contemplating an image of Christ's suffering, a devout Christian might hear the image speak its secrets:

> Well you see this back . . . opened for you and your purification. You count the lashings that they have dealt me, but at the same time you fail to count the ways in which you yourself have offended me. Why do you flee from these bound hands, and hide from the face that has been spit upon and bruised for your sake? But approach my feet with tears and pain in your heart, and with only one glance at my tear-filled eyes and bleeding body I bestow upon you forgiveness for your sins,

as well as all my grace and blessing. If you continue to live, traitor, in
your sins, what do you think my Father will do with you? But I am
your cure, look to me, for I cannot deny you my friendship.[25]

Thus images called out to the beholder, insisting that the viewer fix their gaze.
Note how in San Román's imagining, the image itself commands the beholder
to "see well," not to "hide from the face of Christ," and to "look to me" for
cure.[26] The image then calls for an emotional response, a spiritual posture: a
contrite heart, a sense of individual responsibility for Jesus' suffering; emotions elicited by the prior act of beholding, by the unaverted gaze. The voice of
the suffering Christ rings in accusation and, with the power of just "one glance"
from the devotee, melts into warm tones of forgiveness. The visual image itself
has the capacity to redeem, if the sinner is just willing to look.

Colonial observers, Indian and Spanish alike, noted that some images were
more able than others to elicit response, were more immediately evocative.
This was certainly the case for the Cristo Aparecido, which came to be seen as
miraculous, in part because of the devotion it evoked in observers, not least of
all in Roa himself. In Grijalva's history, Roa offers his own emotional reaction
as evidence of the extraordinary nature of the cross: since the arrival of the
cross he was not able to think about anything else.[27] A nineteenth-century
source confirms that the Totolapan crucifix must be miraculous in origin
because of "the devotion, respect, compunction, and tenderness that it causes...
in the soul [of the viewer]."[28]

Thus, Roa's extreme physical disciplines were called forth by the powerful
and evocative Cristo, even as the friar sought to use these, in turn, to elicit devotion among the local Indian community.

Hijos de dolores: Contrition and Penance

Roa's self-discipline was intended to help the Indians understand the central
tenets of the Christian faith, "that is, the innocence of Christ, the gravity of our
guilt, the redemption by Christ, and that which we should do."[29] Roa engineered
the transformation of his private practices of spiritual devotion into public spec-
tacles, clearly intended to instruct the Indians in key Christian doctrines regarding the meaning of suffering, sin, penance, and penitence, but also to communicate to them their emotional content. The most appropriate emotional
responses to Christ's suffering were contrition and compassion, such as that
elicited so poignantly by San Román's articulate Christ at the Column.

Theologically, Roa labored to illustrate the profound nature of Christ's suffering, pointing to the sinful nature of human beings and the innocence of
Christ. Through this process, Roa and other Spanish evangelizers sought to
transform the Indians into fellow Christian sufferers, hijos de dolores, the sons

and daughters of pain.[30] In Christian theological anthropology, which explains the place of the human person in relation to God, the earth, and the greater human community, humanity itself is defined in large part by its capacity to suffer. Human beings are, by their very nature, liable to suffering, and who better to redeem this suffering humanity than a suffering God? The friars' understanding of suffering did not, obviously, conform to familiar twentieth-century interpretations. They did not interpret suffering as we might today, in relation to physical and spiritual suffering wrought by war, hunger, or poverty; the malaise associated with existential angst; or the collective suffering of oppressed communities in the face of overwhelming systems of exploitation and oppression. What we perceive today as the profound suffering of indigenous communities in the sixteenth century caused by cultural disintegration and death by epidemic disease did not have a primary place, role, or function, within the Spanish missionaries' theological interpretation. There is no evidence that most Spanish friars perceived human suffering primarily as the result of structures of injustice, as liberation-minded clerics and theologians would come to do in the twentieth century. Nor does theodicy (questions about the identity of God, given the suffering of humankind and the presence of evil in the world) enter their extensive writing and reflections. Rather, through the practice of christo-mimesis, they sought to instill in the Indians a profound sense of remorse for their own human sinfulness and a corresponding appropriation of the practice of self-inflicted suffering through the imposition of physical pain. The most veiled aspect of the new Christian identity was that the Indians were to come to see themselves as sufferers, but within the sixteenth-century theological framework, remorse for sin, that is, contrition, was the only appropriate and desirable expression of Christian suffering.[31]

Anthropologist Jorge Klor de Alva has studied in some detail the emergence of a confessorial consciousness among Indians in the first century after the conquest. This self-scrutinizing consciousness, painstakingly cultivated by the friars, meant that Indians learned to systematically and methodically examine their memories, evaluating the smallest deed and most fleeting thought for transgression. These transgressions were then fully disclosed to Spanish priests. The centrality of this process to the missionary effort is evident in the plethora of bilingual (Spanish-Nahua) instructional manuals, or *confesionarios*, written and circulated throughout the colonial period. Klor de Alva argues that, within the context of the colonial endeavor, the purpose of the sacrament of confession was to "affect . . . each word, thought, and deed of every individual Indian," ultimately for purposes of social control.[32] That Indians should engage in this self-scrutinizing practice and then ultimately find themselves to be guilty was key to the evangelization process. Confession was not the only means of communicating the Christian sentiment of contrition; Roa's performances and preaching served a similar purpose. Authentic contrition should inspire Indians to take up penitential disciplines of their own accord.

As a case in point, Torquemada relays a scene that captures, at least in the imagination of the Spanish, the precise moment in which the Christian sense of contrition was communicated to a group of Indian lords. The friar Torquemada recounts how these lords came to express emotional affliction for the offense caused to Jesus by their own sin:

> At the beginning of the conversion of Tlaxcala, the governors had committed certain large sins deserving of punishment. But these were lords who would tolerate nothing since they were unaccustomed to being punished. . . . One [friar] was unafraid and called all the guilty and shut himself with them in the *capítulo* of the convent and compelled them to confess their sin and guilt and to understand that they needed to discipline themselves. So that they would understand that it was not his individual anger at their offense, he desired to scourge himself with them, in the same way a father wants to participate in the punishment of the sons, or as a mother whose child she has raised at her breast is ill and takes the *purga* for the child's benefit. The friar took out a scourge from his sleeve, removed his habit and began to whip himself vigorously. The Taxcaltecans, when they saw him naked and whipping himself for a fault he had not committed, *recognized themselves to be guilty* and were afraid of the act. With great readiness they prostrated on the earth and each one began to whip himself (either with a scourge the *guardían* had prepared for the situation, or with one that they had brought themselves, because in those times due to the great fervor of devotion it was rare not to carry a scourge with you). And they gave themselves many strong lashes for a very long time, until it seemed to the *guardían* that it was enough, and he gave the signal for them to stop, at which these lords were so remorseful that they wanted to return again to the past penitence and they were very thankful to the friar, confessing that he had removed a great blindness and put them in the light.[33]

Through a well-orchestrated drama, the friar succeeds in persuading the Indian lords to feel the burden of guilt and the anguish of contrition, which they then desire to manifest physically through the infliction of pain on their denuded and prostrate bodies.[34]

In this way, colonial friars educated the Indians in the public display of private affliction. Inasmuch as missionaries tended to the formation of the indigenous Christian conscience, they also urged neophytes to inhabit a Christian body. Through encouraging the appropriation of Christian penitential practices, the friars emphasized that human bodies are uniquely vulnerable to pain. Flagellation and other bodily disciplines played with, accentuated, and almost taunted this vulnerability. For many colonial observers, the Indians were "naturally" well suited for penitential discipline. First, they perceived that

Indians were not hindered by a sense of personal modesty. Motolinía explains that when "an Indian awakens in the morning and immediately desires to take the discipline . . . they are neither troubled nor embarrassed with dressing and undressing."[35] Second, Torquemada observes, the Indians "did not have as delicate flesh as others do" and were consequently better able to sustain and tolerate the lashings.[36]

Within the sixteenth-century Spanish Christian framework, Christ's own suffering on the cross seems to have been interpreted almost exclusively in relation to physical pain, rather than in connection to public humiliation, social rejection, political persecution, and a personal sense of abandonment by God. As hijos de dolores, devotees of this pained and suffering Christ, the Indians were to become Christian sufferers whose bodies were defined by availability to self-inflicted pain, who deeply grieved their own sins, and who experienced emotional anguish stemming from a profound compassion for the unmerited suffering of Christ.

Reluctant Tortures: Indigenous Responses to Roa

What sense did the Indians themselves make of the friars' labors, and how did the people of Totolapan respond to Roa, specifically? Although the Christian Indians of Totolapan accepted that there was much about the friar Roa that was extraordinary, the testimonies of Roa's Indian assistants before the Inquisition reveal their uneasiness about Roa's self-disciplines, and their ambivalence toward participating in his ritual practices. In the final analysis, though they accepted and loved both Roa and the Cristo, the Totolapans were not persuaded to transform themselves into hijos de dolores, nor to place the suffering of Christ at the forefront of their understanding of the Christian god. This conclusion is drawn from the experience of Roa's assistants, particularly when, as the intended audience of his daily spectacle, they were obliged, called, and occasionally moved, to participate in the friar's rituals of self-mortification.

The early Spanish colonial record highlights the enthusiasm with which Indians received Christianity, to which, "innocent as children," they were "naturally" inclined. By most accounts the Indians of Mexico readily accepted the legitimacy of the Christian god, even from the beginning of the conquest. This was certainly true of the Totolapan Christians who, according to colonial accounts, manifested a passionate enthusiasm for the new faith. In much of Mesoamerica the "ready acceptance" of Christianity was facilitated by the pre-existing tradition of religious inclusivism in which new deities, especially those of conquering states, were absorbed into existing local cosmologies. But as to the range of beliefs and practices that could be rightly encompassed by the new religion, and as to the location of religious authority within the local practice of Christianity, these were frequently contested, under constant negotiation and renegotiation between lay indigenous believers and Spanish priests. In some senses, then, conversion was the easy part, while evangelization was a more complicated, protracted, and painful process. Though it does not constitute an essential part of the biography of the Cristo Aparecido, in many places, especially the Yucatan, Christian exclusivism was the most devastating and costly lesson that the Indians of Mexico suffered.[37]

Regardless of the friars' intentions, the extent to which the Indians themselves located the religious significance of their penitential performances either in the nuances of Christian doctrine or in the emotional content of such enactments remains an open question. Here, then, we must contemplate how the Indians received, interpreted, and understood the missionaries' performed lessons. Too often scholars have gauged indigenous responses to Christianity along the continuum of accommodation and resistance, a paradigm that follows too narrowly the conquistadors' and missionaries' own insistence on acceptance or rejection as the only possible responses to the call for Christian conversion. The only real place for human agency and integrity in this limited understanding is in the refusal of and resistance to Christianity, an option rarely taken in Mexico, where outright rejection of Christianity was the exception. Here I seek to move beyond the limitations of the accommodation/resistance paradigm by portraying the complexity of the relationship between Roa and the community of new believers of Totolapan as the location of a complicated negotiation of religious meaning that is best comprehended somewhere in the murky terrain between conquest and conversation.

The early colonial chroniclers emphasize indigenous predilection for Christian rituals, processions, and penance. They vividly describe how Indians began to manifest Christian suffering publicly, not only through mass participation in penitential processions, numbering in the tens of thousands, according to Torquemada, but also in the adoption of the embodied gestures of faith, through weeping, sobbing, sighing, verbal expressions of pain, and contorted features that may have been very dissimilar from Nahua culturally determined ritual bodily practice.

Accounts of enthusiastic reception by chroniclers are often epic in scale. One rich description from Motolinía depicts precisely the fervor and zeal with which Indians appropriated penitential practice.

It is very edifying to see how here in Mexico they take the discipline on Holy Thursday—both the Spaniards and the countless Indians. In one section of the city are five or six thousand Indians, in another ten or twelve thousand, while—in the opinion of the Spaniards—the number in Tetzcoc and in Tlaxcallan is fifteen or twenty thousand, although the number of people going in procession seems larger than it really is. The truth is that they go in seven or eight groups and participating in it are men and women and boys, crippled and maimed. Among the crippled I saw one who attracted attention, because both his legs were paralyzed from the knees down. He hobbled forward on his knees and, with his right hand on the ground for support, he took discipline with the other hand, although he had all he could do to help himself forward by means of both hands. Some disciplined themselves with wire scourges and others with cords that do not cause less pain. They carry torches which are made of pitch-pine, are firmly tied together, and produce a good light. Their procession and taking the discipline is a good example and a source of edification for the Spaniards who are present, as well as for the Spaniards who take the discipline with them, and also for those who carry the Cross or hold the torches in order to furnish light. I have seen many Spaniards in tears. . .. The "refreshment" which they resort to after the discipline consists in washing themselves with warm water mixed with chili.[38]

Motolinía's firsthand recollection captures the general feel of this large penitential procession while painting a vivid portrait of one memorable participant in particular. The friar, Torquemada, similarly notes with approval how the Indians woke up at matins to pray and *llorar sus pecados*, cry over their sins, and then disciplined themselves "without being instructed to do so." Most important for the Spanish friars, the Indians came to take up the practice of Christian penance of their own accord, with such passion and fervor that they stood as pious examples for Spanish colonists. Fray Antonio Roa inspired similar zeal among the Indians, at least by some accounts. López Beltrán writes of him that "wherever this holy penitent went, the multitudes of Indians beat themselves, coming out from all surrounding areas, piqued by curiosity, carried by devotion, or impelled by admiration for his terrifying penances."[39]

Even given the transparent biases of Spanish authors, it is not possible to disregard these many accounts of indigenous "predilection" for Christian penance as the pure fabrication of the friars. Fairly soon after the conquest, Indians throughout Mesoamerica came to regard themselves as "good Christians" and, as part of this belief, surely came to grieve their sins and desire punishment for them. Yet this was not the case in every place or in every moment.

Far from evincing the enthusiasm so vividly described by Motolinía and Torquemada, the Totolapan witnessness uniformly express reluctance to collaborate with Roa. They make it clear that they participated in abusing the friar only against their will, at times even disregarding his instructions altogether. Juan de Santa María recalls how when they refused to whip and beat Roa he became angry and threatened them in such a way that it was not possible to "go against his will." Antonio de Luna similarly describes how he and the other youths tempered the punishments, leading Roa to complain that the lashings Luna administered were too "soft," and to insist on the use of more force.

Though more often than not Roa was successful in persuading his assistants to increase the intensity of their efforts, the degree to which these young men (mere teenagers at the time) attempted resistance is remarkable.

Their hesitance to participate is depicted visually in the painting housed today in the Iglesia Parroquial de Totolapan, which shows the participation of young Indian men in Roa's flagellation.[40] In figure 3.1, Roa is naked from the waist up, bleeding from the lashings on his shoulders. As he walks on live coals, an Indian assistant raises a whip high above his head. The person closest to the foreground of the painting is yet another Indian youth who, observing these hideous punishments, clasps his hands together in a posture indicating anxiety and concern. The theme of Roa's "reluctant torturers," here represented artistically, is also predominant in Grijalva's *Crónica:* "For this purposes the holy man trained some of the Indian acquaintances that he always had with him, they were in his company, wherever he went. These tormented his body, *with many tears and with tenderness*: but also with such ferocity that it was like they were his enemies, because this holy man *had persuaded them* to do so."[41] Grijalva goes on to describe a similar response throughout the region, observing that the indigenous peoples reacted to Roa's physical punishment with both alarm and fear.[42] The Inquisition testimonies not only reveal a lack of enthusiasm for punishing Roa but they also contain little evidence that Roa's performances inspired penitential acts like self-flagellation in the Indians themselves.

Though the Totolapans were not inclined to participate in Roa's passion plays or to emulate him by adopting their own penitential practice, there is one lesson that they seem to have internalized. The testimonies emphasize the *lástima*, or compassion, that the witnesses felt for Roa in his suffering; several describe feeling concern for Roa after particularly brutal beatings. Guillermo de San Pedro, the youngest of the witnesses, tells of his pity for Roa after he and other assistants had left the penitent friar in his cell all night with his hands brutally tied and a rope around his neck. He recalls how the next morning *movido este declarante a compasión*, moved to compassion, he could not help but to ask Roa how he was. Francisco de Roa, the witness who had known Fray Antonio the longest, assisting him for fifteen years (and who, it seems, esteemed Roa enough to take his name), repeatedly described the lástima, the pain, or even regret, that he and the other assistants had felt for Roa. Grijalva describes even more dramatically how the Indians reacted with tenderness and pity. "Their feelings became so tender that their tears flowed," he writes, "they were so admiring, and so moved to tenderness that they offered to him their own backs to help him carry the burden of those lashings."[43]

Though at first this may appear to have been an unanticipated and unintended response from the Totolapans, perhaps this is evidence that they did, in one respect, internalize the sentiment of Christian suffering that Roa was working so hard to communicate. Insofar as Roa transformed himself into a "living" crucifix, the youths' sense of compassion and lástima for him was one of the most important lessons. Indeed, these were the very sentiments that were expected to dominate Christian emotional engagement with Christ's suffering and with artistic representations of this suffering, crucifixes most of all. In a Christian framework, pity was a profoundly appropriate and "natural" response to Roa's penance, so much so that, for Grijalva, even the physical environment of the region echoes the Indian's lástima: "The very stones of those mountains even until today are filled with tenderness; today the highest peaks humble themselves in his name."[44]

Though it may seem to be a "natural" or "human" reaction to the self-inflicted pain Roa suffered, pity, or lástima, would not necessarily have been a culturally appropriate reaction for the Nahua-speaking people, given the well-documented and widespread practice of ritual bloodletting in preconquest Mexico. Bloodletting from ears, nose, tongue, fingers, and sometimes genitals constituted part of regular religious observance throughout Mesoamerica, not limited to elites. In her study of Nahua-Christian moral dialogue, Louise Burkhart argues that, in fact, for newly converted Christians, "self-flagellation made a convenient substitute for bloodletting: to bleed oneself with thorns was declared idolatrous, but to flog oneself until the blood came showed devotion to Christ."[45] Certainly this is one explanation for the enthusiasm evident in the penitential procession described by Motolinía, above.

As far as the testimonies of the Indian witnesses regarding Roa's practices, it appears that the pre-Columbian practice of bloodletting did little to make Roa's penance any more comprehensible or acceptable to the Indians of Totolapan. The attention that the witnesses, Juan de Santa María in particular, pay to the spilling of Roa's blood merits consideration in this context. He notes that after one flaying, "the floor had become a lake of blood."[46] As I have suggested, Roa's self-flagellation drew attention to the physical vulnerability of the human body and its liability to pain and suffering. The pain that Roa suffered at his own hands and at the hands of his Indian assistants referred back to the pain suffered by Christ, as articulated in the crucifix. In contrast, from what we know of Mesoamerican bloodletting practices, the intention there was never the deliberate infliction of pain. The various implements for drawing blood—obsidian blades, cactus needles, and stingray spines—were designed to be quick and efficient augers. Crying out, tears, flinching, grimacing, and other expressions of pain and discomfort were not acceptable or desired aspects of the ritual practice. Neither were expressions of compassion or pity for those engaged in acts of bloodletting appropriate or called for. Although both the Christian tradition of self-flagellation and the pre-Columbian practice of bloodletting can be considered acts of auto-sacrifice, in indigenous belief, the blood, and not the pain, constituted the offering. The blood itself, captured on small pieces of paper and set on fire, was seen as a holy sacrifice to the deities. The Christian emphasis on human and divine suffering was foreign to pre-Columbian religious rituals and belief, and therefore to its iconography, as I argue below. One must note here that, even for Roa, the significance of blood within his Christian framework may not have been entirely limited to an indication of pain.[47]

Though the young Indian men who assisted him at times disobeyed Roa, there is some indication that the people of Totolapan indeed came to see Roa as one of Gruzinski's *venerables*, or holy men. The Inquisition testimonies highlight Roa's inexplicable, almost miraculous resilience. After suffering hours of torture, Roa asserts that he is "fine" and even that he has slept well. One witness remembered how after one of these punishments, "without pausing to rest, Roa put on his habit and went to his cell." After particularly brutal beatings, the assistants would often drag the weeping Roa back to his cell. But when they inquired the next morning as to how he was, the friar responded, *bien*, "well," as if nothing had occurred. The witness Santiago recalls that many times, in spite of the many lashings he received, Roa's flesh appeared uninjured and unmarred. The Indian witnesses locate the miraculous in his passion play in Roa's survival of these abuses. Fernández affirms that in spite of the severity of Roa's punishments, "they did not see him faint, nor any signs of weakness . . . neither did the Indians who disrobed him discover any traces of the flames that he had suffered."[48]

Other traditions speak to Roa's saintlike acts of charity. Grijalva writes that Roa always greeted people warmly at the door, and seemed always to bear a happy and contented expression. A twentieth-century history elaborates: "his face always was radiant with joy, and his words were sweet, and all those who saw or heard him took delight in the Lord."[49] In ritualized settings, Roa was known to wash and kiss the feet of Indians.[50] At meals he would serve the poor first at that table, before anyone else. Perhaps these acts of humility, kindness, and generosity are the things that drew the Indians to him. A third set of traditions recount several miracles in which Roa was assisted by Indian angels. In one memory, the friar and several Indians are lost in the desert and are nearly overcome with thirst. Roa prays to God for assistance, offering his life in exchange for water for these "poor Indians." Suddenly, a mysterious Indian with a container of water appears and then, after all drink, vanishes in front of their eyes.

Thus it seems that the Indians were impressed less by Roa's instruction on Christian doctrine than by the evidence that Roa was in some sense divine: "The Indians admired all of this, and declared that it was not possible that he was only human."[51] However, the people of Totolapan do not seem to have preserved or venerated any relics of Roa himself, as was done in Molango, another area where Roa ministered. There, locals venerated pieces of charcoal that survived a church fire as relics of the saint. While Roa lived, he never seems to have been scorched by the fires he often tread upon as part of his penance; so people naturally assumed that in death his body would similarly resist flames.

Whenever they came across a piece of charcoal that refused to burn or could not be reduced to ash, they saved it and would kiss and venerate it as his remains.[52] Similarly, in Meztitlán, the people venerated a cave where Roa was said to have retired to pray.

Severed Goddess, Flayed God, and Long-Suffering Maize: Visual Religion and the Transfer of Affect

Above I have explored how the Indians of Totolapan responded to Roa's efforts to bring to life the Gospel story of Jesus' passion and death, and to persuade them that by the very nature of their humanity they were culpable for his suffering. A more difficult task remains: to draw out or hypothesize how the Totolapans initially received the Cristo Aparecido itself, certainly the first image of its kind they had encountered. Colonial sources focus exclusively on Roa's response to the Cristo and are strangely silent about how the locals of Totolapan reacted to the arrival of the image. What, then, did the Totolapans see in this form when confronted with it for the first time? Did this thin, pale Christ appear much as they had imagined him: the vague, indeterminate figure hinted at in preachers' sermons brought suddenly, finally, into sharp focus? Did they perceive that the Cristo was pained, afflicted? Did the Indians find him astonishing and beautiful, as did Roa and his Augustinian brothers? Or were they outwardly indifferent, the import of the image not immediately transparent to them?

The temptation exists to seek answers to these questions by appealing to the visual-cultural context of pre-Columbian religion as the framework within which crucifixes were originally received, categorized, and interpreted. Such an approach would then proceed with an exploration of the iconographic commensurability of the Aztec and Christian visual universes, and conclude by postulating a crude correlation between Aztec deities and saints of the Christian pantheon as is typical of "syncretic" interpretive approaches. Here, I yield briefly to this temptation, exploring some of the most suggestive and evocative aspects of Mesoamerican religion—considering, for example, the extent to which the practice of human sacrifice and the iconographic representation of wounded deities found parallels in Christianity, as the original missionaries so deeply feared. Ultimately, however, the encounter between Christianity and Mesoamerican religion is best comprehended neither as the collision of two incompatible visual universes nor as the merging of roughly analogous beliefs and religious imagery. In the Christian conversion of Mexico it was not, in the final analysis, the case that the old symbolic apparatus found new application and expression in the novel Christian order. Rather, it was the underlying sentiment that lingered and endured; and the more ordinary and modest, but also more deeply rooted, everyday sensibilities and practices that most framed interpretive engagement with Christian material religion. Simply put, the religious *feelings* that drummed beneath the prior institutional, symbolic, iconographic, and ritual religious complex are what sought (and ultimately found) continuity, purchase, and home within Christianity. This phenomenon begs an affective approach to the study of religion.[53]

The stories of missionaries recall in romantic overtones the pull that the crucifix had for the Indians of Mexico. In other parts of the world, in the same colonial moment, the crucifix was not so readily accepted. In some missionary settings, it was an obstacle to the process of Christian evangelization: the graphic depiction of a suffering god was unacceptable, even deplorable, in some local cultural contexts. The Italian Jesuit Matteo Ricci was faced with just such a response in China in the last quarter of the sixteenth century. Adopting the dress and cultural persona of a Confucian scholar, Ricci sought to impress the Chinese with elaborately embossed and illustrated Christian Bibles and with the sophistication, symmetry, and complexity of Christianity as a philosophical system.[54] Yet, during the many years of ministry among the Chinese, fearing misunderstanding and rejection, Ricci hid from them the doctrine of the passion of Jesus Christ, and especially the moment of the Crucifixion. In one of the most poignant scenes in historian Jonathan Spence's biography of the Jesuit, he tells of the inadvertent discovery of a crucifix by the Chinese. When the image accidentally spilled out of Ricci's knapsack, those present recoiled in horror and revulsion:

> One crucifix, which Ricci was carrying in his private baggage, must have been small yet vividly real in the style of the late sixteenth century, designed to give maximum immediacy to the man contemplating it, in line with Ignatius's injunctions to be present as Christ is crucified. Ricci described it as "beautiful, carved out of wood, with blood painted on it, so it seemed alive." The eunuch who found it, however—that same Ma Tang who had admired the Virgin's picture—suspected black magic and shouted aloud, "This is a wicked thing you have made, to kill our king; they cannot be good people who practice such arts." Soldiers were called up and the baggage of Ricci and his companions was ransacked for further clues to their depraved designs, and they were threatened with savage beatings. The main difficulty was, as Ricci noted with honesty, that the eunuch "truly thought it was something evil" and that in the face of the hostile crowd Ricci found it hard to marshal an adequate explanation of the significance of Christ crucified.[55]

One Chinese colleague tried to explain to Ricci that it was really "not good to have someone looking like that"; and another suggested that the Jesuits "crush into powder any other crucifixes they had with them, so there would be no memory of them."[56]

Across the globe, the Indians of the New World never seem to have recoiled in horror from images of the crucifix. On the contrary, according to the friars, it held a powerful appeal and fascination for them, quickly becoming a potent and pliable symbol and an instrument of evangelization. While Spanish friars celebrated the Mexicans' enthusiasm for Christian images, they also worried that images of the Crucifixion would strike deeper, disturbing resonances for the native peoples of New Spain; that the dead body of Jesus hanging on the cross would rekindle the still very recent memory of the Aztec practice of human sacrifice. The Spanish were repelled and sickened by the ritual murder of victims that they witnessed at the great temples of Tenochtitlán, upon which the Aztec empire relied for its vitality: through these offerings they worked to maintain not only their empire but, even more important, the fragile cosmic order. More than any other aspect of the Aztec state, for the Spanish this practice threw into question the very humanity of the Indians and served as dark evidence that the devil was at work in this strange land. Ultimately it provided the moral justification for the conquest of Mexico and the enslavement of its people.

Yet the language of sacrifice was far from foreign to the Christian religion, which had at its very center a self-sacrificing God who first made himself human and then gave himself up to be tortured and killed in order to redeem his earthly children. The friars were at great pains to explain to the newly converted Indians how this was radically distinct from the grim rituals practiced at Tenochtitlán, and they worked hard to shield the greatest symbol of Christ's sacrifice from misunderstanding and misuse. The fact that some methods of sacrifice, scaffold sacrifice in particular, were eerily reminiscent of death by crucifixion probably exacerbated Spanish fears (figure 3.4).[57] The anxiety that the Indians would collapse human sacrificial traditions with the final, once-and-for-all sacrifice of Christ triggered Fr. Diego de Landa's deadly inquisition in the Yucatan in 1562. The Franciscans believed that this association had led to the actual crucifixion of Mayan children, and their search for evidence of this practice and of continued idolatry gave rise to the worst episode of violence and interrogation of the early colonial period.[58] Clearly the Christian god and the Aztec deities had in common that they sometimes exacted a high price, a heavy human toll.

Modern scholars have allowed their own vision of the past to be clouded by these missionary anxieties. In her study comparing pre-Columbian and Christian cruciforms, Carol Callaway attempts to explain the "widespread acceptance" of the cross in Mexico. Connecting past practices of human sacrifice too absolutely to Christian iconography, she argues erroneously that devotion to the crucifix declined as the collective memory of human sacrifice waned.[59] There is little evidence, however, that human sacrifice was ever the dominant or exclusive interpretive lens for indigenous understanding of the crucifix. In actuality, human sacrifice was a temple practice largely limited to the imperial

FIGURE 3.4. Scaffold sacrifice. Precolumbian. Elizabeth Benson, *Maya Iconography*. Princeton, NJ: Princeton University Press, 1988 (p. 332). Reprinted by permission of Princeton University Press.

center; as such, it may have been quite remote from the everyday, lived religion practiced by most Mexicans.

More likely, for Indians beholding Christian images for the first time, the copious blood depicted in Spanish representations of the crucifix reminded them less of human sacrifice than of the more widespread and common practice of bloodletting and blood offering.[60] These were also common themes in pre-Columbian pictorial representations. However, I have yet to encounter an instance in either Nahua or Mayan iconography where blood is used to represent pain, violence, or suffering.[61] Mayanist David Stuart has found that blood depicted in Mayan iconography is restricted to ritual settings and limited to specific areas of the body (nose, forehead, cheek, chin, or ears). Most frequently it was an indication of the sacred power of a royal figure or deity.[62] In a striking example, blood drips from the fingers of a regally dressed female god into a sacred vessel at her feet: a sign of her royalty and sacred power. Her face is serene, poised, and beautiful (figure 3.5). The Christian artistic preoccupation with human suffering was foreign to pre-Columbian religious rituals and iconography.

Given that, as I have suggested, in Mesoamerican iconography blood was limited to ritualized contexts and was associated with power and not pain, it seems likely that the tears and rivulets of blood represented on Iberian crucifixes did not immediately indicate to the Indians an experience or a narrative of suffering. Take, for example, the Cristo Aparecido as Roa first beheld it: hair crowned with thorns and matted with blood. When Cortéz and his soldiers arrived in the inner sanctum of the Templo Mayor in Tenochtitlán, they were filled with revulsion at the smell of blood that permeated the inner rooms of the temple. They record their disgust at the Aztec priests whose hair was sticky and matted with the blood of sacrificial victims.[63] Perhaps the cloak of blood that shrouded the body of Christ on European-style crucifixes like the Cristo Aparecido actually suggested to the Indians, more than anything else, Jesus' status as a priest rather than as victim, or indicated his royal power rather than his defeat and death.

It was only later, after the Indians encountered Christian imagery, that they incorporated blood as an artistic representation indicating pain and suffering. Take, for example, the reinterpretation of an Aztec warrior pictographic convention in the Kingsborough Codex, a letter of petition sent to the king by the Indians of Tepetlaoztoc, describing pictorially and in Roman script the abuse they have experienced at the hands of a particularly vicious Spanish encomendero. The original pre-Columbian pictograph, shown in figure 3.6, was employed in Aztec histories to relate military victory, and depicts a standing warrior grabbing the hair of the kneeling subject he has conquered. The image is highly stylized, and no evidence of suffering is present. Importing this imagery into the setting of Spanish colonialism, the codex adapts the pre-Columbian convention to depict the abuse of an indigenous community by their encomendero. In many respects the Kingsborough images, one of which is shown in figure 3.7, follow the precolonial convention: the kneeling posture of the Indians along with the manner in which the encomendero grasps their hair indicates a conquered or subjugated status for the Indians and a warrior status for the encomendero.[64]

The Kingsborough images differ from the precolonial original in several important respects. The more recent images are much less stylized and more European (or "realistic") in their technique. Just as conspicuous as the stylistic

FIGURE 3.5. Bleeding Mayan queen. Elizabeth Benson. *Maya Iconography*. Princeton, NJ: Princeton University Press, 1988 (p. 180). Reprinted by permission of Princeton University Press.

differences, however, is the presence of copious amounts of blood. In this post-conquest variation on the precolonial convention, blood is added to represent the pain and suffering of the indigenous community. Additionally, one notes the emotive, pleading expression of the conquered figure in the Kingsborough

FIGURE 3.6. Conquest pictograph. Precolumbian. Drawing by John
Montgomery from *Stories in Red and Black. Pictorial Histories of the Aztecs and
Mixtecs* by Elizabeth Hill Boone. Austin: University of Texas Press, 2000. By
permission of the University of Texas.

Codex, absent in the precolonial warrior convention. The addition of blood in
the Kingsborough Codex images is the layering of Christian iconographic conventions over pre-Columbian ones. It could only have been the (by then)
ubiquitous representations of Jesus bleeding on the cross that suggested to the
Indians this new artistic and symbolic function (the expression of pain and
suffering). The Kingsborough images can, in fact, be read as crucifixion
images, in which the blood of indigenous victims references Christ's own
blood shed on the cross. Therefore, in this codex we encounter one of the rare
examples in the colonial period of indigenous Mexicans framing their own
suffering in relation to the suffering of Christ.

FIGURE 3.7. Encomendero abusing Indians. Drawing, Mexico, mid-sixteenth century. Paso y Troncoso, Francisco del, and Edward King Kingsborough. *Códice Kingsborough. Memorial de los indios de Tepetlaoztoc al monarca español contra los encomenderos del pueblo.* Madrid: Fototipía de Hauser y Menet, 1912.

There are persons in the Aztec pantheon that may have made the Indians more receptive to the suffering Christian god. Xipe Totec, a god of the agricultural cycle, was said to have flayed himself in order to nourish human beings. For Callaway, Xipe, "supreme penitent and personification of victimization," was the deity most reminiscent of Christ.[65] The severed goddess Coyolxauhqui, who appears on the great stone disk found at the Templo Mayor in Mexico City, is another example of a "wounded" deity: her head decapitated and limbs severed from her body by her sibling in a familial cosmic battle. My contention is not so much that Mesoamerican iconography provided a set interpretation of the Christian God, but rather that the presence of these wounded gods in their pantheon made them less likely to reject the crucifix outright, to recoil, as did the Chinese on Ricci's ship. Again, I find little evidence that either the flayed deities or human sacrifice was the predominant interpretive framework for the Crucifixion of Jesus.

There were other, more common and ordinary, aspects of religious practice through which the Indians of the New World probably filtered their reception of Christian imagery. I contend, as have some others, that the most basic resonance was been between images of Christ and the staple food, maize. Torquemada's etymology of the Nahua word for "cross" confirms this interpretation. The Nahuatl word *tonacaquahuitl*, which he translates as "the wooden beam which gives sustenance to our lives," is composed from the root word for corn, *tonacayutl*: "the thing that nourishes our body."[66] In this way, the association of the cross with corn was underscored linguistically. Striking in this regard is a sixteenth-century stone atrial cross from the state of Hidalgo. This cross offers two distinct representations of Christ. Encircling the axis of the cross is the crown of thorns, a reference to Christ's persecution, recalling the mockery of the soldiers who tormented him. The vertical beam of the cross depicts a stalk of maize, referencing the Indian symbolism for the cycle of birth, death, and rebirth. The symbolism of Christ as corn, represented graphically in the Hidalgo cross, may also be at work in the fabrication of the cristos de caña, arguably the most important native artistic engagement with Christian imagery in the sixteenth and seventeenth centuries. Scholars considering the multiple symbolic significances the materials used in the fabrication of these images have postulated that the use of corn in the forms both of paste and leaves for the construction of a frame (*alma de hojas de maíz*) may have resonated with an indigenous religious view of maize as a sacred and life-giving food.[67] As an added interpretive layer, in Nahua belief systems human beings themselves were made of corn.

This brings us to the single most important aspect of indigenous Christianity as reflecting the survival and transfer of pre-Columbian religiocultural elements: namely, affection and tenderness for objects of the natural world. While Christian spiritual postures of the day did allow for the place of tenderness in devotion to Christ, among many others, in short order this sentiment dominated Indian engagement with Christian images. It certainly came to define spiritual devotion to the Cristo Aparecido, as I describe in chapter 8 of this book. In this interpretation, the transmission of religious affect does not only move person to person as if by contagion, as affect theorists have suggested, but is also communicated from one generation to the next, and in this instance imported from one religion to the next.[68] This sentiment of affection emerges from the Mesoamerican belief that the sacred permeated and pene-trated the material world: the ordinary objects and things of everyday life and common use were perceived to be "alive with the sacred."[69] Inga Clendinnen writes that corn, in particular, was regarded with a "special tenderness": "Women breathed softly on the maize kernels before they were dropped into the cooking pot, the warm moist breath giving them courage for the fire. Spilt kernels were carefully gathered up so that famine would not come and every eighth year the long-suffering maize was 'rested' for a period by being cooked without condiments."[70] As Sahagun's Nahua informants explained to him, "we brought much torment to it—we ate it, we put chili on it, we salted it, we added saltpeter to it, we added lime. And we tired it to death, so we revived it. Thus it was said maize was given new youth when this was done."[71]

The religious sensibility of gentle care and kind regard for the sacred most likely found its fullest and deepest expression in native engagement with *tlapialli*, the sacred "bundles" or idols of lineage. For the Spanish friars, the Indians' attachment to these "fearsome" idols was the single greatest obstacle to authentic conversion to the Christian faith. The conqueror Cortés asked of the Indians why they "cared for such Idols which were made of clay and old wood for they were evil things" which deceived them. At an early moment of Christianization, these varied objects of material religion shared, for a short time, a place with the novel Christian saints on small home altars in the homes of ordinary Indian believers—for outside observers, a strange menagerie.[72] The ritual gestures and offerings with which Indian's engaged both Christian and pre-Columbian sacred objects has most frequently been understood in instru-mental terms, as a practice of propitiation in which the devotee appealed to, bargained with, coaxed, and wheedled the spirit within in order to gain some concrete personal or collective benefit. This understanding effectively reduces and flattens indigenous, popular religious faith and practice to the crudest and most base human manipulation of the divine and of the natural world. Here, again, I am in accord with Clendinnen, who argues that the purpose of Mexica ritual was not instrumental, "but rather aesthetic, expressive, interrogative, and creative."[73] Beholding material manifestations of the sacred (such as the *idolillos* and images of the Christian saints), a believer might readily experience a vari-ety of more predictable (to Western eyes) religious emotions and sentiments, among these awe, reverence, fear, love, adoration, humility, and contrition. Instead, I suggest that tenderness for the many material and natural manifesta-tions of the divine was the single most important spiritual posture in Mesoa-merican local religion, and this is the emotion that predominated in indigenous affective engagement with the Christian sacred, like the Cristo Aparecido. It stands in stark contrast to the representation of Mesoamerican religion in the popular imagination, as depicted, for example, by Mel Gibson's 2006 film *Apocalypto*, in which the Mayan culture decays from within, plagued by the "ritual savagery" of its brutal and barbaric sacrificial religion.

Perhaps this tenderness was related to the perceived vulnerability of the cosmos within the indigenous worldview. Where Roa's extreme penitential practices served to highlight the vulnerability of the human body to pain and suffering, indigenous cosmology emphasized the vulnerability of the cosmos and the role of human action in the preservation and maintenance of the delicate order. Between the omnipotence of God the father and the heart-breaking vulnerability of the son, it was the latter that seems most to have captured Indian religious imagination, perhaps because the broken Christ most readily evoked their tender regard for the fragile cosmic order. Though the early record is silent about indigenous reception of the Cristo, I believe that the Aparecido was soon enfolded as their beloved, diminutive *cristito*.

Conclusions

I have argued that crucifixes were not transparently, for the Indians, a depiction of suffering. The sheer intensity of the Spanish effort is testimony to the likelihood that crucifixes, which seem to us today to be so starkly and transparently narratives of violence and victimization, were not immediately recognizable as such in an indigenous cultural context. Hence the need for interpretation, elaboration, and illustration like that provided so expertly by Antonio de Roa. Furthermore, there is little evidence that the Indians filtered their reception of the crucifix through the lens of human sacrifice, as many have argued before. Rather, the Indians soon came to engage Christian images, including crucifixes, with the emotional vocabulary that predominated in their religion before the arrival of Christianity: affection and tenderness toward the presence of the sacred in the humble objects of the material world, and through these for the fragile cosmos. Within this affective framework, the process of Christian conversion necessarily involved modeling for the Indians not only the physical habits of prayer and devotion but also the correct emotional postures required for the expression of Christian spirituality. Thus Roa labored to communicate to the Indians Christian sentiments: contrition and remorse for sin, compassion for the afflicted Christian god, and grief over the liability of the human body to pain. The Totolapans expressed both anxiety and discomfort with Roa's penitential practices and ultimately worked to resist his efforts to associate the crucifix with physical pain, spiritual suffering, and human sinfulness. Their relationship with the Cristo emerged as much in spite of Roa's methods as owing to his Herculean efforts.

The elaborate negotiation of meaning between Roa and the community of new believers of Totolapan is convincing evidence that the Indians' devotion to images of Christ crucified and the cross did not emerge from a "natural" identification of Christ's suffering with their own. There is no evidence in the Totolapans' testimonies or the hagiographic accounts of an explicit identification of the Indians' suffering, brought about by the conquest, with the suffering of Christ. Indeed, nothing in Roa's deeds or actions indicated that this association was appropriate. Colonial friars in general warned against this: "The suffering of the poor is not an appropriate offering to God. . . . To the altar one must only bring the sighs of a contrite heart, not the sorrows and struggles of one who perceives themselves deprived and dispossessed."[74] If anything, Roa's practice urged a profound distinction between human suffering and that of the Lord and Savior: ours is merited, his is not. We are sinful; Jesus is innocent. In this distinction Roa effectively denied the reality of Indian suffering. In any case, the theology of affliction he elaborated could hardly have been helpful in interpreting the Indians' own profound and unprecedented suffering during the initial stages of conquest and colonization.

Nevertheless, for indigenous Christians, their new faith meant that on some level they had to come to grips with the Christian theological emphasis on human beings as constituted, in part, by their vulnerability to physical pain and by their spiritual anguish. This theological engagement was then underscored by their very real day-to-day experience of unprecedented suffering under conquest and colonial rule. The question is not whether or not the colonized Indians suffered but how they understood, experienced, and categorized their newly deepened suffering. The conquest thus represents the convergence of two powerful events: the importation of a potent religious narrative that took as its centerpiece a Christian theological aesthetics of suffering, and the very real experience of unprecedented suffering due to military defeat and ethnocide, and to mass death as the result of epidemic diseases.

A final point is made here. For some contemporary scholars, prior indigenous understandings were in a sense "obstacles" for the indigenous people's comprehension of key Christian doctrines.[75] Recently, theologians as well have revisited this colonial period and puzzled over "cleavages" between Christian evangelization and indigenous understandings.[76] Such an approach makes the same assumption that plagued clergy from the middle of the sixteenth century forward: the widespread conviction that Indians were incapable of comprehending the finer points of Christian doctrine.

In discussing the meaning that the Indians made of Christian practice and Christian visual culture, it has not been my desire to point to a "failure" (or even a success) in communication, nor to assign blame for such a failure. The inherent failures of the missionary effort to Christianize New Spain lie on a much more profound level than one of mere "misinterpretation" or "misappropriation" of Christian concepts. The Indians of Totolapan cannot be assumed to have "misunderstood," missed, or disregarded the key Christian doctrines in which Roa instructed them. This interpretation presumes that the dialogic frontier in a missionary setting is the clash of two static worldviews, a perspective that is too easily appropriated into the discourse of Christendom, for which error (or misunderstanding) exists to be eradicated.[77]

4

The Cristo Comes to Life

Lived Religion in Colonial Mexico City

It was an age that hungered for resemblances . . .
—Philippe Ariés, *The Hour of*
Our Death

Scene 3. "Holy Theft." Iglesia de Totolapan, 1583

The first assault. It is night in Totolapan, dark, warm, and dry. You
rest in your sanctuary, untroubled and unconcerned. And why
not? You are rarely disturbed. The people who pass before you are
no bother; by now their faces have grown familiar, their offerings
anticipated. In hushed voices they bring flowers, light candles,
burn copal. You enjoy the warmth of the candles' waxy glow. And
the tendrils of weighted, fragrant smoke that drift slowly up to you
are also pleasing, coaxing ancient memories of a life long past, all
but forgotten, briefly to the surface. Their murmured prayers to
you, thanksgivings, gentle petitions and repetitions, are also
soothing, in their way. Comfortable, loved, securely ensconced in
these tender ministrations, you drift in and out of sleep.

And then disruption. Firm hands grab hold of you. You are
wrested, pried roughly, from your cross. And then secreted,
hastily, through a high window into the dark, warm night.

This chapter of the Cristo's biography opens in 1583 with an act
of *furta sacra*, or holy theft, in which the Augustinians
transferred the image of the Cristo Aparecido from the iglesia in
Totolapan to their newly renovated convento in Mexico City for
"safe-keeping."[1] According to the living memory of the people of
Totolapan, the friars stole the Cristo from them under cover of
night, for they would never have willingly allowed the image to

leave their pueblo. The locals of Totolapan deeply grieved the loss of their Cristo. Had this project been differently conceived, my attention might have remained with them, to watch and observe as they once again remade their faith, creating a devotion around the Cristo's empty cross that the friars left for them as "consolation," to ease them in their loss. The persistent faith of the people of Totolapan during the Cristo's long absence is treated to a limited extent in the subsequent chapter of this book. Here, however, I follow the kidnapped Cristo to Mexico City, where he remained in the possession of the Augustinian order for 278 years, from 1583 until 1861, before finally being repatriated to Totolapan.

This chapter treats the multiplicity of meanings that accrued to the Cristo Aparecido during the first hundred and fifty years that he resided in Mexico City. At the close of the sixteenth century, one religious critically observed that some of the image's devotees thought of him as alive and able to bestow blessings, while others thought that he was the real Jesus Christ, or even God.[2] In fact, each of these was simultaneously true, and they were not mutually exclusive. For the devotee and believer, the meaning of a particular image at a given point in time is always multivalent, necessarily complex, and ultimately irreducible. To these diverse meanings this chapter adds two others that will also be explored here: the Cristo's value as an object of beauty, a baroque adornment, and his use as a "shield of arms," as protection for the people of Mexico against the repeated waves of epidemics that particularly tormented urban Indians and mestizos during these centuries, especially the typhus epidemic of 1736.

Three dramatic episodes marked the Cristo's sojourn in the colonial center. The first two occurred in the penultimate decade of the sixteenth century. The precipitating event is the one I have just described: the theft of the image from its remote locale on the margins of the province and its translation to Mexico City. The physical relocation of this holy object to Mexico City heralded a profound change in the emphasis of the religious orders in Mexico: as missionary zeal waned, institutional resources were transferred away from evangelizing the missionary frontier and toward ministry to an emerging urban Church, particularly in the increasingly complex, racially mixed, colonial center.

Though the Cristo's removal from Totolapan was surreptitious, his arrival in the city was anything but; with "cross raised high" and great "pomp and solemnity," the pious friars of many religious orders and the Indian Christians of Mexico City assembled to welcome the famous Cristo. Stirred and roused by this show of faith, the Cristo Aparecido blessed those who gathered in his honor with his first signs of animate life, offering the crowd gestures of benediction and other signs of vitality and divine presence. Days later, a procession celebrating the feast of the Holy Name entered the chapel of the Augustinian *colegio*, the Cristo's original Mexico City home. As they approached the image, Indian Christians and Spanish friars together witnessed dramatic alterations to the Cristo's form. In large part owing to pamphlets published and distributed by the Augustinians, news of the Cristo's miracles had spread quickly, drawing more devotees from across the city. Upon these, his newly adopted children, the Cristo bestowed miracles of healing. The Cristo was at the height of his power and influence; from this vantage point the reader encounters a pivotal moment in the consolidation of an indigenous and authentically Mexican Christianity. At this moment of maturation and deepening, the Christian faith of urban, colonial Mexico was not so much imposed or coerced (by the conqueror upon the conquered) as forged in the common and collective experience of the sacred, shared and shaped by European and Indian alike: a mestizo religion for an increasingly mestizo population.

The overwhelming response of the Indians of Mexico City to the Cristo Aparecido quickly garnered the attention of the Franciscans, ever vigilant and frequently anxious about the use and abuse of religious images by the popular classes. Franciscan concerns about the legitimacy of devotion to the Cristo seem to have intensified when the Augustinians requested permission to move the image from their colegio to a more prominent and central location in their convento. The Augustinians' request gave rise to the second critical event treated in this chapter: the Inquisition hearing in May of 1583 that called witnesses, both Indian and Spanish, to testify about the Cristo's origins and reputed miracles. In their hands, the Inquisitors held the Cristo's fate: their task was to judge whether God resided in some unique way in this Cristo, thus marking him worthy of special veneration, or whether he was a common and ordinary image, like any other, deserving of respect but not meriting particular celebration.

The third occurrence that marked the Cristo's centuries in Mexico City transpired more than 150 years later, when the city faced a devastating *matlaza-huatl*, or typhus, epidemic. The epidemic began in 1736 and ravaged and raged until the last months of 1737. The epidemic literally brought the city to its knees in supplication, as the people of Mexico City called on the power of the Cristo Aparecido of Totolapan as part of a massive effort to thwart the onslaught. Our Cristo was not alone, but acted in concert with perhaps as many as a hundred other religious images in the city. In cooperation with these other images, the Cristo Aparecido formed part of a "shield of arms" that successfully halted the disease by the close of 1737, protecting a population that, after more than two hundred years of colonial rule, had little recourse except to depend upon the efficacy of their images for its survival.

If the sixteenth century was the age of the rural doctrina and austere mission convento, the seventeenth century in Mexico initiated the era of the urban parish church and the exuberantly adorned and ornate cathedral; the baroque had dawned on Mexico.[3] With their abundance of images and their "massive, intricate, and gilded altarpieces," the churches of baroque Latin America were regarded as unfamiliar, novel and even a bit peculiar. Described as *rico y curioso*, the baroque church "jolted the viewer into a new experience" of the sacred.[5] These churches were designed to serve a heuristic function, to uplift the popular classes by engaging all of their senses, "intended less to engage the intellect with theological propositions than to provide an experience of divine order and grandeur. They helped to build 'a bridge that reached from the mundane world to the threshold of the divine spirit.'"[6]

Quite comfortably, the Cristo Aparecido occupied and accentuated the landscape of baroque Mexico City. Indeed, it was for this purpose, in large part, that he was brought there. The interplay of shadow and light characterized the art and architecture of the baroque. But in Mexico there were other contrasts, too, that scored these centuries. Perhaps the starkest of these was the mass death of the Indians, whose population was at its lowest in 1620, and the contrasting life and vitality of their beloved images in the same decades. In baroque art the human form garnered a new three-dimensionality: figures in motion seemed to spill forth, reaching out from canvasses and bursting from bas-relief. Even stone columns writhed with movement. So, too, during these centuries, the Cristo Aparecido himself pulsed with life, even as his devotees often languished, plagued by illness, hunger, and the increasing reach of colonialism.

Furta Sacra: Holy Theft

In the year that the Totolapans lost their Cristo to the friars of Mexico City, four decades had lapsed since the image first appeared in their pueblo. Recall that immediately after its arrival, the Cristo occupied Roa's monastic cell, where at least initially the image was the object of the friar's private devotion. Nevertheless, when Roa departed for Molango in 1544 (where he served until his death in 1563) he left the Cristo behind, suggesting that he felt the image belonged in Totolapan.[7] Not long after the friar concluded his formal ministry in Totolapan, the Cristo Aparecido was moved from Roa's private cell to a prominent position in the church sanctuary, where the local community had unhindered access to it.[8]

Over the course of those brief but pivotal decades, the Cristo had become central to local faith and religious practice. Even more striking, during these years it became deeply embedded in the historical and collective memory of the indigenous Christians of Totolapan. As Suárez de Escobar, who orchestrated the transfer of the image observed: the Indians of Totolapan "had *always* held the crucifix in great veneration."[9] That is to say, the image was *theirs*, and had been so as far back as human memory extended. In this regard, the Cristo was not unique; other exceptional images were similarly integrated into indigenous oral, artistic, and written traditions in an historical span that may seem surprisingly short to modern observers. By the close of the sixteenth century, there are several accounts of Indian pueblos that recalled honoring a specific Christian image since *tiempo inmemorial*, time immemorial, though the presence of Christianity in those communities was no longer than thirty to fifty years.[10]

This was the local belief with respect to a collection of three Christian paintings (of the Virgin Mary, the Crucifixion, and the Resurrection) carefully preserved by a community of Indians living in relative isolation along the southern coast of Mexico around the period in question. Though the images could not have been in existence for more than fifty or sixty years, the Dominican friars who first "discovered" them described them as "very old." Even more to the point, the Indians explained that they preserved these paintings in honor of "their ancestors [who] had left them this memory."[11] According to the tradition of this and other pueblos, Christian images were not introduced by the Spanish, but rather constituted part of a sacred indigenous memory, bequeathed to the community by their ancestral legacy. In an early seventeenth-century account, an elderly Otomi Indian recalled to a friar that "a long time ago" his community possessed a sacred book that contained a striking illustration of Christ crucified. The man vividly recalled both the image and the book itself (likely a catechism of some sort), and recounted how his community carefully preserved this inheritance, passing the text from father to child to be "guarded and taught."[12] This understanding persisted. In 1786, the Indians of Cuautitlán, devotees of an image of the Immaculate Conception, argued against the Spanish priest who was trying to remove the image, on the grounds that she belonged to them since they had venerated her since "inmemorial tiempo."[13]

These examples point to the indigenous agency involved in the conservation and dissemination of Christian images only decades after the completion of the "spiritual conquest" of Mexico. Even more striking, they speak of the integration of Christian images into indigenous collective memory, including the projection of their origins deep into the Indian past.

This is to say that by 1583, and perhaps a good deal earlier, the Cristo Aparecido was already part of the religious patrimony of the people of Totolapan. Observers noted that year that the image was already quite old and slightly "worn," indicating ritual use.[14] Fray Pedro Suárez de Escobar, provincial of the Augustinian order, and fray Pedro Coronel, Roa's successor as prior of Totolapan, were aware that Coronel's flock had come to hold the Cristo in high esteem. Nevertheless, together they conspired to bring the image to Mexico City. In December of 1582, the two friars requested and received a license from the archbishop of Mexico, don Pedro Mora de Contreras, to translate the Cristo. The archbishop additionally approved the friars' request to greet the image's arrival in the city with a religious procession, and with all due pomp and reverence.[15] In preparation for the festivities, the image received its first restoration: a varnish was applied to the santo before its introduction to the city.

In a statement given several months later, Provincial Suárez de Escobar explained that from the moment of his election as head of the order he had intended to bring the Totolapan Cristo to Mexico City, though he knew little about the image itself other than that it had been presented as a gift to Fray Antonio de Roa, perhaps even given by God himself. Later he confessed that he had been unaware of the story of the mysterious arrival of the Cristo in Totolapan or of Indian involvement in Roa's penitences.[16] What surely motivated Suárez de Escobar at the outset, then, was the Cristo's association with Antonio de Roa. The image was known to have been the object of Roa's particular veneration; and Roa was, by that time, widely held to be a saint by the Augustinian order.[17] Though the transfer of the Cristo to the capital certainly enhanced Antonio Roa's prominence as a New World candidate for sainthood, the Augustinians were never to achieve this organizational objective.[18]

Suárez felt a particular affinity for Roa: the provincial was also an ascetic who preferred living in isolation and silence to the company of his Augustinian brothers, and the rural mission conventos to the distractions of Mexico City.[19] He had even earned the epithet Fray Pedro the Hermit when, upon his election as definidor of the order in 1578,[20] he immediately removed himself to the remote western convento of Tzintzicastla, where he lived as an anchorite in one of the hermitages.[21] For Suárez, the Cristo must have referenced all that Roa himself represented: missionary zeal, ascetic discipline, and monastic practice. As he confronted an increasingly urban Mexican Church (over which he was a key administrator), Suárez surely hoped to memorialize, or monumentalize, these increasingly marginal traditions by displaying Fray Antonio's crucifix in his order's central convento. Suárez de Escobar himself had no doubt that the convento in Mexico City, where Roa himself had died and was buried, was where the Cristo belonged. Ultimately the transfer of the Cristo reflected the order's conviction that the image was the property of Fray Antonio Roa and his ecclesiastical corporation, and not that of the community of Indian believers in Totolapan who had cared for it during forty years.

The transfer of the image to Mexico City also reflected a growing emphasis on the institutional well-being of the religious orders and their role within urban society, as against their earlier commitment to propagating the faith in indigenous communities. After 1578, the pace of the creation of new Augustinian conventos in *pueblos de indios* slowed considerably: over the course of twenty years only seven were established.[22] In contrast, the Augustinians had already begun a process of institutional consolidation, of strengthening and developing their urban institutions and infrastructure. In 1575, the Augustinians founded the Colegio de San Pablo and assigned multiple friars to minister to the Indians of its barrio.[23] Grijalva boasted of the extensive library that the new Colegio housed, with books on all the arts and in several languages brought from all over Spain.[24] Similarly, in 1579 the acclaimed architect Claudio de Arciniega was at the helm of another series of amplifications to the already impressive Augustinian Mexico City convento. These alterations were so extensive that they were not finally completed until 1587.[25] The new colegio and the vastly expanded convento served to further advance the Augustinian stake in the city.

Throughout the Mexican Church, missionary fervor was on the decline, though not without frequent comment; regrettably, the time of the missionary heroes, of Roa and of the Franciscan Twelve, had begun to fade to a romantic memory. As the sixteenth century drew to a close, the Church emphasized ministry to urban communities of Spanish settlers, the growing mestizo population, and Indians of the city's many barrios. Resources were channeled into the building of urban conventos, metropolitan parish churches, and cathedrals, rather than into ministering to rural doctrinas and missions.[26] Furthermore, after 1570 royal policies sought to strengthen and bureaucratize commercial networks that favored secular clergy (diocesan priests) above the religious orders and their friars. The Third Provincial Mexican Council in 1585 affirmed a vision of an urban Church with bishops (rather than provincials like Suárez) at the helm.[27]

The Church's retreat from rural areas and the concomitant process of its consolidation in urban centers was in great part galvanized by the pronounced decline in the indigenous population as a result of repeated bouts of epidemic disease. Perhaps it is not coincidental that the Cristo Aparecido arrived in the city in the early months 1583, on the heels of the most long-lived and geographically extensive epidemic of the sixteenth century, a typhus outbreak that lasted from 1576 to 1581. The Franciscan Torquemada estimated the number of dead at over two million by the conclusion of the epidemic. On October 26, 1583, Archbishop Pedro Mora de Contreras observed that more than half the population of Mexico had fallen.[28] Surely this staggering loss, more than any other single factor, defined the sociocultural context within which, three months later, the same archbishop made the small but not insignificant decision to grant permission for the Cristo Aparecido do be moved to Mexico City.

The mortality of the Indians during these decades was so pronounced that it threatened the very social and economic structure of the colony. Even after the first major wave of epidemics, in the earlier part of the sixteenth century, Grijalva recalled that there had still remained enough "hands [to create] such magnificent buildings, so great, so strong, so beautiful, and of such perfect architecture that one could hardly desire more."[29] Sixty years later the decline of the Indian population of Mexico was more starkly apparent, more devastating. Those Indians that remained were concentrated in urban areas; perhaps this helped to facilitate their continued survival. This profound demographic shift perforce led to an institutional and ecclesiological one. A colonial chronicle records that at the beginning of the seventeenth century, Augustinian priests were recalled from many pueblos where too few Indians remained after epidemics had decimated the population. These friars were then channeled either to Mexico City or to those largely urban communities where there was still an indigenous population sufficient to sustain them.[30] As the orders recalled their

missionary friars back to the capital, so too the Cristo was compelled to abandon what remained of his rural flock and retreat to Mexico City.

The translation of the Cristo to Mexico City was not just the result of epide-
miological and demographic forces and individual will. An additional historical
impetus was the momentum created by the Council of Trent. The Church's
nineteenth ecumenical council, which met from 1545 to 1563, embodied and
codified the ideals of the Catholic Reformation (or Counter-Reformation). The
concluding twenty-fifth session of the Council, in 1563, issued a statement, "On
the Invocation, Veneration, and Relics of Saints, and on Sacred Images," that
was to have far-reaching impact on the practice of Catholic faith. This statement defended the legitimate use of images in Christian practice and asserted
that "images of Christ, of the Virgin Mother of God, and of the other saints, are
to be had and retained particularly in temples, and that due honor and veneration are to be given them." Trent even clarified the appropriate form and meaning of such devotion: "because the honor which is shown them is referred to
the prototypes which those images represent; in such wise that by the images
which we kiss, and before which we uncover the head, and prostrate ourselves,
we adore Christ; and we venerate the saints, whose similitude they bear." The
teachings of the Council created the theological justification for a new surge in
artistic representations of Christ, Mary, and all the saints for display and veneration in churches, monasteries, and cathedrals. Trent also provided the historical momentum for the gathering of sacra to the Mexican capital that began
in the closing decades of the sixteenth century.

The Cristo was brought to Mexico City during a period in which the Augustinians, caught up in the momentum created by Tridentine teachings, were
accruing relics and other valuable objects of religious art with which to adorn
their new convento and colegio. During these same years they received as a gift
an image of Mary, known as the Virgen del Tránsito.[31] Most noteworthy, in
October of 1573, they obtained from Europe a relic of the Lignum Crucis (the
true cross). In 1581 the convento's ledgers recorded the purchase of six large
and costly retablos, or altarpieces, for the sacristy and refectory.[32] Thus it came
to be, Grijalva writes, that along with the "precious treasure [of the Lignum
Crucis] and relics of other saints, that our convento in Mexico City became
greatly enriched."[33] The Cristo Aparecido, which first graced the colegio and
later the convento, was counted among these "precious treasures": a New World
gem displayed among Old World jewels.

The accrual of sacred objects and religious art to the colonial center constituted a process of "baroqueification," if you will, that extended beyond the
Augustinian order to the Church more generally. William Taylor describes the
angry protest that erupted in Ixmiquilpan when the archbishop ordered their
Cristo Renovado transferred to Mexico City in 1621. Both the Indians and local Spaniards of the pueblo struggled against the removal of their Cristo. In
spite of their best efforts, the image was moved to the capital, where it came

to reside in a convento of Carmelite nuns.[34] In the New World, this process was facilitated in great part by the ties that the growing number of American-born friars of all orders had with New World oligarchs, ties that provided the Church with the financial means to fill their conventos and churches with valuable works of art.[35]

The age of far-flung monastery complexes was giving way to the age of ornate, large parish churches and dizzyingly adorned cathedrals that would characterize seventeenth-century ecclesial art and architecture. These defined the baroque Catholicism that would dominate the seventeenth and eighteenth centuries in Mexico.

The Living Christ in Mexico City

> And they brought the colt to Jesus, and cast their garments on him; and he sat upon him. And many spread their garments in the way; and others cut down branches off the trees, and strewed them in the way. And they that went before, and they that followed, cried, saying, Hosanna; Blessed is he that cometh in the name of the Lord.
> —Mark 11: 7-9

Jesus of the gospels came riding into Jerusalem on a donkey, but the crowds greeted him as king. Just so, with all due ceremony and pageantry, the believers of Mexico City gathered to welcome the Cristo Aparecido of Totolapan at the Augustinian Colegio de San Pablo. The image was presented to the people on March 22, 1583, the Friday preceding Palm Sunday: he had arrived just in time for the Easter week celebrations. The day was unusually warm. Nevertheless, expectant crowds filled the streets, and friars from all orders, bearing high their crosses, assembled in front of the colegio to greet the famed image, welcoming it into Mexico City. News of the Cristo Aparecido's coming had caused much commotion among the people and had even attracted the attendance of several esteemed personages of the city.[36] And then, upon the hopeful people, the Cristo bestowed a miracle. Suffering from the heat of the day, tears of perspiration began to trickle from the Cristo's face. In a gesture of care and compassion, members of the crowd gently dried the image's countenance with a soft cloth.[37] Most compelling and wondrous of all, the Cristo then raised and lowered his arms, giving his blessing. The multitude cried out in thanksgiving for the miracle.

Several days later, after the Cristo's installation on an altar in the Iglesia de San Pablo, the city received another miracle.[38] In the midst of Holy Week celebrations, a procession in honor of the Holy Name of Jesus started out from the Augustinian convento and made its way through city streets toward the colegio. The group included mostly Indians, though they were accompanied by Fray

Juan de Guzmán, whose task it was to encourage and animate the *penitentes* in their discipline. Inside the iglesia, several friars gathered solemnly to wait the arrival of the procession. One of them knelt in prayer at the feet of the Cristo Aprecido.

The procession arrived at the doors of the church and as the faithful pilgrims began to enter, the friars within removed the cover (*velo*) that shrouded the Cristo. Guzmán was the first to observe that the crucifix was much larger than it had been before. Later, he recalled that the nearer he drew to the image, the more it seemed to him to grow "stouter" and fuller. The Cristo also appeared paler and more brilliant than ever, so that the image's skin shone and appeared almost like human flesh.[39] Another witness to the miracle, Fray Simón, later estimated that the Cristo was as much as "four hands" larger than it had been. To a third, Fray Agustín de Carabazal, the Cristo seemed "resplendent," with human-like skin ("carnes que casi eran humanas") and its form more "corpulent."[40] Fray Pedro de Coronel, prior of Totolapan, and Fray Agustín de Golagurto, the rector of the colegio, were present, and both later confirmed the miracle.

The friars fell on their knees and prayed to the Cristo, remaining there for some time. The Indians who had come on procession shouted upon beholding the "terrifying" miracle, so that the friars could barely hear one another for the din. At first, stricken with fear, they cowered at the back of the church, reluctant to approach the image within. But soon, greatly moved by what they witnessed, their fear turned to devotion; they too began to pray fervently and to tear at their own flesh with whips, shedding many tears.[41] Filled with the spirit and with great fervor, Carabazal began to preach in a loud voice about the miracle that the Santo Crucifijo had accomplished: the Cristo was showing himself to be larger than ever before and this was a sign that he would bestow upon them ever-greater mercies.[42] The friars were deeply stirred by what they had witnessed, insisting later that they had never before seen or experienced anything like it.

The Cristo's perspiration, his glowing skin, suddenly corpulent form, and gesture of benediction were signs of divine presence but, just as importantly, also evidence of human life. Perhaps the clearest indication was that his skin appeared to the witnesses in that moment as if it was "human flesh." Though the phenomenon of living images has origins in pre-Christian Europe, the seventeenth century was a period of intensified activity both in Europe and Latin America.[43] In this period in Spain, images of Christ, in particular, were likely to show signs of movement.[44] The theme of images come to life is also presented in several seventeenth-century European oil paintings: a statue of Christ leans forward from his crucifix to embrace St. Francis, or drapes his arm around St. Lutgard.[45] The Cristo Aparecido may have been one of the very earliest New World images that showed signs of life, but this soon became a frequent, although nonetheless extraordinary, miracle. Almost twenty years later, the

Cristo Renovado, Aparecido's neighbor in the city, was seen to tremble on his cross, to bleed, and to open his eyes. Today, the Señor de Chalma bows his head in fatigue from the great spiritual burdens that he bears on behalf of his devotees.

One aspect of the Cristo's construction may have facilitated or accentuated the miracle. The Cristo is an *imágen de vestir*. That is, as a sculpted image he is incomplete, intended to be dressed and adorned. The sculpted figure has no hair, either painted or sculpted. Instead, he is utterly dependent on the generosity of women devotees who promise to him their locks. He also always has worn a fabric loincloth, sometimes decorated with quite elaborate golden embroidery. Many of the first few generations of New World crucifixes were similarly imágenes de vestir, so much so that the Third Mexican Council, which met in 1585, offered prohibitions against the practice. Though some have suggested the practice was a uniquely American innovation, with roots in pre-Columbian religious practice, in fact the tradition of dressing images exists in various religious traditions and has a long history in Europe as elsewhere. [46] The dressing of images clearly assisted in the process of blurring the boundaries between an inanimate object and a living manifestation of the divine. The use of real clothing and human hair on crucifixes in particular not only made them more "agonizingly" realistic (that is, transformed them into more acute representations of human suffering) but also more accurately helped to bring the images to life.

This background does not necessarily help explain what the Cristo's signs of life might have meant for the community of friars and Indians for whom, presumably, they were performed. The skeptical Franciscans, who worried about Indian gullibility, were the ones who reported, as we noted above, that "some think that he is alive and that he is bestowing his blessing upon them. And others think that he is the real Jesus Christ that died in the hands of the Jews. And others think that he is God, and they adore him as a god."[47] Such is the complexity of the mystery of Christ's own person: simultaneously human and divine—a paradox dimly echoed in the Cristo, at once an inanimate statue, the very human Jesus come to life, and God himself. However, it is the Cristo's humanity that is emphasized in the Mexico City miracles.

For Serge Gruzinski, who writes of the procession of the Cristo in Mexico City, the Indians' observation of the Cristo's signs of life "corroborated the sensitivity acquired by Indian communities in the capital to the Christian miraculous." These gestures were dramatic evidence that the Indians had finally adopted Christianity as their own.[48] I believe that for the Indians, who at first shouted in fear and later cried out in recognition at the Cristo's miracles, what was more significant was that the image acknowledged them, blessed them, and recognized them. He showed signs of life in the midst of death, displayed signs of power among the disempowered, and dispensed blessings upon those who most hungered for them. The Cristo was inviting them into relationship, and making himself available to the people of Mexico City. That is, he had become, for them, a "santo," a locally specific manifestation of the divine.

This series of miracles are the product and reflection of a faith forged in common. This was a shared miracle, one that moved and shook both the indigenous communities in the vicinity of the colegio and the friars who lived and worked there. That is, the Cristo's expression of life and divine presence united, even if only temporarily, Indians and their priests into a single, believing, community of faith. As Taylor explains, in Mexico the "will to believe" in animate images was a unifying belief: "If such churches modeled the kingdom of heaven and were charged with the divine presence, then divinely charged images could show signs of life—blinking, bleeding, twitching, shedding tears of perspiration—and could serve as the agents of other marvels. A will to believe in such incarnations bridged ethnic groups, regions, and classes."[49] In this instance, the Indians and Spanish friars of Mexico City were actively creating the sacred in concert.

News of the Cristo's power spread quickly, facilitated by pamphlets distributed by the Augustinians. The incurably ill of Mexico City began to come to him, perhaps in search of the "ever-greater mercies" predicted by Carazabal. One story stands out in the historical record, the case of the widow "Samyn," a thirty-year-old servant and local resident. She had been plagued by a debilitating edema for almost six months, and was unable to use her arms or legs, walk, or even to turn over in bed unassisted. With the help of her daughter and several local Indians who made a chair for this purpose, Samyn was carried to the church so that she could "adore the Santo Crucifixo that had been brought from Totolapan." Her companions carried her to the altar of the Cristo, and two friars, moved with pity, assisted Samyn to her knees so that she could kiss the feet of the image. She remained in that position for half an hour while she prayed the Our Father and then, having adored the Cristo and "kissed his holy feet," she rose *buena y sana*, well and healthy. She stood up of her own accord, unassisted, and "all of those present could see that she was healed of her illness and that the swelling had gone down."[50]

"Behold the Man!": The Cristo on Trial

Then saith Pilate unto him, Speakest thou not unto me? Knowest thou not that I have power to crucify thee, and have power to release thee?
—John 19:10

Artistic representations of the Ecce Homo abound in Christian art, and are ubiquitous in churches and capillas throughout Latin America, and wherever depictions of Christ's passion particularly capture the religious and artistic imagination of the people. Today, an almost ghastly Ecce Homo image of colonial origins keeps the Cristo Aparecido company in the sanctuary of the parish church in Totolapan. The Ecce Homo depicts Christ at the moment in John's gospel when he is beaten and bound, under judgment first by Pilate himself and then by the angry crowd to whom Pilate surrendered the Savior's fate. In the 1583 Inquisition hearing, it was not Christ but the Cristo who was on trial, though his twenty-first-century devotees would not be surprised that the biography of their precious image has at times paralleled the life of Jesus himself as related in the gospels. Though the Inquisition's original charges were against the Cristo's Augustinian guardians, for spreading news of unsubstantiated miracles, in the final analysis, it was not so much the Augustinian order as the image itself that stood awaiting the judgment of the ecclesio-political powers.

Events were set in motion when, realizing the tremendous power of the Cristo Aparecido, Suárez de Escobar determined that the appropriate location for the image was not at the new colegio but rather in the primary convento of the order, their Mexican headquarters. The transfer was to occur on the feast of the Holy Trinity, to what was to be his new and permanent location at the Iglesia de San Agustín. From there, the image could be adored and venerated in the manner that he deserved. Certainly the Augustinians had multiple reasons for being invested in the Cristo and his "performance." The miraculous image provided considerable symbolic capital within the city, and they clearly intended to leverage the image for the greatest yield of power and influence. This is not to suggest that the friars themselves did not genuinely believe the image to be miraculous. But it is probably the case, as one witnessed accused, that the Augustinians quickly came to rely upon the significant offerings they received in honor of the Cristo to help fund the costly ongoing construction of their new and impressive colegio.

Though the Augustinians' official request to move the image was the immediate impetus for the hearing, the Inquisition's scrutiny of the Cristo reflected an institutional ambivalence regarding the proper place and nature of images that had troubled Christianity almost since its origins. This ambivalence troubled Mexico City in particular after the Franciscan friar Bustamante's controversial 1556 sermon charging that the appearance of Guadalupe to Juan Diego was a miracle fabricated by duplicitous priests. With the relatively recent conclusions of the Council of Trent at the fore of their considerations, in particular its cautions around the misuse of images, the Inquisition met in Mexico City and even traveled to Totolapan, where it called upon Indian witnesses and Spanish friars alike to give testimony about the origins of the Cristo Aparecido and his purported miracles.[51]

At the opening of the hearing, don Pedro Garces, treasurer and *provisor* of the archdiocese, listed the archbishop's multiple concerns. First, the Augustinians had neither sought nor received diocesan authorization to publish and distribute accounts of the several miracles that they attributed to the image.

Second, the intended purpose of the meetings was to resolve the question of whether the friars would be allowed to transfer the image to San Agustín. Finally, he accused the Augustinians of brazen self-interest, charging that they had published accounts of the miracles out of vanity, and in anticipation of the offerings they would receive from the large crowds who would surely come in response to such news, which would in turn pay for continuing construction at the Colegio de San Pedro.[52]

Asked if he had had an opportunity to see the Cristo for himself, Garcés responded with scorn: "I have not seen it nor I have desired to. And even more so they say that it raises his arms and then lowering him as if he is giving his benediction to the people. And, as it is well varnished and the varnish melted and dripped in the heat of Holy Thursday, the people dried it with a towel and shouted, as they understood that the Cristo was sweating. And this was published and noted by Pedro de [Gol]Agurto, rector of S. Pedro who said that he had seen him increase in size on that Holy Thursday."[53]

Motivated by their ongoing doubts about the purity and correctness of indigenous Christian faith, the Franciscans stepped forward to express their concern about the "misunderstanding" of the local Indians regarding the Cristo Aparecido. Of his own accord, a Franciscan friar named Gonçales volunteered his opinion on these matters to the Inquisition. As vicar and caretaker of the Indians of the Mexico City neighborhoods of San Juan, San Sebastián, and Santa María, it was Gonçales who testified that the the image of the Totolapan crucifix was alive, and that he was actually Jesus Christ, or even God himself.[54] The Franciscan witness charged the Augustinians with deliberately fostering misunderstanding among the Indians by publishing these miracles, thus weakening their faith.

In the face of the accusations aired before the Inquisition, the friars argued passionately for the authenticity and singularity of their image. Toward this end, the provincial himself testified. The order also helped document the miracles of healing attributed to the Cristo by soliciting witnesses. A little over two weeks before his own appearance, Suárez traveled to Totolapan with a notary skilled in Nahuatl to gather the testimonies of Indian witnesses to the miracle. These witnesses were carefully selected, and their testimonies rehearsed and orchestrated (as is evident in the consistency of their stories). Important as the issue was, they hardly would have left the issue to chance. Of the singularity of the Cristo, the Augustinians argued before the Inquisition "that God should be more manifest in one image over another is normal and occurs in other parts of Christendom."[55] Finally, they also denied responsibility for the pamphlets, saying rather that they were the work of "mugercillas amigas de novedades," young women fond of rumors and gossip.

Nonetheless, the Inquisition handed down a decision that surely disappointed the friars. On May 22, having scrutinized the relevant documents, they decreed that neither the provincial nor any of his friars were authorized to publish accounts of miracles, unless these were authenticated in advance by a competent judge. Suárez was ordered to repeat this pronouncement to his friars when they were all gathered together in *capítulo*. The archbishop gave permission for the crucifix to be transferred to San Agustín for the time being, but ordered that this was to be done without any celebration or fiesta in its honor. Nor were the Augustinians to preach on any subject related to the crucifix. Rather, the friars should "give an ordinary sermon in honor of the feast of the Trinity . . . under threat of grave punishment and censure."[56]

On June 3, the inquisitor in charge offered further clarification. He reiterated that though the friars had been given permission to move the image, it must be done without any publicity so as to avoid stimulating the "enthusiasm" of the people. The image should be placed in a public and appropriate place, and covered with a drape (*velo*), "as were other images of our Lord Jesus Christ." There it should be available and accessible so that "all faithful Christians can see and adore it"; but for the time it should be regarded not as singular or unique, but revered just as any image of Christ would be.[57]

So it came to be that, in spite of the Augustinians' best efforts, the Cristo Aparecido was officially determined to be a common and ordinary image by a decree of the Inquisition. This certainly did not reflect the experience of the residents of the City of Mexico, nor did it deter them in their belief: both pilgrims and passers-by frequented the image for more than two centuries at his home on an altar in the iglesia of the Convento de San Augustin. In perhaps the most final and effective literary vindication of the Cristo, Grijalva's authoritative history of the Augustinian order in Mexico makes no mention of the Inquisition case, effectively deleting the event from history.[58] Whatever doubts were raised by the Inquisition as to the image's singularity were also addressed, definitively for the order, by Grijalva's assertion of Roa's sanctity.

The Baroque Seventeenth Century

Throughout the seventeenth and eighteenth centuries, the Cristo remained one of the most prized religious treasures of the Augustinian order in Mexico, surpassed only by their Lignam Crucis. As such, it was undoubtedly one of the most respected and recognized processional objects in the city. In some ways the Franciscans had won their battle against the Cristo when the Inquisition declared him "common and ordinary." But if the Franciscans won the battle, they surely lost the war. Though he was among the first and most distinguished of the New World images to grace the churches of colonial Mexico City, he was by the eighteenth century only one of many. Over the course of the prolific seventeenth century, dozens and dozens of images had accumulated, as baroque adornments to chapels, barrio shrines, colegios, churches, convents, and cathedrals. This resulted in the concentration of religious capital in the city; it had become again the power center that it had once been as Tenochtitán, the ritual and political center of the Aztec empire, the geographic navel of the universe. The sacred space of colonial Mexico City was marked, bounded, and punctuated by its religious images.

The Cristo was at the center of this landscape. Though the historical record pertaining to the Cristo is relatively thin during these years, Robles's daily record of events in Mexico City mentions two processions with the image in the late seventeenth century. On February 1, 1677, when the friars "took out their two most precious relics," the Lignum Crucis and the Santo Cristo de Totolapa, which they carried with them to the cathedral.[59] On Friday, April 27, 1691, Robles notes a mass and procession in honor of San Agustín that wound its way along the waterfront and concluded at the Santo Cristo de Totolapa.[60]

On December 11, 1676, the Cristo narrowly escaped a fire that leveled the Augustinian convento that had been his home for almost one hundred years. The fire ignited during a celebration in honor of the Virgin of Guadalupe, and although it took a mere two hours for the church and all the altars inside to burn, three days passed before the fire extinguished itself completely.[61] Such fires were commonplace in baroque churches of the mid-colonial centuries, given the high combustibility of the elaborately carved wooden altars and altarpieces, and the many candles and colored paper streamers that decorated them. Because technology for combating fires was limited, there was nothing much that could be done, except to appeal to divine intervention and watch as the blaze burned the church to the ground.

The Cristo was one of the few objects that survived the December fire, among those most precious objects that heroic devotees risked their lives to retrieve in the minutes before the church was completely engulfed by flames. Among those items rescued were two safe boxes, two side altars, and several religious images.[62] A man named don Juan de Chavarría was brave enough to dive into the flames to reclaim the *custodio* that held the Blessed Sacrament from the main altar.[63] By the grace of such an heroic act, the Cristo Aparecido himself was spared a tragic fate.[64] Other cristos did not fare as well as ours during these treacherous centuries, and were in fact destroyed by fires in those years. This was the case with the original Cristo de Chalma, burned to charcoal and ashes in a fire in the late eighteenth century.

The Augustinians did not delay in the project of rebuilding the church. A mere three days later they traversed the city, pleading for alms for the construction.[65] If it was ever in question, the Cristo's status in the order was reaffirmed and amplified in the rebuilding of this structure. Before the fire, it had been housed in a chapel dedicated to Augustinians of the Third Order (lay members who took vows but did not live in the convento). The new church featured a large "Capilla del Cristo de Totolapan," dedicated solely to him.[66] The Cristo had the power to generate generous financial support among the Mexico City population; on one occasion, for example, the large sum of 80 pesos was donated for the purchase of doors to the "Capilla de Totolapan."[67]

The archbishop blessed the new Iglesia de San Agustín on December 10, 1692; and on December 14, the new building was officially occupied. A grand procession marked the formal occupation of the new structure, including cofradías with their banners and the religious orders with their crosses, all "richly adorned with jewels."[68] Certainly on this occasion one would imagine that the Cristo, too, was ceremoniously returned to the convento, and his capilla inaugurated with pomp and honor along with the rest. Here emerges what is perhaps the most striking and impressive aspect of this history: the sheer fact of the Cristo's survival, the remarkable—one might even say miraculous— endurance of this fragile, impermanent object through these dramatic and dangerous centuries.

In spite of the Franciscans' best efforts, Mexico City by the eighteenth century was teeming with images around which swirled an equally rich ceremonial life. A cacophony of processions, both secular and sacred, crisscrossed barrios and moved from sacred landmark to sacred landmark, sanctifying city streets. Pamela Voekel writes of the elaborate and ostentatious public funeral processions, so grand that even those not of the wealthy classes were dispatched by "numerous clerics, friends, beggars, family, clients, and perhaps confraternity members."[69] The city also celebrated five major festivals a year, three of which were secular.[70] The baroque aesthetic was in many ways an ephemeral one. Temporary altars improvised out of doors, delicate paper streamers, processions that filled city streets for hours and then were suddenly gone with little trace—all of these spoke to a transient beauty.[71] Each image, each altar, each barrio capilla and procession marked yet one more "point of access to the sacred," so that the city abounded with sacred sites.[72] The baroque cityscape facilitated the "easy commingling of the sacred and the profane."[73] The very urbanity of this sacred metropolis was defined, in part, by the abundance and availability of these diverse, and sometimes fleeting, access points to the holy.

The many images that came to populate the New World necessitated a system, an organizational structure, for their sustenance. The seventeenth century was the age when the lay religious organizations known as *mayordomías*, *cofradías*, or *hermandades* flourished as relatively autonomous Indian modes of community organization.[74] A European social form, the religious confraternity, or brotherhood, was first introduced to indigenous communities in the sixteenth century by Spanish priests as part of their project of evangelization and acculturation. These were formally organized bodies, largely in service of the local parish, with close clerical supervision. Beginning in the 1620s, just when the indigenous population was at its nadir, central Mexico was the location of a religious renaissance of sorts. From this period onward, indigenous communities seem to have fully appropriated the institution, tailoring it to their own requirements and uses. In the Yucatan in the seventeenth and eighteenth century, the word *cofradía* was essentially synonymous with community.[75] Serge Gruzinski's compelling thesis is that Indian mayordomías and confraternities were flexible institutions, readily adaptable to changing local circumstances.[76]

Most frequently, at their origin these mayordomías were the product of local Indian initiative and organized around devotion to a particular local image, or santo, providing the religiocultural infrastructure for the many requisite fiestas and celebrations. Especially beginning in the mid-seventeenth century, these were founded with relative autonomy from official Church structures and authority, without official license and frequently without formal constitutions.[77] Very few ever petitioned for official status as a cofradía. These lay organizations continued to flourish through the eighteenth century; in 1794 the archbishop of Mexico said that he counted no fewer than 951 such entities in his diocese, 500 of which he quickly determined to be illegitimate. Nevertheless he exercised caution around abolishing Indian confraternities, as the Indians were "very tenacious in maintaining their customs and devotions" and likely to riot if their brotherhoods were threatened.[78]

In all likelihood, within decades of his arrival in the city one such informal mayordomía was organized on behalf of the Cristo Aparecido, though I have uncovered no official documents or constitutions related to its founding. Such a group probably organized and facilitated the collective sponsorship that sustained the Cristo during these centuries, paying for candles and flowers for his altar, sponsoring his fiestas, and otherwise contributing the general maintenance of devotion.[79] As I explore in some depth in the last chapters of this book, in the late twentieth century the mayordomía of Totolapan played a central role in the biography of the Cristo Aparecido.

In the colonial period, mayordomías served a dual purpose: the maintenance of images and the care of the dead. That is, in making a regular financial contribution to their local mayordomía, the Indians of Mexico City not only cared for their cristos and vírgenes, but also assured that there would be resources for their own proper burial. As they simultaneously labored to maintain their beloved cristos and care for the bodies of their deceased members, the mayordomías may have enhanced the associations between the indigenous body and the body of Christ. This conflation must have been very near the surface in the eighteenth century, when the Indians of central Mexico called upon their beloved cristos as they faced a deadly typhus epidemic. Gruzinski writes of the mayordomías that they "could offer a psychological and material response to the epidemics that decimated the Indian population."[80]

A Shield of Arms: The Cristo and the Epidemic of 1736

In 1736 Mexico City faced the worst epidemic the region had suffering in more than a century. Yet again, matlazahuatl, or typhus, filled the city's hospitals and cemeteries. However, by this point in history the people were not without recourse: the city government administration and the Indian and mestizo residents of the urban barrios together turned to the city's many religious images for assistance. This gesture was the culmination of a two-century-long development of a deep and multifaceted relationship between the Indians of the New World and the religious images that had become (among other things) their protection and succor against the repeated waves of epidemic disease that resulted, time and time again, in their mass death. I have already suggested that such epidemics had an impact on the Cristo's biography in the sixteenth century, when typhus may have contributed to the image's removal to Mexico City in 1583. Serge Gruzinski has written compellingly about the "torn net," the loss of cultural coherence and religious meaning that the Indians experienced in the initial phase of conquest and colonial rule.[81] By the end of the seventeenth century, this torn net had been largely replaced with an impenetrable, unassailable shield of arms: a legion of Christian images that the indigenous and (by now) mestizo people of Mexico had assembled for their defense and protection. Here it becomes clear that the Indians understood that their health and well-being was dependant upon the welfare and efficacy of their beloved images.[82] As Gruzinski writes, "Images were the ultimate (sometimes the only) protection and remedy against the illnesses and natural disasters which repeatedly struck the Mexican population."[83] This use of images extends into the present century. In April of 2009 the residents of Mexico City called on their images to help them combat the outbreak of swine flu; an image of Our Lord of Health was retrieved from storage where it had been for more than two hundred years and placed on the main altar of the city's cathedral.

Centuries earlier, in 1736 the city called forth its many images, some well known and some "never before seen" until necessity drew them from obscurity. These filed out of chapels, neighborhood shrines, and local churches, and filled city streets. Among these was the Cristo Aparecido of Totolapan, upon whom the people of Mexico City called for aid against the illness. The Cristo was not the only or even the principal image, but rather part of an ensemble cast to whom the suffering looked for succor and relief. In 1736-1737, the combined force of Mexico cities images was unleashed to stem the tide of disease and death. Through prayer, processions, and penitence the potency of these images was called upon by the Spanish, by the city administrators, and by the residents of the Indian barrios, who fell in the greatest numbers before the onslaught. The sum total of this effort constituted "a shield of arms," which is the title of Cabrera's massive tome cataloguing both the city's images and its multipronged efforts to defeat the epidemic.[84] Cabrera's work is at once a history of the epidemic, a celebration of the defeat of the illness, and a treasury of information about religious images in Mexico City in the eighteenth century. But more then these, it is a proclamation of collective of faith in the face of disaster. Some might see it as a defense of the very existence of God necessitated by the massive human loss; Cabrera notes the presence of the divine in every corner of the city. Similarly, he documents the deep-felt penitential faith of the people of Mexico City.

In the second half of the seventeenth century, Mexico saw the first significant period of population recovery since the arrival of the Europeans. Though the pace of recovery slowed, the population increased incrementally during the first three decades of the following century. The matlazahuatl put a halt to this process of recovery: in some locales it would be decades before the slow progress would return.[85] Ironically, this very process of growth and recovery contributed to the spread of the disease, which moved along new and heavily trafficked commercial routes.[86] In particular, through the process of urbanization, the population of Mexico City had increased exponentially in the decades immediately prior to the epidemic, especially among the poor and disenfranchised classes. Indians displaced from rural areas by the disruption caused by the emerging hacienda system swelled urban streets. Typhus is a disease that flourishes under conditions of extreme poverty: it is the affliction of prisons and concentration camps. Mexico City's poor neighborhoods were rife with misery, and the first reports came from the periphery of the capital, where living conditions were the worst.[87] The epidemic reached its peak in the first months of 1737. At the beginning of that year, the Hospital of San Hipólito cared for only 100 Indian (and *casta*) patients with the disease, but by March this number had surged to 896. The Hospital Real de Indios counted almost five hundred Indians who died within its walls in the month in which the illness peaked.[88] At its conclusion, death registers totaled over forty thousand, including almost fourteen thousand Indians.[89]

City administrators offered no facile explanations for how the illness took root and spread, nor did they offer simplistic proposals for how the city should best respond to care for victims, dispose of the dead, and deter the illness's progress. Contemporary observers, like Cabrera himself, contended that the matlazahuatl was caused in part by social factors and the physical environment.[90] Poverty increased the reach and devastation of the illness, they understood, as did density of population, health compromised by drinking and alcoholism, and most important, by bad or contaminated air. Indians were perceived as particularly vulnerable because they "ate poorly, dressed worse, and worked too hard."[91] Both Spanish and the Indians had theories of contagion: the Spanish had long used the vernacular *pegar* (to stick or adhere) to describe how disease spread from person to person.[92] But these more pragmatic attributions of origins were also combined with those of an explicitly theological nature: the Indians' continued "idolatry" was frequently blamed as one of the root causes for the devastating disease.

Given their complex understanding of how the epidemic came to have a hold on the population, city administers advised a multipronged attack on the spread of illness. They recommended the use of scented luminaries to clear the air (a sort of colonial aromatherapy), but also counseled improved sanitation, the disposal of clothing and blankets belonging to the sick, and a new attention to personal hygiene. In addition, they empowered a committee of doctors and surgeons to study the problem, and opened new hospitals and rededicated others for the new purpose.[93] In addition to general policies of public health, city officials advocated prayer, penance, and processions. Images themselves were seen to purify the sick air and to offer immunity to disease. At the height of its course, when prospects for defeating the disease seemed most grim, the viceroy wrote to the Council of the Indies to explain: "In addition to these human interventions, we have also solicited divine providence, with public prayer, novenas, and pleading to God, his Holy Mother, and particular saints, who are the counsel of this city and its people. We have sought to placate His justified anger with processions and public penance, but it has not been enough. How great our sins must be, or how weak our repentance, that His mercy is deaf to our pleas."[94]

If drunkenness and idolatry were among the spiritual causes, than penitence was most certainly a powerful cure. Religious processions to halt epidemics were common practice in Europe during the Middle Ages and early modern period, so their use for this purpose was not a Mexican innovation.[95] For the believing Catholics of the city, epidemic disease did not lead to a crisis of faith but rather signaled a greater need for the protection offered by Christian saints and for more dramatic displays of devotion. So although the local government worried about the spread of disease by large gatherings of people, they nevertheless "authorized and organized" processions, novenas, and rosaries that brought together crowds of people from all over the city. Over thirty religious events were sponsored by the city government over the course of the epidemic; most of these were concentrated in a three-month period, from January to March of 1737, when there were seventeen government-organized celebrations.[96] These numbers reflect only those that were officially sponsored; others were initiated by individual mayordomías, the religious orders, and may even have been improvised in the moment.

A novena and procession of the Cristo Aparecido was among the countless ceremonial events orchestrated to protect the city's residents in 1736. Cabrera describes how the Augustinian order brought out their most "trusted" image in supplication. They celebrated the Cristo Aparecido "for a full nine days, with the greatest devotion and culto in his chapel of the same name where the faithful crowd attended the solemn devotions." The novena concluded with a procession that was as large in scale and as aesthetically appealing as it was deeply penitential (*mortificada*). Cabrera thus finds a corresponding fervor and intensity between the order's "great desire for the health of Mexico and the veneration that they have always shown to this image . . . [as] from this and from other assaults he had protected them, as a shield."[97]

Believers not only drew on tried and true religious techniques, but improvised and marshaled new religious strategies against the epidemic. This is noted by historian Paul Ramírez in his treatment of the procession of Santiago Tlatelolco on March 5, 1737, which disturbed Cabrera for its strange creativity.[98] The devout of Tlatelolco processed with their image adorned not as the victorious "Moor slayer," but rather dressed in the garb of the contrite penitent, bearing a scourge where he should have wielded a sword. For Ramírez, the barrio's conversion of their image "may reflect the active reception of another sympathetically suffering penitent, participating as a member of the community," ultimately underscoring the profound identification between the image and his community of devotees.[99] Images could simultaneously be the ones to whom penance was directed, the audience for (and object of) ritual acts of devotion, and also ritual actors in a religious drama, themselves expressing gestures of faith alongside their devotees.

Nevertheless, neither the Cristo Aparecido nor the faith and improvisation of the devout of Mexico City was able to stop the progression of the illness, which continued through much of 1737. True, Cabrera's history narrates the eventual success of these many images, working in unison, in eventually defeating the epidemic. For him, the Cristo Aparecido figured in this ultimate (if delayed) triumph. But even many months after the Cristo's procession, the numbers of the dead continued to rise, the pestilence undeterred. For some, this might be seen as his greatest moment of failure.

One image emerged as truly victorious, finally giving relief to the populace: the Virgin of Guadalupe. Where the Cristo and other images failed, Guadalupe prevailed. At the beginning of the epidemic Guadalupe was only one of three prominent Marian images in the city of Mexico. In fact, processions honoring the Virgin of Loreto in December of 1736 and then Our Lady of Remedios, considered then to be the city's patron, were paid for out of public coffers before attentions turned to Guadalupe as a source of assistance. In February of 1737, the faithful gathered at Guadalupe's shrine at Tepeyac, praying for relief, pleading that the image be moved to the cathedral where she might exert more influence against the plague. In March of that year the city council petitioned the archbishop to have Guadalupe recognized as the patron of the city. This was finally accomplished, and in May the city held a large-scale procession and lavish celebration.[100] It appears that the *tilma* (Juan Diego's cloak upon which the image of Guadalupe was imprinted) remained at the sanctuary at Tepeyac. Perhaps this was because the archbishop worried about damage that might be caused to the historic image. In 1677, the archbishop ordered that the glass box in which the image was housed be kept shut, presumably to protect her against potential damage by eager devotees.[101] Instead, the mayodomías marched carrying a great silver statue of Guadalupe through city streets, and the image was greeted by myriad replicas that hung on every building, "their omnipresence multiplied by countless mirrors, so that the whole city appeared to exhibit but one likeness."[102] The Guadalupan celebration finally turned the tide: a few short weeks later, in June 1737, the disease began to subside. This display of power, protection, and care for the people of the city was the defining moment for Guadalupan devotion, the beginning of the consolidation of her prominent place as the national symbol for Mexico (figure 4.1).[103]

FIGURE 4.1. Guadalupe protects the City of Mexico. Print, Mexico, 1739. Cabrera y Quintero, Cayetano, and Víctor M. Ruiz Naufal, *Escudo de armas de México*. Ed. facsimilar con un estudio histórico y una cronología de Víctor M. Ruiz Naufal. Mexico City: Instituto Mexicano del Seguro Social, 1981.

Conclusions

The Cristo Aparecido's arrival in Mexico City in 1583 signaled the beginning of an aesthetic shift: during the seventeenth century, Christian images accrued as baroque adornments to Mexico City's cathedrals, churches, and capillas. The sixteenth-century friar, Roa, was the first to proclaim the Cristo's beauty, but in baroque Mexico City the Cristo accumulated significance as an aesthetic object, although not precisely as a "work of art". The example of devotion to the Cristo Aparecido suggests that that the emerging faith of early-seventeenth-century Mexico City was a faith forged in common, between Spanish friars and urban Indians alike. Together they brought the Cristo to life and saw to his maintenance and care. In this respect, baroque religion was also surprisingly local and highly popular in its origins. Believers from the barrios surrounding the Cristo's chapel held that the image was not only alive but but also the historical Jesus come among them. This chapter suggests that certain events in the life of the Cristo echo those in the life of Christ himself: his triumphant arrival in Jerusalem and his trial before Pilate finding parallels in the image's celebratory reception in Mexico City and in his subsequent judgment before the Inquisition. In this context the Franciscans, as the likely instigators of the inquisition's scrutiny, emerge as the Cristo's first and primary antagonists.

Together, the Cristo and his many hermanos came to define the very urbanity of the city. As if they had indeed anticipated such a need, in the eighteenth century these accumulated sacra served a deeper and more urgent purpose: the protection of the citizens against the worst epidemic they had seen in over a hundred years. Thus, the Cristo was, perhaps, where his presence was most required during these centuries.

Though I would not necessarily describe these centuries as a period of decline for the Cristo it is the Virgin Mary in her apparition as Guadalupe who was ascendant in these years, surpassing both the city's many images of Christ and its other virgins to claim her title as patroness of the city, and finally of Mexico itself. The most pronounced decline in the Cristo's status comes in the nineteenth century, when his hold on Mexico City is loosened by Bourbon-era reforms and the full weight of secular nationalism, as the following chapter describes.

5

Repatriation

Christ Comes Again to Totolapan

In the midst of violent tempest and turmoil,
Your tender and loving Father returns to you.
Oh happy people of Totolapan!
                    —Anonymous, 1861

Scene 4. Homecoming. Entrance, Totolapan, March 1861

How does one welcome Christ, long lost, finally home? Gather
together your children: small angels resplendent, arrayed in
glory, luminous white. The little ones will be the first to receive
him. They are proud of their feathered wings and gingerly
raise the beribboned hems of their satin skirts above the dusty
earth.

  And, then, all turn to greet him: savior, survivor, persistent
saint. He has risen like a phoenix from flames, and falls into the
arms of his beloved. At last.

Many historical forces combined to allow for the Cristo
Aparecido's return, finally, to Totolapan in March of 1861.
Most important of these was the changing relationship
between the church and state that began with a movement of
reform initiated by priests and prelates within the church. As
addressed in the previous chapter, the matlazahuatl epidemic
of 1736-1737 was the occasion for the fullest expression of
baroque religion to date. The people of Mexico City unleashed
the considerable power of their saints and, in concert with
emerging medical strategies for combating disease, defeated
the deadly typhus outbreak.

Nevertheless, within two decades of these events, the Mexican Church made a decided shift against this baroque sensibility and was embarking on a process of internal reform and "modernization." Most pertinent to our purposes here, the hierarchy advocated an individual, interiorized piety as against the kind of public acts of corporate religion that it had successfully marshaled against the epidemic.

These and other religious reforms paved the way for, and dovetailed neatly with, a program of "defensive modernization" adopted by the Bourbon monarchy that ruled Mexico through the course of the eighteenth century until Mexico won its independence in 1821.[1] Most of all, the Bourbons enacted policies effecting the subordination of the church to the state, a process that culminated in a critical period of state appropriation of church property in the second half of the nineteenth century. The year 1861 saw the nationalization (the state appropriation) of the great Augustinian convento that was the Cristo's home for 278 years—a crisis that freed the Cristo to be returned, finally, to the people of Totolapan.

The pueblo of Totolapan welcomed back their image in grand style: they authored poems, printed invitations, and dressed their children as angels to ceremoniously greet the Cristo, their "tender and loving father," back to his pueblo of origin. The people of Totolapan had preserved a memory of their Cristo for centuries: for them his return, though delayed, was inevitable. So, in addition to exploring the historical movements that facilitated the Cristo's return to Totolapan, this chapter also refocuses attention on his pueblo of origin. Here I trace the faith of the people of Totolapan since the Cristo's departure, and conclude this portion of his biography with the Cristo's triumphant and ceremonious homecoming.

Another, distinct phenomenon may also have contributed to the loosening grip of the Augustinians on the Cristo of Totolapan. During the mid-colonial centuries, the Augustinians turned their attention away from the Aparecido and focused instead on building up the cult of another Augustinian Christ, the cristo known as the Señor de Chalma, whose shrine was to become (and continues to be) the second most visited pilgrimage site in Mexico. This chapter therefore contrasts the fate of the Cristo Aparecido of Totolapan with his most famous cristo hermano, sibling santo, the Señor de Chalma. At the same time, here the reader discovers that though the Cristo Aparecido has many hermanos, many kin, each with his own distinct biography, that for the devotees of Mexico, *Cristo es uno*: these images are, on some deep level, truly one and the same.

With our attention focused squarely on the Cristo, here we must dispense of traditional periodizations of the history of Mexico. Mexico's independence from Spain in 1821, for example, can for most historical purposes be understood as the pivotal event during this period, the great divide marking the transition from colonial to post-colonial society. Yet independence seems to have had very little discernable, immediate impact on the Augustinian order, on popular devotion to the Cristo, or on the well-being of the image itself. Perhaps this chapter's most substantive theoretical contribution, then, is that these larger-than-life political events are not always of consequence for local religious practices.

The Cristo in Decline: The Bourbon Church and the Rise of Liberal Secularism

During the almost three centuries that the Cristo was in Mexico City, he was hostage to the Augustinian order and simultaneously minister to and protector of the Indians of the neighborhood barrios. In Mexico City, devotion to the Cristo Aparecido, who had become known as the Cristo de Totolapan, had continued uninterrupted. Believers arrived regularly from the surrounding barrios to visit the image in his home at the Convento de San Agustin in Mexico City, where he occupied a prominent side chapel built and named for him. By the middle of the eighteenth century the Cristo was still potent, but his power was wielded in unison with others, as "one of many" holy images worshiped in the city (as in the defeat of the epidemic). Furthermore, the memory of the friar Roa and the story of the Cristo's exceptional origins had been largely forgotten. Perhaps this was the long-term consequence of the Inquisition's sixteenth-century pronouncement that the image was to be regarded as "common and ordinary."

Separated from the local context of his pueblo of origin, the significance of the story of his miraculous appearance waned over time. One mid-eighteenth-century source records that the Santo Cristo of Totolapan was held in much veneration in the "Convento Grande de San Agustín" in Mexico City, but in this report Roa's name is forgotten all together; the legend of the Cristo's appearance speaks only of a generic "Fray Agustín Varón."[2] In 1755, another source mentions the veneration of "the miraculous image of Nuestro Señor Jescristo Crucificado, with the name of Totolapan," but again, makes no mention of Roa or the legend of the image's appearance.[3] In fact, in these centuries the Cristo was not even known by the name of Aparecido, effectively erasing all memory of his miraculous origin.

The symbolic capital of the image surely declined as clerical sensibilities and taste turned against the baroque and with the invention of the "Bourbon Church." Modernizing clerics in the late eighteenth and nineteenth centuries emphasized an individualized and interiorized piety and an unmediated relationship with the divine. In her groundbreaking study of Bourbon Mexico, historian Pamela Voekel writes of the reformers' mission to "return the Church to its early pristine purity, to remove the centuries' accumulated clutter that stood between God and the individual."[4] The preponderance of saints' images that crowded church altars came under particular attack, and though the statues were not banned from church sanctuaries entirely, their numbers were radically reduced (at least for a while) and their role reassigned. That is, no longer were they to be brokers of divine power and munificence, but rather they were to "serve as moral exemplars, paragons of the now supreme virtues of moderation and restraint."[5]

The cleansing from churches of the excesses of the baroque was the aesthetic expression of a theological shift among the Church hierarchy and among more elite Catholics. The new bourbon piety yielded, belatedly, to the basic premise of the Protestant Reformation: "God did not erupt into the world at multiple points, for He was always already there in the reformed believer's heart."[6] The sacred cityscape of baroque Catholicism, defined by multiple points of access to the sacred, punctuated by cathedrals, shrines, altars, santos, barrio capillas, and processions, was no longer to anchor Catholic faith and practice. Rather, reformist Catholic leadership worked to "limit the manifestation of divinity in the world" and in particular to calm the performative and liturgical expression and celebration of divine presence.[7] The Bourbon body in prayer was characterized by quietude, stillness, and contemplation.

This Enlightenment Catholicism also found institutional expression. Reformist attitudes were consolidated in the Fourth Provincial Council of 1771 and embodied in the episcopacies of Francisco Fabíana y Fuero (of Puebla) and Francisco de Lorenzana (of Mexico). These were the first bishops to advocate "the application of modern, enlightened ideas to church institutions and practices and to call for an activist clergy that would spearhead necessary changes."[8] This era saw the escalation of the ongoing process of secularization of the Mexican Church, in which responsibility for individual parishes and even missions was wrested from the religious orders and turned over to diocesan priests. By 1740 the number of central Mexican parishes in the hands of secular clergy had risen to more than half.[9] Between 1749 and 1753, King Fernando VI directed the bishops of New Spain to hand all parishes remaining under the jurisdiction of religious orders over to secular clergy. This program met with very little resistance; and it had the ultimate effect of forcing the withdrawal of doctrineros from their rural parishes "back to their city priories." The Augustinians of Michoacán, for example, lost some thirty-two parishes at this early stage and were forced to close their novitiate for ten years in order to reduce their numbers by the requisite amount.[10] The convento of Totolapan was transferred to diocesan priests sometime soon after 1766; the last Augustinian prior arrived in the pueblo that year.[11] The monastic orders were fast losing their grasp on New Spain.

While it may seem contradictory or surprising, the two "regalist bishops," Fabían y Fuero and Lorenzana, supported a vision of a modern Church "removed from secular affairs" and, though it may have been for strategic

purposes, even endorsed a strengthened and fortified monarchy.[12] The resulting "royal absolutism" ultimately led to the expulsion of the Jesuits from the
Spanish empire (and from Spain itself) in 1767, as that order was perceived by
the crown as having too deep a stake in the colony, with their wealthy hacien-
das and their domination of educational institutions. At any rate, Voekel argues
that it was precisely the "Enlightened Catholicism" endorsed by the Church
hierarchy in the second half of the eighteenth century that provided the religious impetus for the rise of liberal secularism.[13] That is, while some might
imagine the birth of Latin American liberalism as an inherently secular movement, in actuality its origins lay in a prior shift in the religious sensibilities of
the ecclesial hierarchy (priests and bishops).

None of these social, political, and aesthetic changes boded well for the
Cristo's continued tenure in the viceregal capital. In an environment that was
decreasingly hospitable for the Cristo, an Augustinian priest named Manuel
Gonzales de la Paz y del Campo set for himself the goal of reviving interest in
the saintly Antonio de Roa and, to a lesser degree, in the Cristo himself. As I
have said, the image was still in active devotional use, to be sure, but somehow
the excruciating memory of Roa seems have waned among the Augustinians.
Gonzales, who was elected as prior of the order's Mexico City convento in 1750,
felt called to intervene. Taking up the task of official chronicler of the order, a
position once held by Juan de Grijalva, Gonzales wrote an extended hagiographic account of Roa's life and ministry. He also commissioned at least two
paintings of the heroic missionary friar. In a macabre graveyard rite, Gonzales
attempted to exhume Roa's remains from the Mexico City convento cemetery
and convert his bones into sacred relics. In some ways, Gonzales's actions were
emblematic of a last-ditch effort among the religious orders to salvage and
restore the memory of their role in the missionary past, though given the
concerns of this period, this revitalized memory recast the early Augustinian
missionaries as the founding fathers of a new "creole nation."[14] In any case, his
labors were certainly a response to, and defense against, the shifting religious
culture wrought by the Bourbon reforms. A recent catalogue of art from this
period describes the Augustinians at the forefront of the artistic reaction to
Bourbonism.[15]

Gonzales undertook the exhumation of Roa's bodily remains in 1740.
A description of the grisly event concludes his several-hundred-page history
of the order in Mexico City. The project was doomed from the start due to the
lack of substantive institutional support from the archdiocese; the constant
problem of flooding that plagued Mexico City also greatly aggravated the process. The lands around the convento were thick with mud, and the ill-skilled
laborers sent by the archbishop to assist with the digging were clumsy and
careless, much to Gonzales's consternation. In despair, he watched, helpless
as the skeleton of his beloved saint emerged from the muddy earth in bits and
pieces:

> I desired only to dignify God by revealing that Hidden Treasure. . . .
> I was there, with much pain and suffering during the entire act. I
> observed that the laborers worked without skill or familiarity. . . . The
> largest piece that was removed intact were Roa's feet: the toes, the
> nails, muscles, and tendons. Thanks to the grace of God these
> seemed as if they were formed from a mold intended for this
> purpose. . . . Another piece revealed half his skull, another was his
> hand, from the wrist to the first knuckle of his fingers. . . . How
> painful it was to observe [this exhumation] knowing that they would
> not be able to accomplish the removal of the skeleton in its entirety,
> but rather torn forth [from the earth] in pieces. . . . Nothing I did
> made a difference [to the laborers]; neither my tears, nor my pleas
> [could convince the diggers to have more care] . . . all of it was so
> poorly treated that it seemed as if it had been done by Roa's enemies
> so that his devotees, and the province itself, would be bereft of this
> venerable treasure.[16]

A vigorous debate about the authenticity of the remains followed in short order.
The diocesan authorities "dared to doubt" that the disinterred body parts truly
belonged to Roa. To the horror of Gonzales, who had already penned an admiring epigraph for the would-have been tomb of his saintly predecessor, the bones
were deposited in an unmarked, common grave.

Given the consensus among church and royal reformers that popular veneration of the objects of material religion was antithetical to a modern church
and state, it is perhaps not surprising that (what was quite likely) Roa's
exhumed body met with such casual disregard. His effort to obtain actual relics
of Fray Antonio de Roa a dismal failure, the undeterred Gonzales sought other,
less materialist, methods to raise him up in the eyes of the Mexican faithful. He
commissioned or (or perhaps simply inspired) the artist Francisco Antonio
Vallejo to execute two large paintings of Roa; these are reproduced and discussed in the opening chapters of this book (figures 2.1 and 3.1). Vallejo's pair
of paintings depict the moment of the Cristo's apparition in Totolapan and Roa,
naked from the waist up, burdened by the weight of a large cross. Vallejo was a
protégé of the most esteemed baroque painter of New Spain, Miguel Cabrera,
whose most famous work is a portrait of Sor Juana Inés de la Cruz, as displayed
on the cover of Octavio Paz's biography of the scholar-nun. Vallejo himself was
not as respected as Cabrera: "without strength or market personality: he is a
second [that is "second-rate"] Cabrerra."[17] Nevertheless, today Vallejo's large
canvases have been carefully restored and hang in a place of honor in the nave
of the Totolapan iglesia.

A third painting probably resulted from Gonzales's efforts. In the same
period, the indigenous artist Carlos Clemente López produced a work similar
in composition to Vallejo's, but set in the convento in Molango. Roa, fully

clothed in his habit, carries a cross, though he appears less burdened than in Vallejo's rendering. Today this image hangs in the Museo Nacional del Virreinato in Tepotzotlán. In commissioning these works, Gonzales clearly had a political as well as spiritual agenda. In particular he struggled with the diminished stature of religious orders and with the Episcopal turn against images and the baroque. He was surrounded by the regalist era's general disinterest in the ascetic practices and sacrifices of the first generation of missionaries. An art historian puts it bluntly: "At a time when the Bourbon crown tended to promote a more rational piety and criticized Christian practices such as those of fray Antonio, the work of fray Manuel became a criticism against these new tendencies. By exalting figures such as the missionary friar [Roa] . . . Bourbon secularization was itself criticized, and with it the secular bishops who [in spite of Gonzales' best efforts] paid such little attention in the promotion of the venerable Augustinian."[18] Gonzales, failed, ultimately, in securing for his saint the kind of hierarchical recognition that he hoped. However, it may be may be owing to his efforts that the memory of Roa persists today. If the people of Totolapan did not preserve a memory of Roa in the seventeenth century, they certainly learned again of their Cristo's miraculous arrival when, in 1758, Gonzales took over as prior of Totolapan, one of the last Augustinian friars to serve in that capacity before its secularization.

El Cristo Hermano: The Señor de Chalma

The most venerated image of the crucified Christ in Mexico today is another Augustinian Christ of colonial origin, the Cristo known as the Señor de Chalma. The Cristo Aparecido was historically prior to the Chalma Christ and was a model for the subsequent devotion. At some historical junctures the two are rival christs, competing for a place of honor in the history of the order. At other moments, the two cristos are conflated into a single shared historical memory and devotional tradition.

The Cristo Aparecido shines in Augustinian histories through the middle of the seventeenth century, which are seemingly indifferent to the Señor de Chalma. Most notably, Grijalva makes no mention of the Chalma image. In all likelihood, then, it did not exist until very late in the sixteenth century or early in the seventeenth. This not withstanding, in the late seventeenth and early eighteenth centuries, the Totolapan Christ came to be overshadowed by his larger but historically subsequent brother. So by the eighteenth century, chroniclers began to claim that the Chalma Christ was historically prior in origin. This claim emerges in the period that the *santuario* of the Señor de Chalma was growing in fame and becoming a supralocal shrine, drawing multitudes of pilgrims from across the central provinces of New Spain. In the same period the Cristo Aparecido, in comparison, seems to shrink in stature, his brilliance dimmed ever so slightly.

Nevertheless as the Señor de Chalma gained prominence both within the Augustinian order and beyond, the historically prior Cristo Aparecido was the standard against which the Chalma image's power was perforce measured and compared. The legends and traditions that grew up around him were often modeled after those of the Cristo Aparecido, and much energy was spent on explaining the absence of the Señor de Chalma from Grijalva's official history.

The Chalma image is a Cristo *aparecido* in his own right. According to official "hagiographies," the image appeared by a miracle in one of the caves at Chalma, where the local indigenous communities had continued to worship their traditional deities despite constant warnings, admonitions, and threats on the part of their diligent friars. The Augustinian friars Nicolás de Perea and Sebastián de Tolentino, among the first missionaries in the region, are said to have discovered the image there one morning. The story is a substitution legend. The friars entered the cave to encounter the triumphant crucifix, emanating a brilliant light; the "idols" he displaced lay broken and disempowered at his feet. José Sicardo's earliest account of the Chalma image, *Interrogatorio de la vida y virtudes del venerable hermano fray Bartolomé de Jesús María*, written in 1683, does not associate its origins with the labors of Perea and Tolentino, Augustinian missionaries to Mexico in the 1530s. These friars appear as protagonists only in the eighteenth century with Magallanes's account of the appearance of the Chalma image, and then in the nineteenth century in Joaquín Sardo's *Relación histórica*. From a historical-critical perspective (which here is distinct from the perspective of faith), the incorporation of Perea and Tolentino is a subsequent addition (or fabrication) designed to lend authenticity and weight to the image so that it might, among other things, measure up to the distinguished origins of the Cristo of Totolapan, which was without question tied to a known missionary.

The crucifix was certainly well established in the caves above Chalma by the time that the mestizo lay brother, Bartolomé de Jesús María (d. 1658) encountered it, sometime after 1620. Fray Bartolomé is often identified as the founder of the community of hermits at Chalma, and in all likelihood he was also the originator of the cult.[19] He began his relationship with the image as an independent lay ascetic, but eventually became an Augustinian; he made his final vows in December of 1630 in the presence of Grijalva himself.[20] Writing in the first half of the eighteenth century, Matías de Escobar argues that Bartolomé's decision to take the Augustinian habit was made under coercion: had he not joined he would have lost access to the cueva that had become his literal and spiritual home. Escobar understood that Bartolomé, like the other mestizo hermits he had gathered around him, "had found in the retreat of this sanctuary the possibility of exercising a religious authority that would otherwise have been denied to them on the basis of their race."[21]

With his "assimilation" into the Augustinians, Bartolomé became, not unlike Roa himself, a powerful force for evangelization. Though the image was venerated before Bartolomé, the numbers of visitors to the cave grew exponentially after Fray Bartolomé took up residence. Large crowds of local Indians gathered around the cave, drawn as much by the intensity of the hermit's devotion as by the image itself. In 1810 Sardo characterized Bartolomé's devotion to the crucifix: "his efforts were singularly dedicated to drawing into his heart the wounds and the pained breaths of that blessed and broken corpse, a mysterious text with meanings written within and without."[22] Pilgrims responded to the friar's relationship to the image, but also to his famed pastoral sensibilities, including most of all his generosity to the poor.[23] They came to visit Bartolomé, to seek his counsel and his healing, which was frequently of a miraculous nature. In 1729, Matías de Escobar wrote that "the mestizo Bartolomé fulfilled the function of intermediary, much needed by the friars so that they could attract indigenous communities [to the faith]. He was a 'Christian shaman' who had become a friar, and as such . . . he could also supplant the Indian witchcraft with his own form of 'magic.'"[24] Rubial García, modern historian of the religious orders of Mexico, argues that by this point hermits in the style of Fray Bartolomé had vanished entirely from New Spain.[25] Not only was Bartolomé the most famous of the Señor de Chalma's colonial devotees; he was the most famous hermit of New Spain's seventeenth century, at a time when the age of asceticism seemed to have passed.

The process of institutionalizing both the cult and the growing community of hermits at Chalma continued long after Fray Bartolomé's death. The *reducto* of hermits was transformed into a community of friars through a protracted process that began in the 1680s. In the same period, construction began of a convento and church fit to house both the esteemed image and its growing number of pilgrim devotees. In 1683, some twenty-five years after Bartolomé's death, the crucifix was ceremoniously moved from the cave where it had originally appeared to the newly constructed church shrine.[26] José Sicardo's *Interrogatorio* was published in honor of the transfer of the image, as was a sermon given by José de Olivares.[27] Not only was the image "domesticated" by moving it to the new setting, but by 1690 individual hermits living in solitude at Chalma had also all been "settled" at the convento. The language employed in these documents suggests a fascinating parallel between the domestication of the autonomous mestizo hermits, the transfer of the cave-dwelling cristo to its new (more appropriate and fitting) church structure, and the *reducción* of "uncivilized" Indians into Christian settlements: all three, once dangerously unwieldy, now tamed and safely encompassed within the ecclesial fold. Housed in a church and attended by a community of religious, much as the Cristo Aparecido de Totolapan before him, the Señor de Chalma could now take center stage as the premier image of the friars of Saint Augustine in New Spain.

The problem remained of recording the history of the image and its sacred site. Above all, its clerical devotees were at great pains to explain how such an important and esteemed image, which they attributed to the first decades of the

sixteenth century, had been ignored by the early Augustinian chroniclers of
New Spain. The friars who administered the Chalma shrine were obliged to
grapple with the prominence of the Cristo de Totolapan in the sixteenth century.
Sicardo's 1683 hagiography of Fray Bartolomé seems to have been modeled
after Grijalva's history of Roa and his miraculous crucifix. But it was Juan de
Magallanes, writing in 1721, who first explicitly compared the Chalma Cristo
with his counterpart in Totolapan.

Magallanes's supercessionist history proposed that the Chalma image was
even more worthy of veneration than the Totolapan cristo, using Grijalva's
standards for the Aparecido as a measure. Grijalva determined that the Cristo
of Totolapan was of divine provenance because it could not be proven to be of
either Spanish or native origin, given the paucity of artisans in New Spain and
the difficulty in transporting such images from Europe. For Magallanes, this
argument "has even more force for the Santo Cristo de Chalma, which
appeared at least three years prior to the Santo Cristo de Totolapan."[28] Grijalva
additionally found the Totolapan image to be miraculous because of its evocative power to elicit devotion in all who saw it. Magallanes therefore argues that
the Señor de Chalma had even more emotional impact on visitors: "If the majesty of the santo Cristo de Totolapan owing to its singular design and the devotion that it causes reveals that it is the work of angels, the same can then be said
of Chalma. And if our venerable fray Antonio deserved, owing to his virtues,
such a celestial benefit in Totolapan, were the virtues of Padre Nicolas Perea
any less?"[29]

A century later, the prior of the convento at Chalma, Joaquín Sardo, reiterated (almost verbatim) this comparison of the two images, but extended Magallanes's supercessionist claims, declaring the Chalma image superior in all ways
to the Totolapan Cristo. Sardo devotes an entire chapter to demonstrating how
God, for "inexplicable" reasons, favored the Augustinians with many porten-
tous images of Christ Crucified, but ranks the Señor de Chalma first among
these many gifts.[30] Sardo writes that the image is "so unusual, so unique, so
admirable, that I do not believe that there is another in the Catholic world that
is its equal."[31] This cannot be read except as a veiled comparison to the (here)
unnamed Cristo Aparecido, the Chalma image's most prominent rival. Sardo
feels compelled to argue for the Chalma Cristo's singularity and divine origin:
it was indubitably created by "the hands of the Omnipotent One." In Sardo's
schema of the Augustinian cristos, the Cristo de Totolapan falls in second place,
with the third place occupied by a painting of a crucifix that appeared miraculously in 1699 on the stairs of the Augustinian convento in the town of Atlixco—
though here Sardo argues that this two-dimensional image is no more than a
mediocre copy of the Chalma crucifix. The fourth place in this schema is occupied by the "Santo Cristo de Yxmiquilpam."[32] In ranking the spiritual and artistic
value of these images, Sardo posits the various cristos as each possessing a
distinct identity, history, and merit—they are rivals, competitors.

There is one other quality upon which Sardo basis his assessment of the quality and value of these images. Recall how for Roa the Cristo Aparecido represented the most pained and realistic depiction of Christ's suffering that he had beheld. For Sardo, the Chalma image surpasses Roa's crucifix and all others as a uniquely graphic and profound representation of the suffering of Christ on the cross:

> First, consider attentively the entire sacred form; note the size, the proportions, and the likenesses, which together are a perfect representation of Christ dead on the Cross. Note the posture, so naturally representing a corpse hanging from only three nails; the gesture of the head, so utterly characteristic of one deceased, totally collapsed toward the right upon the chest, at once completely mysterious and completely natural. And the movement of the arms, the left taught and strained toward the body, and the right slightly curved, indicating that the entire body has given in to the left side, as if it is suspended from the left arm. Even more persuasive is the bend at the knees that manifests precisely the position that one would expect after three hours on the cross . . . as if at any instant the entire body might tear and be freed from the nails, and the holy body collapse on the ground. Note as well the emaciated pallor of the entire body, and the cadaveric quality of his holy face; and the different shades of blood: here purple and vivid, there already denigrated and coagulated. And note the horrible damage done to his shoulders by the fierce cruelty of the whips. Observing this, one will come to see that the resulting form is so perfect, so natural, so true to life a depiction of a God-man dead and hanging from a cross, [that it is fully] understood only from the requisite reflection upon this sorrowful spectacle.[33]

In the vision of this friar, every inch of the image's body is associated with a narrative of suffering and pain. Every aspect of the Cristo is referred back to the gospel narrative of Jesus' torture. The Señor de Chalma lends himself to this kind of meditation defines, and this marks the image as miraculous.

Modern scholars have also related the Cristo of Totolapan and the Señor de Chalma. In the mid-twentieth century, Gonzalo Obregón wielded the Cristo de Totolapan to disprove the miraculous origins of the Señor de Chalma: "It is regrettable that the date [1537] is totally unacceptable. Regrettable as well is that modern researchers have proven that the Cristo de Totolapan is made of indigenous codices. This same Cristo de Totolapan offers to us another argument to deny the authenticity of the Chalma legend. . . . It is natural that a relic of such worth was preserved in the most important church that the order had in all of New Spain. Here it was kept in a special chapel and surrounded by an uninterrupted cult."[34] Obregón argues that if the Chalma image were indeed of early colonial origin, it would have been similarly preserved and cared for, given a privileged place in the order's Mexico City headquarters, as had been the Cristo de Totolapan.

Most contemporary historians tend to posit a date of origin for the Señor de Chalma somewhere in the late sixteenth or the very early seventeenth century.[35] Here, I concur that the Cristo de Totolapan was historically prior. To a large extent the Augustinians modeled devotion to the subsequent Señor Chalma on the traditions surrounding the Totolapan Cristo that had become the paradigmatic Mexican crucifix. Therefore, in keeping with the Totolapan prototype, esteemed cristos should be attributed to the period of the earliest missionaries and associated with famed friars. They should be an *imagen aparecida*, that is, of uncertain provenance, and should offer the most detailed depiction of human pain and suffering that was technically achievable.

The question remains of how the Chalma Christ came to surpass the Cristo de Totolapan. A few texts dating into the first decades of the nineteenth century note active devotion to the Cristo de Totolapan from among the surrounding barrios. These documents continue to describe him as "resplendent in miracles." Nevertheless, within Mexico City the image's meaning and significance could not finally transcend the limits of his peculiar and particular relationship to the Augustinian order. He had become to some extent more a relic of Augustinian history than he was an image with transcendent and universal appeal. In part, I argue, this weakened and diminished state resulted from the decision to remove the image from the cultural and geographical context from which it derived its original meaning—the places, buildings, and people that together associated it with a living memory of the history of its appearance. That is, the removal of the image to the Augustinian convento in Mexico City had the eventual effect of linking it too intimately, and too strictly, with the identity of the order.

In contrast, the Señor de Chalma remained at the location of his miraculous appearance while the Augustinians positioned themselves around it. In fact, as I have discussed here, the cave where the crucifix was said to have shattered and felled "pagan idols" attracted a string of hermits and ascetics long before the existence of an Augustinian convento in the vicinity. With respect to Chalma, rather than "kidnapping" the image and installing it as an adornment at the center of their power, as had been done with the Aparecido, the Augustinians established their convento and eventual shrine around the image, maintaining it in the context of its original sacred geography. Moreover, they succeeded in incorporating into their own ranks the band of hermit ascetics who had begun independently to gather around the Chalma image from its earliest days. Furthermore, that the Señor de Chalma remained in the rural areas lent the image protection against the most dramatic challenges of the Bourbon reforms that were focused on urban areas. That is, on the margins of the colony, he was less likely to feel the impact of changing attitudes toward baroque piety in the eighteenth century, buffered from the most aggressive aspects of reform. Together, these factors explain why, in contrast, none of the urban chapels housing the Totolapa crucifix ever achieved the status of *santuario*, or shrine, whether officially or unofficially. Nor have I come across any mention of "pilgrims" or *romería* (pilgrimage) in relation to the Señor de Totolapan during the years of his exile, while these words are frequently used in association with the Chalma Cristo from the first half of the seventeenth century.

The Cristo de Chalma maintains his prominence today. He is not the Cristo that Bartolomé adored; the original was all but completely destroyed in a fire at the end of the eighteenth century. The charred remains were used in fabricating the image that is venerated today. This fact seems to have had little weight or relevance for devotees in any age. Sardo's *Crónica*, including his vivid and emotive description of the Cristo, was written just decades after the fire that struck the iglesia. Yet the chronicler never mentions the fire, nor does he discuss the reconstruction of the santo itself. The symmetry, grace, and majesty that he perceived in the new Cristo are inseparable for him from those possessed by the original image.[36] Today's pilgrims, who travel to Chalma to pay homage to their Señor in greater numbers than ever, have no knowledge of the lost original; nor would such knowledge be likely to make a difference to them. Mexican anthropologists Robert and María Shadow noted this in their ethnographic study of the shrine, observing that the pilgrims were unaware of this history. When visitors learned (through the anthropologists' questions) of the destroyed original, this knowledge "did not diminish the veneration that they felt for their Lord . . . [as] popular devotion to this image is not based on familiarity with it in historic terms, but rather solely on emotional meanings."[37]

In Totolapan today, the locals struggle to make sense of the way that the Cristo de Chalma seems to them and others to have surpassed their own. They explain that in the beginning the Señor de Chalma, disguised as an ordinary man, passed through Totolapan on his way to Chalma in search of a place to rest. He considered making his home among them:

> They say that the Cristo in Chalma was the Cristo that was here.
> Some men from the pueblo had taken their flocks up into the hills.
> An old man, a stranger, approached them and said that they should
> build a temple for the Cristo up in the hills. You see he wanted to be
> in the hills. The men from the pueblo sent a messenger down to the
> Augustinians but the friars did not listen. So the Cristo, in the form
> that he had taken as an old man, walked all the way to Chalma
> looking for a home. Now, when you walk the pilgrimage to Chalma
> you can see very clearly the footprints that the Señor left behind as he
> passed through Totolapan.

Time and space collapse as the Cristo de Chalma and the Cristo de Totolapan are conflated in this vision. It is easy to imagine that, having lost their image in the sixteenth century, and possibly learning of the existence of a miraculous crucifix in Chalma by the beginning of the eighteenth century (long before their own santo was returned to them in the nineteenth), they came to think of the Chalma image as their very own Christ, who had simply found a more hospitable place for his shrine.

In the last several years, under the leadership of a powerful woman *mayordoma*, the people of Totolapan have instituted a collective pilgrimage to Chalma. Even those most active in this annual event, however, express a more intimate bond and connection to the Totolapan image. Those who frequent the pilgrimage often feel compelled to explain their dual devotion, "Well you know, *Cristo es uno*, Christ is one," they say as they shrug their shoulders, articulating their own version of Christian monotheism. "Really, there is only one Christ," Doña Bonifacia concurs. One devotee, Doña Luz, elaborates: "Ours is smaller than Chalma, but if you look closely you will perceive that they are in fact they same. The two are cousins." The Señor de Chalma and the Cristo de Totolapan are venerated today as cristos hermanos in the local cycle of fiestas.

The Icon and the Iconoclast: President Benito Juárez and the Nationalization of the San Agustín Convento

Our attention now returns to our very own Cristo who, at the middle of the nineteenth century, remained ensconced in his capilla at the Augustinian convento. All this was to change in 1861, with the chaotic and sometimes violent process of nationalization of Church property, in which the Augustinian convento and all of its contents were confiscated from the Church and appropriated by the secular nationalist government. Surprisingly, the very reforms that targeted the power of the religious orders and the Church itself in Mexico actually freed the image to return to its original religious and geographical context, thus breathing new life into the local expression of Catholic folk religion and lending the image new power and prominence. Thus, 1861 was a pivotal year in the life of the Cristo Aparecido: the occasion for his repatriation, to borrow current-day language, to the people of Totolapan.

The nineteenth century saw the mounting friction between the Church and an increasingly secular state. Having achieved independence in 1821, the new national government continued its process of decolonization. The destruction of the conventos and appropriation of Church property can also be understood as a continuation of the work of the Bourbon secularizers. Within an increasingly nationalist framework, the Church was comprehended as the quintessential colonialist institution, deeply entrenched in the very systems of power that had led to the impoverishment of the Latin American people. While the exploited indigenous and mestizo peoples of Mexico grew poorer and more broken, the Church had grown wealthier, as was most conspicuously evident in their ostentatious and ornate, silver- and gold-leaf baroque churches and cathedrals. The new nation thus sought to curtail the authority and influence of the Roman Catholic Church as an institution: a laborious, erratic, and painful process that especially targeted the religious orders as iconic ambassadors of the colonial church. This process, culminated in (but was not concluded with) the effective dismantling of the religious orders and the seizure of ecclesial property under president Benito Juárez's Laws of Reform at the middle of the nineteenth century. As one modern scholar has observed, "the partial transfer of sacrality from systems of religious ideas and forms of worship to the cult of the nation-state marks the passage of Mexico from colony to nation."[38]

The Constitution of 1857 was the product of bitter and armed conflict between defenders of the old regime, in which the Church was an integral part of the state bureaucracy, and defenders of the new liberal order. When the constitution's anti-ecclesial provisions became evident, a conservative coalition of clergy and military joined in open revolt against the constitutional government. The War of Reform, between liberals and conservatives, raged from December 1857 to January 1861. Benito Juárez had been made provisional president; but in short order he was forced to flee Mexico to Vera Cruz, where he established a temporary governmental seat. From this precarious position, Juárez did not shy away from his project of reform. In July 12, 1859, he propagated the liberal reforms that would nationalize church property. These initial laws targeted the religious orders in particular, largely sparing the secular church and exempting diocesan buildings suitable for public worship. The following day the "Reglamento para el Cumplimiento de la Ley de Nacionalización" was passed, intended to guide the expropriation, inventory taking, and sale at public auction of the property of the religious orders—much as had been done following the expulsion of Jesuits from the colonies under the Bourbon regime in the 1760s.[39]

Juárez's exile from the capital caused a delay in the implementation of nationalization of church property. It was only after the Liberal army reentered Mexico City on December 27, 1860, that the full weight of these laws could be brought to bear on the orders. These laws suppressed both the cofradías (mayordomías) and the conventos that had preserved and maintained the rich traditions of the cults of saints for centuries. Other laws passed in 1860 prohibited religious ceremonies outside of churches, and subjected even the ringing of church bells to police regulation. Most relevant to the fate of the Cristo de Totolapan, the laws mandated the transfer of antiques, works of art, and books from the suppressed conventos to the national museums and libraries.[40]

Absent the once-dominant Jesuits, the Augustinians, for all their diminished status in the new republic, were the wealthiest of all the religious orders facing dissolution.[41] They were therefore subjected to the most rigorous and extensive process of amortization. Through the process of the appropriation of ecclesial properties, all of the orders lost their wealth, though it seems that the Franciscans may have been slightly buffered because of the sentimental place that they held in the collective memory of the Mexican people.[42] Nevertheless, the convento of San Francisco in downtown Mexico City was demolished to make way for Gante and Sixteenth of September streets; and the convento de Santo Domingo made way for Leandro Valle Street. Perhaps owing to its imposing size, the convento de San Agustín was spared complete demolition, though nevertheless subjected to the process of nationalization.[43]

The Augustinian convento and its contents were confiscated in May of 1861. Some of the buildings were immediately destroyed, while part of the property was divided into parcels for resale to private buyers at auction.[44] The buildings were defaced and their contents dismantled. Soldiers entered the church and used ropes to topple the saints' images that occupied the main altarpiece. Art historian Romero de Terreros records how the statues smashed as they hit the ground: "They destroyed the altarpieces with axes, and at times used horses to ply them from the walls."[45] Almost twenty altarpieces were destroyed in the Augustinian convento alone, and in all about 350 gilded altarpieces were lost throughout the city.[46]

Observers mournfully recorded the looting of the fine library of the Augustinian convento; the doors were flung open and books and manuscripts left to the mercy of soldiers and thieves. Rivera Cambas, writing less than two decades after these events, recalls how: "The library was entirely abandoned, the doors wide open and the books and manuscripts at the mercy of whoever wanted to take them, a multitude of books destroyed and strewn in the cloister and the monastic cells, and others littering the floor of the library in the most complete disorder . . . it was as if in the time of the barbarians"[47] Other libraries were similarly pillaged, including the exceptionally fine library of the Franciscan convento, which may have had in its possession as many as 16,000 volumes dating from the sixteenth century. These tomes were driven away in carts, and countless volumes "fell onto the road at the mercy of whoever would take them."[48]

Mexico City periodicals from the month of May, when the destruction was at its most fevered pitch, describe the impact of the physical dismantling of the many conventos on the city at large. An editorial begged the government to desist from the process of demolition:

> The destruction of the beautiful seminary building continues. We think that this is an act of barbarity that has no possible explanation. Could it possibly serve to make the plaza more beautiful? No. . . .
> What could the destroyers of a building that cost hundreds of thousands of pesos possibly hope to achieve? [Rather] it would have been more useful to convert it into a hall of justice or into the government seat of the capital?
> The destruction of the beautiful temples of the Franciscans and of Santa Isabel continues as well. Why this labor of annihilation that fills the city with repugnant ruins when some of these temples

should be preserved as monuments of art, and some are necessary for Catholic worship? We invite congress to demand the suspension of this destruction that has no object other than enriching a very few ... [at least] they should determine which of the buildings should be destroyed and which of them preserved."[49]

Another editorial expressed little regret or sentimentality but rather complained that the stones and rocks from the demolished conventos littered the streets of the city, causing a public nuisance: "The stones and rubbish from the conventos continue to litter [the city]. Wouldn't it be more useful, for example, if the stone tiles were used to shore up the curbs and sidewalks of the city, which are in constant need of repair. This would also prevent the later necessity of cleaning up the streets."[50] Criticism came not only from the public but from within the Church as it tried to defend its property; in particular, the prolific bishop Garza y Ballesteros of Puebla, was a vocal critic of the Laws of Reform.

The demolition of these buildings and the haphazard looting of their contents became for some an issue of national identity. Art historians have come to criticize the destructive aspect of nationalization as paradigmatic of the relationship of Mexicans to their past:

> Since the Conquest, we Mexicans have nurtured the bad habit of devoting ourselves to iconoclasms of various kinds, and we have forgotten how to build without first destroying, as the case of the High Temple of Tenochtitlán clearly demonstrates. We Mexicans still believe that it is necessary to destroy the past to make way for the present. More than just a bad habit, this is a serious problem of national identity. However, let us return to the destruction of the art of Mexico City and jump ahead to 1861. In the preceding decades, little was destroyed. . . . But in 1861, a true "feat" was performed: dozens of buildings were demolished in just a few months. The inhabitants of the city grew accustomed to the sound of pickaxes and crowbars, the crash of collapsing buildings, and other typical sounds of demolition. Soldiers entered San Agustín with ropes and pulled down the burnished gold and polychromed figures of the main altarpiece, which smashed as they hit the ground. They destroyed the altarpieces with axes, and at times used horses to ply them from the walls. . . . The sale of Church property was a comedy of cunning buyers and name-lenders; a truly dramatic case of defrauding the state.[51]

Art historians thus accused the nineteenth-century bastions of liberalism of a modern iconoclasm of the sort epitomized by Fray Diego de Landa in the Yucatán, in which colonial friars engaged in the wanton destruction of indigenous icons and religious art.

How was it possible that the Cristo Aparecido survived this iconoclastic revolution? Where was the image when the soldiers entered the Augustinian convento and toppled the saint, or when those images that remained were auctioned to the highest bidder? Early in 1681, at least two months before the soldiers arrived, an anonymous rescuer, perhaps a prescient priest or devotee, acted in flagrant disregard of the law and smuggled the Cristo Aparecido out of his chapel before the destruction began. Perhaps it was the order itself that targeted the image for rescue and removed it to safety, while other images, other treasures, were abandoned to the soldiers. According to oral tradition, the Cristo was moved from the Augustinian convento soon after Juárez's original reforms in 1859, transported first to Iztapalapa, south of the city, where it remained for two years until the people of Totolapan petitioned successfully for its return. This story, for which no corroborating documentary evidence has come to light, would explain the participation of Iztapalapans in the annual celebration of the image today, as I discuss in chapter 8. Whether in 1861 or earlier, the Augustinian friars probably orchestrated the covert removal of the image from the convento, perhaps in collaboration with the local parish priests of Totolapan or with the community of Iztapalapa.

By these means, the Cristo returned to Totolapan much the way that he first departed the pueblo, through an act of furta sacra, though in this case the Augustinians stole the image from the state and returned him to the safety of Totolapan.

Art historians reflecting on the fate of the Augustinian convento rarely list the Cristo Aparecido among its great treasures. Manuel Romero de Terreros's study of the history of the convento does not mention the Cristo at all.[52] Of his generation of Mexican scholars, only Manuel Rivera Cambas, in his *México Pintoresco* (1880), mentions the Cristo in the context of the Augustinian convento, recording that he was celebrated there with fiestas and solemn processions, and that he had a special chapel devoted to him.[53] Of all of the lost contents of the convento, the most lamented by art historians is the finely sculpted *sillería del coro* (choir seats). Romero de Terreros declares the sillería "undoubtedly the most important work of art that the convento possessed" and records how the soldiers "began to destroy the magnificent church in May of 1861: they destroyed the altars, and the choir seat was roughly dismantled and haphazardly cast aside in a basement. The temple was left abandoned and even flooded."[54] Nonetheless, the Cristo survived, while the order's library, archives, and its silleria de coro were neglected and destroyed. In the very fact of his rescue we seem to find evidence for the Cristo's privileged status.

The rescue is also suggestive of the modes of resistance employed by conservative Catholics during the nationalization process. The friars were not, in principle, allowed to remove objects of value from their conventos. Those who did were sometimes denounced by entrepreneurial laypeople seeking to claim the rewards offered to informers (amounting to a certain percentage of the value of the "recovered" objects). In fact, Augustinian friars were involved in many subversive acts during this period. A police report from May charges several friars who, disguised as soldiers, attempted to recruit a municipal squadron for service in the conservative armed forces.[55] By whatever means, the Cristo was removed before the ransacking and subsequent government auction that would surely have led him to another, less agreeable, fate.

The convento of San Agustín itself, home to the Cristo for almost three centuries, was sold at auction, purchased by a man named Pedro Labat. He was obliged to resell the building several months later, when he was unable to meet the negotiated "bargain basement" price. The new bidder, Vicente Escandón, was a conservative entrepreneur who intended to redeem the convento, to return it to its religious purpose.[56] Escandón's plan never came to fruition: the Juárez government determined that he had purchased the property at below-market rate, accused him of speculation, and imposed a substantial fine on the property. Escandón was unable to pay and, having briefly passed through private hands, the convento was eventually returned to the state.[57]

An initial plan designated the convento for government offices, but ultimately the building was put to a more auspicious use. On November 30, 1867, the restored president, Benito Juárez, decreed that the iglesia de San Agustín was to serve as the new national library.[58] Architects and builders were then assigned the difficult work of refitting the heavy, old ecclesial structure into an edifice befitting the newly constituted secular state. García Icazbalceta complained in 1875 of "the vast sum spent in converting it into the Biblioteca Nacional, a destiny for which it would always be inadequate."[59] Manuel Romero de Terreros described the alterations in detail: "The architects sought to hide, to whatever degree possible, the religious character of the building. For example, they worked to eliminate as much as possible the "church" aspect of the interior. They closed off the arms of the cross, building in each one a wall as a continuation of the nave. . . . Through the windows little light now entered because above each chapel had been built another floor to serve as a book depository."[60] In addition to these structural alterations, seventeen heroes of classical history were erected where Christian saints once adorned the nave. Confucius, Homer, Plato, Aristotle, Cicero, Virgil, Dante, Copernicus, and Descartes now loomed imposingly where diminutive virgins once consoled sinners. So it came to be that for many decades the national library of a secular state occupied the chapel once erected to house the Cristo Aparecido de Totolapan. At length a more fitting location for the library was found: since 1979 the bulk of the library's collection (including many volumes reclaimed from the great dispersal of 1861) has been housed in impressive new quarters on the campus of the Universidad Autónoma de México.[61]

Repatriation and Cultural Heritage

The following poem appeared in a pamphlet in 1861:

> The image of Jesus Christ appeared
> To his beloved servant, the venerable Antonio Roa,
> Was lost in the opulent capital
> For more than two hundred years.
> A thousand pious attempts and
> Every human diligence were made
> Because to his original pueblo he would return,
> For his return they groaned and sighed.
> In the midst of violent tempest and turmoil,
> Your tender and loving Father returns to you.
> Oh happy people of Totolapan!
> To preach to you his protection and his piety
> To banish horrors and calamities!
> Surrender to him your heart, in simplicity and innocence.[62]

The theme of contested ownership is a dominant current in the biography of the Cristo. Claims to ownership, explicit or implied, were made from many quarters: the community of Totolapans who first received him, the friar Roa who was his first devotee, the Augustinian order, the secular, nationalist state—all vied for possession. In spite of these competing claims, the image eventually expressed his own will in the matter. For local devotees of Totolapan, it was inevitable that the Cristo would return home and resume his proper and rightful place among them. Here I have dubbed this process "repatriation." Though this political terminology usually describes the return of refugees or human remains to their community of origin, there are instances in which it has been applied to the restoration of sacred objects to native communities.[63] As such, it is apt language for expressing the significance to the pueblo of the return of their imagen: they received it as one long lost, finally returned home.

After the loss of their Cristo to the friars of Mexico City, the people of Totolapan had once again remade their faith, creating a devotion around the Cristo's empty cross which the Augustinians left for them as "consolation."[64] In truth, the sources for reconstructing the course of local faith during the Cristo's long absence are few and far between. Under ideal circumstances, namely, a more complete historical record, one could retrace the entire lineage of cofradías and mayordomías, the religious brotherhoods around which they organized and anchored their collective faith, following the Totolapan's devotion to the Santa Cruz Aparecida and to the many other saints' images that came to repopulate the iglesia in Totolapan.

The locals of Totolapan certainly grieved the loss of their image. More important, they preserved a memory of their absent Cristo over centuries; the ongoing relationship between the "satellite" convento in Totolapan and the Augustinian community in Mexico City insured this. In 1655, the bell from the iglesia in Totolapan was brought to Mexico City and, in spite of Franciscan protests, installed at the cathedral. When the bell was declared by the archbishop to be of inferior quality, the Augustinians reclaimed it and installed it at their urban convento.[65] The circulation of friars from the colonial center to the convento on the periphery and back to the center again also certainly helped to keep the memory of the Cristo alive. Each successive generation of priors in Totolapan would have been familiar with the famous Cristo of Totolapan that occupied a privileged place in their Mexico City convento. That is to say, over the course of centuries friars played a significant role in preserving the memory of the Cristo for the people of Totolapan.

The Augustinians, as we have seen, never doubted that the crucifix was theirs, or that they had the authority to transplant it. But according to tradition, the people of Totolapan were convinced that the image belonged to them, the image was theirs, and had been removed without their consent. The collective memory of the event as theft was very much in evidence during Lauro López Beltrán's tenure as priest in the pueblo of Totolapan during the 1930s. A community elder, who had been present as a child for the return of the Cristo in 1861, recalled to López Beltrán her understanding of the tradition that the Augustinians "secreted away the Santo Cristo." He writes, "The uninterrupted tradition of the sons of Totolapan is that they took him without their consent . . . that they removed him at night and furtively so no one would know."[66] But this memory has even deeper historical roots. López Beltrán cites an *Itinerario parroquial* from the first bishop of Cuernavaca, Fortino Hipólito Vera y Talona (appointed 1894), that records that the people of Totolapan, affirming the tradition of their parents and grandparents, unanimously agreed that the friars had removed the image in secret, and they even indicate the precise window through which he was removed.[67] Tracing this sentiment even further back, into the sixteenth century, brings a new lens through which to read the testimony of the Indian witnesses in the inquisition hearing in 1583. On the surface, these witnesses seem to make no explicit claim to ownership of the Cristo. However, it is possible that their emphasis on their participation in Roa's penitences is meant to assert the primacy of their relationship with the Augustinian saint, and therefore their entitlement to his image.

Totolapans today assert local ownership of the image by emphasizing indigenous protagonists in recounting the appearance. Not only do contemporary devotees describe the beauty and strangeness of the Indian angel who brought the Cristo, but they emphasize that it was one of their very own, an Indian portero, and not a friar, who first received both the stranger and the santo. Locals today also certainly hold to the idea that the Augustinians removed the Cristo in secret. They themselves would never willingly allow the image to leave the pueblo; even restorations must be performed on site. They cannot imagine their ancestors feeling otherwise.[68]

A recent local history of Totolapan, published in collaboration with the mayordomía, imagines Antonio de Roa as the founder of a cofradía in honor of the Cristo Aparecido—a sodality that continued to function even after the removal of the image itself. There is little documentary evidence that founding a religious brotherhood was the friar's intention, or that one existed continuously in the seventeenth and eighteenth centuries. Clearly Roa desired to communicate his own respect, devotion, and awe to the local community: a devotion that could reasonably have been formalized by the creation of a mayordomía in the Cristo's honor. It is possible that the distinction between culto and cofradía, between devotion and the institutional apparatus developed to support ritual observance of devotion, was, at that point, a mere technicality for the people of Totolapan, as it surely is to some extent for them today.

Evidence suggests that a cofradía in honor of the abandoned cross was founded shortly after the removal of the image. The late nineteenth-century Itinerario parroquial mentions the founding of a cofradía de la Santa Cruz in 1583, but it cites no original source. A pastoral visitación by Bishop Lanciego to the pueblo in January of 1716 notes the existence of six different cofradías in the parish, including one founded in the iglesia parroquial and dedicated to the Santísima Cruz (Holy Cross). The same report records two others, also founded locally, devoted specifically to images of Christ's Passion: the Christ Entombed (Santo Entierro de Cristo Nuestro Señor) and Jesus the Nazarene (Jesús Nazareno).[69] Most suggestive are the Relaciones Geográficas of 1743, which recount that the people of Totolapan, having remained with the cruz aparecida as memoria y consuelo, guard it on their altar for the remedy of their infirmities and defense against calamities.[70] This seems conclusive evidence that the people of Totolapan were caring for the empty cross at least 150 years after the Cristo had been taken from them. Finally, a pastoral visit from the archbishop's office in 1779-1780 records that, at the time, there were three cofradías in Totolapan and that the "faithful there give considerable financial offerings for the veneration of the Santo Cristo Crucificado."[71] As I discussed in chapter 3, there is no evidence that Roa himself was ever an object of local devotion, as was true in Molango, where people venerated pieces of charcoal as his relics.[72]

Today the believers of Totolapan speak of the period that the Cristo spent in Mexico City as a time when he was lost to them, and utterly inaccessible. One mayordomo explained to me: "While it was in Mexico City the Cristo was in a private chapel. The public could not go there and visit it. You could say that it was being stored, or protected. Those were difficult times and there was persecution in the Church. But also, we couldn't and we didn't go visit it then." Another elaborated that the celebration of the Cristo continued even after he departed for Mexico: "after he left we continued to celebrate his annual fiesta, on the fifth Friday of Lent." Yet still another resident imagines a return to pre-Christian roots after the loss of the image: "How did we survived all those years without the crucifix? We did what we had always done: we worshiped the sun, and the moon!"

It is stunning to contemplate the possibility of a community whose religious life for almost three centuries was organized, at least in part, around worship of an object in absentia. The sequence of cofradías and mayordomías attests to this extraordinary tradition in Totolapan. Frequently in Christian iconography the empty cross signifies the resurrected Christ, the Christ who conquered death. Rather, for the Totolapans, the empty cross (the one left behind for them by the Augustinians) guarded the memory of the missing Cristo, signifying not Jesus' Resurrection, but the Cristo's absence and the theft itself. It is no wonder then that they welcomed back the Cristo as their long-lost santo, finally come home.

Conclusions

Mexican cristos derive their deepest significance from their local context, in relation to local actors and sacred geography. This is true even when, like the Señor de Chalma, they achieve regional devotion or even national significance. Perhaps their profound local identification explains how it is possible that two images could be "rival christs" as the Aparecido and the Señor de Chalma have been at times, vying with each other for prestige and influence. Nonetheless, Mexican images of Christ gain power both from their singularity and their multiplicity. Each image has its own history, its own identity; each is *único*, or unique. But sometimes individual images like the Cristo Aparecido are enfolded within a network of "cristos hermanos," linked in a regional web of devotion in which identities of various images are muddled or even collapsed. This, in part, explains how an image can be replaceable, again as was the Chalma cristo after the fire.

The extraordinary material survival of the Cristo Aparecido in these treacherous centuries marks his biography. The image was even impervious to movements of religious reform. In the final analysis, the liberal reforms of the nineteenth century may, in some cases, have had an outcome opposite to what they intended. These reforms, which were intended to secularize and nationalize the colonial churches and religious art of Mexico, unintentionally facilitated the return of the Cristo to his pueblo of origin by emancipating him from the Augustinian order and thereby lending renewed vigor to local, religious identity. The Aparecido survived fires, natural disasters, and nationalization, where other cristos fell in these centuries. The government confiscated hundreds of cristos; and today these colonial images are displayed in government-run museums throughout Mexico. Some house dozens upon dozens of images, becoming veritable mausoleums for "dead" christs, which, removed from their cultic function, have been divested of their religious significance. Once at the center of local devotions, these hermanos now languish in museums and private collections. The Cristo Aparecido only narrowly escaped this fate.

The iconoclast impulse has been present in Mexico for centuries, brought by the first missionaries to the New World as they sought to erase the visual-religious universe of the indigenous people by mass destruction of their "idols." In this chapter I have described how iconoclasm surfaced in a new form in the nineteenth century as Mexico sought to define its identity as a nation by destroying and secularizing Catholic saints. The impulse persists in the present: in April of 2009, the government of Mexico with the support of the Catholic archbishop attempted to strike a blow to narcotics traffickers by bulldozing some thirty shrines to Santa Muerte.[73] The popular "Saint Death" appears as a female skeleton and is said to be the patron saint of drug traffickers. The following chapter discovers a twentieth-century version of iconoclasm in the tendencies of Vatican II and the theology of liberation.

6

The Red Bishop, the Cristo, and the Aesthetics of Liberation

The dolorous Christs of Latin America, whose central image is ever the cross, are Christs of impotence, an impotence interiorized by the oppressed. Defeat, sacrifice, pain, crucifixion. . . . Defeat is not perceived as a temporary reversal to be overcome in struggle, it appears as an inevitable necessity, a precondition for the privilege of living.

—Hugo Assman

"Jesus Christ, Liberator!"
    —Leonardo Boff

Scene 5. Main Road, Totolapan, 1954

On an ordinary Friday in April of 1954, the zealous new bishop of Cuernavaca set out from his cathedral in a chauffeured car to tend to the flock of a humble and unassuming corner of his diocese. It had been barely two years since don Sergio Méndez Arceo's consecration as bishop, and yet he had already distinguished himself for the serious, devout, and hands-on style of his ministry. That is why it is only mildly surprising that the good bishop took it upon himself personally to bring the Cristo Aparecido back to Totolapan. The imagen had recently undergone a major restoration in Cuernavaca, a process that took nearly a year, and was ready at last to be returned to his people. Whether he knew it or not, on that auspicious day the seventh bishop of Cuernavaca became for the people of Totolapan the theotokos, the god-bearer, bringing the divine into their pueblo.

Appropriately enough, it was the week of the fiesta patronal of the Cristo. His annual celebration falls on the Quinto Viernes, or fifth Friday of Lent, marking the day of his original appearance in Totolapan just over four centuries before.

"Look," the crowds murmured, "here he comes!" Don Sergio carefully, protectively, cradled this Christ in his arms as his car made its way up winding roads, over potholes, higher and higher to Totolapan. The santo was too large to be fully accommodated by the car; part of the cross projected precariously through the window. But the bishop cushioned his precious cargo from the inevitable jolts, bumps and quick stops of the rural mountain road. The car made its gradual approach to the entrance of the town where a crowd gathered in anticipation, anxiously awaiting the Cristo's arrival. It had been nearly a year since he left; the people of Totolapan missed him sorely.

"Don Sergio had much faith in our Christ. He had *mucha ley* and *mucha fe*," recollects don Tolentino, mayordomo and community elder. At the entrance to the town the bishop stopped, stepped gracefully out of his car, paused briefly to remove his shoes, and came barefoot, carrying Christ into the town. Like Fray Antonio de Roa four centuries before, this prince among men humbled himself before the Cristo. The people bowed their heads and smiled at the respect and love he showed for their santo, and, through him, for them all. It is a beautiful moment, and they will love and remember the bishop forever for this gesture of love. Don Tolentino explains, "This is why I say he is a man of much faith. There were stones in the road, and he came without socks even. I saw this, I was there in the church waiting for him and saw him arrive." Don Tomás, long-time member of the mayordomía and don Tolentino's colleague, also remembers that day with fondness and longing: "He walked almost a kilometer to the center of town carrying the Christ. He sang the songs of the Via Crucis, and the Oración de la Pasión. I was there. I took pictures of this and saved them; but that was long ago, and now they are buried away somewhere."

His purpose in Mexico City accomplished, and his tenure there brought to a dramatic end by Bourbon-era religious reforms, the Cristo Aparecido was smuggled out of the city and returned ceremoniously to his pueblo of origin in 1861. The people of Totolapan successfully protected their image from the turmoil of the revolution of 1910–1920, during which, for a time, the Cristo abandoned his altar in the local iglesia. Morelos was the epicenter of the revolution and it was a native son, Emiliano Zapata, whose army was largely responsible for bringing an end to Porfirio Díaz's thirty-five-year regime; through manipulation and outright violence he claimed the presidency of Mexico almost without interruption from 1876 to 1911. Revolutionary soldiers occupied the Cristo's sanctuary, using it as a temporary garrison. The image found refuge from the sometimes unpredictable soldiers in the homes of local devotees, under the protection of one young woman in particular who bartered and bargained for the image's continued safety.[1] The Cristo also survived the postrevolutionary period in which antireligious campaigns sometimes took a violent turn and images of saints were burned publicly in the process of creating a "revolutionary civil religion."[2]

At the middle of the twentieth century, Mexico, and Latin America generally, was on the brink of another revolution that potentially threatened the welfare of the Cristo Aparecido, this one fomented from within the Church. The Second Vatican Council, which met in Rome in 1962–1965, defined the meaning of modernity for the Roman Catholic Church, charting a new course for radical change within the Church liturgically, theologically, and socially. Three years later, in 1968, at a gathering in Medellín, Colombia, Latin American bishops sought to concretize the advances of Vatican II in the sociopolitical realities of their respective countries. In particular, they felt an urgent need to respond to the crushing poverty suffered by the vast majority of Latin Americans and to the increasing political instability of their governments, many of which were succumbing to military dictatorships.[3] Medellín marked the beginning of a new era for the Church. From its colonial origins, the hierarchy of the Latin American Church was more often than not identified with the interests of the economic and political elite. The Medellín documents represent a radical rupture with this history: they contain sharp criticisms of Latin America's ruling and middle classes, of foreign capitalism, endemic poverty, and social injustice.[4] Above all, the concluding statements articulate the Church's primary commitment to the material and social liberation of the impoverished masses of Latin America. With these declarations, Medellín became the location of the first official, systematized articulation of the theology of liberation.[5]

On the eve of this ecclesial and theological revolution, the Cristo was returned to Totolapan from a major restoration in the state capital, in the embrace of the man who one day would come to be both revered and excoriated as the famous "red bishop" of Cuernavaca. In this moment the biographies of two figures, a four-hundred-year-old icon and a visionary bishop, intersected and came to overlap for three decades. As don Sergio lovingly bore the Christ into Totolapan, he also carried the faithful of Morelos and the Cristo Aparecido himself into the life of the Vatican II church, and subsequently into the church of the utopian vision of liberation theology. Today don Sergio Méndez Arceo (1902–1992) occupies a crucial place in the pantheon of Latin American liberation-minded bishops, alongside Hélder Câmara of Brazil, Samuel Ruiz of Chiapas, and Oscar Romero of El Salvador.

Liberation theology, in theory and practice, was not only a prophetic and revolutionary project but also a distinctly modern one that posed dangers to the Cristo not dissimilar to those he faced by the secular modernizing project of the bourbon reformers a century earlier.[6] For some priests and theologians, liberation theology was a means to modernize the faith of the poor, to guide and coax it away from the pitfalls of "superstition" and "idolatry," and to transform Latin American Christianity from a "folk religion" which, according to them, mired believers in resignation and passivity, into an instrument for personal and social transformation. In many instances, local interpretations of liberation theology were pitted against traditional practices that were inherited from the colonial Church: religious fiestas, devotion to saints, mayordomías, and the cargo system, in which adult males assumed financial responsibility for sponsoring elaborate and expensive community religious fiestas. Today, where the Church has continued to persue a progressive vision, its liberating project rarely finds fertile ground when clerics and bishops tether their liberationist agenda to a parallel project of purifying the Catholicism of the poor classes from the taint of "folk religion." This dynamic is precisely what anthropologist Kristin Norget discovered in her research of the Nueva Evangelización movement in Oaxaca in the 1990s, where the priests' insistence on identifying popular religion as the "corruption of faith" hindered the "transformative promise" of their sociopolitical agenda.[7]

On some level, the concerns of progressive and leftist priests were justified. Historically, local religious practices were perhaps just as frequently vehicles for colonial rule as they were instruments for the assertion of local autonomy against colonial domination. Sometimes modern communities and images have succumbed to this ambiguous legacy. In the late twentieth century, specific local saints were often said to prefer reactionary political parties or even military regimes. For example, one conservative Nicaraguan priest persuaded his flock that a miraculous sweating Cristo was expressing anger at the revolutionary Sandinistas.[8] Owing to this checkered history, traditional popular religious practices were frequently challenged within the liberationist framework, and devotion to saints in particular was perceived as the primary cause of spiritual resignation, resulting in political passivity. In this modernist, liberationist vision, images of the Christ's suffering, especially crucifixes like our very own Cristo Aparecido, were particularly suspect, as indicated in the epigraph that opens this chapter, in which Brazilian theologian Hugo Assman decries the political impotence resulting from popular devotion to the crucifix.[9]

Liberation-minded priests and theologians challenged what they perceived as traditional and oppressive conceptions of Christ's affliction on the cross, reframing the theological interpretation of crucifixes primarily in relation to social suffering. This liberationist Christology pointed to the sociopolitical causes, rather than the redemptive value, of the suffering of a very earthly, very human, Jesus. The image of Christ raised up by liberation theology is of a Jesus who was on the side of the poor, the disenfranchised. Jesus himself made a "preferential option for the poor." He desired not only their spiritual salvation but, more urgently, also their earthly liberation from systems of injustice and inequality. As he continues to bear witness to the suffering of the oppressed masses, so too Christ condemns their tormentors: the wealthy, the politicians, the military dictators, the agents and beneficiaries of global capitalism, and the governments of the first world. After all, the liberation theologians reason, the historical Jesus himself was born of a persecuted, enslaved people living under colonial rule. The Kingdom of God message that Jesus preached was not the promise of a life hereafter, but rather a vision of right relationship and social justice on the earth here and now. The Jesus of liberation theology was a preacher, a laborer, a fellow traveler, and sometimes a guerrilla revolutionary struggling on behalf of his people.[10] This was the vision of Jesus that liberation theologians sought to bring to poor communities across Latin America in the 1970s, 1980s, and 1990s, and don Sergio came to be among his most passionate and effective prophets.

Totolapan was among the most receptive communities in the state to don Sergio's liberationist message. The pueblo welcomed three successive diocesan priests trained in Medellín-inspired philosophies and methods. These ministered effectively in Totolapan over the greater part of the 1980s and into the early 1990s. As a result of their labors, the Totolapans raised and contributed more money to the fledgling democratic socialist Sandinista government in Nicaragua than any other parish in the diocese. All the while that they labored on behalf of the radical vision of Jesus as Liberator, the people of Totolapan continued to worship and care for their anguished and suffering Cristo. Under their attention and protection, the Cristo weathered, survived, and sometimes thrived under the great upheavals in the Mexican Catholic Church in the twentieth century: the ongoing process of the separation of church and state, official anticlericalism, atheistic public education, liturgical renewal, the Second Vatican Council, a new emphasis on ecumenism coming from within the Church, and even the politically radical message of the theology of liberation.

This chapter explores how these historic movements, and liberation theology most of all, play out in and play upon the particularity of a local context. Liberation theology was and continues to be not just a global movement and an institutional transformation within the Church but also a local and lived religion. That is, it is a personal and collective practice of faith that is lived out in the diversity and particularity of local cultural contexts, all the while in dynamic engagement with both the rich religious traditions and the ambiguous history of Christianity in Latin America. The specific example of Sergio Méndez Arceo's episcopacy in Morelos, and the impact of his ministry on Totolapan and on devotion to the Cristo Aparecido, is also lens through which to examine the encounter of liberation theology with popular piety, sacred art, and traditional religious institutions.

This local encounter provides a helpful context within which to test and challenge accepted interpretations of liberation theology and its legacy. In their critical evaluation of the movement, subsequent theologians and social scientists have argued that one of its great failures was its antagonism toward popular piety and inherited cultural forms like the mayordomía, the lay organizational structure around which local religious life was organized for centuries. These local organizations were colonial in origin, and thus in some cases wedded to structures of inequity inherited from the colonial church and society—the very structures that liberation theology challenged. In some contemporary contexts, mayordomías have been linked to a conservative, even right-wing political agenda, further exacerbating tensions with the liberationist political project. While attentive to the consequences of the friction between liberation theology and popular religion for the people of Latin America, here I will argue for a more nuanced understanding of the complex historical relationship between these two powerful religious forces and traditions. In particular, in the second half of this chapter, I will demonstrate how in the case of Totolapan the traditional mayordomal structure dedicated to the care and maintenance of the Cristo actually facilitated the development of the *comunidades eclesiales de base*, the basic organizational unit for the practice of liberation theology.

Though my focus is on the local working out of these historic movements, I do not mean to underestimate the global significance of local events. As I describe below, don Sergio's innovative and modernizing experiment with the Cuernavaca cathedral, and his subsequent interventions at the Second Vatican Council, ultimately helped shape the council's vision for architectural and liturgical renewal within the Church, a vision that was then disseminated and implemented worldwide, including parishes throughout the United States.[11]

Don Sergio and the Cristo

Don Sergio's loving embrace of the Cristo at the entrance of the pueblo of Totolapan in 1954 is now inextricably a part of the biography of the imagen itself, just as are Fray Roa's abundant tears. But what meaning did don Sergio intend to assign to the Cristo, and of what consequence is that intention for devotees themselves? The questions posed by don Sergio's affection for the Cristo Aparecido lead us to probe his early orthodoxy and the slow maturation of his own faith from traditionalism to liberation; to observe his much-criticized and oft-regretted renovation of the Cuernavaca cathedral; to eavesdrop on the familiar meals and gentle humor he shared in the humble homes of the *campesinos* of Totolapan; and with them to celebrate the rise and mourn the decline of liberation theology and the base community movement.

By all conventional wisdom, the moment in 1954 that opens this chapter should not have occurred. The first decade of Sergio Méndez Arceo's episcopacy was marked by friction with the popular piety of his flock, and in particular with their devotion to images of saints. His ambitious renovation of the sixteenth-century Franciscan convento that since 1891 has served as the cathedral of Cuernavaca began in 1957, and was intended to curb what he perceived to be the excesses and "exaggerations" of the cult of the saints. Toward this end, the bishop had almost a dozen side altars stripped from the nave, and removed the baroque images that had occupied them. The cathedral basement became a mausoleum for these saints *retirados del culto*, that is, removed from their cultic function and retained merely as artifacts of an earlier devotional practice.[12] This renovation anticipated and, as we shall discover, even influenced the liturgical reforms brought about by the Second Vatican Council. In the following decade, the bishop encouraged his parish priests to do likewise, to purify the faith of the people by "sweeping clean" the churches of Morelos of their many images. In this way, in keeping with Vatican II, he hoped to make way for a new, twentieth-century "modern" piety which, paradoxically in its Mexican expression, was to be based in part on the resurrection of a reimagined sixteenth-century, pre-baroque, monastic austerity.

With this dramatic entry into Totolapan in 1954, however, don Sergio participated whole-heartedly for a moment in the religious life of the people, offering deeply evocative and heavily weighted symbolic acts. The removal of his shoes, in particular, resonated with the people of Totolapan. This gesture begs a more complex understanding of the "people's bishop's" pastoral project for the people of Morelos, and the trajectory of his own faith and piety. Given his ongoing support of the people of Totolapan in their veneration of their Cristo—he returned frequently to celebrate the Quinto Viernes fiesta with them—one cannot speak merely of his "antipathy" toward popular devotion.

Just as as Don Sergio's pious and penitential entry into Totolapan was an expression of personal faith and devotion, it also was a calculated and dramatic act of religious street theater. The people of Totolapan could not fail to see the resonances between don Sergio's arrival in their pueblo and the familiar oil painting of Roa that still hung in their parroquia. In that well-known image, Fray Antonio Roa carries a heavy cross upon his shoulders as he makes his way barefoot through the very same streets. A church historian by training (he held a doctorate from one of the Pontifical Universities in Rome), don Sergio was certainly familiar with the Roa paintings. And he would probably have read the work of Lauro López Beltrán, one of the most prominent and active priests in his diocese.

López Beltrán's historical study of Roa, researched and written during the time that he himself had served for several years as parish priest in Totolapan and published in 1969, was most likely written to bolster and publicize the cult. He was a passionate *aparicionista*, an enthusiastic traditionalist who adhered to belief in the Virgin of Guadalupe's miraculous appearance to Juan

Diego at Tepeyac. As one of her more earnest clerical devotees, López Beltrán served as instigator and spiritual director for the first diocesan-sponsored pilgrimage to the Guadalupan Basilica in Mexico City in May of 1961.[13] Like many clerics, López Beltrán was less interested in the Cristo than he was in the person and ministry of his predecessor Fray Antonio de Roa. His book sought to demonstrate the veracity of Roa's "miraculously" brutal penitences.[14] Don Sergio, who was a staunch *anti-aparicionista*, nevertheless held the energetic López Beltrán in high esteem. They often worked collaboratively; the bishop accompanied López Beltrán and the people of Morelos on their first formal diocesan pilgrimage to Guadalupe's original shrine at Tepeyac. The respect was clearly mutual, as López Beltrán fondly recorded the events of don Sergio's consecration as bishop in 1952.[15] It was probably through López Beltrán that don Sergio first learned of the existence of this unique crucifix in a dusty corner of his diocese.

By imitating the friar's gesture, evoking the memory of Roa depicted in the painting that hung in the parroquia of Totolapan, don Sergio simultaneously recalled and superceded Roa's own efforts to attribute meaning to and define appropriate religious devotion to the Cristo Aparecido. What he accomplished, ultimately, was to assert an alternative interpretation. In this way the bishop added his own response to the thick layers of meaning that had accumulated during centuries of successive engagements between the Cristo de Totolapan and representatives of the Catholic clergy seeking to mold the community's relationship to him. That he was in fact seeking to marginalize Roa's interpretation and substitute his own is underscored by don Sergio's putative removal a decade or two later of the Roa paintings to his cathedral in Cuernavaca. When the paintings disappeared from Totolapan, the mayordomos tried unsuccessfully for weeks to determine their whereabouts. Today the people of Totolapan, including the man who served as *primer mayordomo* at that time, recall distinctly that it was their beloved bishop himself who removed them. However those "keepers of the flame," seeking to preserve an untarnished memory of their patriarch, now argue that it was not don Sergio but a disgruntled and vengeful parish priest who sold the two paintings to a wealthy German collector in an effort to frame the bishop.[16] It was don Sergio himself, say these defenders, who actually rescued the paintings from this fate, redeemed them with his own private funds, and kept them safe until they could be restored. However this may have transpired, the paintings were warehoused at the cathedral for more than twenty years, along with dozens of other "retired saints" withdrawn from public devotion, and dozens of other liturgically questionable religious works, until the Instituto Nacional de Antropologia e Historia was finally granted access to them in 1990, at which point they were restored and returned to Totolapan.[17] This was a decision based on new curatorial theories (discussed in the following chapter) rather than on theological or liturgical considerations.

From Traditionalism to Liberation

Méndez Arceo returned in 1939 at the age of thirty-two from twelve years of advanced study in Rome. Eager to begin his ministry in Mexico, the young cleric set about an ambitious and formidable task, to address the consequences of some eighty years of particularly pronounced anti-Church policies in Mexico.[18] In an extended interview with journalist Gabriela Videla given in the last year of his episcopacy, don Sergio explained how for three long decades he had grappled with church institutionalism, introversion, and the sense of victimization that resulted from the peculiarities and traumas of the separation of church and state in Mexico.[19] His desire to challenge and engage the Church and the larger society on these issues shaped and defined his agenda throughout his ministry.

In particular, the Cristero War from 1926 to 1929 most affected and shaped the early years of don Sergio's episcopacy. Tensions mounted with the Constitution of 1917, which included a number of articles that reflected the anti-clericalism and anti-Catholicism of the revolutionary Mexican government.[20] Provisions limited the number of priests per diocese, outlawed parochial education, and forbade public expression of religion, such as processions in honor of saints. In protest, the Church went so far as to declare a self-imposed moratorium, withdrawing priests from their parishes and suspending all religious services throughout Mexico—an aggressively defensive action taken by Mexican Catholic prelates with the pope's approval. Needless to say, both priests and the priesthood itself suffered under the state's repressive legislation as well as the Church's extended nationwide boycott. Méndez Arceo felt that both the government's pronounced religious persecution and the Church's self-defensive posture had left deep wounds upon ecclesiastical discipline, wounds he desired to heal in his ministry.[21]

Don Sergio began his career as bishop not as a political conservative per se, but as an enthusiastic guardian and preserver of the "traditional" church, a "sentinel" of orthodoxy with a paradoxically critical and modernizing edge. By the end of the first decade of his episcopacy, his emphasis on priestly formation began to take on a modernizing aspect, impacting even the religious orders; in 1961 he controversially incorporated Freudian psychoanalysis into the spiritual preparation of the brothers in the Cuernavaca convento. Above all, he sought to *enoblecer el sacerdocio*, to return dignity to a largely degraded priesthood. The first phase of don Sergio's ministry as bishop was devoted to the recruitment and formation of his diocesan priests.[22] He worked to reinvigorate seminary education, setting rigorous standards for formation, theological training, and academic preparation. Under his guidance, first as spiritual director and professor of ecclesiastical history and liturgy at the Seminario Menor de México, and then during the first ten years of his episcopacy, vocations and seminaries thrived. Attentive to the public perception of his clerics, during this time don Sergio also set new, stricter guidelines for clerical behavior, especially with regard to dress, public comportment, and contact with women.[23]

Around the time of don Sergio's entrance with the Cristo into Totolapan, perhaps for the first time since the revolution the state was softening some of its more aggressively anti-Church policies. Moving to occupy space created by this relative opening to religious faith, and trying to regain ground lost in the course of the religious persecution of the 1920s, including the course of the Cristero Rebellion, Catholic intellectuals began embarking on a project of asserting and defending what they called *la cultura católica*.[24] The new emphasis may also have been a response to state efforts, in the 1920s and 1930s, to encourage the development of a revolutionary cultural nationalism through a process of standardization of folk culture.[25] By appropriating sanitized and secularized regional traditions into national events and celebrations, the government worked to co-opt local cultural practices and incorporate these in the construction of a cohesive national cultural identity. Therefore the Church's assertion of la cultura católica was a defensive posture, an effort to control the interpretation of local cultural traditions in the face of a secularizing nationalism.

Don Sergio took a leadership role in this movement as director of the Church's Commission on Education and Culture in 1953. In that capacity, scarcely a year before his act of ritual performance in Totolapan, he delivered a lecture to the first National Congress of Catholic Culture in which he emphasized the importance of culture, arts, and human sciences as "mediations for a better expression and '*vivencia*' of the Christian faith."[26] By reasserting the presence of the Church in public culture and strengthening traditional institutions like the priesthood, Don Sergio intended to rebuild what he felt had been undone in the first third of the twentieth century.

Don Sergio's participation in the celebration of the Cristo of Totolapan gains new significance when placed against this backdrop of a church-state contest over the collective display of popular culture and ritual. That is, not only is his a meaningful and weighty act but also a very public, albeit highly local, one. In sanctioning the celebration of the Cristo, don Sergio acted to reclaim public space for Catholic ritual, culture, and sensibility.

At the same time, with the same gesture, don Sergio also located himself squarely on the "side" of the people of Totolapan, claiming an allegiance with them and their faith. In this way he both anticipated one of the primary methods of evangelization of liberation theology and simultaneously addressed the anticlericalism that defined the culture of his new diocese. Don Sergio was struck in Morelos by what he perceived as the peoples' "arrogance" in relation to their priests.[27] In response, upon his arrival as bishop, he offered a ceremonious gesture of humility that won over the people of the state. He recalls: "I walked barefoot and I knelt and kissed the earth, the land, of Morelos. This was my entrance into Tres Marías. Do you call these gestures conservative? Well, they are not conservative. Do you call them liberal? Neither are they liberal. They reflect the desire to immerse myself in what I had come to do."[28] The bishop's genuflection and obeisance marked the beginning of his career as bishop and set the tone for his ministry in the diocese. His episcopacy was punctuated throughout by ritual acts through which he sought to "immerse" himself in the life and culture of the people of Morelos. His entrance into To-tolapan with the Cristo can be counted among these. After Vatican II, these acts of "immersion" also came to shape and sharpen his commitment to the libera-tionist practice of solidarity with the poor of his diocese, and those of Central America during the 1980s, a period of regional political crisis and turmoil. Thus the journalist Videla is able to declare the remarkable achievement that "in an anticlerical society, don Sergio was able to make of himself a legend."[29]

Perhaps it was due to don Sergio's own ministerial style, folksy and hum-ble, that the people of the state came to expect a similar demeanor from subse-quent bishops. Decades later, in 1994, when the people of Tepoztlán wrested control of their pueblo from the civil authorities in the well-known "golf course rebellion," the unpopular, politically conservative bishop, Luis Reynoso, made a pastoral visit to the town. Armed locals standing guard at the entrance of the pueblo insisted that the bishop get out of his car, remove his shoes, and enter the community barefoot, in this case forcing an act of ritual humility. Fortu-nately for the bishop, he complied.

Here I have sought to contextualize don Sergio's act of devotion to the Cristo Aparecido, framing it in terms of the political, pastoral, and biographical valences that it may have carried for the bishop himself. But his respect and af-fection for the Cristo Aparecido of Totolapan did not necessarily lend immunity to other valued santos, nor even to the cristos hermanos in other Morelos towns, when the bishop embarked upon his great works of parish modernization and cathedral renovation. One of the most painful consequences of the renovation, for many Morelenses, was the "exile" of the cathedral's imágenes. The banish-ment of Morelos's cristos to basements, storage closets, and museums provides the occasion for a more sustained reflection upon the relationship between Vati-can II, liberation theology, and popular devotion to images of Christ crucified. In many ways, the story of don Sergio's modernization of the cathedral and other churches of the diocese highlights the uniqueness of Totolapan's beloved Cristo, and reveals not so much an antagonism as a complicated ambivalence toward local religious practices on the part of Bishop Sergio Méndez Arceo.

Saints in Exile: The Renovation of the Cuernavaca Cathedral

> That cathedral which you stripped, denuded, so that it could become song
> and welcome, mariachi and community, life and resurrection . . .
> —Poem in honor of don Sergio by Pedro Casaldáliga[30]

Don Sergio's renovation of the cathedral, which began in 1957 under the direction of the architect-liturgist Fray Gabriel Chávez de la Mora, was driven by a vision that was artistic as well as catechetical and liturgical.[30] Perhaps the most ambitious articulation of the Catholic liturgical renewal movement anywhere in the world up to that point, the vision that don Sergio developed and implemented for the Cuernavaca cathedral would eventually come to be a defining influence on the Second Vatican Council's statements related to modernizing liturgy and liturgical space. The bishop's intention was to create a liturgical space that on the one hand communicated an unequivocally cristocentric theology, and on the other returned the cathedral to an idealized and modernized version of its "original" sixteenth-century form. This involved, among other things, stripping the architectural and artistic traces of subsequent centuries, and in particular the baroque-inspired retablos (also referred to as reredos, altarpieces, or retables in English) and the "ignoble," neoclassical modifications of the liberal nineteenth century.

Don Sergio's alterations to the cathedral grew out of a local movement for liturgical revitalization spearheaded in Mexico by a group of Benedictine monks, many of whom sought to bring a version of Eastern Orthodox spirituality to Mexico. Their innovations included the distribution of Orthodox, two-dimensional flat icons to some of the most traditional parishes in Cuernavaca. In the Benedictines' view of that day, contemplation of such Eastern-style icons was more beneficial spiritually than the popular local devotion to sculpted imágenes. Father López Beltrán was outraged at one point when a visiting English friar substituted flat icons for the local santos in the parish church of Ocotepec, a traditional community on the outskirts of Cuernavaca. Tempers flared, to the point that don Sergio himself felt obliged to send an assistant to step in and mediate the dispute between the two hot-tempered clerics.[31]

Keeping in mind that the cathedral had first been built as the church of a particularly impressive Franciscan monastery (the fifth in New Spain), don Sergio explained that the faith inspired there was to be shaped by the "cristocentric renewal of evangelical Franciscanism" during the sixteenth century.[32] Here, Méndez Arceo's vision anticipated the idealized and romanticized place the sixteenth century would come to hold for an entire generation of liberation theologians. These theologians preferred to identify themselves with the (admittedly short-lived) utopian vision of the mendicant friars who first sought to evangelize the Americas, the vision of Valades's "Atrio Ideal" discussed in the second chapter of this book. In written works, these twentieth-century scholars often posit their project as bringing to fruition the "incomplete" evangelization begun the sixteenth century, which, as they saw it, had been hindered by four centuries of colonialism and capitalist imperialism.[33]

One task of the renovation was to adapt the physical plan of the great sanctuary so as to better suit its function as a cathedral.[34] The space was to be adorned simply but not austerely, so that the Eucharistic table, as the primary symbol of Christ, stood clearly as its visual and spiritual center.[35] In this way, even in its capacity as a cathedral, it was to maintain the imagined "simplicity" of the Franciscan monasticism that had shaped and defined its original architecture. Don Sergio specified three guiding principals for the renovations: (1) to treat with respect everything that possessed artistic or historic value; (2) to renovate the space in a way that was liturgically functional and also typically modern; and (3) to use the renovations to "orient" popular piety.[36]

An *Exhortación Pastoral* published upon the completion of these renovations prepared the people of the diocese to encounter the radical transformation of their cathedral for the first time. In this pamphlet, don Sergio offered a pastorally minded explanation for the dramatic changes he had decreed. Before the renovation, the baroque-inspired retablo behind the main altar, "crowded with flowers and candles and images, [had] overwhelmed the physical space," detracted attention from the Eucharistic altar.[37] Furthermore, he argues, it had "neither artistic nor historic merit" that would indicate the need for preservation. While he acknowledges those whose faith had been nurtured at the foot of the retablo, he explains that he had it removed for the spiritual benefit, for the sake of the souls, of his entire flock. Not insensitive to the fact that people would experience the dramatic change as a loss, he referenced the absent gold-leaf altarpiece (and the faith it had nurtured) by painting the back wall where it had once stood in a subtle, golden hue: a golden ghost of an age past.

With respect to the many of the retablos that lined the walls of the cathedral sanctuary, don Sergio was convinced that none of these possessed any artistic, historic, or material value whatsoever. They were not only poorly made works, he felt, but their installation had destroyed the primitive frescos of the church, diminished the number of the windows and the physical capacity of the space while stifling the circulation of air. Determined to return the cathedral to its "original" form, don Sergio found it significant that "the primitive church, as is evidenced by the precious frescos, did not have any retablos in the nave."[38] Ultimately, then, not only the main retablo behind the altar but also all of the side altarpieces were removed, as well. To gain access to them, don Sergio approved the removal the corresponding side altars, as well as the individual santos that rested upon them. None of these, once more, in his estimation, was of any artistic merit.

For poor believers of the diocese this last intervention, the removal of almost a dozen side altars from the nave and their saints, was the most controversial modification of the cathedral by far. It was upon those capilla altars, each with the image of its particular saint, that the faith of the people had rested for centuries. In their original function, side altars were used by each friar for the celebration of his own private Mass. Later, each came to be occupied by a single community santo under the care of its own mayordomía, which bore responsibility for maintaining the altar and caring for the image. Because the bishop found neither of these uses to be satisfactory from a liturgical point of view, he removed the altars and banished dozens of images of the saints to the cathedral basement.

This he justified by pointing out that neither the altars themselves, the corresponding retablos, nor the saints were original to the colonial church. Their origins were not even attributable to the baroque period; the retablos were disappointing replacements for the apparently quite spectacular seventeenth-century gold-leafed retablos and reredos that had been discarded in the late eighteenth and nineteen centuries as clerical taste rejected the baroque. They were, the bishop deemed, of such poor quality that were not worthy of placing in storage. Also in the nineteenth century, the original colonial santos, hand carved from cedar, had been replaced by mass-produced (factory-made) plaster and chalk statues.[39] Don Sergio did, however, note two exceptions that merited preservation in the church sanctuary: an image of San Cristóbal that had not been especially esteemed by the people, and an image of Our Lady of the Assumption, the patroness of the original church, which he believed to be the earliest image of her created in the New World.[40] Don Sergio's criteria for the "artistic" and "historic" over the popular functioned quite independently of the peoples' own estimation. Most important, the santos that the people held in high esteem, he deemed unworthy.

Given the bishop's criteria, which privileged the historical and colonial, we can easily see see how the Cristo Aparecido of Totolapan won and maintained the bishop's respect. Precisely because of its documented sixteenth-century origins and its connection to the exemplary Roa and the missionary endeavors of the early friars, this santo was exempt from the bishop's efforts to purify the piety of the believers of Morelos. In fact, don Sergio often returned to the people of Totolapan to tell them how in all of his travels he had only ever encountered one other image (in Austria) that was even vaguely similar in quality and style to theirs, an image that so "perfectly captured Christ at the precise moment of his death."[41]

After removing the altars, retablos, and the many saints' images from the cathedral, don Sergio inscribed biblical verses from the Gospels on the walls behind where these altars had once stood. In his *Exhortación* to the people of Morelos, he explained and defended his actions:

> This multiplication of altars and retablos is not a good thing, my beloved children. In the first place, for reasons of space, because it greatly reduces the capacity and the ability to circulate in the church, including for processions. But principally because it divides attention and creates a lack of reverence for the main altar, because on these side altars people place candles, flowers, vases, and even objects of personal use, and people even lean on them to rest. What is one to think upon seeing this spectacle? That the Eucharistic altar is the center of the church? The most precious jewel? The location of Christ's Sacrifice?[42]

The Cuernavaca cathedral renovations, in particular the removal of the saints and the positioning of images of Mary and Jesus, anticipated and influenced the reforms propagated by Vatican II. Don Sergio attended the council and, though initially skeptical about what it could accomplish in terms of reform and renewal, he made several interventions that guided the discussion about liturgy. He spoke in the sessions about his concern for the devotional practices of the Latin American people, especially expressing his anxiety about the inappropriate popular celebration of saints as "mediators" to God.[43] Ultimately, the council's conclusions were very much in keeping with don Sergio's own vision: the images in a church should be "few, appropriate, and placed in a clearly hierarchical order."[44] Liturgical preference thus came to require that each parish would have an image of Christ crucified at the back of the nave, an image of the Virgin Mary to his left but nearer to the people, and finally an image of the patron saint of the church on his right. This is certainly the case in the Cuernavaca cathedral, where the colonial image of Our Lady of the Assumption was carefully installed on the left. Today, from her perch, where she hovers in clouds surrounded by angels and cherubim, she can gaze up with ecstatic adoration, or perhaps in deferent homage, at the incongruously modern crucifix that now hangs in the center of the nave.

In the context of Vatican II, as an alternative to churches crowded with saints, don Sergio recommended that a single altar should be dedicated to all the saints, and occupied by one image at a time, as appropriate to the feast day.[45] This was indeed what he had intended to do in Cuernavaca with the saints he had removed from the nave. His vision was to place a placard describing the life and actions of the saint beneath the image of the day, to locate him or her within a specific historical context. But in this regard the display of saints was to have a heuristic rather than a particularly devotional value, a strange echo of what the Bourbon reformers had imagined for the role of Christian images two centuries earlier.

Méndez Arceo's *acción litúrgica*, or liturgical action, that is, his experiment with the Cuernavaca cathedral and his interventions at Vatican II, were a powerful force in shaping a global movement toward liturgical, architectural, and aesthetic modernization within the Church. Feminist Camille Paglia attacked this modernized Catholic aesthetic in an interview in the Jesuit journal *America*, in 1992, in which she mourned the implementation of this vision in the United States during the late 1960s and 1970s. She attributed her own alienation from the Catholic Church to these reforms. Critical of the renovations of Catholic churches then sweeping neighborhood parishes throughout the United States, Paglia condemned the mass removal of saints as a sort of ethnic cleansing:

> . . . [the] snobbish purgation of the ethnic origins of the parishioners in these churches. . . . They remodeled the church from the inside.

The statues were taken down to the cellar and out of sight. I couldn't believe it. The whole altar, of course, they dropped a bomb on the altar, which is what they've been doing for the last 25 years. . . . It's all open, like a Chamber of Commerce/guild hall in the front. . . . It's totally sanitized. . . . Now we have this abomination in America of these shells of the old churches with these barbecue-pit interiors! These airline-terminal interiors. What does this do to young Catholics? I think it just removes any visual culture.[46]

Even the crucifix that Don Sergio installed in the cathedral seemed to reiterate and underscore the physical absence of the exiled saints. Today it remains the only image of Christ in the cathedral, and in design and function it is almost aggressively modern, blatantly defying use as a devotional object. Even so, it is the central image: don Sergio imagined that, hanging as it was from the "triumphal arc in between the sanctuary and the nave, it would dominate the whole church."[47] Stylistically modern, this Christ is suspended, as if floating, high over the congregation. Alive, head raised, eyes open, this is an image of the resurrected, triumphant Christ, not the suffering Jesus. Wounds, blood, nails, and other indications of pain, distress, or death are conspicuously absent. This Cristo hovers, unbound, in front of the cross. The horizontal beam (*patibulum*) itself is positioned quite low, so that Christ's arms angle downward, palms forward, hands open, as if assuming a position of blessing and invitation.[48] Thus positioned remotely, high above his people, it is impossible to feel the comforting gaze of this Christ upon you. Nor is it feasible to light a candle so that he might savor the warmth of its glow. From the perspective of would-be devotees, there is no use in burning a little *copal* (incense) to stimulate his senses; the thin curls and tendrils of smoke could hardly rise to meet him. Poor Cristo Moderno de Cuernavaca: his skin will never be darkened by centuries of loving devotion like so many images transfigured by layer upon layer of dust, smoke, and ash.

The new cathedral Cristo reflected the bishop's own personal predilection for the modern, especially in sacred art. The pectoral cross that he wore represented a pelican with wings outstretched, an historical allegory for the crucified Christ. Copied from the image on his episcopal shield, this cross was a modern articulation of an ancient association between the pelican and Christ based on the legend that if necessary, the bird will tear its own flesh to feed its offspring, thus sharing with Christ a willingness to self-sacrifice.[49] The ring that don Sergio insisted the seminarians kiss while genuflecting was in the style of modern sacred art. In the bishop's room in Ocotepec, there hung a very expressive Christ on the cross, a modernist image gifted to him by a sculptor who had at one time been his student at the seminary. So unusual was the representation that one of the bishop's colleagues at the seminary worried privately that the "image seemed to him to be terrible and he did not understand how such an orthodox bishop could like such a work of art, because to him it seemed to be a deformation of the crucified."[50]

Most controversial about the modernist crucifix that don Sergio commissioned for the cathedral may have been that it was designed to be suspended, to hang, free-floating, in the center of the nave. In the town of Atlatlaucan, less than a ten-minute *combi* ride from Totolapan, this was the central point of contention that caused a permanent and seemingly irreconcilable rift in the town. In 1966, in the wake of Vatican II, a modernizing priest from the United Staes, perhaps inspired by the very crucifix that hung in the cathedral, decided to remove the local cristo from its customary place in the *nicho* behind the altar, and replace it with one that hung in the center of the church. This innovation was accompanied by several others, including alterations to the traditional liturgy and a liberationist practice of Bible study, but the "hanging" crucifix was, in the mind of local traditionalists, the final straw. The resulting, painful civil dispute culminated in the forced exodus of nearly half of the members of parish. Those that opposed the innovations ran the priest out of town and took control over the parroquia. Their first act was to remove the *cristo colgado*, the hanging Christ, and reinstall their own cristo behind the altar. Those who preferred the newer liturgical forms and who saw no real cause for objection to the hanging crucifix made their exiled home in one of the small barrio chapels. Both liturgical communities functioned for perhaps twenty years without a priest. Eventually, the traditionalists came to identify themselves as *lefebristas*, after Walter Lefebre, the French cardinal who dissented from Vatican II and established a neo-orthodox splinter group within the Church.[51] Several years ago, Atlatlaucan finally received its lefebrista priest who, to this day, celebrates Mass in Latin with his back to the congregation.

Those who did not oppose the Vatican II reforms are referred to disparagingly in Atlatlaucan as *los colgadores*, those who "hung" Jesus. This epithet reflects the angry perception that their Cristo was twice-punished: crucified once by his Roman persecutors who hung him from the cross, and, to add insult to injury, strung up anew in Atlatlaucan by those who at one time had claimed to be his devotees and protectors. Today, both lefebristas and colgadores make their annual pilgrimages both to the Señor de Chalma and to the nearby Cristo Aparecido; but they do so in two separate groups. At the annual fiesta in honor of the Cristo in Totolapan, they were able to point each other out to me from across the *atrio*, church courtyard. The story of Atlatlaucan bears mention here, because the conflict in this pueblo is an important point of reference for the people of Totolapan as they negotiate their own disputes, as we will see in the following chapter.

In retrospect at least, one of the great successes that don Sergio claimed for the new cathedral was its ecumenism. Stripped of these folk Catholic elements, it now offered to non-Catholic Christians "a sheltering space where they could sit and offer their prayers in an environment more centered on Christ."[52] The substitution of passages of biblical text for the santos is perhaps the most starkly symbolic manifestation of this ecumenical spirit, given Protestantism's concentrated emphasis on "the word" and its preoccupation with what they often perceive to be the idolatry of Catholic devotional practice.[53] Local anxieties about the "Protestant bishop" were exacerbated when, in 1961, don Sergio requested and received permission from the pope for Catholics in his diocese to use the more readily accessible and affordable protestant Bibles.

Defenders of the restoration explained that the previous cathedral was a reflection of "our badly developed faith . . . *mucha veladora*, many candles, but nothing about the sacraments, nothing about participation in Mass understood as the mystical body of Christ."[54] I have often heard the faith of Mexican people described as non-Eucharistic. Some have argued that their faith, organized around processions and fiestas, is primarily liturgical and so they have been disparagingly called *ceremoniáticos*, addicted to Catholic ritual.[55] Observing the easy coming and going during Mass and individual engagement with the saints, others have concluded that the spiritual practice of Catholic Mexico is inherently individualistic, as well.[56]

United States Catholics in particular are frequently struck by how few of the faithful receive communion in Mexico. In fact, a minority receive any of the official sacraments at all, except perhaps for baptism, a fact that has long troubled their clerics. At the same time, priests and bishops have done much to discourage the universal reception of communion, insisting that communicants be in compliance with all rules of the church. Surpassing even Church teaching on the subject, it is commonly assumed in Mexico, by laity and clerics alike, that only those who confess regularly, whose marriage has been blessed by the Church, who have been baptized and even confirmed in the Church, are entitled to receive the Eucharist. One priest told me that the current bishop is displeased if he arrives in a parish and discovers that "too many people" are receiving communion. For centuries, it seems, Catholics in Mexico have found themselves caught between a rock and a hard place, with the Church both insisting upon the centrality of the sacraments and simultaneously withholding access to them from most people.

In his plan for the restoration, the bishop gave significant weight to what he determined to be those objects possessing "artistic" or "historical" value. But in determining the fate of the saints and other religious objects (the retablos and side altars in particular), don Sergio did not consider their sacramental value for the people. His plans for the renovation disregarded the possibility that the piety of ordinary Mexican Catholics was already deeply and profoundly sacramental and even Eucharistic; a sacramentality expressed precisely in devotion to the saints. Historian David Brading comes to a similar conclusion in his reflection on sacred images in the early colonial period: "If the Son of God had become man and the bread and wine of the Eucharist the body and blood of Christ, so too the material images that represented Christ and his Mother equally became invested with a numinous quality which at times formed the conduit of miraculous powers. . . . After all, had not the Greek Fathers argued that the veneration paid to ikons was an affirmation of the reality of the incarnation?"[57] A theology of transubstantiation and divine presence is visible in both the bread and wine as in the many santos.

In a practice that is acutely individual and at the same time inherently collective, believers in the cult of the saints do indeed engage the sacred in a Eucharistic sense. They are touched by and can touch the divine as they "take Christ" within them by lighting candles, touching the foot of a *santito*, gazing into his or her eyes. In those moments they are communicated, that is, they have "received." From a theological perspective, one could argue that this Eucharist of communion with the saints is more true to Jesus' own sacramental ministry than the more formal one of universal Catholic liturgy. That is, no one here is excluded; all are worthy, and no one is judged. Indeed, it could be argued that the theological truth of the Eucharist lies as much in Jesus' perfectly inclusive feeding of the five thousand with the multiplication of the loaves and fishes as it is does in the rehearsal of the intimacy of the Last Supper.

I have attended recitations of the rosary in the humble homes of devotees to the Señor de Chalma and other local cristos that were in essence lay-led Eucharists. The traditional *pan dulce* and *atole* served in the succeeding peaceful quietude very much enhance this sense of their meaning. Such Eucharists, with their shared prayers, songs, and meal, not dissimilar from the Moravian Love Feast, are often led by laywomen and they are available to saint and sinner alike: all are welcome, and any may participate. One may reasonably conclude, therefore, that while generations of missionaries and clerics fretted over a population seemingly resistant to enlightenment, all the while a deeply sacramental and Eucharistic piety was evolving among them, one that is expressed in adoration of images of the saints. In spite of don Sergio's insistence that the saints and retablos of the cathedral had no aesthetic value, the experience of beauty in the santos, flowers, and candles may in fact have functioned as a sacrament for the poor. In this theological interpretation, they were not a distraction from the symbolic imagery of the Eucharistic table, as don Sergio argued, but actually called attention to the sacred beauty of the divine.

Criticism of the exile of the saints from the cathedral came from various sectors of the community. Affluent Catholics and conservative journalists, already sensing the beginnings of a leftward shift in the bishop's ministry, suddenly claimed to be defenders of popular religiosity and attacked the bishop for turning the cathedral into a "work of art" or a "museum."[58] This was a particularly poignant criticism, given that under the strong secularism of the Mexican state, many of the colonial monasteries had become "ex-conventos," relics of colonial religion, functioning as museums administered by the Instituto Nacional de Antropología e Historia (INAH). Indeed, observers today recall that one of the plans that don Sergio had for the "treasures" he carefully safeguarded in the cathedral basement was to open a museum of religious art, perhaps in Tepoztlán, although considering the low estimation in which he held of most of the cathedral imágenes, it is difficult to imagine which of these he would have deemed worthy for inclusion in the collection.

In one case of twentieth-century furta sacra, don Sergio convinced the people of the pueblo of Hueyapan to lend INAH one of their beloved images for an exposition of colonial art. After the close of the exhibit, INAH failed to return the saint; and given don Sergio's rumored antipathy toward the peoples' santos, the locals came to understand this loss as the "premeditated theft of their image." The bishop was never again welcome in the pueblo. Eventually, after ten years of petitions and complaints, the image was finally repatriated, returned to its home.[59] Don Sergio was startled to discover that criticism came as well from agnostics and atheists. After his release from prison, where he had spent four years on charges of subversion, the muralist and communist militant David Alfaro Siqueiros went to live in Cuernavaca. Though an avowed atheist, he often visited the cathedral; he was so disturbed by the removal of the saints there that he challenged the bishop to his face.[60]

In addition to disapprobation from members of the cultural and intellectual elite, the bishop also carefully noted criticism that literally came from the "pews" of his cathedral. He carefully preserved these messages, written by ordinary believers on the backs of offering envelopes. One such note charged: "Your Excellency . . . with all respect and frankness, I tell you: this cathedral is horrible, and everyone says that that which was once a work of art is now a mixture of things from the time of the idols. It seems as if it is from the time of idolatry. Why in the church do they profane the figure of Christ with this frightening modern art?"[61] Thus ordinary believers themselves wielded clerical language against him, accusing him of the very thing of which they themselves have for so long been accused: idolatry and disregard for the artistic. In the colonial period in Mexico, evangelizing friars pitted icon against idol. Modern priests and secular observers have at some points rehearsed this distinction, in emphasizing the saints' status as art versus their status as icons.[62] But this hand-scribbled note left in the pew of the cathedral encapsulates an important clarification: the conflict between bishop and believer was the clash between two opposing aesthetic sensibilities, and not a clash between an artistic and an anti-aesthetic vision.

Ultimately, for the people of Morelos the saints themselves did not passively accept their exile from the cathedral. The process of removing the side altars, saints, and nineteenth-century retablos from the walls of the nave revealed mid-seventeenth-century frescos that had been hidden for centuries. These frescos represented the occasion of the martyrdom of the Mexican Franciscan friars in Japan by crucifixion, and don Sergio had them carefully restored. For some believers, the frescos represented nothing less than the banished saints themselves, who had reappeared on the walls of the cathedral, rebelliously defying the bishop's own power and authority, and reoccupying the church.[63]

Throughout the 1960s, don Sergio worked to implement this aesthetic reorientation in parishes throughout his diocese, directing parish priests to relocate the saints' images to church basements and storage closets. The most humble devotees of the diocese thus came to worry over their saints who had been "disappeared," borrowing the eerie language used to lament the kidnap and murder of political activists under repressive military regimes in Central America and Argentina. The colonial origins of the the Cristo Aparecido of Totolapan lent him and the other images of the parroquia of Totolapan artistic immunity, so that together they survived the rash of "disappearances." Don Sergio's early ambivalence toward the santos and to other expressions of popular religiosity is not part of the story that the faithful of Totolapan tell about their favored bishop. In fact, they can hardly imagine that it would have been possible for don Sergio to do such a thing. It is don Sergio's respect for the Cristo that they remember; and his stature as "people's bishop" and champion of the poor, achieved during the 1970s and 1980s, that they lovingly invoke today.

From the Bishop's Crozier to the Pilgrim's Staff: The People's Bishop of Morelos

In March of 1973, the bishop once again immersed himself in the life of the people, this time by paying homage to the much-celebrated Señor de Chalma. Again he ceremoniously departed his cathedral and, accompanied by his secretary Padre Baltasar López and several seminarians, he made his way by foot to Chalma, the most visited pilgrimage site in Mexico after the basilica dedicated to the Virgin of Guadalupe.

Unlike the basilica, where pilgrims from diverse classes and backgrounds mix and mingle with foreign tourists, at the Sanctuario of Chalma one will find *pura gente humilde*, as one frequent pilgrim observed to me. At the *hospedaje* administered by the Augustinian friars who care for the shrine to this day, pilgrims crowd the floors on bedrolls and in sleeping bags. Today the pueblo itself offers thousands of private hotel rooms. But the construction of these "hotels" is haphazard and chaotic, and the rooms that advertise hot water and individual toilets are the exception. One will find few foreign tourists there beyond the occasional new age backpackers, interested in venturing to the shrine. Certainly, this U.S. researcher and her young family seemed incongruous and out of place.

The narrow streets meandering mazelike down to the sanctuary are crowded with innumerable vendors from whom one can as easily purchase tequila, a decorative roach clip, or a key chain engraved with a bare-breasted woman as one can a replica of the Señor himself. The shrine is alarmingly crowded during certain feast days; several years ago a dozen people were killed as pilgrims jostled and pushed to get closer to the santo. An unlikely place for a bishop, one might imagine.

Nevertheless, on that day don Sergio left behind forever his bronze bishop's crozier, and took up in its place the simple wooden staff of the humble pilgrim.[64] This single gesture symbolized the shifting commitments of the Church as a whole. Swept by the liberationist current, the institution itself often made a "preferential option for the poor." The journey was rigorous and demanding; and yet is it possible, as priests today recollect, casting the radiant glow of sainthood upon their beloved leader, that he made the twenty-mile journey barefoot? If not, we can certainly imagine that before he entered the sanctuary he removed his shoes in homage to the sacred within. But this act of ritual humility and presence now took on significance distinct from his previous gestures of a similar nature.

It had been almost five years since the pivotal and history-altering gathering of bishops and priests at Medellín in 1968. There, don Sergio's colleagues had set the agenda for the implementation of Vatican II in a Latin American context. What resulted was the first systematic articulation of the theology of liberation. That same year don Sergio had agonized over the massacre of students at Tlatelolco. In its wake, in 1970, he declared himself a member of the Socialist party. In 1972, don Sergio was the only bishop in attendance at the first Latin American Encounter of Christians for Socialism (Encuentro Latinoamericano de Cristianos por el Socialismo) held in Santiago de Chile. Upon his return from this conference, as he arrived at the airport, a group of irate conservative teenagers doused him with red paint in protest of his turn toward the left. It was from then on that he was derisively, or admiringly, referred to as the "red bishop" of Cuernavaca.

By the time don Sergio entered Chalma with his simple pilgrim's staff made of pine, he had cast his lot with the workers, the poor, and the left, and had become known by even the most cynical pundits as the *obispo de los pobres*, the bishop of the poor.[65] Each increasingly radical step that he took brought him a step closer to the poor, and perhaps to a deeper understanding of their faith. One may imagine that his familiarity with and respect for the Cristo Aparecido of Totolapan had helped prepare him for this moment. The crowd was unusually quiet as don Sergio stood before them, beneath the watchful gaze of the Cristo de Chalma, and began his homily.[66]

> I have not made my pilgrimage here today to complete a religious promise (*manda o promesa*). In immersing myself in this religious activity, I am journeying toward you, and in doing so I am on pilgrimage toward God. I have made this pilgrimage to understand its meanings, its positive aspects and its negative aspects, in the hopes of being able to "evangelize" this search for God in the light of the Word of the God who himself is on a journey, a journey in which

he searches for us. I have walked as so many pilgrims have walked, because I desired to encounter God in the most humble of my brothers and sisters. It is to this sanctuary that the most humble come, those most in need of mercy.

I have not come in order to make a sacrifice, to suffer the troubles of the way, as if God was a vengeful God, only satisfied with the pain of those who have offended him. I have come as we all should come, to encounter God on the *camino*, on the path.

Don Sergio's fellow pilgrim and assistant, Padre Baltasar, continued the sermon: "What use are superficial acts of devotion if we do not enter into the Christian task of transforming the relations of hate, injustice, vengeance and exploitation? We need to sojourn together from this world toward a new world, a world built on new human relationships with families, coworkers, friends. Because for us they are truly the living Christ, the Christ of community." Don Sergio then concluded his reflections, addressing the crowd directly: "What is the imagen of God that God himself has made?" "*¡El hombre!* [Man himself]," someone called out boldly from the crowd. "Yes!" Sergio affirms: "In our brothers and sisters we encounter God; it is toward them that our true pilgrimage should move. Here in Chalma we experience the special presence of God, not because God has made himself manifest in an image, but because historic and cultural forces have transformed this place into a location where human beings united in faith, united in love, encounter one another."

Don Sergio's homily at Chalma, given relatively early in the liberation theology movement, reflects two seemingly paradoxical approaches contained within this new mandate with respect to popular piety. Don Sergio was unable to shun, at this early date, the corrective and moderating role of the cleric as he sought to "evangelize" the faith of the poor, to shape and form it along increasingly liberationist lines: to coax popular faith away from seeing God in the image, and toward seeing God in each other. This commitment often led him to recast his earlier apprehension about traditional practices in anti-colonialist and Marxist language. INAH Anthropologist Miguel Morayta recalls a painful conversation with Méndez Arceo in which the young, eager anthropologist defended the social and cultural value of the veneration of images. "The bishop's answer thundered like lightening: 'Images and mayordomías were and remain instruments of colonization. Beliefs and principles, are what matter, not images! Anthropologists are the worst offenders, they simply want to maintain everything exactly the way it is. They want nothing to change or improve.'"[67]

Nevertheless, don Sergio's pilgrimage to Chalma, his taking up of the pilgrim's staff, and even his homily signaled a turning point for the bishop, the beginning of a deeper engagement with popular piety, a more deliberate rapprochement. The practice of solidarity extolled by liberation theology brought priests into a new degree of intimacy with the lives of the poor, in the sense of *convivio*, of living alongside and with the most struggling communities. The bishop's commitment to this expression of the "preferential option for the poor" led him to join them for a while on their spiritual journey. The deeper the bishop's praxis, and the deeper his commitment to the pursuit of an earthly justice imagined in social and political terms, the less inclined he was to "tinker" with the faith of the *más humildes*, as he so often called them. This is a path that ultimately brought don Sergio to retire to the very traditional pueblo of Ocotepec where, during the last years of his life, he participated wholeheartedly in the ritual life of the community, embracing practices he had previously rejected, including traditional ceremonies honoring the dead.[68]

This evolution of don Sergio's attitude toward popular religion, specifically the resolution of his earlier ambivalence, reflects a larger shift within liberation theology globally. This is a change described by the Uruguayan Jesuit theologian Juan Luis Segundo. Segundo argues that the first wave of written liberation theology was directed toward intellectuals and the middle-class, and appropriated the Marxist analysis of class and other structures of oppression to construct an ideological critique. This approach, argues Segundo, contributed to a widespread increase in suspicion toward popular religion as participating in the maintenance of structures of oppression. In this first phase, liberation theologians like Leonardo Boff of Brazil therefore sought to correct the theological "misunderstandings" of the poor. In an article puzzling over challenges he faced while theologizing with members of a Christian base community (CEB) in one of the poorest states in Brazil, Boff worried that "a Jesus who only suffers is not liberating; he generates the cult of suffering and fatalism." Thus the role of the theologian remained a corrective one: "to relocate within the mind of common people the cross in its true place."[69]

Segundo then points to a second line of liberation theology that abandoned its more strictly ideological project and "accepted the religion of ordinary people as a generally liberating element."[70] In this subsequent phase, liberation theologians claim to have been "evangelized by the poor," even allowing for the possibility that they themselves might be evangelized by "a passive and fatalistic conception of God," a challenge represented most acutely in popular devotion to images of Christ's passion.[71] In his pilgrimage to Chalma, don Sergio opened himself to precisely such a transformation, in which he allowed his own faith to be touched by the folk beliefs and practices of Mexico's poorest believers, as he put down his golden bishop's crozier and took up the staff of the peasant pilgrim.

Liberation Theology in Totolapan: The Mayordomía in the Postconciliar Context

On a grassroots level, liberation theology found its greatest expression in the *comunidades eclesiales de base* (CEB), the small subparochial neighborhood groups devoted to Bible study, community organizing, and sometimes political action. As the local manifestation of the new liberationist church's preferential option for the poor, the CEBs took root in impoverished and persecuted communities (both rural and urban) and provided the context for a multileveled practice of solidarity. Drawing on the Vatican II notion that the Church is defined not so much by its hierarchical structure as by the more inclusive notion of the Church as the "people of God," the CEB movement was based on the principle of lay empowerment. Armed with the mandate of Vatican II, radicalizing clerics thus sought to transfer authority for biblical interpretation and theological reflection, as well as for social transformation, to the laity.

In Totolapan, however, as in many other communities throughout Latin America, there already existed a model and structure for the participation of a self-empowered laity: the mayordomía. In the case of Totolapan, the local mayordomía parroquial informally absorbed the running of the CEBs into their other duties. This is surprising, given the vehemence with which Méndez Arceo expressed his apprenshions about mayordomías to INAH anthropologist Morayta. In the case of Totolapan, don Sergio's earlier engagement with the Cristo simply set the stage for a deeper engagement in the pueblo through his work with the local CEBs. That is, it seems that the bishop's appreciation for Totolapan Cristo predisposed him to a more collaborative relationship with his devotees. In turn, the CEBs in Totolapan proved to be among the most effective and vibrant in his diocese. Elsewhere in Mexico and Central America, there was friction between the liberation theology movement and the mayordomal structure, as I explore below. But in Totolapan for the most part neither the mayordomos nor the clerics seemed to perceive any contradiction or conflict in the overlap between the traditional structure and the novel ecclesial communities. In my interpretation, the fact that they functioned interdependently and in relative harmony contributed in large part to the local success of the CEB movement. Absent also in Totolapan was the antagonism that some of the more traditional communities in Morelos felt toward the innovations of liberationist priests and to their bishop in particular. To some extent, as explored in the previous section, the Cristo Aparecido was immune to, or exempt from, the efforts of liberationist clerics who otherwise sought to purify the popular faith of their flock, to strip away the more "folkloric" practices.

Don Sergio's practice of "immersion," expressed so poignantly in his ceremonial arrival in Totolapan with the Cristo, dovetailed naturally with the commitment that animated the CEBs. From the mid-1970s through the 1980s, the people of Morelos recall a very concrete change in their bishop: he simply spent more time with them. They explain that he visited them in prison, attended their labor meetings, showed up at their fiestas: "Vino a convivir con nosotros, los pobres," he came to share himself with us, to live alongside us, one CEB member recalls.[72] In keeping with his earlier commitment, don Sergio embarked upon the foundation of CEBs first and foremost as part of his project of clerical formation and training. Thus, at some point in the first half of the 1970s, he began to imagine and implement a new vision for the seminaries in his diocese, using them to train priests as community organizers motivated by a passionate commitment to the preferential option for the poor.[73] Local CEBs emerged under the direction of these newly trained priests and, in turn, their work was supported by a newly formed national organization of clergy called Sacerdotes para el Pueblo.[74] Indeed, throughout Latin America during this period, seminaries were in many respects the epicenter of the liberation theology movement, preparing both priests and lay leaders who had risen up through CEB networks. CEBs were present in Mexico from at least as early as 1972, though this is relatively late when compared to Peru and Brazil, for example, where the formation of CEBs predated the council at Medellín in 1968. Individual base communities in Mexico waxed and waned in the following two decades. Sociologist Michael Foley describes the efforts of a young couple in the diocese of Cuernavaca who, under Sergio Méndez Arceo's auspices, attempted to revive a moribund base community in 1976.[75] As late as 1989, the Mexican bishops, in language that was at once desperate and euphoric, encouraged priests "take up their commitment [to the CEBs] anew."[76]

In Totolapan, as long as there were liberationist priests at the helm, the community (for the most part) was actively engaged in the base community movement. The mayordomía posed no obstacle to the work of the CEBs, but rather incorporated some of the duties into their structure. As discussed in chapter 4 of this book, Serge Gruzinski has argued that, at least in a colonial setting, Indian mayordomías and confraternities were inherently adaptable institutions, which indigenous communities tailored to their own requirements and uses.[77] The case of Totolapan during the era of liberation theology certainly underscores Gruzinski's thesis, extending it into the modern period.

Today, as in the colonial era, great local variation in function, role, and organization marks the diverse lay ecclesial entities that may roughly be grouped together as "mayordomías."

Most scholarly interest in the institution to date has focused on the economic impact of the mayordomía, its capacity either to redistribute wealth or to consolidate wealth, power, and prestige. Anthropological studies have similarly focused on the role played by the mayordomias in civil-religious hierarchies, in relation to a ladder system of advancement and increasing financial responsibility, specifically fiesta sponsorship.[78] In the case of Totolapan, the emphasis of the mayordomía, at least in living memory, is almost exclusively on its religious and ritual functions. That is, at least in the last forty to fifty years, the local mayordomía's link to civil authorities is tenuous at best. It is true that most of the men who serve in the local government have at one time or another also participated in the mayordomía parroquial, or at the very least in one of the lesser barrio or saints groups that are also sometimes called mayordomías. This is to be expected, given the small size of the pueblo and the disproportionately large membership of the mayordomía parroquial. But these roles, one civic and the other religious, are only loosely related. In Totolapan the function of the mayordomía is largely understood as defending and preserving the cultural and religious "patrimony" of the pueblo, although this specific word is avoided, as will be explained in the subsequent chapter. For the most part this broad responsibility is focused on a singular duty: the care of the Cristo Aparecido. Fiesta sponsorship is collective, rather than a costly burden shouldered by a specific individual or family at a given point in time. In this regard, the mayordomía in Totolapan more closely resembles those of the colonial period; some scholars today argue persuasively that the mayordomías' link to the cargo system and the civil-religious hierarchy is not an adaptation of a pre-Columbian cultural form or a holdover from the colonial period (as was previously believed), but rather a more recent, postindependence innovation.[79]

In addition to tending to the nuts and bolts of the annual cycle of festivals devoted to celebration of the Cristo, the activities of the mayordomía are analogous to those of other contemporary lay organizations within the Church. They might be likened to a community-appointed vestry, a parish council, or an altar guild, for instance. In Totolapan, the mayordomos serve simultaneously as community elders, cultural ambassadors, deacons, and in their less glamorous capacities as sextons, janitors, and night watchmen. As defenders of tradition, they can become community spokespeople and advocates in times of extracommunity conflict. They also can step in as judges and even would-be executioners in instances of transgression, as was the case several decades ago when mayordomos thwarted thieves from Mexico City who were attempting to steal three of the community santos under cover of night. As we will see in the following chapter, one of their most important roles may be as brokers between the ecclesial hierarchy (priests and bishops) and the lay community at large. Perhaps this is why people often explain that "the mayordomos speak for all of us, for the whole pueblo."

Totolapan's mayordomal structure is noteworthy with regard to its size. At any given time there are roughly ninety mayordomos who compose the mayordomía parroquial, the parish-wide structure under which other subordinate mayordomías cluster: for example, those related to barrio identity, and those dedicated to the Virgin of Guadalupe and the Señor de Chalma. Of the ninety members, each year four are selected, through a process of group and self-nomination and then election, as head mayordomos. Of these one is named the primer mayordomo, the leading mayordomo of the pueblo. There have always been lesser religious organizations as well, which sometimes call themselves mayordomías, but the mayordomía parroquial is the largest and most dominant of these structures. But there are no jealousies between them. One mayordomo today explained to me that "the mayordomía parroquial does not try to compete with these other groups—rather, its function is to serve and support the others." In their own self-description, they see themselves not so much as jefes (or bosses), but rather "servants" of the community.

Here my intention is to underscore the striking flexibility, mutability, and diversity of the mayordomal structure and function within a single community, a fact that has insured its ongoing cultural usefulness and guaranteed its historical longevity. A recent study shows that mayordomías are even effective in the movement for environmental protection.[80] At its most effective, the mayordomía can and does, in fact, adapt readily to the shifting organizational needs of the community. I emphasize this easy adaptability because it helps to explain how in the 1970s and 1980s, under the influence of liberationist priests, the mayordomía parroquial in Totolapan became a comfortable home for the CEBs and served as a solidarity group for peasant struggles in Central America. All the while it continued to fulfill its primary purpose: to maintain the cult of the Cristo Aparecido.

Padre Gonzalo Ribero, working with the strong encouragement of Bishop Méndez Arceo, was the first of their parish priests to introduce the concept of the CEBs to Totolapan in the late 1970s. Given the role of the various mayordomías in tending to the collective life of the pueblo, no one found it unusual that several members of the mayordomía parroquial took it upon themselves to serve as leaders and organizers of the ecclesial base communities. The mayordomos were, after all, already accustomed to working collaboratively, negotiating complex relationships with priests, and distributing information to the pueblo. They were also the ones who had most familiarity with the inner workings of the church.

Now well into their seventies and early eighties, these men recall wistfully and with nostalgia an era now past. "We mayordomos were the coordinators of the CEB groups," don Tomás, much-esteemed community elder explains. "I myself was responsible for three or four of them. All the other group coordinators of the CEBs were also mayordomos. We both cared for the Cristo and worked with the CEBs. One woman worked with us on the CEBs; but then she got married and after that she stopped."

Don Tolentino, also now in his eighties, is as respected and oft-consulted on matters of custom and religion as his colleague. He has left off watching his favorite team play in a major soccer tournament on television to reminisce with me. Walking slowly, with a cane to support a long-ago-injured foot, he wore the straw hat of the campesino and spoke clearly and deliberately, for my benefit:

> There were five of us in charge of the CEBs and each one had their groups that they ran. We were also mayordomos, but at the same time the group was independent. The CEBs themselves were not related to the celebration of the Cristo; the CEBs were one thing and the mayordomía another. The duty of the mayordomía was to organize the fiestas. But Padre Gonzalo also named the mayordomía as an ecclesial group—to assist him with the work of the CEBs. He

also supported our work as mayordomos; it was with his approval and support that we organized our fiestas.

From the perspective of Totolapan priests advancing a liberationist agenda, the mayordomos were an obvious pool from which to select and recruit leaders for the base communities. Today Padre Gonzalo is a monsignor, *vicario general* of the diocese. But he too is an ailing and elderly man. He makes his home in the town of Yecapixtla, some forty-five minutes beyond Totolapan and further into the hinterlands of the diocese, occupying one of the rooms in the imposing ex-convento there. In spite of poor health, he continues valiantly to tend to the pastoral needs of his flock as part of a team of priests. When I ring the large bell, the frail priest makes his way cautiously down the large stone stairs to meet me. He recalls the time he spent in Totolapan, from the mid 1970s to the early1980s and his vision for developing the base communities in those days:

> When I got to Totolapan the plan was to turn the mayordomía into a pastoral team, to give them a new focus. I wanted to shift it from an emphasis on simple religiosity (*pura religiosidad*), popular piety, to an interest in the holy Bible. I tried to communicate to them the mysticism of liberation (*la mística de la liberación*). I began meeting with the mayordomos as a group in the convento and I tried to turn the mayordomía into a *consejo de pastoral*, a pastoral team.
>
> At the same time, I also accompanied them in their religiosity. I joined them when they distributed the programs for the annual fiesta for the Cristo. I offered support and hospitality for the pilgrims who came for the fiesta. Yes, it is true that the people of Morelos are rebellious, on all levels. As a priest it is difficult and frustrating to work with the mayordomías, one always has to struggle to maintain a sense of equilibrium.

Padre Julio Tinoco followed Padre Gonzalo as parish priest, and continued the project of building up the base communities. More youthful than his predecessor, he is an active and energetic priest—now the sole párroco of a neighborhood parish in the Colonia Juan Morales in Cuautla. Reflecting on the nine years he ministered in Totolapan, Padre Julio recalls a strategy similar to Padre Gonzalo's:

> Many of the leaders of the CEBs were mayordomos, but all the leaders worked basically the same way. That is, even those that were also mayordomos were engaged in the process of forging a new consciousness, a new mentality that was based on a different sort of commitment. I gave the mayordomos a different focus. I called them the consejo parroquial. In the United States you might call them the

parish counsel. When I was there they accepted this change; but now I am not so sure, they may have returned to their previous understanding. And even though the leaders were mayordomos, almost all of the participants in the CEBs were women.

Padre Gonzalo initiated his work with the CEBs with a process of group biblical reflection. He explains: "Together, we began reading the Bible. At first they were resistant to beginning that process because they knew that in their neighboring town of Atlatlaucan the people there had become divided because of a conflict emerging over Bible study. And so they were cautious at first about this process of reading the Bible for fear that it would lead to conflict within the pueblo. For two years the group remained in the convento, continuing to meet and reflect, but then we went on a mission during Lent into peoples' homes."

Building on the work that his predecessor had begun, Padre Julio gave the CEBs a more concrete direction and focus: "I thought, their practice of faith in the Cristo needs to be enriched with works. And so I did two things, I gave workshops about the cultivation of soybeans and the other project I worked on was solidarity with Central America. The intention of the *talleres de soya* that I gave was to provide an *alternativa popular de salud*, because soybeans are more complete, more nutritious, for an impoverished population. With the solidarity project, we tried to motivate the communities to raise money for the Sandinistas, for the Nicaraguan people. We would send the money that we raised to the Diocese and then don Sergio would collect all the money and send it on. And we got cards from Nicaragua and a letter from don Sergio saying that we had given more money than any other community in the diocese. That was during the times of the revolutions in Central America. So I encouraged people to read *literatura popular*, literature published by popular presses, as part of a process of consciousness raising, *concientización*."

The mayordomía in Totolapan was not unique in its function as a means for organizing around current political issues. In nearby Tepoztlán, for example, in 1994 the influential and defining barrio mayordomal structure served as an effective mechanism for mobilizing the community against the construction of a luxury golf course within the boundaries of the pueblo. The *No al club de golf* campaign, in part a modern-day water rights struggle, forcibly removed the Mexican government and police from the pueblo and eventually succeeded in blocking the controversial construction project.[81] During the same period, mayordomal structures in Tepoztlán were also used to marshal financial support for the Zapatistas in Chiapas. Lancaster gives the example of the Nicaraguan town of Masaya, whose famously devout Indian residents organized their collective life around at least a half-dozen local religious fiestas but which was simultaneously "also a militant stronghold during the 1979 revolution."[82] In these examples, traditional local religious structures and institutions were put at the service of a liberationist, or otherwise politically radical, agenda. That is to say, Totolapan was not entirely exceptional in this regard.

Elsewhere in the diocese of Cuernavaca, however, liberationist priests working to evangelize parishes along the lines of Vatican II and the theology of liberation found themselves at odds with local mayordomías. An unpublished essay by Miguel Morayta dedicates a small section to the intracommunity conflicts created by such priests when they refused to collaborate with mayordomos, *rezaderos* (lay leaders of community prayer) and religious brotherhoods, or attempted to prevent access to religious images for devotional purposes. In essence, they sought to liberate believers from their devotion to the cult of the saints, which they saw as enforcing oppressive social structures. This especially was true in the case of the traditional pueblo of Acapantzingo, today part of Cuernavaca. In 1980 the parish priest there prohibited the celebration of an important local fiesta to San Isidro Labrador. The people of the parish were so outraged that they forcibly removed the priest from the parish and kept a twenty-four-hour-a-day watch in the atrio to prevent his return and to protect their saints. This stalemate lasted more than a year. Eventually, the community permitted a lefebrista priest to enter the church and celebrate Mass, which meant reverting to the pre-Vatican II style of liturgy in Latin.[83]

The friction between traditional practices and liberation theology was even more pronounced in Indian Chiapas and in the Indian western highlands of Guatemala. In Chiapas, for example, continuing a process of modernization that began in the 1950s, liberation theology was posited as a modernizing alternative to local customary practices, in particular to the burdensome cargo system. In many communities the excessive drinking related to fiestas and the weight of the cargo stimulated Protestant conversions in indigenous areas. The liberationist program of indigenous deacons that flourished under bishop don Samuel Ruiz purposefully undermined traditional practices in the highland villages.[84] Ruiz's version was voluntary, rather than obligatory, and provided an honorable way to remove oneself from the heavy demands of the cargo and fiesta system. Simultaneously, it also afforded enterprising young indigenous men educational opportunities and contacts with the Spanish-speaking world at the same time that it encouraged the use of indigenous languages, dress, and customs in a liturgical context. However, even in this instance in which liberation theology and mayordomías were seen as juxtaposed, Ruth Chojnacki's research on the Indian deacon program in modern-day Chiapas suggests that the work of these catechists was understood by the community and the catechists themselves as a sort of "cargo," with its own set of costs and sacrifices.[85]

This tension was played out most tragically in Guatemala, where revolutionary Catholic Indians, mobilized in part by the CEB movement and liberationist priests, publicly executed the head mayordomo of the Ixil region. The Ejército Guerrillero de los Pobres (EGP) had partially succeed, for the first time in Guatemalan history, in mobilizing Catholic Indians and their Spanish priests in the highlands along Marxist revolutionary lines in response to the murderous policies of the Guatemalan military government. As the most *principal de principales* (the mayordomo of all mayordomos), Sebastián Guzmán was a defender of Ixil tradition, culture, and custom, including devotion to local Catholic saints, and the one "upon whose shoulders the future life of the community fell."[86] When the CEBs became active in the region and began to organize cooperatives and educational programs, it brought them up against Guzmán who, exploiting relationships he had made related to the cargo system, had become one of the top contractors of labor for the brutally exploitative coffee plantations of the coastal region. There the cargo system had become, as Marvin Harris described it, essentially "a mechanism of domination and exploitation."[87] The CEBs also challenged Guzmán's religious authority, insofar as they "exposed the hidden ties between a [political] slavery inspired by religious fear and the practice of [traditional Ixil Catholic] custom."[88] The EGP also accused Guzmán of being a traitor, of turning over the names of modernizing (i.e., "anti-tradition"), revolutionary Catholics to the Guatemalan Army for execution. In 1979, apparently in the presence of a Catholic priest who had been "converted" to the EGP cause, members of the EGP publicly executed Guzmán.[89]

In Totolapan there was no such civil war, nor were the religious cargos particularly heavy or costly. Instead, the focus of the mayordomia was on brokering the collective, rather than individual, financial responsibility for fiestas. Leftist theologians writing within the Church sometimes cast liberation theology as a modernizing force against the magical thinking and "false consciousness" represented in popular religiosity. As a result, in some local contexts liberation theology pit itself against traditional, religious practices that were seen as irredeemably linked to a colonialist and conservative political agenda. I have shown that this was not the case in Totolapan, where liberation theology dovetailed quite naturally with local religious practice, thus underscoring Lancaster's powerful thesis that liberation theology was, in some times and places, "an outgrowth or subset" of popular religion.[90]

Cristo Aparecido Libertador: The Liberating Christ of Totolapan

Partly owing to their close association with the mayordomos, and in part because of the centrality of the image to the spiritual life of the people they sought to evangelize, Totolapan's liberationist priests were forced to grapple anew with the significance of the Cristo Aparecido. While Padre Gonzalo offered practical support to the mayordomos in their preparation for the fiesta, and graciously welcomed pilgrims to the parish, he also tried to influence the significance of the devotion: "Maybe today the people in Totolapan still celebrate their santo in the same manner. For example, the theme of death is very prominent because the people themselves have long been enslaved. But I hope that over those six years that I was priest there, I helped to give their devotion an aspect more in keeping with the gospel, more *evangélico.*"

A pamphlet that Padre Gonzalo wrote in 1983 and distributed during the fiesta celebrating the 440th anniversary of the miraculous appearance of the "Santo Cristo de Totolapan" reflects both the cleric's respect for the traditions of the people of the pueblo and his effort to shape their interpretation of those traditions along liberationist lines. Padre Gonzalo shared with his predecessor, Padre Lauro López Beltrán, a particular interest in the ministry of Fray Antonio Roa; and so this pamphlet recounts the missionary history of the pueblo and details Roa's efforts to evangelize the "natives." Several pages are devoted to a respectful treatment of the Cristo itself: its sojourn in Mexico City, its ceremonious return, its restoration, its second return in the arms of Bishop Sergio Méndez Arceo. But the pamphlet also reflects the ambivalence of liberation theology toward popular faith, and toward devotion to the crucified Christ in particular. Thus, the theological and pastoral reflections that conclude the pamphlet are an effort to shape that devotion; to imbue the cult with a liberating content. Padre Gonzalo writes:

> For our devotion to this Holy Image to become a force that drives our faith it is necessary that it is grounded in an appreciation of the Word of God through constant reading of the Bible and reflection, both individually and as a group . . . [and] that the Image is not the end point or goal of our faith, but rather a means of assistance and support on our path. Our faith [in the image] should lead us to understand who Christ was and why was he crucified, and how his crucifixion continues today. These reflections will lead us to discover that we are living in an unjust society and will ultimately bring us to denounce all injustice as contrary to the will of God.

The pamphlet echoes liberation theology's emphasis on the earthly life of Jesus and the sociopolitical roots of his execution. It also seeks to instill in the minds of the devotees an association of Jesus' suffering with the persecution and struggles of poor people everywhere in the present day.

Padre Julio Tinoco also explored with me how he had grappled with the centrality of the Cristo for the faith of the people of Totolapan:

> When I arrived in Totolapan I encountered a deep piety in the devotion toward the Cristo de Totolapan. I didn't really understand at first, but then I realized, that this Cristo was really something special. That is, don Sergio did a study, *una investigación*, about the Christ and he discovered that there is only one other Cristo in existence that is like this one, in Europe, that resembles so exactly a person that has just died. When I arrived in Totolapan, I tried to enrich the practice of faith with works, and to fortify and give life to the CEBs.

For the fiestas and the restorations I was the one, as priest, who always had to lower the Cristo and take it out on procession. Well, you know, the priest who wants to convert a pueblo also must himself be converted to the pueblo.[91] This is what Jesus did. When the time came for me to remove the Cristo for a procession, I always felt filled with respect and honor for what I was doing. Above all because it is an historic work of art, very old. It is made of caña and it weights almost nothing, but the cross itself is a little heavy.[92]

The mayordomos who participated as leaders of the CEBs today remember their liberationist priests with great fondness and speak of the "beauty" of their work in the comunidades eclesiales de base. Tolentino Vergara expresses this enthusiasm:

As a leader of the CEBs, I was like a professor, giving classes in different barrios of Totolapan. It was our job to transmit something to the people. We talked about problems within the family, social problems, and problems on the level of the community and the pueblo. There were lots and lots of people here involved in the CEBs (harta gente). We, the leaders, were the ones who traveled all over to go to meetings of all the [base community] groups. I went to meetings with priests in Toluca, Tepito, Guerrero, and other places. We also had meetings with the bishops. I talked with don Sergio a lot. With all due respect, of the bishops the best was don Sergio. I have a great deal of respect for him. And I loved him precisely because he always respected las gentes humildes. He was muy pacífico, muy tranquilo. He was beautiful, era bonito, don Sergio. He came and walked alongside, y convivió con, the people.

Don Tolentino recalls with great affection how they used to bring food to don Sergio when he would come to visit, "Most of all he really loved to eat antojitos. We would always bring him food, even if the place where he was staying would prepare him something. And he would always say to us, 'Look, I will eat what you have brought for me.'" Don Tolentino's voice fills with sad longing as he continues, "I was with the CEBs and I traveled all over. I went to meetings in Aquitlapan, Guerrero, in Río Blanco, Vera Cruz, in San Luis Potosí. In Río Blanco we were five thousand people, divided into twelve groups. We spoke about liberation; it was truly a beautiful thing. I spoke also with Bishop Samuel Ruiz of Chiapas at these encuentros, we were like a familia—all at one table."

In Totolapan, although the CEBs functioned under the auspices of the mayordomía parroquial, it is also clear that both priests and mayordomos often perceived caring for the Cristo and carrying out the duties of CEB leadership as distinct and unrelated, religious tasks. One did not necessarily influence the other. For the most part, therefore, it is difficult to trace the extent to which the process of liberationist concientización affected local spiritual engagement with the Cristo. Occasionally, in describing their relationship to the Cristo, today one hears mayordomos adopt phrases and themes from liberationist discourse. One elderly mayordomo who had been active in the CEBs explained to me, "You know, it is one thing to *rendirle culto al cristo*, to offer him our devotion, and it is entirely something else to *adorar*, to worship him. What we do is *rendirle culto*. To adore is to be like the rich who adore their gold, for example. We, let me tell you that we do not adore, in that sense." In this case it is possible that a Marxist critique of class found its way, through liberation theology, into the spiritual vocabulary of devotees. But it would be difficult to argue, on the other hand, that such critiques of wealth were not present even before the arrival of don Sergio and his priests; as Lancaster suggests, "traditional religion already embodies a strong if indirect class consciousness."[93]

Another mayordomo, in response to my probing, explained that "in the time of the CEBs the priests did say that Cristo came to liberate the people. Before it was always that the church had no reason to be involved in matters of politics. But liberation theology taught us that yes, in fact Jesus came to help those in need; and that is why they crucified him. That is why Pilate washed his hands, and we remember this to this very day." At that moment, I wanted desperately to ask if the Jesus who came to liberate people was one and the same as the Cristo Aparecido. But I could not bring myself to ask what seemed to me to be too pointed, and in some ways too forceful, a question.

Liberation theology's critique of popular religiosity did profoundly affect the faith of one Totolapan mayordomo in particular, don Julio. Julio is similar to his colleagues in many ways; he too is a campesino who works long hours on a small plot of land from which he harvests food for his family and a few peaches to sell. But he is more of an intellectual, and indeed more versed in the formal discourse of liberation theology. Books by Carl Sagan and Jon Sobrino line his small bookcase. He cultivates a sort of bohemian air, donning mod-style, thick-rimmed glasses for our meeting. We eat sweet canned peaches harvested from his land while he holds forth about his understanding of faith:

> The hierarchical church is still in diapers. It does not accomplish anything—only celebrations, baptisms, and *quince años*. This is not what God expected from the hierarchy. God wanted the institutional church to commit itself to what Jesus Christ wanted. Don Sergio was the bishop for the state of Morelos, and he was the bishop most committed to evangelization. The bishops today are very passive, not involved with the people at all. I was head mayordomo for one year, many years ago, but I didn't like it. I didn't like it because what mayordomos do is drown the people in traditions; and traditions are not always good. Let's say I am a mayordomo and I organize a fiesta and I have to ask each person for 150 pesos. And what if these are

very burdensome times for people? Then this poses a problem. Don
Gonzalo (notice how I don't call him "padre"—I never call a priest
"padre," I just call them don So-and-so) who was the main priest who
worked with us in the communities, he didn't like the fiestas. Well,
yes, he did like them but only if they were spontaneous, that is to say,
voluntary. Say, one year I don't pay the mayordomos because my
harvests were poor: either I don't pay or I don't eat. Once I was head
mayordomo. And in addition to this I have also been an organizer of
fiestas, but not as a mayordomo. I also worked with the Grupo de
Catequista y Evangelización. All that I am explaining to you is the
way that I have felt about things since I was evangelized with don
Gonzalo. I came to these understandings with him. It was with don
Gonzalo that I evangelized myself.

For several years now I have not gone to Mass. It is because these
new priests, they do not reflect on the Bible. They read it but they do
not reflect on it. I do still celebrate the Cristo. I don't have any
problem that the mayordomos organize fiestas for him. But that they
should place quotas on the people? This is not agreeable to God! It
should all be voluntary. All fiestas can be pleasing to God when they
are organized justly.

Finally, with don Julio I broached the question of Jesus' suffering directly;
I asked him whether indigenous people had seen in the image of the crucified
Christ a reflection of their own suffering. I asked him if people in Totolapan felt
that their suffering was connected to the suffering of Jesus:

The question of Jesus' suffering? Well the truth is Jesus even suffered
more than the indigenous people because he continues to suffer
when he sees our suffering at the hands of politicians and the United
States, which is the country that most screws with the rest of the
world. All the suffering that we pass through, Jesus sees it and
suffers also. But most people here in Totolapan, they don't realize
this; they don't understand that Jesus suffers because of our
suffering. This is a concept that is the culmination of a process of
education and evangelization, and for it one needs a good preparation
[i.e., along liberationist lines]. But this preparation doesn't just
happen from one day to the next. Here in Tototlapan we never got to
finish our process of evangelization and preparation because we lost
our liberationist priests.

When liberation theologians and politicized artists in the twentieth century attempted to recuperate the image of Christ crucified, they imagined that
poor and struggling believers suffering under conquest (both spiritual and
military) recognized in the image of Christ a mirror or reflection of their own

suffering. Or they posited that Christ's suffering might be able to represent or stand for the suffering of an oppressed and colonized people. Perhaps the experience of the Totolapans are a corrective to this view: don Julio's reflections challenge the notion that poor Mexican Christians necessarily understand their suffering and Christ's as related or analogous. For the people of Totolapan, identification with Jesus' suffering on the cross is neither the starting point for, nor the origin of, their relationship to their Cristo. Rather, this identification is the as yet unrealized endpoint of an interrupted process of liberationist evangelization, a process that may never be fulfilled or come to completion.

Conclusions: The Other Saints in Exile and the Undoing of Liberation Theology

In the late 1970s, Rome began to grow anxious about the increasing radicalism of the base community movement and begant to withdraw support and even to embark on a process of "dismantling the infrastructure" and underpinnings of liberation theology. The Vatican attempted, and failed, to endorse a more conservative agenda at the bishop's conference at Puebla in 1977, seeking to temper the more radical declarations of Medellín. In 1984, Cardinal Ratzinger (now Pope Benedict) issued his "Instruction on Certain Aspects of the 'Theology of Liberation,'" which was a lengthy critique of what he perceived as the errors of liberation theology. Ratzinger targeted theologians of the movement for censure and gave orders to close down some of the most politically engaged liberationist seminaries. In 1995, the Vatican formally silenced Brazilian theologian Leonardo Boff, in particular for his criticism of the power structures of the institutional church.[94] Throughout Latin America, radical bishops and priests were forced into early retirement or thrust into the margins of their respective dioceses, and replaced with political conservatives.

The aging priests and elderly mayordomos who shared their memories with me are the badly weathered face of liberation theology today. They are today's "saints in exile," simultaneously languishing on the margins of a Church that has turned its back on them and at the same time struggling to keep the tradition and commitments of liberation theology alive through their own work. They mourn the decline of the liberationist Church. With the passing of the time of the base communities, they have been left with a deep sense of nostalgia that comes with the experience of personal loss. Heavyhearted, don Tolentino concludes: "The time of the CEBs passed with the change of the bishops. The ones that came after don Sergio didn't want it. When Padre Gonzalo and Padre Julio were here things were improving for the people; but when they left, the meetings stopped. We were just getting started when we ran into problems. Now it is like we have lost our leader, our spiritual guide. But I still have all the materials from the CEBs meetings; and every once in a while I take them out and read them, even today." Padre Gonzalo, from his remote parish on the margins of the diocese agrees, "Certainly today liberation theology is not as strong as it was. It does not have as much institutional support. Just the opposite, it was repressed. It was a painful thing to see all of our hard work undone." But don Julio, for his part, insists that liberation theology is not a thing of the past:

> No! This never passes. It is like saying the scriptures are a thing of the past. There are no longer comunidades de base because there are no longer *luchadores sociales*. There is no one to organize them. And we are worse off for it. If there are communities mobilized, if we were organized, the governors would tremble. The government of the United States would tremble before us! Some day, when there are again priests that involve themselves in the life of the community, then the comunidades de base will return. Let me tell you, even if I was in my grave, if the comunidades came back, then I myself would rise from the dead to work with them!

What these people of Morelos remember as extraordinary about don Sergio Méndez Arceo is not that he had threatened their devotion to their saints but that in some slow but resolute way he became theirs, the bishop of the poor, *el obispo de los pobres*. Padre Julio recalls that don Sergio was always supportive and respectful of *la religiosidad popular*, imbuing it with positive value. Most important for the people of Morelos was the sense of convivio described above. What mattered was that the bishop spent time with them, accepted their invitations, attended their fiestas, and ate in their homes. They, in turn, became for him a beloved cathedral. When, in 1983 don Sergio went into forced retirement, people gathered at a celebration of his life and ministry in the parish of San Pedro Mártir in Mexico City. They greeted him with signs reading, "We, the poor, are your cathedral, each of us a founding stone . . . a cathedral that is taking root among the poor of Latin America, who struggle for a world of peace and justice."[95]

He was not just the "pope of Morelos," as one social scientist called him; rather the large numbers of the people of his diocese had come to absorb don Sergio into their own religious framework. In the end they cared for him much as they have always cared for their beloved santos; the bishop became the object of their affection, protection, and concern. One afternoon in the early 1980s, don Sergio descended the steps of the Cuernavaca convento surrounded by a large group of very humble, concerned, and intent peasant men. "We will protect you, don Sergio!" they declared with indignation. "Whatever they try to do to you, don Sergio, we will be there watching your back."[96] As to their numerous cristos, the people of Morelos were fiercely loyal to their bishop: in him the *gente rebelde* found, once again, their rebellious priest. Like their santos, for the people of Totolapan the bishop is often described as "beautiful." Listening

intently and attentively to humble people recount their struggles and tribula-
tions, the bishop's face would so often "cloud over" with concern.[97] Observers
noted how "don Sergio himself suffered with the pain of the other: the pain of
hunger, repression, and persecution; the affliction of each individual child,
woman, peasant, laborer, the affliction of entire pueblos [became his own]."[98]
His face became for them the countenance of the compassionate and suffering
Christ.

In the end, they did literally watch over him. At his death in 1993, a vigil
over the bishop's body was held at the cathedral. Around midnight, the staff
there advised the mourners that the cathedral was closing, and that they would
have to return the next day to continue their watch. At this, the people of Ocotopec gathered around the body of the man who had chosen their pueblo for
retirement. They could not bring themselves to leave their bishop alone through
the night: so they requested permission from then bishop Luis Reynoso to
bring the body back to their parish church where they could continue the wake
without interruption. The bishop granted their request, saying to his assistant,
"Let them them take him. If not, these Indians are capable of taking him by
force."[99]

In this chapter I have explored the aesthetics of liberation. By this I mean
not only the aesthetic project that don Sergio embarked upon in his diocese,
and empowered his priests to bring about. This was indeed significant, as it
implied a novel way of valuing the artistic within sacred art at the same time
that it worked to define the content of spiritual engagement with Christian
iconography. But I have also indicated the aesthetic value that participants in
the base communities attributed to their labors. They understood their participation in aesthetic terms—not only is their Cristo beautiful, but the sense of
community and of familia in the CEBs was frequently described as beautiful as
well. *Bonito* as well was their bishop, as he carried their Cristo home: beautiful
were the meals he shared with them.

In fact, today the aesthetic and artistic project may constitute the most
important institutional legacy of liberation theology in the diocese. Padre
Baltasar López, who served as Don Sergio's personal secretary and accompanied the bishop on his pilgrimage to Chalma, is today the minister of sacred art
for the diocese. Single-handedly he has sought to rejuvenate two important
neighborhood parishes in the city of Cuernavaca, by building modern "open
air" chapels next to the older, colonial structures—in part a creative response to
INAH's prohibition against major renovations to colonial buildings. In collaboration with INAH Morelos and the U.S. Federal Bureau of Investigation, Padre
Baltasar has embarked on a process of cataloguing all the santos in Morelos, as
part of a theft prevention and recovery program.[100]

The consequence for the people of Totolapan of the official discontinuation
and disassembling of liberation theology is instructive here. Theologians, clerics,
and secular critics have long worried that the worship of a "dead" and "defeated"

Christ leads people to internalize a sense of defeat. But I argue that the disappointment and despair experienced by marginalized communities does not result so much from the specificities of their spiritual practice, even when those entail devotion to an image of a crucified God. Rather it stems from real, concrete, and repeated experiences of defeat in political, social, economic, and even ecclesial arenas. More than their devotion to their Cristo, the undoing of liberation theology in Totolapan has led many people to a sense of despair and hopelessness.[101] These frustrated hopes were one factor that contributed to their confrontation with the explicitly anti-liberationist Franciscan friars who were sent to reside in the community by the conservative bishop who replaced don Sergio, as I explore in the chapter that follows.

7

The Gentle Devotions of a Rebellious People

The Phenomenology of a Santo

Scene 6. Atrio, Iglesia de Totolapan, 1998.

An angry crowd gathers in the walled monastery garden, in front of the colonial church of Totolapan. At the close of the twentieth century, the passionate local devotees of the same Cristo have locked shut the doors of their church, trapping their parish priests inside. The hostages stand accused of offending and insulting the precious image. Inside, under the watchful gaze of the Cristo Aparecido, the friars kneel to pray. Outside, the crowd debates whether to run the priests out of town or hang the offenders.

In the fall of 1998 the reverent believers of Totolapan rebelled against their parish priests. The Cristo Aparecido, their beloved patron saint and symbol of their collective identity, rested uneasily at the center of the conflict. At stake, the people believed, was their ability to celebrate their santo in the manner to which they and he were accustomed. Also at issue was lay access to the church and adjoining "ex-convento" which, in addition to serving as the parish church and rectory, function as a sanctuary for the santo.[1] Here the Cristo makes his home and receives his faithful; here the fiestas in his honor are planned and executed, and here pilgrims find shelter. From the perspective of the current local priests of the parish, a small company of Franciscan friars who have served since 1993, the ongoing devotion to this ancient representation of Jesus' suffering and death was hindering the development of the peoples' faith in the "living Christ." They therefore withheld their support from the annual celebration of the crucifix, preached against the cult, and turned away people bringing candles, flowers, and other offerings to the Cristo. The Franciscans were the Cristo's original critics, stimulating the Inquisition's scrutiny of the image in the sixteenth century. In the late twentieth century, the Franciscans again become the Cristo's primary antagonists. In the process of transforming the crumbling 450-year-old ex-convento into a functioning home for a modern religious community, the friars had also greatly limited the community's previously unrestricted access to church buildings.

In October of that year, roused by righteous indignation on behalf of their Cristo and hoping to defend and preserve their *usos, costumbres, y tradiciones*, the community attempted forcibly to remove the priests from their charge of the parish. So troubling was the clerics' perceived offense to the Cristo Aparecido that at the height of this conflict the mayordomos held the priests and two dozen of their loyal supporters prisoner, locked inside the church with the very Cristo that they were accused of offending. The drama of the incident even briefly captured national media attention.[2]

In the months leading up to and immediately following this decisive moment, the mayordomos, in their capacity as defenders and protectors of tradition and as community-appointed caretakers of the Cristo, sought a nonviolent resolution of hostilities. The mayordomos deftly solicited the intervention of the Instituto Nacional de Antropología e Historia (INAH), the national government-sponsored body mandated to protect the architectural and art historical legacy of the nation. Beyond its local significance for believers, on a national level, the Cristo Aparecido, like countless other objects of colonial sacred art, has been designated part of the *patrimonio nacional*, the collective legacy of a decidedly secular nation. Adding to the complexity of the conflict, which was in essence a local power struggle, the Cristo Aparecido, the church, and the ex-convento of Totolapan all fall under INAH's jurisdiction as the government body designated to safeguard this heritage.

The conflict in Totolapan thus came to reflect the fissures and fault lines that have riddled the religious and social landscape, shaping the history of Mexico since its inception as a nation. And so the diminutive Christ, *pobre de él*, was buffeted and jostled as three powerful sociocultural forces chaffed and rubbed: a secular, nationalist state; an institutional Church that still perceives itself as threatened and marginalized; and a popular, and to some limited extent autonomous, syncretic lay Catholicism. At the same time, these age-old frictions were rediscovered and reinvented in locally specific and novel ways. And so, in the name of the national patrimony, INAH wielded the force of state anticlericalism against modernizing friars and in defense of the Cristo Aparecido and the customary practices of local religion.

As authorities were challenged and allegiances made over the course of many months of tensions, varied and sometimes incompatible meanings of the Cristo were negotiated in the nexus of church-state-local religion. Though the friars remain as párrocos of Totolapan under a fragile peace, the mayordomos achieved a partial victory: the INAH intervened on behalf of local popular religious practice over and against the institutional church, affirming the may-ordomos' authority over the celebration of the Cristo, and even over the church and ex-convento.

In written pleas soliciting outside intervention, the mayordomos, on behalf of the community, strove formally to articulate to the secular govern-ment as well as to the ecclesial authorities the precise nature of the priests' transgression and the importance of the Cristo for the community.[3] They also circulated widely a questionnaire designed to buttress their case against the priests, the results of which were sent to then bishop of Cuernavaca, don Luis Reynoso Cervantes. The conflict with the friars also defined the content of col-lective public discourse in the pueblo for more than two years. Even several years later, questions I asked regarding the events that transpired that fall have the power to elicit anger and anxiety (but now also humor as well)—as emo-tions that have been repressed for the sake of harmony return quickly to the surface. The written correspondence, answers to 840 completed question-naires, and interviews with the leaders of the rebellion, the friars, lay people on both sides of the conflict, and INAH officials provide a revealing lens for accessing the varied and sometimes clashing meanings that the Cristo Aparecido holds for people on all sides still, in the early twenty-first century.

Against the backdrop of this contest, those aspects of local devotion expe-rienced as the most crucial stand out in relief as local devotees asserted and defined the significance of their Cristo, as against the interpretations and understandings of both INAH and the friars. The meaning of the Cristo for the people of Totolapan is evident also in the routine repetition of the annual cycle of fiestas, as the following chapter will assert. But these significances become even more starkly apparent, in a context of conflict and crisis in which emotions are intensified and division magnified. Not only are the shape and depth of the peoples' faith in their Cristo exposed in this dispute but the limits and parameters of this devotion become dramatically manifest as well. One meaning emerges as predominant: the otherwise elusive sig-nificance of the Cristo's status as a santo, a manifestation of the divine for the people of Totolapan and the central symbol of local religious and cultural col-lective identity. Through an analysis of the conflict in Totolapan in 1998, this chapter describes the phenomenology of the santo: first articulating the per-spective of the friars, then those of INAH, and then finally homing in on the understandings of devotees themselves.

Above all, in the nexus of this conflict, the theme of Christ's affliction comes suddenly, strongly to the fore. The motif of Christ's suffering erupts not with respect to the long-past persecution of the historical Jesus on the cross, but rather with respect to the perceived mistreatment and mishandling of the carved Cristo in the present time. In their devotion to the Cristo Aparecido, it is not the suffering of Jesus but rather the vulnerability of the material image itself that is the primary motif defining the relationship between believers and their image. For the people of Totolapan, at least in the context of crisis, the Cristo serves as a poignant metaphor for the vulnerability of their own embattled faith. This faith, still both potent and profound, has nevertheless been rendered fragile, in the experience of the believers themselves, by the collective memory of centuries of outside evangelization and the legacy of conquest.

In the Shadow of the Popocatépetl: Ethnographic Sketch of Contemporary Totolapan

This study is not primarily an ethnography of the pueblo of Totolapan, though I do seek to introduce you to some of local actors, and to give you, to the best of my abilities, a feel for the people and place itself—to share with you the sense of pride that people have in their community and their traditions. Today, the town of Totolapan itself is homely and humble, almost charmless some might say, a poor relation to neighboring Tlayacapan and Tepoztlán. Local businessmen lament that the two guesthouses remain empty while Tlayacapan, less than five kilometers away, has a thriving tourist industry, drawing weekend shoppers in search of bargains on locally produced pottery. Tepoztlán, some thirty kilometers away, is Totolapan's most glamorous neighbor. Dramatically nestled in the mountains at the foot of a pyramid, Tepoztlán has been studied, restudied, and studied again by anthropologists. It is ethnographic ground zero, if you will.

As a community that preserved a strong sense of its indigenous origin, Tepoztlán was the site of Robert Redfield's and later Oscar Lewis's groundbreaking anthropological studies. Today it is a Mecca for hippies, new agers, and artists, both Mexican and international. Pilgrims from diverse religious traditions also come to climb the steep rocks to the pyramid to receive its "healing energies." I myself regularly made the rigorous sojourn up the mountain with my husband and eldest son. Once, we trailed behind a Moslem sheik who, perfumed and adorned, labored up the rocky mountainside and then removed his shoes to pray at the top of the ruins. On another day a college group of evangelical Christians gathered in the same spot to sing, clap, and shout their praises to Jesus.

In contrast, Totolapan, also a pueblo proud of its indigenous origins, has been neglected for the most part by outsiders. Occasionally a bus full of tourists, mostly European, or groups of Mexican school children arrive in Totolapan as they travel the *ruta de conventos*, the self-guided tour of colonial conventos and churches in the region. But for the most part Totolapan attracts no hippies to draw on the energy of the place; no generations of foreign anthropologists and their intellectual interlocutors; no artisans, no weekend tourists from Mexico City. Archeologists as well have found little of interest in the area. The literature included in an information packet distributed by the local City Hall laments, "The municipio of Totolapan is one of those territories forgotten by the government scheme to recover and rescue historic sites. Apparently, this neglect is due to the fact that in Totolapan there do not exist any obvious archeological ruins or even any evidence that would motivate further research or exploration in this zone." Studies of Totolapan completed in the past century are by affectionate parish priests with an eye toward popular religiosity, like Lauro López Beltrán, and self-studies written primarily for local consumption, like a collaboratively authored volume published in 2000.[4]

In these histories, the Cristo Aparecido looms large, as he does in a chronology of the history of the town distributed by the City Hall. In this list of major events affecting the pueblo there are a mere twenty-two entries. Beginning with the arrival of Toltecs to the region in the twelfth century, the document marks such notable events as Cortez's conquest of the region, the arrival of the Augustinians, and Roa's tenure in the pueblo. Revealingly, at least three entries concern the fate of image of the Cristo Aparecido himself. And the chronology concludes, quite abruptly, with the arrival in 1935 of Lauro López Beltrán, the parish priest who was to become Roa's twentieth-century biographer. The same materials include a section designated for "famous personages of the municipio and their works." Under this category the author has written, almost forlornly, "In Totolapan, to this date, there has not existed a single illustrious person."

By pointing to the neglect of the pueblo by outsiders, I do not mean to give a "lost-in-time" feeling to the town. On the road leading to Totolapan one will find shops dedicated to the latest global fads, including one hawking whatever accoutrements are necessary to "Feng Shui" your home and life. There is easy access to the internet in Totolapan, and the children of more affluent families turn in their high school essays computer-printed with full-color graphics. Some families make periodic trips to shop at the Wal-Mart in Cuernavaca. There is also a small but fairly constant flow of migrants and reverse-migrants back and forth from the United States, mostly to San Juan Capistrano, in southern California. They continue to participate in the annual fiesta in Totolapan, as I discuss in the following chapter.

The municipality of Totolapan has maintained a stable population of between 7,000 and 8,000 residents for the last several decades at least, though only some 4,000 of these live in the pueblo proper. Unlike Tepoztlán, Totolapan has not yet, after all these centuries, recovered its antediluvian population (that is, before the flood of illness and destruction brought by the conquest), estimated at about 20,000 at the time of the conquest.[5] Today the people of Totolapan, who have not spoken their ancestors' Nahuatl for at least three generations, describe themselves as peasants and farmers. The population of the town is characterized by an increasing economic diversity. But locals often explained to me that though they now count among their numbers a handful of doctors, shopkeepers, and schoolteachers, still "we are all *meramente del campo*, a country people."

Every family, even those trained in other professions, harvests at least their share of crops produced on their *ejido*, or collectively owned plot of land. And many hold private lands in addition to these, where they also grow tomatoes, onions, tomatillos, corn, peaches, and other fruits to sell at the local market, or at the larger markets in Mexico City, and always for their own table as well. My research was slowed during the intense harvest season (mid-September through the beginning of November) when the entire community, even those well into their seventies, work from dawn to night, seven days a week. The poorest and most marginal members of the community are migrant agricultural laborers from the nearby state of Guerrero, who work for the locals for about nine dollars a day and live in makeshift camps on the outskirts of town. Many of them speak little Spanish; and for the most part they do not participate in the local cycle of fiestas, though I did on a few occasions observe women and children from the camp who had come to pray in front of the Cristo. With the obvious exception of the migrant laborers, the community explains that they have experienced increased economic prosperity in the last thirty years.

The people that I interviewed for this study were largely from the petit-bourgeoisie living in the center of the town: the proprietor of the successful "mini-super," small shopkeepers selling dry goods and snacks from their front doors, the owner of a successful tortilla factory run out of her home, a woman who ran a small vegetable stall at the market. But among my informants were also several who had never known any work other than agricultural labor. I also interviewed members of the local mayordomía, which includes a surprising degree of economic diversity in its ranks.

Though the town crouches low in ancient mountains with a smoking volcano, the Popocatépetl, looming in the distance, the locals seem to worry little about the threat of volcanic eruption.[6] As I will suggest, there are other threats that they experience as more acute: the constant fear of drought that might blight their crops, and anxiety about a plethora of perils that menace their beloved Cristo Aparecido and, by association, the integrity of their community as a whole. If the volcano is at risk of eruption, then so too are Totolapan and the surrounding pueblos periodically explosive, disrupted by intracommunity conflicts of the micropolitical sort.

With respect to the religious context of the community, by and large, the people of Totolapan are, in broad terms, Roman Catholics. But against the sense of a homogenous religious landscape that this would seem to imply, is the reality of diverse identities, sometimes of a polarized and conflictive nature, that define the religious culture of the pueblo. The broad category of people categorized as Catholics is ruptured by a dizzying variety of distinctions. There are Guadalupanos and mayordomos (those principally devoted to the Virgin of Guadalupe, and those more exclusively dedicated to the Cristo Aparecido); leftist cynics and agnostics; charismatics; those who favor the current priests and those who oppose them; those who defend the reforms of Vatican II and those who regret them; and, finally and most definitively, there are *creyentes* and then there are *católicos*, that is, "believers" and "Catholics." But almost without exception all of these subgroups are devotees of the Cristo Aparecido. Nevertheless, the last of these distinctions requires explanation.

Though Mexico is, according to all sources, an overwhelmingly "Catholic" country, I never actually met a single person in Totolapan who willingly claimed the designation "católico." Doña Bonifacia, who spends a good portion of her life organizing the community-wide pilgrimage to visit the Señor de Chalma, a nearby Catholic shrine, was typical in this regard. She explained to me that she calls herself a creyente because she does not go to church much: "Often the católicas are those women without husbands, so they have time to be at church constantly. They have time to pray morning, noon, and night." Doña Bonifacia estimates that only about 20 percent of the population of Totolapan was actually católico. Doña Erlinda, who has had several miraculous experiences mediated by the Cristo Aparecido, also identifies as creyente. She agrees with Bonifacia that "those who are católicas are the ones who are always in church." And, in her experience, they are, without exception, women. For Bonifacia, Erlinda, and many others, the term *creyente* provides a certain dignity to a spiritual practice that seemed (to them) to fall short of ecclesial expectations. That is, *creyente* is a claim to faith, to belief, though in the most modest and humble terms. Bonifacia and her daughters laughed gently at the "antics" of the católicas, who, in less flattering terms, might be referred to as "church mice." In this context, the designation *católica* contained a jab, an edge of mild derision. But at other times I also heard a note of deference, respect, and admiration in the use of the term, as if it was synonymous with "good Catholic" or even "good Christian." Conversely, people shied away from claiming the title for themselves, lest they be seen as arrogant or putting on airs.

The sense of *católico* as being applicable only to those singularly devoted to God was expressed most forcefully by community elder don Bruno. He insisted that, "Here in Totolapan were are all creyentes but we cannot rightly call ourselves católicos by any stretch. Not even one hair on our heads is católico. To be católico you have to focus completely on religion, on faith, on God. Here we are pure devils, *diablos bien hechos*, because we devote ourselves not to God but to drink, women, and vice."

For some in the community, the rejection of the term *católico* was of a more explicit and definitive nature. This is true, for example, with don Felix, who explained that after some disappointments he had faced with the bishop and local priests in the late 1990s, he had "had it" with the Church. He said, "I am a Christian, *creyente pero no católico*." That is, "I am a believer, a person of faith, but not a Catholic." He went on to explain: "You see, to be a Roman Catholic means that you go to mass every single Sunday, that you tithe to the church, that you confess regularly and receive communion. Creyentes, we do go to Mass but not because it is an obligation. We go only when we want to, when we feel drawn to go. We creyentes, we have only God and our images. That is what we care about, that is the religion of the creyentes." For don Felix and for others claiming the term, *creyente* sometimes seemed to level a critique of the institutional Church and the "impossible" demands of its clerics on its very human flock. Of the ninety men serving as mayordomos in the pueblo, don Felix estimates that perhaps 15 percent are católico.

But where were these católicos? Eventually, through much diligence and effort, I was able to meet with two women identified by the rest of the community as definitely católica: doña Isabel and doña María de los Ángeles. Even they shied away from the word, reluctant to claim the epithet for their own. "Well, there are many ways of being católico," doña Isabel explained, "One way is to be a 'committed layperson.' That is what we call ourselves. We are not católicas but *laicas compromitidas*. "What does it mean to a be a laica compromitida?" I asked. "Well, we go to mass every day, or at least once a week. And we keep all of the fasts indicated in the church calendar. We are also part of the parish school for evangelization."

While the distinction between creyente and católico may be particularly pronounced in Morelos, which has a long history of anticlericalism, it was a distinction that I encountered wherever I traveled in Mexico. Its origins may date to 1940 when, in a gesture of rapprochement with the faith (though not necessarily with the Church), Manuel Ávila Camacho famously referred to himself as *creyente* in his campaign for the presidency.[7] Here he sought mostly to distance himself from the explicit atheism of many revolutionary leaders, most notably Francisco Mujica. Perhaps what I encountered today in these rural communities was a popularized appropriation of this distinction. It is possible that the distinction has older origins, a current rearticulation of a prior sentiment along the lines of that encountered among colonial Yucatecan Indians. Frustrated with the endless efforts of the Spanish to dictate the norms of Catholic belief and practice, the Indians insisted that they were in fact the true Catholics. In all its various uses, it seems to me that the term *creyente* allows believers to define the parameters of their own spiritual practice while simultaneously preserving a relationship with the tradition and with other people of faith.

With respect to religious diversity outside of these diverse expressions of Roman Catholic faith, both Pentecostals and Jehovah's Witnesses have found recruits in Totolapan. The Jehovah's Witnesses, whose local founder was for many years among the most committed devotees of the Cristo, count perhaps some three or four dozen members. Though a Pentecostal church occupies a store front in the town plaza, evangelicals have not found fertile ground in the pueblo. After almost forty years of effort, they claim a mere fifteen members and among these, says the pastor, are only a few who actually are truly living according to the dictates of the Bible. In spite of his best efforts, many continue to honor the Cristo Aparecido. Possibly the most vibrant alternatives to conventional Roman Catholicism in the region are those traditions that offer high and richly aesthetic liturgies. In the 1970s, followers claiming allegiance to an anti-Vatican II splinter group founded by the dissenting French Cardinal Walter Lefebvre took control of the parish church and ex-convento in neighboring Atlatlaucan, leaving the Catholics marginalized to a small neighborhood chapel. And in nearby Tlayacapan an impressive Iglesia Copta Ortodoxa, Coptic Orthdox church, was under construction at the time of my research. I believe that the popularity of these alternatives stems from the fact that they possess an even more pronounced emphasis on tradition and liturgy than that provided by contemporary Mexican Catholicism.

Though there is no single local ritual or practice that I encountered that is immediately identifiable as pre-Columbian, the people of Totolapan understand themselves as both syncretic and traditional in their beliefs and practices. They are wedded to their customs just as they are wedded to one another, and they are prepared to go to "extremes" to defend both their traditions and their community. Nevertheless, the careful listener observes that their discourse bears the imprint of successive waves of evangelization, just as they maintain a collective memory of conquest that continues to affect their relationship to outsiders.

The Anatomy of a Conflict: The Friars and the Cristo

The Franciscan friars came to Totolapan in 1993 from their house in Mexico City, a small community founded by a group of Italian brothers only twenty-five years earlier. Their arrival in Morelos, scarcely a year after don Sergio Méndez's much-mourned death, both coincided with and contributed to the final stages of the official undoing of the theology of liberation in the diocese of Cuernavaca. The friars literally displaced Padre Julio Tinoco, the liberationist diocesan priest who had preceded them as párroco of Totolapan. On August 28, 1993, the very same day that the Franciscans took possession of the ex-convento, Padre Julio packed his bags and left the parish where he had spent ten years evangelizing the community along liberationist lines. Under his ministry, the people of Totolapan had, as we have seen, lived out a praxis of solidarity with their brother and sister struggling peasants in Central America. Padre Julio packed ten years worth of weekly CEB reflections (literally thousands of them) into boxes, distributed some of his liberation theology texts to the local leaders of the CEBs, and departed. It was, or so it seemed, the end of an era.

Handsome, dynamic, *morenos*, sometimes brandishing a down-to-earth folksiness, the Franciscan friars are theologically conservative and have been experimenting with charismatic Catholicism. They brought to their ministry among the traditional people of Totolapan a distinctly modern cynicism regarding the popular faith of Mexican country people and in particular a deep skepticism toward the "miraculous" as understood by their flock. Most possessed little understanding of the liberation theology that had shaped the religious life of the people for the last two decades, nor is it part of their curriculum of seminary study. "Liberation theology? Isn't that when the priests helped people find jobs in factories?" one young novice answers me quizzically. One of the more seasoned friars, however, expressed an explicit tension with the theology of those who had preceded them:

> When we came here to Totolapan we had to deal with the priests who
> came before us. Liberation theology was the problem. You see they
> preached that Christ was a revolutionary and that we should take up
> arms and kill the rich—they preached that Christ was against the
> rich. Well, maybe not exactly in those words. But when we came and
> talked about a God of love, forgiveness, and sacrifice and a God who
> wants the rich and poor to be equal, the people here said, "This is not
> the God that we know." They didn't exactly say to us that God was a
> revolutionary, but they didn't understand our message either. They
> do not accept a Christ outside of the cross.

Nor did the friars know much about the community of Totolapan itself before they settled there. They came in search of a quiet and tranquil place where they could found a seminary, and where they could live together in contemplative community, engaged in theological training and in silent prayer. "Our idea was to have a convento for novices, where we could give classes," Padre Salvador explains. Unlike their Augustinian predecessors who founded the monastery almost five centuries earlier, these friars did not come as zealous missionaries with a concrete or specific vision for the evangelization of the people of Totolapan. Nor did they have any particular interest in the cult to the Cristo itself or in administering a sanctuary. In fact, ministry to the locals seemed to be for the most part incidental to their initial vision.

Some of the friars' local supporters imagine that they were sent to Totolapan by don Sergio Méndez Arceo himself; the supposed association with the much beloved bishop lent legitimacy to their presence as ministers in the town. But Padre Salvador himself explains that it was instead his successor, Bishop Luis Reynoso, the less popular and archconservative bishop, who had welcomed this small group of friars to the state of Morelos. Luis Reynoso, bishop of Cuernavaca from 1987 to 2000, was appointed to the diocese by Rome with an unofficial mandate to rein in the radicalism that don Sergio had inspired. Reynoso's episcopacy was also hostile to local traditional organizations like mayordomías—and the use of charismatic priests to undermine these organizations was part of his general strategy.[8] In February 1992, Reynoso found himself in the awkward position of presiding at the funeral of the bishop emeritus. The cathedral was literally packed with don Sergio's friends and admirers, come from around the globe to grieve his death and mourn the institutional dismantling of liberation theology. When Reynoso had tried to speak to don Sergio's social justice vision, cynical crowds shouted him down, chanting, "We want bishops on the side of the poor." They shouted until "the walls of the cathedral shook," and don Reynoso was forced to fall silent.[9] The plaintive question hanging in the air that day remained unanswered, "don Sergio—and now who will opt for the poor?"

Bishop Luis Reynoso and Padre Conrado, the Italian friar who then headed the Franciscan group, had met years earlier in the course of their seminary training. So the bishop had gladly granted his friend permission to occupy one of the ex-conventos in his diocese, and to return it after centuries of "secularization" to its original function as a priory. Padre Salvador explains, "don Luis Reynoso offered us various options and we had to evaluate the best one for us. Although Totolapan was not on the original list, we had passed by it on our way to Tlayacapan and went back to have a closer look. We chose Totolapan because we were looking for a quiet place, appropriate to our need for silence." Padre Salvador looks at me sheepishly, "What can I say, we first visited Totolapan after the annual fiesta had come and gone," he explains, referring to the explosive and deafening *cohetes*, the fireworks, that are an integral and constant part of local religious celebrations. Laughing, he adds, "Here there is much noise and it is far from tranquil," alluding to the ever-present specter of the conflict.

According to the friars and those who support them, they found the parish church and ex-convento in total physical disrepair. "There was not even a place for them to cook," recalls María de los Angeles, an active member of the parish sympathetic to the friars. "It broke one's heart to see them cooking outside on an open fire, their faces covered in soot. The poor novices! The upstairs rooms where they were to live were completely deteriorated. There were no doors or windows. They saw all this and suffered very much—the young novices were afraid that there were ghosts in the convento. They would joke and say that they had only a rock for their bed—they would sleep on the floor because Padre Julio, when he left, had taken everything with him. He didn't leave beds or blankets or even a radio for the novices." Another laywoman disdainfully describes the convento's practical functions during the principal fiesta honoring the Cristo: "Before the time of the friars the church was nothing more than a public bathroom, a cantina, and a hotel." The *huerta*, traditional monastery garden, that is one of the few in the nation to remain intact (in most pueblos and cities the expansive and valuable land was sold off during the years following the Reforma of the 1850s) was to them no more than a "jungle" littered with trash and garbage, waiting to be tamed and recovered. It seemed that the generation of liberation-minded priests who had occupied the church for almost two decades had shown little interest in maintaining the physical grounds.

The Franciscans' vision was to transform the four-hundred-and-fifty-year old ex-convento into a functioning modern monastery for two or three priests and four novices, and a modest center for theological education. This was no easy task, given the challenges of rehabilitating and maintaining such an old building (the church was originally constructed in 1535); and the limitations on restorations and alterations were carefully legislated and monitored by INAH. In any case, the friars and many of their local lay collaborators failed to perceive the extreme age and heritage of the building as an asset. Rather they saw it as a hurdle, an obstacle to the ministry they sought to develop. The black and ochre sixteenth-century frescos that adorned the walls of the convento, probably painted by indigenous artisans, did not elicit in them the romantic memory of valiant and pious missionaries who had come before them. They know only a little about Roa himself, but basically consider that his ministry to the people of Totolapan was a failure, as is clearly evident to them in the persistence of "pagan" customs among the local population. As the friars saw it, the frescos gave the building a ramshackle, impoverished, and worn appearance: "You should have seen how ugly it was before," explained the church secretary who, having observed my comings and goings with much suspicion, had watched like a hawk while I talked to the priests and seminarians. Clearly not the types to shy away from a challenge, these men had their work cut out for them.

When I first arrived in the convento in September of 2003, I found two young seminarians overseeing the destruction of the sixteenth-century frescos. Flagrantly disregarding the authority of INAH in the matter, they were haphazardly dismantling the early colonial works that had successfully weathered an independence war and a revolution. In other colonial churches in Morelos, I had observed students from INAH's National School of Restoration in Mexico City laboring over the same type of frescos with fine paintbrushes, painstakingly working to preserve the national patrimony.[10] The young seminarians supervising the demolition in Totolapan were gregarious, smiling, and interested in my questions. "Really," one confided as the stucco wall crumbled behind him, "we are here to break up the power of the mayordomos, to get these mayordomos in line a little bit."

Yet one sees that these energetic brothers are trying to bring a new vitality to their church, in their own way. The comments of the current minister of sacred art for the diocese, articulating the issue more generally and from a liberationist perspective, are illuminating: "The Church has a different perspective than INAH on these matters. INAH wants to preserve everything at all costs. For us the church is not an architectural monument, it is a living community. And so, if a renovation gives the community life, you have to do it. Even if it means tearing down a colonial building; if it brings new life to the people, then it must be done." In Totolapan, where the graceful frescos once recalled an earlier time in the history of the Mexican church, Roa's time, and the time of the origins of the cult to the Cristo Aparecido, today the walls are freshly plastered and whitewashed. Corkboards adorn the walls, advertising upcoming retreats and recalling, in clumsily hand-lettered slogans, the message of St. Francis. Two corridors still retain most of the original frescos intact: INAH inspectors arrived in time to rescue these from the friars' modernizing vision.

The mayordomos describe the first year that the friars occupied the ex-convento as relatively harmonious. The friars promised that they had not come to challenge local customs, that they would respect the traditions of the people. In fact, their focus was really more internal, on establishing their community. Eventually, though, the friars' plans for the ex-convento collided with the mayordomos' sense of entitlement to the use and maintenance of the physical grounds.[11] For the mayordomos, this included use of rooms both upstairs and downstairs for planning meetings and as art studios for creation and storage of *adornos* (decorations) for their fiestas, and use of the old cloister garden for socializing and strategizing. They also made use of the roof of the ex-convento to launch their cohetes, beginning in the wee hours, for more than a dozen annual fiestas.

One former mayordomo, once an active leader of the base community movement, traces his disillusionment with the friars to an encounter that occurred toward the end of their first year in the parish:

> I began serving as a mayordomo in 1962. But I left in 1993. During
> all that time, I was always there in the church, tied to the apron
> strings of the priests, *pegado a las faldas de los curas*. When one priest
> arrived I attached myself to him until another came; then I attached
> myself to the next. How did I leave the mayordomía? One evening, in
> 1993, there were about four of us mayordomos talking in the *claustro*
> garden. It was about eight o'clock and we were hanging out and
> waiting because we had a prayer to lead at eleven o'clock that night. It
> was Holy Thursday. And there we were just talking, outside. Of
> course, we know that if mass is starting we shouldn't talk too loudly.
> So we were *tranquilo*, talking calmly and quietly. But then the priest
> came out and shouted at us "Go outside!" But we were being very
> quiet. This was before the conflict with them really got started so we
> were a little surprised and offended. We didn't leave so he turned out
> the lights on us, trying to force us out. So then one of the mayor-
> domos got up and turned the light back on. The friar came back out;
> he was really angry and yelled at us to leave. We said to him: "Why
> should we leave if this house isn't even yours: it belongs to us all."
> And from that time, we have had bad faith in the friars. From that
> moment, I left the mayordomía and stopped being so attached to the
> church.[12] That was really the end. We were betrayed by the friars. The
> day that Padre Conrado came to take charge of the parish, he told us
> that he came to serve, not to take away our customs. With all the
> previous priests, they always did what the people wanted, but not the
> Franciscans.

Another community elder had left the mayordomía to devote himself to directing the Moros y Cristianos play that is performed each year at the annual celebration of the Cristo.[13] He explains, "We used to have our meetings in the rooms upstairs in the convento. When don Sergio was bishop, they even used the convento for classrooms for the children while the high school was being built. And now, *ya todo invadieron los padres*, the priests have completely taken over the place. It is like when someone comes to your home, takes over and moves in."

Friction also mounted as the priests began to develop a concrete pastoral plan for the community. "If we could teach the people here one thing, it would be for them to learn that faith does not rest solely in the cohete, in the firework," Padre Salvador explains. "They should know that for every cohete they launch into the sky, God would be even more pleased with the prayers of a repentant heart floating up to heaven." The friars then began to preach against the cult, trying to shift attention away from the Cristo and toward what they perceived to be a more doctrinally correct devotion to the Santísimo Sacramento, the consecrated Eucharist which they keep in the tabernacle behind the altar, right below the nicho where the Cristo resides. "When we got to Totolapan, the people didn't even know what the Santísimo Sacramento was," Salvador explains. We were really surprised when they asked us, 'But *who* is the Santísimo Sacramento?'"

A laywoman now working closely with the friars who is one of their staunchest supporters explains the content of their ministry:

> They came and said the Cristo was a work of art that was made by an artist; it was a monument, a statue. Or as our brother Protestants would say, an idol. They came to teach us to believe in the Jesus of the Eucharist, Jesus that lives. They told us that we were worshiping a dead Christ. And that because Christ has risen, that we should not be stuck with an image of Christ deceased. These lessons were very hard for us and at first they didn't explain themselves so well. At first it made me angry because I had seen my parents kneel before the Cristo and honor it. So I didn't like what they said. It took them a while to explain it all to us, to explain that Christ has risen. Now the center of our faith is the living Eucharist.

In spite of the friars' repeated invectives against what they saw as local preoccupation with the "dead Christ," I arrived one day to discover that the Franciscan seminarians had adorned the parish church for the Feast of Saint Francis. Most impressive was a large tomb they had elaborately constructed with the corpus of the deceased Francis inside. Once could actually enter the tomb and bring offerings to the saint. The irony of the friars' devotion to their dead founder, given their frequent criticism of local devotion to the "dead Christ," was not lost on the local community.

My primary intention here is to point out the way in which the friars' understanding of the Cristo oddly overlaps, at least for a moment, with that of the INAH, as they appropriate a secular, art historical language to deride the cult. The santo is a mere "object of art." It is not of divine origin, but was created by human hands. In this regard, the friars stand in the long line of "enlightened" clerics seeking to moderate popular devotions that stems back at least to the Bourbon reforms of the late eighteenth century.[14] The INAH, for its part, has deliberately moved away from such language in its search for a vocabulary that is less overtly antagonistic to popular practice. One mayordomo explains, "They called our Cristo a work of art, a statue, like any old statue of Zapata, or a bullfighter." In this assertion he casts aside two icons of Mexican cultural nationalism, asserting a local religious identity over and against the secular national identity propagated in the public schools and television.

The distinction between art and icon introduced in the previous chapter is perhaps most clearly apparent in the story of doña Mara and her crucifix (figure 7.1). Doña Mara, spry at ninety-eight, lives in Tepoztlán, some twenty miles from Totolapan, where she has been the guardian, caretaker, and principal devotee of another miraculous crucifix since her adolescence. Hers is also probably of colonial origin, though later in the period, and is larger than that of Totolapan, almost life-sized. Today the Cristo resides in her living room, and the shrine devoted to him overwhelms the space. She has created not just a domestic altar but a home chapel. She was first introduced to this Cristo when, at the age of fourteen, she married and went to live in the home of her mother-in-law. She is fond of telling the story of the narrow escape of the image from a foreign art collector, and of her abusive husband's mysterious death at the Cristo's hands:

After I went to live with my mother-in-law, my husband would beat me, sometimes with his belt. I still have scars and dark marks on my shoulders and back and chest where he hit me. Once I ran home crying to my mother and she said, "You wanted to get married this young, it was your decision, go back to your husband." I was afraid of him, the way he used to hit me. I had a sister-in-law also who lived in the house but she didn't really care for the Cristo. But I always brought him flowers and lit candles for him. So when my mother-in-law was dying she said, "I give him to you."

People come to me and I cure them, I rub flowers on the body of the Cristo and then I rub them on people to do a cure. I cure many things, and also calm cranky children who don't sleep. People used to come a lot and visit the Cristo but not for the last few years—they don't believe anymore—they prefer to live like animals. I hate to say it but I am a bit crude that way. They used to come from all the barrios and brought flowers. Without the flowers it is really ugly. One

FIGURE 7.1. Doña Mara and her cristo in her living room chapel, Tepoztlán. Photo by author.

day some gringos came to visit him and they gave me some money. With that money I bought a new cross for him. And once, I sang in Nahuatl at Bellas Artes and I made a good amount of money and so I bought his silver crown of thorns.

When I have no money I eat just bread, but when there is money I make tamales. When there is nothing I cry to him, to the santo, "¡Ay papi, I don't have any tortillas!" And then he takes care of me. And someone comes and leaves ten pesos as an offering. My husband used to beat me all the time; he was a drunk, a *borracho*. We were married for forty-eight years. One day I came home to find that he had sold the Cristo to some gringos. I yelled at him, "How could he do that?!" He said, "The Cristo is mine, not yours," and then he called me *una cabrona vieja*, a cantankerous old bitch.

Doña Mara pauses and has a good laugh over that one and continues with her story:

Then I said to him, "Get out! And I hope the dogs on the street eat you alive." When I got home I saw that they had pushed aside all of the Cristo's flowers and had taken the mantilla off of his head. The gringos had come with a big truck to get him. At first I told them that no, they couldn't have him. But then I said that if they must take him, that they had to take care of him, that he had belonged to my mother-in-law and that they should light candles for him and make sure that he always had flowers. And so in the end they left without him.

And at that very time, that very day, my husband got sick. He couldn't urinate for three days and his stomach was huge and swollen, he was all stopped up. And his daughters came and took him to the hospital but it was too late. That is how he died, because he tried to sell the Cristo. And let me tell you, I did not even go to the funeral and to this day I don't know where the man is buried.

Tensions between the mayordomos and the friars increased as the clerics disappointed community expectations that they would extend concrete support to the cult, in particular to the annual fiesta. Their traditionally assigned role was not only to celebrate the masses, of which there are almost two dozen over the course of three days, but also to greet the pilgrims from various communities upon their arrival, to welcome them and offer each group an individual blessing. They celebrated the masses, begrudgingly and for a fee, but they declined on principle to greet the pilgrims as they arrived. The friars also refused to allow the mayordomos to set off cohetes from the roof of the ex-convento, with the excuse that the explosions potentially weakened the structure of the colonial building. Even after several representatives from the group in charge of fireworks went to petition the priests, the friars continued to deny access, and today the cohetes are launched from the ground, in front of the public bathrooms, an area unquestionably within the mayordomos' jurisdiction.[15]

The friars also discouraged and sometimes even turned away devotees bringing flowers or candles for the santo. Today, having learned something from the conflict, Padre Salvador has adopted the language of "catechizing" popular religion rather than eradicating it. He explains, "At a certain moment the people thought I would touch their faith in their Cristo, that I had come to change their traditional customs. The thing is that you need to shape and give direction to popular religion. Ideally, you can keep the devotion to Christ or popular religion but you have to direct it. For example, there are many wasted flowers at the fiesta. And so I suggested that perhaps instead of flowers people could bring rice and beans as an offering to the Cristo. And then afterward these could be divided and shared among the people. But they didn't like this idea. I am not sure why they rejected it."

Tensions between the friars and the mayordomos escalated in April of 1998, when some mayordomos discovered that one of the oldest santos in the community was missing from the church.[16] That very afternoon, the mayordomos, who suspected foul play, visited Padre Salvador to bring to him their inquietudes regarding the missing imagen. The missing santo was an image of Christ at the Column (though his column is long since missing), which the people call the Señor de la Preciosa Sangre. This image is brutalized and baroque: this Christ's wounds are particularly deep, ribs exposed. "*Le abrieron,*" one man observes, "they opened him up." "This is the most famous and valuable Cristo in our community," don Felix explains. "When groups of tourists come, mostly Europeans, he is the one that they really want to see. It is because he is made from real human skin, his skin was donated by a Moor who converted to Christianity, or maybe it was an Indian. He is made with real human bones and real teeth." The Totolapan's Cristo de la Purísima Sangre appears alongside at least two other local images of Christ's passion in Roziére and Moyssen's art historical overview of Mexican christs, while the more famous Cristo Aparecido himself is strangely and inexplicably absent.[17]

"He is the *santito feíto.* The little ugly one. You know the one: a squinty-eyed santo. When I was a girl my grandmother used to take me to see him and I would be afraid," another parishioner observes. "If you wait patiently, praying, and look at him for a long time, just in the right way, his skin almost looks like it is alive. It looks like real skin." Another woman explains, "It is not that he is ugly really, but he has a bad appearance, it is a bit scary, he looks like he has been burned."

The santito feíto, the ugly little saint, did not hold a particularly prominent place in the pantheon of Totolapan imágenes. They are not always certain that he is a cristo at all. He did not even reside in the nave of the church, alongside the Cristo Aparecido, Mary, Christ Entombed, Christ on the Road to Calvary, and San Isidro Labrador, patron saint of campesinos. Rather, he had been housed in one of the storage rooms in the ex-convento when he disappeared. In spite of his relatively marginal status for the community, the mayordomos took immediate action, only to discover that Padre Salvador himself had taken the Cristo de la Purísima Sangre to INAH Morelos, in Cuernavaca, for a restoration paid for out of the priest's own discretionary fund. The pueblo's dwindling confidence in their priest was thus further shaken by the fact that he had taken this initiative without consulting with them. And so, at an emergency meeting that very evening, the mayordomos voted to accompany Padre Salvador the following day to INAH to discover for themselves the whereabouts of the saint. At this meeting, the mayordomos also began to organize a *junta vecinal,* a civic neighborhood organization that they later used to initiate their own ties with INAH, thereby strengthening their position against the friars.

INAH restorer José Nao explains what occurred the day that the mayordomos arrived at the INAH Morelos offices in Cuernavaca:

> In the case of Totolapan we were in error. One of the errors we made was that we worked directly with Padre Salvador and bypassed the mayordomos. You see he came to us with a santo that he wanted restored that he was going to pay for himself. It was the Cristo de la

Columna. But then, one day fifty mayordomos from Totolapan showed up asking where the santo was and saying that it had been taken without their permission. And then we at INAH realized our mistake and we apologized and asked their forgiveness and once they saw the santo was here they felt better and even contributed money to the work. Since then we have worked directly with the mayordomos, always in communication with them.

This encounter marked a turning point for INAH Morelos's relationship to the Totolapan mayordomía, a turning point reflecting a national shift in INAH's attitude toward these lay religious authority structures. In the last several years, all across the nation INAH has sought out a more collaborative rather than adversarial relationship with local cultural leaders in their efforts to coordinate care for sacred art. In this regard, INAH is participating in a global trend among directors of museums who seek to handle objects of religious significance with more sensitivity toward their cultural uses.[18] INAH has moved to actively endorse the idea of popular devotions as composing part of the cultural patrimony of Mexico.[19]

The Irruption of the Mystical in the Modern: INAH Cares for Christ

> The aesthetic and the iconic are two worlds of thought. In the case of works of art they are bound one to the other by the physical object, the artifact, which is, as it were, a body in which two souls dwell.
> —Robert Redfield[20]

INAH was already deeply involved in the spiritual life of the community as modern-day *santeros*, restorers of saints. It was inevitable, then, that INAH enter the fray over devotion to the Cristo. INAH did not posit itself as a neutral mediator between local and institutional religion, but rather as champion of the cultural patrimony, seeking to rescue the living traditions that provided local cultural context for the Cristo's continued national significance from the intervention of the institutional church, and most of all its meddling clerics.

Still, the mayordomos' alliance with INAH was both a cautious and at times uneasy one. They perceived that INAH's approach to their Cristo differed profoundly from theirs, and thus they were careful to delineate the parameters of INAH's authority in the community. And for INAH too, such allegiances were relatively new to them and thus a bit awkward and fraught with ambivalence. In conferences and a series of articles written by restorers, published on INAH's official Web site titled "Letter from the Restorer," INAH grapples with what it means to care for these images with profoundly religious significance.[21]

These reflections compel us to consider as well what it means when objects of active religious significance, and the Cristo Aparecido in particular, come under the care and jurisdiction of a revolutionary, secular state that has long been antagonistic to both local and institutional public expressions of religion.

Created by state decree in 1937, INAH's primary mandate was to care for and preserve the extraordinary pre-Columbian archeological legacy of Mexico.[22] INAH probably had a de facto authority over colonial church buildings from its inception, but there was little interest in interpreting or valuing these structures as part of a national legacy until the 1930s, when nationalist fervor stimulated a reexamination of sixteenth- and seventeenth-century ecclesial structures.[23] Certainly by the time that don Sergio began to plan his radical restoration of the Cuernavaca cathedral in the mid-1950s, INAH had become a force to be reckoned with. INAH was originally skeptical of the plans, and the bishop was obliged to exert his considerable powers of persuasion to gain their approval and consent.[24]

It was not until 1972, however, that INAH's jurisdiction over churches and ex-conventos was codified in law. The Ley Federal de Monumentos y Zonas Arqueológicos, Artísticos e Históricos clearly designates all existing structures built from the sixteenth to the nineteenth centuries, as well as their contents, as historical monuments and therefore considered "inalienable property of the nation" under INAH's jurisdiction.[25] It also includes within its purview all church documents, written communication, and archives from those centuries. While in some ways analogous to being declared a national landmark, the designation is not necessarily a formal process or procedure but is assumed for all churches and their contents from all but the twentieth century.[26] Under the 1972 law, INAH became an instrument in the ongoing administration of state-appropriated Church property. Through extending INAH's mandate to include preservation of churches and conventos, alongside the nation's tens of thousands of identified pre-Columbian archeological ruins, the state signaled the incorporation of these structures into a valued place in the historical legacy of the nation while simultaneously affirming its jurisdiction over what was until the 1850s church property.[27] INAH represents, among other things, the institutionalization and formalization of state secularization of church property.[28]

Plaques and placards bearing INAH's name now mark the entryways to major ex-conventos throughout the country. As visual markers of the state's solicitous presence, they define the place of ecclesial structures within a secular, nationalist framework. In this way, INAH engineers the transformation of ex-conventos into state-run museums. At the Museo del Ex-convento de San Juan Bautista en Tlayacapan, near Totolapan, colonial santos that have been appropriated and restored by INAH are now displayed alongside macabre mummies of the key personages of local colonial society, exhumed from the church crypt in the recent restoration. This is a tragic fate for the santos, images once revered and celebrated as manifestations of the divine. Often inadvertently but sometimes deliberately, the Church's own historical process facilitated INAH's efforts. Vatican II's removal of the images of saints from churches, anticipated by and then implemented enthusiastically in the diocese of Cuernavaca by Bishop Méndez Arceo, freed up many santos to be available for incorporation into INAH exhibits.[29] In any case, on a sunny Sunday morning in Tlaycapan, museum patrons study the mummies in a room that still functions as the church sacristy. The recessional procession of presbyters, acolytes, and colorful *estandartes*, or banners, of a mid-morning Mass winds its way through glass museum cases and past the cluster of disheveled backpackers. Don Sergio himself gazes down from a large color portrait hung on the wall, as if studying the bewildering scene that he may well have helped to create.

From behind a desk in her bustling office, Teresa Loera, national director of INAH's Department of Restoration, explains: "There are two ways to value these things, one is the value of faith, and the other is the value of the patrimonio cultural." For INAH the images are not santos, as they are for believers, but neither are they simply *obras de arte*, works of art esteemed for their aesthetic or commercial value alone. Instead, INAH regards them as artifacts similar to historical documents: "Conservation is a social, scientific, and technical process whose goal is to preserve the patrimony as resource for understanding the past, a means of confronting the present, and a tool for building the future."[30] INAH's method of restoration reflects this approach. Loera explains:

> We are trained to prevent and deter the deterioration of the saints. We restore according to both the aesthetic and historic value of the work. When you do a restoration you have to be careful to preserve the work as an [historical document]. For example, if there has been a fire and the saint has been burned, it is important that when you do the restoration that you can still see that the saint has survived a fire. *Hay que dejar vestigios.* If it is missing a foot or a hand you don't just add a new one because you don't really know what that foot or hand was like before. The images need to be preserved as documents that *platican una historia*, communicate a story, even when it is a history of abandonment and neglect. This is what should remain for subsequent generations. Even works that have no apparent beauty at all are cared for as part of the patrimonio cultural.

Employing social-science paradigms, INAH restorers imagine themselves as cultural workers with a pedagogical function. In a sense their goal is to "elevate" the faith of the popular classes, imbuing religious rituals and traditions with a legitimizing revolutionary nationalism, in which restoration is conceived of as a process of consciousness raising.[31] Today INAH restorers do in fact engage the participation of local populations in restorations, but mostly so that these communities come to understand their santos in what they would view as a modern and rational way, as "testimonies of the history of their country and as part of the patrimonio nacional."[32] Thus, INAH has its own project of evangelization. One restorer explains, "only if we approach our work as restorers by way of a deep iconographic analysis of works of sacred art . . . only then will we be able to understand the cultural weight and significance contained in that patrimony, and only then can we direct it, *dirigirlo*, and project it, responsibly, into the future."[33]

In this sense, the professionally trained INAH restorers who work "according to international norms of restoration and conservation," differ dramatically from their predecessors, the traditional santeros, those who were entrusted by the community of believers to create and maintain saints according to the norms of lay, folk culture.[34] According to Loera, the santero is one who simply "dedicates himself to repainting the saints. And if the arm breaks off they don't repair it or preserve it, they just make a new saint." But the role of the santero is perhaps more nuanced and complex than she admits. Unlike the INAH restorer, the santero was of the same faith and mindset as the communities who employed him. His goal was to preserve the saint for its cultic function, to keep it in active use and circulation. At times this meant preservation and conservation; and at other times it meant the creation of a new saint in the likeness of the expired one.[35]

In one sense, however, INAH restorers are not utterly dissimilar from their santero counterparts and the believers themselves. The restorers do, in fact, honor and esteem these images also, paying them homage not with candles and flowers but with fine paintbrushes, delicate instruments, and long hours of painstaking effort. In an INAH studio, or on site in communities, one can observe the restorers as they dote on and labor carefully over a santito, all the resources of a modern nation at their disposal. The image is x-rayed, laboratory analyses are done, biologists and chemists and other experts are consulted; a national school of restoration has been created to teach careful methods. Is it not possible that the imágenes themselves might in fact appreciate these ministrations after all?

Still, INAH's scientific attitude toward the Cristo Aparecido is clearly revealed in the comments of an INAH restorer from the most recent restoration. "The Cristo of Totolapan is made of *quiote de maguey*," explains José Nao, as he draws me a sketch of the maguey plant with an arrow indicating the long woody shaft that emerges only every twenty years from its center. This is the part of the plant that was used in the construction of santos. "That is how we know that this Cristo was made here, in the New World, and not brought from Spain, because it was carved from a native plant." A recent art historical study of restoration methods of the *cristos de caña*, the original New World crucifixes, includes photographs of the nearly clinical and scientific setting of mock autopsies performed in order to understand the caña technology. The broken bodies of *cristos* and other saints are exposed to harsh lights upon operating tables in what appear to be surgical theaters. Samples of the images' "flesh" are taken, examined under microscopes and diagramed.[36] For the believers of Totolapan, devotees of the Cristo, this technical, medicalized, and art historical treatment of the saints is anathema.

The Totolapan mayordomos are well aware of the INAH's secular approach to their beloved Cristo, and to village santos in general. Perhaps this is the cause for local concern over and ambivalence toward the official restoration of religious objects that is prevalent throughout the state of Morelos. The negative effects of INAH's interventions on their Cristo have long troubled devotees. They perceive restorations as traumatic to the santo, at best a necessary evil, and the people of Totolapan fret over the trauma caused to the Cristo by the many restorations that have sought to preserve him from deterioration. The Cristo is watched carefully at all times throughout these restorations, attended by a group of mayordomos who keep vigil, monitoring the restorers during every minute of their work. Part of the task of the mayordomía is to insure the santo's comfort and modesty; they are careful to prevent his being unnecessarily exposed. As is true elsewhere in Mexico, in Totolapan women are not traditionally allowed to be present during the restoration of a male saint and, according to the staff at INAH's Morelos office, during the restorations of male saints anywhere the state, even women restorers are only barely tolerated.

Often it seems that the restoration is unwelcome, and is rejected by the saint itself. The Cristo Aparecido is said to shed new layers of paint or protective finish within a matter of days. Doña Alejandrina recalled that on one such occasion some seventy years ago when she was a little girl: "He shed the restoration, just like you shed a nail or the paint from a finger nail. They tried to paint him but it just didn't stick. But ever since then the Cristo changed colors. He used to be a lovely kind of wooden color and now he is sort of *cremita*, cream colored." Sometimes the Christ acts preemptively to ward off a restoration. Once, he broke a little finger as he was being taken down for a procession. The day before he was to leave for INAH, the people found that the Cristo's finger had miraculously regenerated, thus narrowly escaping a harrowing restoration.[37] In fact, part of what often marks a sculpted image as a "saint" is this self-renovating capacity. There is a tradition of *Cristos renovados* throughout the history of Mexican folk piety. Images of Mary often reveal their miraculous nature not in regeneration but rather in their incorruptibility, their ability to maintain a pristine appearance over time. William Taylor suggests that the ability of a sculpted cristo to self-restore may be related to the theology of the resurrection, whereas Mary's incorruptibility relates to her ever-virginal state.[38] In either case, the miraculous nature of saints often makes the work of INAH restorers extraneous or obsolete in the eyes of the true believer.

In Totolapan, where high value is placed on the historical originality of the church and the Cristo for their association with weighty and miraculous events, restorations are sometimes seen as detracting from the originality of the image. Don Bruno, who directs the annual performance of the "Doce Pares de Francia," the local version of the traditional Moros y Cristianos pageant, explains what happened when the eighteenth-century oil paintings of Fray Roa were restored:

> Yes, one day Sergio Méndez took them away. According to him he was going to restore them. But then three or four years passed and they were not returned. So we organized a group, we were told that maybe the retablos were already in DF [Mexico City] but he couldn't say exactly where. When the retablos were finally returned they had been retouched. Before that you could really see the original work. Now you can't see original paint anymore. *Perdió su originalidad, ya es cosa moderna*, they lost their originality and they are now modern things. They are not as beautiful as they once were, before they were really beautiful. Now it is like when you shine your shoes, there is another layer on top of the original.

In Totolapan, devotees' suspicions about INAH's true intentions were also expressed in the process of ascertaining the whereabouts of the Roa paintings: "Certainly they were stolen from us for a restoration," they surmised. And indeed INAH's frequent removal of local colonial saints to Mexico City for restoration and "safekeeping" might be understood as modern-day examples of *furta sacra*, as practiced by the Augustinians of yore. Vallejo's paintings of Roa were, in fact, warehoused for many years in the Cuernavaca cathedral, long deemed of inferior quality and dubious spiritual content. The canvases were rediscovered by the engineer Juan Dubernard, subsequently restored, and returned to the parish church of Totolapan in 1992.

To a great extent, however, the Totolapans share with INAH a desire for the preservation of the Cristo. Totolapan may be unusual in this regard. Often the art historian's desire for preservation of sacred objects of historical value works at cross purposes with an image's ritual or cultural use. Preservation is not always the highest good from a cultural perspective. In one U.S. instance, the Zuni agitated for the return of their war gods fashioned from wood. The museum eventually returned the objects, and the Zuni placed them once again in sacred caves, where the "hand-carved figures gradually aged and deteriorated, reaffirming the cyclical nature of all man-made objects and perpetuating the delicate balance between omnipresent spirits and the foibles of humankind." For the Zuni, maintaining the deities in archival conditions (acid-free boxes and climate-controlled containers) was a violation of their sacred purpose.[39] In Mexico, in other pueblos where less value is placed on historical originality, believers have found themselves at odds with INAH for an analogous reason. Their preference is that the colonial images look "new" and "attractive," and so frequently repaint them in vibrant colors. INAH staff often find themselves confronted with the challenge of a colonial image to which thick layers of bright paint have been added, to prepare the saint for processions or feast days.[40]

An ambivalence toward INAH's project persists in Totolapan, nonetheless. One community elder, don Otilio Adaya, attributed a loss of respect for the Cristo Aparecido to a recent INAH restoration. He observed to another researcher: "Before [the restoration] you never used to hold the Cristo with your hands, there was a special cloth that you used to pick it up. Now he has lost the people's respect. Before we didn't used to see the Señor Aparecido all week long, there was always a curtain up in front of him and we would get to see him only in Mass on Sunday. Not long ago the Señor went to be restored, *y ahí se le perdió el respeto*, that was where he lost the people's respect."[41] Elsewhere in Morelos, often an image will need to be "resacralized" or reconsecrated upon its return from a restoration, suggesting that the restoration itself is a desecration.[42] This must have been one of the understood effects of the ceremonious return of the Cristo Aparecido from restoration in 1954 by don Sergio, the chief sacralizer of anything in the diocese of Cuernavaca in 1954.

INAH does try to bear in mind the potential reaction of devotees to their restorations. In the case of the Señor de la Purísima Sangre, for example, José Nao explains the care he takes to make his restorations acceptable to believers, even as he appeals to scientific authority:

> One of the beliefs that the people of Totolapan hold is that the Señor de la Columna (also known as the Señor de la Purísima Sangre) is made from the skin of a converted Jew. But that is not true. We took x-rays around eight to ten years ago. The ribs that you see are not human, as the people believe; they are from a cow. The teeth are a child's baby teeth. The wounds are lined with paper of the amate plant to simulate jaggedness. When we received that santo it was very dark, *de piel oscuro*, from all the incense and candles and dust accumulated over centuries. And when we cleaned it and painted it we tried to keep it a little bit dark so that the people would not be so startled by the restoration.

In spite of INAH's efforts, people were unhappy with the restoration of the Cristo de la Columna. Doña Luz recalled how after the restoration of the santo, which she had affectionately dubbed the "santito feíto," they even gave him a new red-and-gold skirt. Even so, his appearance was only slightly improved: "Basically, he is still ugly," she concluded. Bonifacia says of him, "He was restored and now he is lighter. But we didn't want him restored, we wanted him how he was, *morenito*, with dark skin."

Even though they are sometimes dissatisfied with INAH's involvement in the care of their saints, the entire community of Totolapan contributed financially to the restoration of the Roa oil paintings. Teresa Loera describes how she arrived in the pueblo one day and was surprised to receive several large baskets from the mayordomos, woven hampers containing several thousand dollars entirely in loose change. "It created a dilemma for us," Loera explained, "I was very moved, shaken by their generosity, but I couldn't find a bank that would accept all of those coins." Even after this experience of collaboration, the mayordomos maintained their suspicion of INAH's motives. For example, recently INAH requested permission to borrow the two oil paintings of Fray Antonio Roa for an exhibition in Mexico City. The mayordomos refused. If people wanted to see the paintings, they said, they could very well get on a bus and come to Totolapan. "And we don't charge anything either," they added.

Beyond the process of restoration, INAH's efforts to protect the Cristo Aparecido from the loving ministrations of his own adoring devotees has caused other sorts of friction with the community. Believers struggle to maintain an active devotion to the image as a processional object, in spite of its physical deterioration over almost five centuries of liturgical use. At the same time, in the interest of preserving the nation's patrimonio cultural, INAH restorers have actually worked in conjunction with parish priests to moderate the cult. In the last several years, for example, they have requested that processions be reduced from four times to merely twice a year. Most devastating for believers, they have discouraged devotees from touching or kissing the image on his annual feast day, as has been their custom from time immemorial. It is noteworthy that a similar decision was made centuries prior with respect to Juan Diego's tilma, the Virgin of Guadalupe at Tepeyac. In this case, in 1677 the archbishop handed down a decision that the glass case in which the image was housed not be opened, presumably to protect the image from repeated ritual engagement by devotees (touching and kissing).[43] Similarly, INAH restorers worry that these reverent kisses and caresses will corrode the Cristo Aparecido's delicate surfaces and that each procession exposes the Cristo to the potentially harmful elements. Here INAH's concern about the corroding oils of human hands parallels and reiterates the peoples' own anxiety about the damaging effects to the Cristo of restorations at hands that are spiritually "unclean." But when the priests adopted the use of toilet paper to wipe away the "damaging" saliva from kisses left on his cross, as an intermediary step before eliminating the ritual altogether, the people themselves worried over the offense that might be caused to the saint by the liturgical use of such an obscenely mundane implement.

The parameters of INAH's authority in the community were made clear to me at a recent celebration of the Quinto Viernes festival. When I observed that devotees were not going to be granted physical access to the image, I inquired of one mayordomo whether this was because INAH had prohibited it. "¡INAH no manda acá! INAH does not give the orders here!" was the sharp reply. "The santo is of the people, it is owned by the community. And it is very old and very fragile and therefore *intocable*, untouchable, because it could be damaged and corrupted by the sweat on peoples' hands. It is *we* who decided this, as a community, to protect our santo."

Recently, INAH has also been involved in moderating the cult rendered to the Señor de Chalma. The annual number of pilgrims who come to honor this Cristo is second only to the faithful who call upon the Virgin of Guadalupe at her Basilica de Tepeyac. In the last decade or so a sheet of protective Plexiglas has been placed behind the nicho of the Señor de Chalma. Pilgrims to Chalma from Totolapan explain that the Plexiglas now present at the shrine is there to protect the saint from defilement by their own peccant hands, rather than as the priests have said—to safeguard him from the slow wearing away caused by the endless file of pilgrims who reach out for a moment to touch the *piesitos* (feet) of the image, rubbing away infinitesimal particles and leaving oils that corrode the paint. The Augustinian friars who administer the sanctuary explain that INAH placed the glass there to protect the famous crucifix from such injurious devotions; but Loera denies INAH's participation in this. "Possibly our restorers made that recommendation, but ultimately it is not our decision," she explains. "The priests do as they like and then pin the blame on us. We value the images for the care with which they are made, for their historical value, but also because of their association with living traditions. What do I care if the Cristo's foot gets a little messed up? That doesn't matter to me so much—what is important is that we help maintain the living value of the object." In any case, INAH does not claim authority or power to legislate over popular practices and devotions for either for Chalma or the Cristo Aparecido. José Nao said explicitly that it is not within his jurisdiction as a restorer to require alterations to the cult.

INAH has similarly intervened in preserving a colonial image of Christ as an infant, the Niño (or Niñopan) de Xochimilco. With this image, the local community seemed less resistant to incorporating INAH's protocols. In fact, the community saw INAH's prohibitions against flash photography and touching the image as an aid in creating an appropriate attitude of reverence toward their Niño. The INAH prohibitions were posted there in front of the image, alongside others advising the faithful "not to eat or drink" in front of the saint.[44]

My suspicion is that the practices of locally based INAH restorers have not kept pace with their director's more conciliatory attitude toward the active devotions of the people. At the same time, however, it is likely that at Chalma, as in Totolapan, friars seeking to moderate the cult appealed to INAH's authority in the matter, using an art historical rationale to further their own theological agenda, in this case restraining the enthusiasms of popular devotion. In the case of the Cristo Aparecido, we have seen how the Franciscan friars appropriated art historical discourse to deride the cult; even where INAH worked to subvert the friars' authority, there were areas of collaboration. The shared agenda stemmed from the fact that both restorers and modernizing friars share a more strictly "secular," "rationalist," and "non-miraculous," attitude toward the santos. Neither, of course, relates to the Cristo as a santo—as the object of devotion and veneration he is for the people of Totolapan.

The Totolapan mayordomos thus brought to the conflict in 1998 a history of collaboration with INAH, but also a strong dose of suspicion of this government agency. Even as the mayordomos appealed to INAH for assistance, they sought to define the significance of their Cristo and its cult as against INAH's more secular understanding. In this regard, their relationship with the friars was strangely similar: the mayordomos' tensions with the friars grew out of a relationship characterized by intimate collaboration, mutual dependence, and a deep mutual distrust.

On the deepest level, the devotees diverged with INAH in their final assessment of the image's value. Devotees themselves seem entirely unimpressed by the INAH's notion of their Cristo as part of the patrimonio nacional. In fact, I rarely heard them employ the term *patrimonio* at all, and never in reference to their Cristo. There were a few occasions, however, in which believers spoke with some pride of their sanctuary as belonging to the *patrimonio de la humanidad*, thus circumventing the question of nation altogether, to place their sanctuary (UNESCO-style) within a global human heritage.

The Cristo and His People: The Community of Believers

On July 20, 1998, just two months after the friars refused to offer a ceremonial welcome for the returning Cristo de la Columna, the mayordomos drafted a letter to Bishop Reynoso in which they clearly articulated the source of their disaffection for the friars. They did so in the hopes that he might intervene, and send them new pastors. "We have a Cristo . . . in which our grandparents, our parents, and we ourselves have tried to inculcate respect and veneration," the letter begins. It then articulates four key areas of contention:

- The [Franciscans] treat him very poorly, as any old worldly object. And they almost all have said that he is an idol of wood that has no value because the real God is found in the sky and in our own hearts. But especially the older people felt attacked by this sort of attitude to our Imagen; and this has been the cause of many people distancing themselves from the church.
- On the day of his traditional feast day, the 5th Friday of Lent, the friars are very bothered by the burning of cohetes, the participation of *bandas musicales*, and by other things to which the people are accustomed.

- The pilgrims and dancers who participate in the celebration are accustomed to receiving a small message from the priests at the beginning and conclusion of the festival—of encouragement, peace, and blessing. But the friars refuse to offer this blessing, and by so doing hurt the feelings of these persons who leave the fiesta very disappointed.
- They place many obstacles to our preparation of the decorations used to venerate the santo Cristo, making this labor tedious and difficult. Some who bring flowers to the altar are questioned about why they do this, and are told that it would be better if they brought *dispensas*. All these traditions are neither from this current time nor limited to this pueblo. They are practiced throughout the region, from the time that we had the use of reason and they have been inherited, passed down from generation to generation. And for this to end is in the first place very sad, and in the second, almost impossible because of the hold they have upon us.[45]

The bishop did not offer any immediate response. Unsatisfied with his silence, in August of 1998 the mayordomos formed a Junta Vecinal por el Bienestar de tu Comunidad. The constitutive document declared that the junta's principle objective was the preservation of the traditions and customs of the community (*usos y costumbres*), and of religious festivals in particular. Second, it claimed responsibility for monitoring all projects and modifications of the ex-convento, insuring that the original style remain intact.[46] Marshaling articles from the national constitution, federal laws legislating the "Preservation of the Patrimonio Histórico," and local municipal government edicts, the mayordomos argued the validity of their case against the friars. Among the junta's elected members are several of the most influential mayordomos but, interestingly, the list also includes a young woman who was working at the time as the assistant to the municipal president.

At the end of August, the junta mailed a copy of its constitution to the INAH in Morelos, in the hopes of making of them an ally against the friars— which may indeed have been the primary purpose in forming the junta.[47] In a parallel strategy, the mayordomos founded an *asamblea comunitaria* with the intent of impelling local government support, as well. Within two weeks INAH responded to the mayordomos' request by sending an official letter granting institutional legitimacy to the junta as an auxiliary organ of the INAH, renaming it the Junta Vecinal Pro-Conservación del Exconvento de San Guillermo en la Población de Totolapan. INAH's letter marshaled specific provisions of the federal law regarding "Monumentos y Zonas Arqueológicos, Artísticos e Históricos" to add weight to its determination. This was the law that had first codified INAH's national jurisdiction and instructed it to make precisely this sort of alliance wherever it deemed it appropraite.[48] INAH now empowered the

Totolapan junta to care for the ex-convento, to educate the community about the importance of the preservation and conservation of historic sites, and to promote all activities that contributed to the growth and enrichment of local culture. Finally, the letter requested the junta to advise INAH authorities of any unauthorized construction or rehabilitation that might occur within the ex-convento.[49]

In effect, this letter lent state sanction and protection to the local fiesta for celebrating the cult of the Cristo in its traditional form. Even more damaging to the friars' authority, it asserted the mayordomos' control over church buildings as INAH's "watchdogs." Largely due to this allegiance with INAH, the friars came to see their dispute with the mayordomos as a church-state issue, rather than as a more complicated problem internal to the church, one that might be posed in terms of laity versus clergy, or local versus institutional religion. Bishop don Luis Reynoso's written response to the mayordomos, when it came, was defensive rather than pastoral. He regarded them not as disgruntled members of the Church community but as outside agitators. Appealing to state laws protecting religious associations and public worship, the bishop argued that "the mayordomos may not interfere in questions internal to the Church, least of all in its internal governance."[50] For the bishop, the source of the mayordomos' alienation was the very success of the friars in "fortifying the faith of the people of Totolapan." Finally, the letter curiously referred to the mayordomos as *hermanos separados*, separated brethren, the Vatican II term for Protestants.[51]

Tensions finally exploded on Friday October 9, when Bishop don Luis Reynoso arrived in Totolapan in person for the first time since receiving the community's letter. He came, in principle, to celebrate several long-overdue confirmations; but his main purpose was to respond formally to the mayordomos' request that he remove the friars from their ministry there. After celebrating the confirmations, the bishop asked to meet with a small group of representatives, the members of the *directiva* of the mayordomía. But for the people of Totolapan, the time for such polite communication had passed. By now, a large crowd had gathered in the atrio; and they were agitated, insisting on hearing the bishop's letter read to them all, then and there. After the bishop addressed the crowd they became even more agitated and angry. "His letter did not make any sense," they later reflected. "He was being deliberately indirect and evading the key issue at hand."

Those in support of the friars and those against them jostled and shoved one another—shouting threats and jeers. Upon seeing this agitation, the bishop did not hesitate to make a quick exit. He fled ensconced by a circle of loyal local churchwomen, "católicas," who, arm-in-arm, surrounded the bishop and guided him unharmed to his car. With attention momentarily directed away from him, Padre Salvador retreated into the safety of the church, sequestering himself away from the angry mass. Further enraged by their pastors' retreat, the mayordomos frantically rang the church bells, signaling an emergency to the rest of the community, who quickly poured into the church atrio. The last time such an alarm had been sounded was several decades prior, when two thieves had been discovered long past midnight in the act of stealing three santos from the church (the Cristo Aparecido was not among them). On that occasion the community was in the process of lynching the criminals when the police arrived. In the situation at hand, where much of the local community perceived that the honor of their Cristo had been affronted, such a grim outcome was also not entirely outside the realm of the possible.

The ringing of the church bells signaled the mayordomos' decision to take action, finally, against the Franciscans. They locked the doors of the church from the outside, trapping Padre Salvador and the several señoras who defended him inside the sanctuary. There they remained captive for perhaps two hours while the crowd outside considered seriously the possibility of running the priests out of town. In the end, the crisis was averted as those outside decided that even though the group sheltering the friars was a small minority, the issue should not be allowed to divide the community.[52] Specifically, they wanted to avoid the fate that had befallen the people of nearby Atlalaucan, which had turned against one another, run their priest out of town, and then spent more than twenty years without a pastor. And so, the doors were unlocked, the friars were released, and the crowd eventually dispersed.

In the perception of the women who were inside the church with Padre Salvador, this moment was a turning point for the friar. "It was at that moment," they explain, "that the Padre finally came to believe in and honor our Cristo." "We love Padre Salvador, but we didn't always like how he treated our santos," doña Luz explained. "When he was locked inside the church, Padre Salvador fell on the ground before the Cristo, he kissed the ground, repenting, saying that he had failed, that he never meant to divide the people." Salvador himself claims no memory of his own supposed conversion: "It wouldn't have occurred to me to kneel in front of the Cristo," he insists. "Perhaps I knelt to pray awhile in front of the Santísimo Sacramento (the consecrated host) and the people were confused." However, for Luz and for other women supporters in Totolapan, this was a conversion moment for Salvador and even more important, a sign of the Cristo's persistent and unflagging power. This is a Christ that for centuries has brought priests to their knees; even bishops are compelled to humble themselves before him. The Cristo's power is not so much the power to crush or to control but to inspire awe and veneration, tenderness and devotion. None is immune, not the zealous colonial missionary, not the intellectualizing liberationist bishop, and not the skeptical, modernizing friar.

In the days and weeks following the October 9 rebellion, the mayordomía met with the municipal president, multiple letters were sent to the governor of the state, and in December another meeting with Obispo Reynoso was held.

The ultimate outcome was that the mayordomos and the padres reached a fragile peace. The frailes were persuaded, for the time being, to respect the traditions of the people. But, under the bishop's threat of excommunication, the people of Totolapan were forced to tolerate their continued ministry in the town. "It is either the Franciscans or no priest at all," the bishop further threatened. Not an empty warning, they knew, as neighboring Atlatlaucan had gone for some two decades without a priest after running their priest out of town. Some, like the católicas, feel that Salvador has come to understand the pueblo better, and even some of the mayordomos concede that Salvador is a "good guy" after all.

Una Gente Rebelde: The Rebellious People and the Myth of Quiescence

The rebellion against the parish priests in Totolapan was far from unprecedented in Morelos. More than in any other region in Mexico, from at least the mid-eighteenth century, anticlericalism, traditionalism, and a robust sense of local autonomy have frequently led to locally bounded disputes and skirmishes. Even when motivated by a strong sense of community identity, these disputes were often complicated by an unstable factionalism, as even small pueblos were fraught with internal divisions.[53] Because they are as factious as they are intensely communitarian, the experience of these communities is only partially captured by the anthropologists' notion of "closed corporate peasant community" (CCPC). This model, first suggested by the research of anthropologist Robert Redfield in his analysis of the regional culture of Tepoztlán during the 1920s and later formalized by Eric Wolf, posed a sense of local coherence and homogeneity arising from a united opposition to "outside" urban and modernizing influences. More recently, Wolf himself acknowledged the failure of the CCPC system thesis to account for intracommunity conflicts within closed corporate communities.[54] Thus it only partially explains the complex dynamics at work in rural Morelos.

This region was also the site of a key moment in the war for Mexican Independence, when the insurgent commander Father José María Morelos and his followers withstood for many months the royalist siege of Cuautla in 1812. Anenecuilco, not far away, was the birthplace of Emiliano Zapata, beloved hero of the Revolution of 1910. Padre Baltasar, parish priest to an urban poor parish in Cuernavaca and minister of sacred art for the Diocese of Cuernavaca explained this legacy: "The people of Morelos are very rebellious, *una gente rebelde*. Present in them is the spirit of Emiliano Zapata, the Zapatista spirit."[55]

Issues of land tenancy and ownership, water rights, and fees for religious services were often the immediate cause of local conflicts with parish priests.[56]

A fair number of these skirmishes were also sparked by actual and perceived threats to religious ritual and practice. In Tlayacapan, just a ten-minute combi ride from Totolapan, in 1756 the local Indian community almost killed a priest when he tried to prevent the bullfights traditionally held in celebration of the Candlemas fiesta.[57] And again in nearby Yautepec, in 1761 a priest attempted to disband a prayer group meeting in a private home in honor of a miraculous image of the Virgin Mary. When the police arrived and arrested the host, belli-cose devotees came after their priest with machetes drawn.[58]

In the present context, as well, Totolapan is not alone in its assertiveness and defiance (when necessary) in the face of clerical authority. The present-day párroco of Yautepec recalls the first weeks of his ministry in the town: "One of the first times that I celebrated Mass here I was blessing the people, sprinkling them with holy water. And I did not quite have time to make it all the way to the back pews. When Mass was over, a group of men came up to complain. They asked me, 'What is the problem? Are you worried about wearing out your shoes?' And right then and there they demanded their blessing too. They don't let us get away with much."

With the upheavals of Vatican II and liberation theology an anticlerical sentiment and strong sense of local autonomy remained, but were cast along new lines. Some of the liberationist priests, particularly when accommodating the liturgical requests of the people, fared better than many of their predeces-sors. But liberationist clerics in Tlayacapan struggled to remain in their parish.[59] As I have already mentioned, in Atlatlaucan innovating priests after Vatican II were run out of town for removing the traditional crucifix and install-ing a modern one in its place. When a new priest was finally sent to them, they promptly ran him out of town, too.

Neither the Franciscan priests nor many of the locals in Totolapan seem aware of any cultural or historical precedents to their dispute, beyond that which occurred in nearby Atlatlaucan almost fifty years earlier and which was a major point of reference throughout. It would be a mistake to think that because these conflicts are recurrent that they are somehow less painful and poignant. In a sense, each experience of betrayal (for that indeed is what the people of Totolapan felt) is as the first: characterized by shock, disillusionment, disgust, sadness, and grief. The piercing disappointment has not dulled for all its repetition over centuries. As the Totolapan's describe, the pain of feeling "invaded" by the Franciscan charismatics is just as pronounced as it was when the first Augustinian friar arrived in Totolapan.

But do the people of Totolapan understand themselves as rebellious, vola-tile, or unruly, as their clerics and outside observers perceive them? Concerned about possible misconceptions resulting from their action, in the weeks follow-ing the confrontation with the friars they tried to explain the character and disposition of their pueblo to the governor of the state. Their self-description is revealing: "The town of Totolapan has always been characterized by the tranquil character of its people, which nevertheless has brought us, on more than one occasion, to face the consequences of the attitudes of people who confuse this tranquility with indolence and ignorance, thinking they can thus impose their personal interests above those of the community."[60] Thus, though they see themselves as essentially a peaceful people, they are by no means "long-suffering" or inclined to tolerate offense lying down. In spite of the pueblo's factionalism, characteristic of pueblos throughout the region, it is an important clarification that in the case of Totolapan the community's unity was considered the supreme value. Ultimately, critics of the friars backed down from the conflict, not because they lacked courage in the face of power but when community unity itself seemed to be at risk.

Criticism of popular devotion to images of Christ crucified has come from various quarters within (and from without) the Church. One of the most damning critiques has come from liberation theologians who, neglecting the particularity of local cultural context and interpretive engagement, have associated devotion to images of Christ crucified with the passivity and resignation of poor and suffering people.[61] Brazilian theologian João Dias de Araújo's thesis is typical: "Crucifixes, whether they hang around the neck, on the walls of home and schools, from bedsteads, or in shops and churches, have created in the mind of the people the image of a Christ who is dead, nailed to wood, rendered incapable of reacting, wasted by the forces of evil—defeated."[62] For Araújo, the helplessness of this "Spanish" Christ is completely internalized by those who are the most powerless in society: "The Indians, defeated and subjugated, gaze upon the sad and defeated image of the Spanish Christ and behold, reflected there, their own selves and destiny. In the agonizing and dying Christ they confront a reason for resigning themselves to their lot and accepting the fate of a conquered, beaten, a subjugated people."[63] The assumption that devotion to the suffering Christ necessarily causes resignation to suffering goes largely unchallenged both in theological and in secular (historical, sociological) literature.

Here I want to trouble this myth of quiescence, the idea that resignation and passivity are the inevitable products of a "cult of suffering" that results from devotion to Christ crucified. Instead, I hold up the primacy of the image of the crucified Christ for the local identity of the people of Totolapan as a gente rebelde, a rebellious people. Their devotion to the Cristo takes place within a specific cultural context that, in part, is characterized by a restless sense of justice and of local authority and righteousness, even in the face of clerical, ecclesial, and state power. The letter quoted above could have been written in their own defense against this myth. "Look," they say in essence, "we are tranquil but not passive, peaceful but not lazy." These loving devotees of a miraculous, and fairly bloody, tortured crucifix, the image around which their collective life is organized and structured, are hardly the long-suffering, passive, defeated people that some theologians have described. In fact, in this particular instance their "rebelliousness" is expressed on behalf of the very image that is supposed to give rise only to resignation and inertia.

Conclusions. The Finger of Christ: The Vulnerability of a Sentient God

Missionaries, theologians, and historians have imagined that the theme of suffering and affliction dominates popular engagement with the crucifix in Mexico and elsewhere in Latin America. In the answers to questionnaires circulated by the mayordomía in the wake of their action against the Franciscan friars (of which more below), it is not the suffering of Jesus but rather the vulnerability of their Cristo that is the primary motif defining the relationship between believers and the image. For the people of Totolapan, at least in the context of crisis, the Cristo serves as a poignant metaphor for the vulnerability of their own embattled faith. This faith, still both potent and profound, is perceived as fragile by believers themselves. They trace this fragility to the collective memory of the initial experience of spiritual conquest and then to successive waves of evangelization, a memory revitalized by the "new" and "foreign" methods of evangelization employed by the current group of Franciscans. The frequent suggestion that the new Franciscans represented another wave of conquest was captured in a caricature published in the state newspaper that accompanied a story about the Totolapan conflict (figure 7.2).

Their militant action having failed, the mayordomos returned to more "peaceful" and bureaucratic means, petitioning and appealing through official channels. At the end of October, they circulated a questionnaire to which they received about a thousand completed answers, reflecting the opinions of about perhaps a fourth of the adult population of the town. This was not a random sample, nor was the questionnaire anonymous. People on both sides of the issue did express themselves, however, some with an impassioned honesty. The conflict was articulated in part along gender lines—especially by the mayordomos, who blamed the católicas, loyal to the priests, for dividing the community. Some of the most vitriolic opposition to the friars articulated in the questionnaires nevertheless came from women. "If they won't go of their own free will, we will kick them out by force," wrote one in her late fifties. A much younger woman agreed: "Yes, we need to remove them, through the means of physical force, since we obtained no results following legal means." Another woman added, "It is like the passage in the Bible says . . . hypocritical Franciscans, outside you are like well-painted sepulchers but inside you are full of bones and all classes of rot." Men sometimes expressed equal vehemence: "They deserve their punishment . . . to burn with a fire that never goes out."

The one-page questionnaire consisted of four queries: Do you want our community to continue preserving our traditions and customs (yes or no)?

FIGURE 7.2. Friar of Totolapan in conquistador's helmet. October 16, 1998.
By permission from *Regional del Sur de Morelos*.

Who do you want in charge of our parish (with checkboxes for the Franciscan
Order or a diocesan priest)? Do you agree that the Franciscans should definitely
remove themselves from our community (yes or no)? And finally, Do you have
a proposal to resolve the conflict arising from the methods of evangelization
employed by the Franciscans? In providing a space for a written response, the
final question afforded the opportunity for lengthier reflection and comment
and is therefore where the greatest value of the questionnaire lies. In these
answers we encounter bitter diatribes against the priests, criticism of the mayordomos and of the questionnaire itself, and poignant pleas on behalf of the
Cristo.

Though the open-ended commentaries resulting from the first question are the most useful for accessing the depth of community sentiment, the second question also merits explanation. In framing the issue in terms of a preference for secular or regular clergy, an historically significant distinction gets reinterpreted in contemporary categories. As explored in some detail in the first half of this book, since the latter half of the sixteenth century the state has been concerned to replace "regular" clergy (that is, members of the religious orders) with diocesan priests in the administration of parishes. Diocesan clergy were perceived as being more responsive to pressures from rich and powerful parishioners and more readily controlled by the state. This movement became more systematized with the regalist Bourbon reforms in the eighteenth century. There oftenwas local resistance to this transition. In 1775, a community of Indians near Cuernavaca requested the removal of their diocesan parish priest and his replacement with friars who would be more inclined to "work wholeheartedly for the good of our souls."[64]

In current-day Totolapan, the mayordomos have come to associate secular, or diocesan, clergy with the several generations of liberationist priests who had proceeded the friars. The elders of Totolapan now recall with nostalgia the time of the *comunidades eclesiales de base* (Christian base communities), remembering that these flourished "during the time of the *curas diocesanos*."[65] In the pueblo's recent memory, diocesan priests were also more compliant and obliging to the ritual needs of the community. In the minutes of a meeting early in the campaign against the friars, the community evaluated their past relationships with their parish priests, remembering that the last three diocesan priests were "amables, cordiales, y atentos," working in accord with the mayordomos and participating in all of the fiestas. The mayordomos are careful to point out that their dispute with the friars is the single disruption in a long history of positive and productive, mutually satisfying, lay-clergy relationships. This brings us to a useful correction to the notion of "anticlericalism." The fact is that communities rely heavily on their priests, who play a fundamental role in the celebration of religious festivals. At best, as was the case with one of Totolapan's most beloved liberationist curas, Padre Gonzalo, priests can serve as life-changing "spiritual guides" and companions. But at the very least, the people expect them to be pliant and compliant "accessories" to religious rituals organized and orchestrated by the laity. Indeed, in Totolapan the successful celebration of their Cristo is dependent on clerical participation and support. It is not that they reject the notion of clergy in general; rather they require the right kind of priest, one who meets the needs of the community as they themselves define them. As one local young man commented in his answer to the questionnaire: "A people without a pastor cannot rightly call themselves a people." While the parish priest is integral to the identity of the community as such, simultaneously the people have a strong sense of their own permanence vis-à-vis the transience of the their clerics: "Priests, like soldiers, come and go. But we, the people, are always here."

The primary concern expressed in the questionnaires is that the Cristo has been offended by the friar's disrespect. "We beg you, Franciscans. If you possess even the slightest fear of God you will remove yourselves for the good of our town, seeing as how you have offended our Cristo Aparecido in a manner that no other priest has ever dared to do." The friars' irreverence was manifest in many ways, but most distressing to the people was their persistent reference to the materials used in the construction of the Cristo. The friars intended to emphasize that the image was made by human hands, belying the santo's miraculous origins. One young woman, just twenty years old, worries "They mistreat our santitos by saying that they are just stones."[66] And a young man objects to the friars' pronouncement "that our saints are made of wood and plaster." Another man in his thirties protests: "they speak badly of the saints, saying that they are statues made of stone." And another, a good bit younger, suggests: "They really should leave because they say that the Cristo that is in our church is not really Christ but just a statue made of clay, they actually said this during a Mass." For believers, the Cristo is not an inanimate object of art but is a sentient, reactive deity.

There is also concern about the refusal of the friars to participate in the celebration of the Cristo. A woman in her late fifties writes, "when we request a Mass, they don't want to do it and when we try to make our processions they do not want to take out the Cristo Aparecido, [perhaps they mean] well, but in the end they are doing a harmful thing." Another argues with an edge of biting sarcasm: "They judge us badly for taking out our Señor Aparecido for the processions. Who do they want us to celebrate? Saint Francis?" In all of this the people express genuine concern and worry over the perturbation caused to the Cristo and the other saints. "They should leave," one woman writes, "so that the saints can be *tranquilos.*"

The Cristo Aparecido is thus negatively affected, harassed, offended, disturbed, by the irreverence of the Franciscan friars who treat him "as if he is an obra de arte, a work of art." But the people of Totolapan are also troubled that the Cristo Aparecido is vulnerable to mishandling and mistreatment of other kinds. He "suffers" potential injury by many hands: the clumsy hands of eager and nervous believers who knock off the little finger of one hand while taking him down from his perch behind the altar for procession; the clinical, cold, and sometimes invasive hands of INAH restorers, the sinful and yet adoring hands of his own, humble devotees; and for so many other Cristos. the greedy hands of private collectors—especially of wealthy foreigners. Recall here doña Mara's harrowing story of her Cristo's narrow escape from this very fate. In Totolapan they are well aware that other Cristos have met a tragic fate, appropriated into an art museum or into a private art collection. For example, the vast majority of cristos de caña, once devotional objects as well as curiosities (from their time of their origins in the sixteenth century they were brought to Spain as New World curiosities), are now in private collections.

Like his cristo hermano, the Señor de Chalma also is not immune to the world around him. Guides at the shrine explain that the weight of all the requests and needs the pilgrims lay before him has actually caused his head to hang lower. So burdensome are these petitions that, suffering from divine "compassion fatigue," he is barely able to lift his weary head off of his chest. And indeed, comparing photographs of the Señor de Chalma over the last several years, the change is perceptible.

In addition to these psychological vulnerabilities, the Cristo Aparecido is also susceptible to physical deterioration over the course of almost five centuries. Just as he is subject to the trauma of the many restorations that have sought to preserve him from that very deterioration, he is also vulnerable even to the reverent adoration of his people whose kisses and caresses corrode his delicate surfaces and whose processions expose the Cristo to harmful elements. In these cases, the fragility of the Cristo arises from the very physicality of the thing: they are weaknesses arising from the paradox of the divine made manifest in a physical object. These are the risks inherent to the Cristo's very materiality.[67] In this sense, the peoples' anxiety for their Cristo arises from their daily confrontation with the theology of the incarnation. Is the paradox of God made thing really that much different from that of God made flesh, the divine made manifest in a human being? As they behold the crumbling corpus of their beloved, eternal Santo, do they not also grasp more immediately and experience more sharply than many believers the contradiction most starkly manifest in the crucifixion of an omnipotent God?

Yet, the Cristo, which seems to depict so starkly a narrative of torture and violence, is actually as surprisingly resistant to a strict, formulaic association with human suffering as it is to the many layers of restorer's paint that the santo casts off so easily. Here the power and function of symbol (if devotees will forgive me this word) are laid bare. When I pushed the topic of Christ's suffering in conversations with people of Totolapan and Tepoztlán, I was eventually able to steer the conversation in that direction. "Oh, yes, Jesus suffered terribly," they would concede. But I felt that this theme was ultimately a dead end in our conversations; this agreement was arrived at mostly out of polite deference to me, or to demonstrate their familiarity with the biblical story of the life of Jesus. It became clear that for devotees of the Cristo de Totolapan, the story of Jesus' suffering is merely a secondary, less vibrant, narrative associated with any crucifix.

Most pressing for the people of Totolapan is the suffering of the Cristo in the present: he breaks a finger; he "fractures" an arm; he takes offense at the friars' casual disregard. "To look at the Cristo, some people might think it is an image of suffering," I offer tentatively, a statement asking for response. "I don't know why *anyone* would say such a thing," don Bruno wonders, puzzled and disturbed by the thought, hearing in my clumsy query an unintended accusation— you have neglected him, you have permitted him to be abused, you have failed him in some way. "Maybe because once, when we took him down his little finger

broke," he suggests, apparently relieved to have found some reasonable explanation, "He is deteriorating. That must be why they say that."

On another occasion I inquired about the Franciscans' insistence that
in their devotions to the Cristo they are worshiping a dead Christ, where as
Christians, their faith should rest on the living Christ, Christ resurrected. The
people understood this slight not in reference to the historical death of Jesus on
the cross but rather as the greatest disrespect and insult to their most precious
imagen—what they heard and understood was an assertion that their santo
was dead—that is, inanimate, powerless, lifeless. Indeed, Spanish the term
vida muerte describes an artist's rendering—a still life. The epithet may have
other resonances as well—in the colonial period friars derided the ongoing
devotion to pre-Columbian images by disregarding them as *simulacros muertos*,
as dead representations in contrast to the "living" images of Christian saints.[68]

Even INAH has come to adopt anthropomorphic language for the "works
of art" that they restore. An image is referred to as *viva*, as living, if it belongs
to an active devotion.[69] And INAH also frets, in terms similar to those used by
devotees, over the "suffering" of these *cristos torturados*. They write about the
"modifications" that these sculptures have "*suffered* over time." For example, in
the case of one image of Christ crucified in which the body (the corpus)
had been moved at some point in its long history onto another ill-suited cross,
restorers explained that the arms of the image "had *suffered* deformations, to
the point that they became dislocated from the body."[70]

The observations of don Julio, respected community elder in Totolapan,
liberationist, and ever the voice of reason as the most intellectual of his peers,
are particularly revealing. "The Cristo Aparecido? I don't believe that he suffers.
He doesn't suffer because he is simply an image; he is there so that we might
learn what he suffered for us. I do respect the image. But if I break off his little
finger it won't hurt him. He won't bleed. He won't cry out because he is *un
cristo muerto*, a dead Christ. But even so, I won't do this, I won't break off his
little finger because I respect him."

I fell in love with a photograph taken by local photographer, Arturo Medel
(figure 7.3). Here he has captured in black and white a grave on the Día de los
Muertos. The stone is decorated with the traditional festive flowers, turmeric-
colored marigolds and gladiolas. Incense clouds the picture. And, most strik-
ingly, at the top of the stone, a small Cristo has been attached with cord. But this
cristo has been freed from his cross, and thus freed, arms outstretched, he appears to be mid-flight, angled hands guiding him into a graceful and majestic
swan dive off the gravestone.

For whom is the Cristo dead? For those who lack the eyes of faith? For the
devotees of the Cristo Aparecido he is not dead but his eyes are simply closed,
merely an indication that he is sleeping. But if you wait and watch you will see
that he opens them sometimes, too. And he often descends from the cross,
walking the earth in the form of an old man, intervening on behalf of his flock.

FIGURE 7.3. Swan Dive Cristo. Photograph by Arturo Medel, 2003.

Sometimes he is angry, yes, or pained at what transpires around him. But often he is happy too: "Sometimes his cheeks are quite flushed, *chapeadas*, and then you can see that he pleased," doña Luz explains.

The fact that for devotees the Cristo is a reactive, sentient being seems to have eluded both academics and clerics. The liberationist priests' efforts to "radicalize" the faith of the people of Totolapan and Padre Salvador's desire to "evangelize" popular faith can hardly have found any resonance with the community itself. In each case they began with the discourse of a dead and defeated Christ rather than from the discourse in which the people themselves locate their own faith. This Cristo is anything but dead: he lives and breathes and is active in the world.

The people of Totolapan do express anxious concern, not pity, not compassion, for their santo, as they seek to shield him from these many threats. It is easy to see how the long-ago, remote suffering of the historical Jesus on the cross might pale in comparison to these very real, actual threats in the present time. Rather than an identification between the suffering of Christ and the suffering of his people, I see a parallel between the vulnerability of the Cristo Aparecido and the peoples' concern over the vulnerability of their own faith. Answers to the questionnaires reveal that people also worry over the damage the friars' style of evangelization might do to their faith in their Christ. One young man suggests, "The Franciscans should remove themselves from this church, and leave the people of Totolapan with their faith in the Cristo [intact]." And a woman similarly worries, "I have no proposal of how to resolve the conflict with the Franciscans, the only thing is that they shouldn't take away our faith in our Church and our faith in our images." Another similarly observes, "We don't accept the Franciscans because in Mass they criticize our Cristo, and instead of showing us how to love him more, they distance us from him. Rather, it is better that they should distance themselves from us." A middle-aged man concludes, "They should preserve our respect for our images and above all for our *santo cristo*." Finally, another longs, "What I wish is that the priests should always work in agreement with the mayordomos, they represent the whole pueblo and there shouldn't be divisions. I also hope that we don't forget our customs and traditions; that we don't forget to adore our Cristito."

Another parallel anxiety concerns the integrity of the community itself, and the adverse risks of the friars' ministry upon the people of Totolapan and their unity: "If this conflict continues something disastrous and lamentable may happen—we want the people of Totolapan to continue with their customs and we no longer want to be sad"; "Disorder in the pueblo of Totolapan"; "You cannot change the customs of a people because a people without customs and without traditions is a people without a past, without history, without roots, and without legends";[71] and, "we should put an end to this farce because what these people are going to achieve is to divide the people, and this is why we should run those friars out of town, because soon they are going to leave the pueblo in bad shape."

Finally, "I feel that the town should resolve this problem itself—because it is not the responsibility of one but of the whole pueblo."[72] "They have offended God for making the people fight among themselves." And herein, perhaps, lies the only limit to devotion to the Cristo, the only boundary line marking the limits of the people's faith: that is, the identity of the community as a people, as a "pueblo," must not be jeopardized. That there were those who, from within the community, actually supported and offered protection for the friars, is why the friars were allowed to remain, even in spite of the offense that they caused the Cristo.

A final theme emerging from the questionnaires bears mention here: the collective memory of conquest and a sense of historicity and repetition. They perceive themselves as a community besieged: "We don't want them to come and impose their own laws because the time of the *hacendados* is past. Run the lazy bums out!" "This *encuesta* is a good idea but I no longer belong to the Catholic community for the reason that I never liked to live as one deceived, because only people that are blind, that continue believing in false priests who deceive the people, just as was done from the beginning by the Spanish *conquistadores*." "Well, I was a mayordomo many years ago and I have seen that the priests who come to our parish *always* have wanted to take away our customs and put themselves in charge of our parish." "The Franciscans don't come to evangelize but to conquer temples and [take that] which belongs to the *nación mexicana*," "First, they teach us to accept their beliefs, and now they want to take them away from us." Thus the vulnerability of the santo serves as a potent metaphor for a people whose faith has been embattled over the course of centuries.

As with the theme of Jesus' suffering, the paradox of the incarnation is still present in Totolapan. That is, the Cristo's vulnerability does not imply impotence. Far from it. Part of the story that the people of Totolapan tell is of his resilience: his ability to triumph over these potential injuries. He survives, resisting even restorations, shedding the layers of paint and reverting to his prior form. He returns inevitably to his people after nearly three centuries in Mexico City; he survives the Revolution protected by his devotees who move him from home to home when soldiers occupy the church. In the case of other cristos, like the black Christ of neighboring Juitepec or the cristo of the barrio Santa Cruz in Tepoztlán, a soldier is struck dead as he attempts to steal the cristo's silver crown of thorns. The Cristo Aparecido also survives the clumsiness of devotees (his little finger regenerates), and punishes offenders of his dignity (as doña Mara's cristo, who causes the death of her husband). The faith of the people in their beloved santito also endures; and they are always ready and able to defend it—imposing their will even on the intractable Franciscans, who were finally obliged to compromise in order to sustain a strained peace with the mayordomos. He resists, above all, soaring above (as in Arturo Medel's photo) those interpretations that would reduce his existence to a crude and simplistic representation of violent suffering.

8

Beauty, Affection, and Devotion

Fiesta at the Dawn of a New Millennium

Scene 7. Atrio, Iglesia de Totolapan, 2004.

On Sunday morning during the week of the annual fiesta celebrating the Cristo Aparecido, a lone penitent labors arduously on his knees, slowly shuffling down the main path through the atrio toward the altar where the Cristo awaits (figure 8.1) Thin, face worn and furrowed, knees knobby and exposed, he makes his slow, painful way down the aisle. A dramatic figure, but at this fiesta he is the exception. As the penitente makes his gradual approach toward the Cristo, he passes a group of women. Oblivious to the plight of the man behind them, the women laugh and smile as they rest on their knees to decorate the paved path that extends through the atrio to the front door of the church. They kneel not in penance, but rather to express their faith in Christ through the creation of beautiful mosaics that will carpet the path that the Cristo sojourns on his annual "pilgrimage" through the pueblo.

The Cristo and the people of Totolapan survived the conflict of 1998 with the Franciscan friars who were serving, and continue to serve today, as their parish priests. These priests had attempted, in vain, to withdraw their support from the annual fiesta, refusing to welcome pilgrims or even to say masses in the Cristo's honor. Today, with the participation of the chastened friars, the Cristo Aparecido continues to be celebrated, honored, and engaged in the annual cycle of communal celebrations. Of no fewer than twelve religious fiestas celebrated by the people of Totolapan each year, four are dedicated to the Cristo. The largest and most important of these falls on the

FIGURE 8.1. Lone *penitente* at annual fiesta honoring Cristo Aparecido. Photo by author.

Quinto Viernes, the fifth Friday of Lent, and commemorates the date of the Cristo's original arrival in the pueblo.[1] This chapter takes a careful look at the Fifth Friday celebration of the Cristo in the contemporary moment, employing an affective and aesthetic approach that allows me to remain close to devotees in my interpretation. In the previous chapter, I argued that suffering, compassion, pity, and remorse were not the definitive emotions mediating collective devotion to the Cristo Aparecido. This point is reiterated and underscored at the Fifth Friday celebration at which the people of Totolapan do not mourn the death of Jesus, but come together to celebrate their beautiful, living santo. The fiesta is therefore aesthetic rather than penitential in nature: the theme of beauty predominates.

This chapter thus brings us full circle, back to the friar Antonio de Roa's declaration of the singular beauty of the Cristo when he first beheld the image in 1543. The significance of the Cristo as an aesthetic object was heightened in the mid-colonial centuries when baroque sensibilities flourished. This accrued aesthetic value is both preserved and reinvented today, at his annual fiesta, when the Cristo is celebrated as a source of beauty in the world. Correspondingly, the correct spiritual posture in relation to the image is affection, warmth, tenderness, and love. The themes of penance and pain are not absent; they are merely muted in these celebrations; as one devotee explains, "This is a day for us to enjoy ourselves. Yes, we are here for the Cristo, and we do venerate him, but we do it *our* way, with happiness and joy."[2] The figure of Fray Antonio de

Roa is present in the decorations at the annual fiesta but ultimately the memory of Roa and his extreme penancearemarginal to the celebration.

Finally, the focus on the Cristo's contemporary celebration brings our attention to the community of immigrants from Totolapan to the United States. In 2007, Totolapan immigrants began to formalize their ongoing contribution to the celebration of the Cristo in the creation of a *mayordomía de los migrantes*. Though most of them have settled permanently in the California coastal town of San Juan Capistrano, for them the Cristo represents the powerful emotional pull of home, and the fiesta is the occasion for an annual return-migration to Totolapan. The final and concluding moment in this biography of the Cristo thus provides an opportunity to engage with the very recent literature on transnational religion.[3] As his devotees cross the border, the Cristo has become part of the complex, porous and living religious landscape of the contemporary United States. The Cristo's devotees now groom golf course lawns and build new homes not too far from my own southern California home.

In emphasizing the affective aspects of the Fifth Friday celebration, I necessarily distance myself from the main thrust of the scholarly literature on Latin American fiestas since the middle of the twentieth century. Traditionally, ethnographers have offered materialist interpretations of fiestas, debating the extent to which local feasts serve as mechanisms for the exchange and (re)distribution of goods.[4] The relationship of believer to image has similarly been reduced to a calculated negotiation in which ritual engagement serves to provide a material benefit for the devotee. This approach continues to hold sway among some scholars of transnational religion, who focus on the material impact of transnational sponsorship of local fiestas. In my attention to the aesthetic, I have been guided by a body of theological literature written by U.S. Latino and Hispanic theologians. Over the last several years, they have focused their thinking and scholarship on developing a theological aesthetics capable of interpreting and engaging popular practices, including especially devotion to the Virgin of Guadalupe and other saints.[5] The corpus of works on the Virgin of Guadalupe produced by these scholars is very much in keeping with this approach: the sum total a sympathetic, affectionate, aesthetic, and complex portrait of popular devotion that argues everywhere for its theological integrity and authenticity. From them, I have gained my interest in the aesthetic and the affective and my attention to the theme of beauty in popular devotion,

This is not to suggest that there is not a strong economic component to the Totolapan fiestas. During the Fifth Friday hundreds of vendors line the streets with their small *puestos*, selling T-shirts, children's toys, and bric-a-brac. Food is in plentiful supply, as well. Peeled, sweet mangos are cut like flowers, sprinkled with chili, and presented to clients like succulent, edible blossoms. Most of the vendors come from outside of Totolapan, and rely on the circuit of such fiestas to make their living. Some enterprising local merchants do seem to benefit from the throngs, as well. Doña Bonifacia, for instance, does not pause from making her tortillas during the entire fiesta. She recruits her extended family and transforms her home into a busy restaurant. At the annual celebration of the Cristo in 2004, a group of women religious, Sisters of the Holy Cross, arrived in a sporty red car and unpacked their wares in a small stand at a privileged spot in the atrio, at the doors of the church. They were friends of the friars from Mexico City, and they too came to hawk their wares: crosses, rosaries, pictures of the Cristo, prayer books, candles, T-shirts, and other religious paraphernalia.

In Totolapan, the intense rhythm of the festal cycle defines the daily in-and-out of devotion. Anywhere from a dozen to two dozen fiestas are celebrated annually, depending upon who one asks.[6] The locals sometimes also count national holidays within their liturgical calendar, in particular those in honor of Mexican Independence in mid-September, neatly folding secular nationalism within their religious celebrations. Three of the traditional fiestas that honor the Cristo Aparecido are explicitly related to the agricultural cycle. At each of these, traditionally, the Cristo leaves the safety of his sanctuary and is brought outside into the streets of the pueblo. The first is an occasional feast, a procession of the image throughout the pueblo that happens only in case of drought and only at the request of the mayordomía. Another, in December, gives thanks for the harvest. Forty days after Easter, on the day honoring Jesus' ascension into heaven, the image is taken into the hills so that the following year's harvest will be plentiful. The frequency of these outdoor processions has decreased in recent years, as concerns about potential damage to the image have risen. In 2008 the image was taken on just one outdoor procession, during the Fifth Friday fiesta, but it was enclosed within a specially designed glass case to protect it from the elements.

This added protection is necessary in part because the image is associated with rain, and it is understood that bringing him out of the church will usually summon a downpour. One man explained to me how the procession of the image helps to end drought:

> Sometimes in July we begin to think that it won't rain, and people begin to be anxious about their crops. Once it was already July 7 and it had not yet rained. That day there was not even a single cloud in the sky. The mayordomos organized themselves and we went to the priest and told him that we needed to take the Cristo out on procession. We were not even half way around the pueblo when ¡Ay! ¡Caray! A downpour was unleashed upon us. It had been pure sun, and suddenly it poured rain. We huddled in a doorway so the Cristo wouldn't get wet. In other years when there has been no rain and *ya empezaron a dormir las plantas*, the plants had already begun to wilt, we have taken the Cristo on procession and it will always rain within two to three days.

In this instance the procession of the Cristo is not so much an event in his honor, nor is it only a plea for divine intervention. Rather, exposing the Cristo to the elements, to the bright sun, the heat, and the cloudless sky appears to be intended to wake him up, to catch his attention and elicit a response. These gestures appeal to the Cristo's sentience. For example, in many parts of Mexico there is a practice of turning santos upside down or even burying them if they seem indifferent or immune to a devotee's petition. I believe that these practices are not intended to punish the saint (i.e., for a past offense), but are rather designed to provoke a response. The lighting of candles and incense before saints sometimes has a similar function, that is, these are intended to rouse the image, much as smelling salts might awaken someone in a faint.

The complex processes of planning, organizing, preparing for, and celebrating these many fiestas constitute an important part of daily life in the pueblo. Mayordomías are elected, and leadership is ceremoniously transferred. Monies are collected, allocated, and accounted for. Musical and theatrical pieces are studied and rehearsed. Actors are chosen. Elaborate adornos, decorations, are imagined, designed, created, and finally installed. High school reports on the Quinto Viernes fiesta are completed. Each of these acts as a constitutive part of the collective devotion; and in a sense, each of these tasks is consecrated in the Cristo's honor. In this way the fiesta is not felt as a time outside of time. Rather, by helping define the calendar of the liturgical year, it marks all time as sacred, and infuses each day and each moment with spiritual value. As a complement to these collective celebrations, the santo is also engaged by individuals in moments of personal crisis: after the death of a parent, or during the serious illness of a spouse. During the principal procession of the image on his feast day some people have powerful emotional responses as personally painful memories such as these are elicited.

Although the Fifth Friday fiesta is dedicated to the Cristo Aparecido, the event has no single focus. The fiesta spans twelve days, and culminates on the final weekend, that is characterized by frenetic activity, a flurry of simultaneous, parallel events, though there is a planned effort to alternate music, masses, processions, and the arrival of pilgrims. At any given moment there may be a Mass inside the iglesia, explosive fireworks being launched from behind the convento, four or five bands playing simultaneously (each of these with their own amplified music), school children performing a dance, and, almost unceasingly, the reenactment of the Moors and Christians pageant, a thirty-six hour performance. All of this occurs within the relatively limited space of the atrio, where the dizzying array of activities, sounds, and music produces a constant crescendo. Though foreigners may find the resulting experience overwhelming, the intended effect on local people is to create a baroque sense of abundance and joyful exuberance that fills every space with color and sound. A degree of anxiety underscores the planning and execution of the fiesta; it is important that it be celebrated in a manner proper and befitting both to the

Cristo and to the pueblo. Tradition is crucial, but innovation is also highly valued, particularly in the creation of elaborate decorations.

"Your image still lives, Lord": The Fifth Friday Fiesta

In March of 2004, the fiesta of the Quinto Viernes fell on the very weekend that
Mel Gibson's controversial movie, *The Passion of the Christ*, opened in Mexico.
Though I had intentionally missed the film's U.S. theater run, I was curious to
track its reception in Mexico. Therefore I was not chagrined to discover that, as
I settled back into my seat in the second-class bus from Mexico City to Totolapan, the film just beginning on the bus's VCR was a "bootlegged" copy of *The
Passion*, at least forty-eight hours in advance of its theater premier. In spite of
myself, I leaned forward eagerly as the film began. Several minutes passed before I looked around me to see how the other passengers, many of who I knew
to be on their way to the Fifth Friday celebration, were reacting to Gibson's
gruesome portrayal of Christ's flaying by the Roman soldiers. Given the stir
and disruption that the film had caused in the United States, I was surprised at
first to note that I was the only one in the bus who was actually watching the
film. Some slept; others chatted quietly with their neighbors; others stared out
of the window. They did not need Mel Gibson to interpret this story for them;
they had decades, if not centuries, of an interpretive tradition that engaged both
the Gospel narrative of Christ's suffering and a variety of artistic renderings of
his crucifixion.

On the final Thursday of the fiesta, anticipation mounts and there is a bus-
tle of preparatory activity. Inside, the iglesia overflows with white and pink
gladiolas. White and pink neon lights, permanently installed in the iglesia but
rarely illuminated, cast a rosy sheen on the entire nave. The Cristo has been
lowered from his remote nicho behind the altar, brought down among the people where, even if they are not permitted to touch him, at least they can draw
near to him and behold him from up close. He will remain there in his adorno,
his newly constructed decorative setting, until the middle of Holy Week, when
he will again be returned to his nicho. There is no passion play tradition in
Totolapan; Easter week is a fairly subdued affair. In fact, it almost seems as if it
simply signals the close of the Cristo's fiesta. There is an Easter week procession of the other local images, but the Cristo himself will not participate.

An old woman, body curled and hunched, long silver braid falling gracefully down her back, spends many minutes on her knees in front of the Cristo.
Kneeling, arms outstretched in an ancient posture of prayer, the woman gazes
up to contemplate the face of her santo, then down at the floor, lips moving
quickly and quietly in petition, prayer, or thanksgiving. Later she explains that
she has come from a neighboring town, Tepetlixtipa, to pay tribute to the Cristo,
as she does every year. Her son has been ill; and today she is giving thanks for

his successful surgery. She will not stay for the rest of the fiesta but returns home today, having paid her respects. She looks for a priest to hear her confession, but none can be found. In fact the confessional boxes will remain empty and unmanned throughout the weekend; penitence must await the pueblo's return to the routines of quotidian life.

The following day, Friday, eight masses are celebrated, music trumpets, and pilgrims from various pueblos are welcomed. At the noon Mass the church has standing room only: at this service the Cristo will be presented in his adorno and the much anticipated event, ritually rehearsing the image's original appearnace in the Pueblo, has drawn the largest crowd yet this year. Each year the mayordomos design and create a novel, decorative setting for the presentation of image. This year the fragile Cristo has been placed on a mechanized, moving platform that can be raised and lowered. At the beginning of the mass he hovers above a great stone chalice constructed from large cubes of Styrofoam that have been painted to resemble grey, mottled stones. Roa's name is written on the chalice, along with the date of the Cristo's appearance, 1543.

The chalice rests on the banks of a smoking pool—an artificial fountain complete with running water, rocks, flowers, and a mist created with dry ice. The scene is of natural beauty, cast in mystical, Arthurian overtones. Many feet above the great chalice, the mayordomos have erected another independent scene, creating a life-size image of Antonio Roa, a cardboard cutout representation based on Carlos Clemente López's version of the friar that hangs in the Museo Nacional del Virreinato. Fully dressed in his habit (rather than bare-chested as in the painting with which they are most familiar), the cardboard Roa carries a cross upon his shoulders, though in this local reproduction he looks decidedly less burdened than in the original painting. In the adorno, as in the original, Roa treads upon live coals—an effect created with the use of electric flickering lights and translucent red film.

A large, glittering banner draped all along the main altarpiece declares, "Tu Aparición Sigue Viva, Señor!"—Your Image Still Lives, Lord! It is a defiant statement, in the face of the recalcitrant Franciscans. This declaration seems to capture the essence of the fiesta: it is not so much Christ resurrected who lives on, but rather the Cristo Aparecido himself who survives, as does their culto, their devotion to him. The people are well aware that he endures most of all through their celebration of him. It is they who buoy him up and sustain him: without their faith, devotion, and protection the Cristo might well cease to exist. The fiesta provides the Cristo with a crucial transfusion of life force and vital power. The stakes in maintaining the traditional forms of this fiesta are extraordinarily high.

Several mayordomos gather at the image's side, *vigilando* the devotees; they observe as visitors approach the saint, and drop their pesitos, their small coins, into the alcancía. The mayordomos, identifiable by the thick, beribboned medallions they wear on their chests, distribute small prayer cards with the

Cristo's image printed on them. One of them stands to offer me his chair. But an older one says, "You can sit here for a moment; but soon we will have to ask you to leave out of respect for the people." He asks if I am an anthropologist. "No," I reply, "a theologian." He nods his head, slowly. When he inquires my age, thirty-four, he also seems satisfied: "If you were just beginning your studies we would not think that you were up to the task of writing about our Cristo."

As the noon mass begins, the chalice breaks open, almost like a flower, or a great stone shell, and the Cristo slowly, shakily descends into the cup and closer to the pool. On either side of him simulated flames leap and flicker. The moment of the Cristo's descent into the chalice is a great unveiling; both a dramatic presentation of the image and a revelation of the tremendous ingenuity of this year's mayordomos. The people applaud quietly, their response more solemn than rousing. Later in the liturgy, a handsome young priest gives a sermon about how Christ draws near to us, just as the Cristo descends from the chalice to be close to his people. "God is always close," he reminds his flock.

In a subsequent mass the same day, Padre Salvador, at one time the Cristo's primary antagonist, presents a less well-received homily. Still recovering from a stroke he had several months earlier, Salvador is present at the festivities but unable to exert himself. Confused about what the mayordomos' adornos represent, and mistaking the chalice for a baptismal font, Salvador preaches about the "baptismal font that is the source of our faith." Then he proceeds, in his sermon, to offer an endorsement for Mel Gibson's film: "Everyone should go see the movie about Christ's passion. This is an important movie and though it shows Christ's suffering we have to remember that it captures only a small part of what Christ actually suffered for us. It is very important that you not simply buy a bootlegged ('pirated') video of the movie. Make sure that you pay to go see it in a movie theater, so that you can offer your financial support to the work itself, to those good people who made the movie. And besides, 'piracy' is a sin." At this I glanced at the woman next to me, to gauge her response. She is in her thirties, humbly dressed, a peasant from one of the outlaying towns, perhaps. Capturing my inquiring glance, she offers me a cynical, dubious smirk and rolls her eyes slightly at Salvador's invective. In centuries past, Roa and other friars punished their own flesh to highlight the suffering of Christ. The modern-day priest can simply offer a plug for Gibson's big box office film.

Though Roa figures prominently in the adornos, there is a sense in which both he and his penitential exercises are marginal to the fiesta. In fact, though the people of Totolapan have a tremendous faith in their Cristo, they bring a significant dose of rational skepticism to Roa's "miraculous" penitences, in defense of which priests (from Juan de Grijalva in the sixteenth to López Beltrán in the twentieth) have offered volumes. His figure hovers over the iglesia, some twenty feet in the air, gliding over glowing goals that flicker with life. But don

Bruno, one of the primary creators of adornos for the pueblo, insists firmly that Roa is not the one being venerated here:

> Roa was not really a saint. Here you have to read the story about him written by López Beltrán, who was at one time also a friar here. According to the story Roa was in Totolapan just as any other priest. Of course we were not around then so we don't know for certain, but they say that he was very anxious to obtain a cristo so he did penitences in the atrio. An Indian brought a cristo covered with a cloth. When they went to pay him the Cristo had been left in the door of the clock tower all alone, and the Indian was gone. Roa was a friar, nothing else. One day maybe he could be like Juan Diego, made into a saint. But here we don't celebrate Roa; we celebrate the Cristo Aparecido.

When I inquired as to whether the people of Totolapan continued Roa's penitential tradition in any form, don Bruno corrected me hastily, "We read the story of Roa's penances; we know this story. But does it have some significance for us today? No!" Others agree that there was nothing miraculous about Roa's penitence. A local schoolteacher explained that Roa's ability to walk on hot coals stemmed from will power and strength of mind, an indication of his mental discipline. Don Felix, who served as head mayordomo for several years agreed: "Roa was a person, nothing else. He came and left us with the Cristo. The Cristo is the one in whom we have faith. His penitences, which he performed, were simply *psicología profunda*, deep psychology. This was his method of converting the Indians, walking on coals, that sort of thing. But when he left, the Indians discontinued these practices. In other places they still do this, like Taxco where they wear a silver crown of thorns." And another adds, "We have no need for such things [penitential practices], we are a modern people, after all!"

On Saturday, the fiesta proceeds much the same, with the alternation of masses, *salvos de cohetes*, and *bandas*. But on Sunday the pitch again heightens. There are only five masses said, but on this day the Cristo makes his peregrinación, his much-anticipated pilgrimage around the pueblo. In preparation for this procession, the humble town is transformed—transfigured and glorified. Every street is decorated with colorful plastic streamers, and every foot of the path that the Cristo will take is prepared with a decorative carpet.

On Sunday, the day of the culminating procession, the lone penitent who appeared at the beginning of the chapter labors arduously on his knees, slowly shuffling down the main path through the atrio. Though he has not come far, perhaps some twenty meters, his way is slow, face pained. He is assisted by a younger man, his son, perhaps, who coaxes him along his way toward the Cristo Aparecido, gripping his hand for support. The man pauses, and collapses against his son to rest a while. Who knows what promise he has made, what peccadillo he has committed. He seems to weep with pain, agony, his face contorted. He is the exception; most devotees have spent many hours resting on their knees as they adorn the Cristo's path. In fact, each barrio has spent several hours engaged in this endeavor, each trying to outdo the others. Some use the more traditional alfalfa and rose petals, others the innovative colored sawdust, yet others roll out a factory-made green carpet, liturgical Astroturf. But every inch of the Cristo's path will be adorned and decorated. The streets that once streamed with Roa's blood in homage to the Cristo Aparecido are now decorated, for his pleasure and in his honor, with brightly colored sawdust and flowers.

Feo and *bonito*, *ugly* and *beautiful*, are two key words for people in this region, as in many rural parts of Mexico, part of everyday, casual discourse. And at the fiesta beauty proliferates: in the stunning adornos, in the competing music of the various bandas, in the glittering costumes of the Moors and Christians, in abundant arrays of flowers. Even the annual programs, in full color with golden flourishes, are works of art. There is an unexpected beauty as well in the solemnity of cohetes; their explosion is a sonorous "music," a disruption boldly announcing the rupture of the sacred into the world, as George Foster describes it.[7] The full significance of these thundering fireworks was made clear to me months earlier when I observed a funeral procession as it made its way through another small pueblo. As middle-aged men solemnly carried the casket through the town, older men walked both in front and behind launching the fireworks, announcing the solemnity of the occasion. At the Cristo's fiesta, the men in charge of the fireworks arrive cradling armfuls of the missiles, which they embrace as gently as one might a bundle of calla lilies offered before an altar. And they set them off, one after another, without a break, until the whole town is blanketed in dust and ash. Indeed there is something truly volcanic about the explosions, which drum deeply as rolling thunder, and seem easily capable of shattering a sixteenth-century monastery or even the great stone mountains themselves.

But most of all beauty lies in the numinous face of their Christ, from which gentleness and love flow abundantly. The beauty of the saints appeals to all the senses. An old peasant woman negotiates several large bundles of redolent herbs and grasses into a crowded combi. "They smell very good," I smile amiably. "Ahhh . . . yes, they smell santito," she replies. "Santito?" I ask. "Yes, as if there is a santito, a little saint nearby." One woman tried to explain to me what it means that the Cristo is beautiful. Her voice fills with emotion, "When I see the Cristo Aparecido, I love him. I behold him with love and faith, and it fills me with the desire to weep." "What does it mean when we sing to the Señor de Chalma of his beauty?" I ask the seventy-year-old laywoman who leads the weekly rosario to him in Tepoztlán. "But I thought you had been there!" she exclaims, surprised and confused. "Didn't you see him? Ah! He is beautiful," she cries, as if this should have been transparent even to the most imperceptive beholder.

But then what of the "santito feito," the poor, ugly santo, who the people of Totolapan also care for attentively? The Señor de la Purísima Sangre shares his quarters with his handsome cousin, the Cristo Aparecido. Hands bound, eyes wide with surprise, his skin, darkened from so many centuries of candles burned in his presence, often appears to crawl with life. "It gives you chills," they say. He is so grim looking not even his festal purple garb seems to brighten his disposition. Yet the people still express a sense of fondness, warmth, and tenderness for this homely saint. And here, finally, one encounters a trace of *piedad*, pity, not for the agony of his suffering, but for his unpleasant appearance: "Pobrecito," they say, "Poor thing, so ugly."

The people of the pueblo have rejected the alterations to the fiesta proposed by the friars. For example, they briskly dismissed the friars' suggestion that they offer beans and other dry goods to the Cristo, instead of flowers, so that these could later be distributed to the poor. In his own defense, the Cristo himself intervenes when the fiesta is not celebrated properly, and when he does so he is called *cristo castigador*, the punishing Christ. Stories about the Cristo's punishment of those who shirk or disrespect his fiesta circulate in the community. One of these tells the story of a son who is smitten dead because of his father's reluctance to attend the fiesta: "One boy came every year on the pilgrimage, walking to Totolapan with his family. One year his family did not want to come, but the boy did. He insisted and insisted. Finally, his father grew angry and said, 'Get along with you, away from here, and I hope you don't come back.' So the youth came to the fiesta on his own. But while he was here he went for a swim in a pond and drowned. From that time the father repented, and he comes every year because he knows that his son drowned because of his harsh words."

Most of the stories are of a less severe nature. One woman explains that the Cristo punished her father when he tried to add bulls to the fiesta events: "Once my father was mayordomo and he tried to introduce a bull ring and bull riding competition into the fiesta. But on the day that the competition was to take place, it rained tons, a complete downpour, and then he realized that the Cristo disapproved of the bulls. This is why, from that time, you will never see either bulls or cockfights at a religious fiesta in Totolapan, as you sometimes do in other pueblos." In a final example, a woman recalls the Cristo's negative response to her uncle's entrepreneurial focus: "My uncle always sold ice creams at the fiesta. And one year he refused to participate in the preparation of meals for the pilgrims. He was so busy making money with his ice creams that he did not want to participate. So, on the day of the fiesta he got very, very ill. And every since then he always participates in the fiesta."

Yet, in spite of the Cristo's ability to bring storms, illness, or even death to offenders, the people of Totolapan never describe feeling fear, guilt, or dread in relation to the Cristo. Propitiation is the wrong word to describe their celebrations. Absent is the sense that they need to appease or coddle an angry, unpredictable, or fickle God. "Are you afraid of him?" I often asked. "No, quite the contrary!" they would say, voices filled with tenderness and affection, in their eyes the glimmer of a tear, on their lips a wistful smile. Rather they desire to please, not appease; to offer something beautiful, something for his pleasure and theirs. They are thankful, moved, at the chance to give back just a little of what they have received from him. Yet at the fiesta they ask for his blessing as well: "Vendícenos, Señor," Lord, the hand-lettered sign reads: send us your blessing.

At the same time that "tradition" courses throughout the preparation and celebration of the fiesta, innovation also has its place. But these innovations must be of the pueblo's own inspiration, and determined by the community itself. For example, the use of colored sawdust to create the *tapetes*, the carpets for the Cristo's pilgrimage, is a recent tradition, a technology imported from a neighboring community some six or seven years ago. Yet people are enthusiastic about this addition. One community elder explained: "There are many new things at the fiesta. The colored sawdust is very beautiful, we make a mosaic with it. We didn't always do that, but the fiesta is always changing and *mejorando*, improving." Innovation and novelty are obviously crucial to the adornos inside the iglesia, especially with respect to the setting for the image himself. No setting may be repeated in subsequent years.

This is not to say that there are not occasions in which people express a sense of decline in the fiesta, as well. Community elders like Don Otilio Adaya lament that it used to be that the Señor Aparecido was the only image that was ever taken on procession, "whether it was to venerate him, to ask him for good weather, or beg him for rain." More recently, they charge, "any old image" is taken out on procession through the pueblo, for example during Holy Week. Don Otilio particularly worried that this practice could "lead the community from authentic veneration into *fanatismo irracional*, irrational fanaticism."[8]

Monica, a young woman with an interest in feminism who has temporarily left Totolapan to complete a masters degree in Mexico City, caught my attention when she explained that the fiesta was a time of *tristeza*, great sadness for the people. I had never heard this sort of language used before, in relation either to the Cristo or to his fiesta. But she quickly clarified my misunderstanding: "You see, people are sad because the fiesta has not been well organized this year, the municipal government has not done a good job."

The Friars and the Fiesta

The primary role of the friars at the fiesta is as accessories to the various liturgical events. This is not to suggest that this role is somehow extraneous; far from it, the fiesta could hardly proceed without their participation. They are inserted into the proceedings at the various moments in which their presence is considered necessary. For the most part, this means that they celebrate dozens of masses, ceremoniously greet and bless the groups of pilgrims as they arrive at the iglesia, and carry the Cristo on his peregrinación, his pilgrimage, through the pueblo.

At the beginning of October 2003, the Franciscan friars offered the people of Totolapan a rather dreary celebration of their patron, St. Francis of Assisi, perhaps in the hopes that the pueblo might adopt that celebration as their own, maybe even as an alternative to the Fifth Friday. As the feast day approached, they draped from the front of the convento a large, attractive banner of Francis, represented more as an Indian than as a European. At the rear of the nave, to the left of the altar, they installed an adorno of their own creation: an intricate reproduction of a stone tomb, with a life-size corpse of St. Francis lying eerily inside. Inside the tomb, skillfully constructed of brown paper bags that had been stuffed and painted, the friars lit candles around the body of their patron. Even so, the gloom of the tomb was hardly lifted; inside it was so dark that it was difficult to discern the features of the saint's face; making the scene even more lifelike and macabre. The friars' version of fiesta stands in stark contrast both to the buoyant celebration of St. Francis in Christian churches in the United States, often marked by the exuberant and unruly blessing of household pets, from hamsters to pot-belly pigs, and to the Quinto Viernes celebration of those native to Totolapan. Needless to say, the locals did not enter the make-shift, temporary shrine to venerate the effigy within.

The friars now participate, and sometimes with great reverence if at other times less than wholeheartedly, in events honoring the Cristo. The católicas in the pueblo argue that the friars have always honored the Cristo on his feast day: "since the time they came we saw that they had much cariño and much devotion. For example, when Padre Salvador carries the cross, he doesn't touch it with human hands, he puts on his stole and only handles the Cristo with his hands around his stole. They do respect him! They have always bowed down low before him." But for other observers, the friars' willingness to participate in the fiesta was delayed and resulted purely from self-interest. Doña Bonifacia explained to me in a matter-of-fact, not particularly critical tone:

> At first the friars didn't really support the fiesta. The pilgrims from each community would bring their nichos [miniature shrines] with an image of the Cristo inside. The friars didn't want these in the church; they didn't want to find a place for them. But that was because they didn't know that there was money inside. Each community placed their contribution to the santo inside of the alcancías [large boxes]. When the friars realized that there was money in there, well they quickly made a space for them. Now that they have learned that through the Cristo much money enters the church, and now they love him. When the priests saw the large alcancías arrive, full of money, they really changed their tune.

Another woman sympathetic to the friars proposed an alternative source for their initial resistance—the fear that they might drop and damage the image: "At first when they arrived they did not want to carry the santo up to the hill. They were worried that it was too heavy and that because it was very old that the Cristo would be damaged. But they saw that it wasn't hard for us. And now they carry him with much devotion."

The young seminarians observed the fiesta goings-on with curiosity, but the priests joked casually and cynically with me about the faith of the people in their Cristo. In discussing the legend of the Cristo's broken finger in which the digit miraculously reattached itself, one friar made a gesture suggesting that someone had simply glued the finger back in place. Another offered a series of jokes about "Christ disappeared." Nevertheless, in whatever spirit they offer it, during the procession of the image, the friars take their turns belting on the leather holster that serves to bear some of the weight of the image, and diligently carry the Cristo through town.

The Twelve Pairs from France

The pageant of the "Doce Pares de Francia," the Twelve Pairs (or Peers) from France, also known locally as el Reto and elsewhere in Mexico as the Danza of the Moros y Cristianos, the Dance of the Moors and Christians, is an essential part of the festivities in honor of the Cristo. The Totolapan presentation, which spans four stages, three days of performances, and includes some thirty actors, is a loosely historical reenactment of Charlemagne's eighth-century struggle against Moslem incursion. The inclusion of the dance as part of the festivities in honor of the Cristo dates at least to the first decades of the twentieth century.

Drawing on an eleventh-century courtly tradition, and then recast with new significance after the Spanish "reconquest" of Spain from the Moors, the performance of the battle between Christians and Moslems is a tradition that is eight hundred years old. According to historian Max Harris, it has never been more popular or more widespread than it is today.[9] But in Totolapan this theatrical representation has little, if anything, to do with historical memory.

In the opening scene, each actor in turn offers the Cristo his or her opening lines, dedicating their performances to him. The actors are divided into a dozen Christian warriors and their king all dressed in vivid royal blue, and a parallel group of Moorish warriors and their queen dressed in red. In addition to these are also several children who play the roles of trouble-making devils and beatific, winged angels. Though the general theme and basic plot of the performance are familiar to all, the precise content of the play, the speeches and dialogue, are largely inaccessible to any but the actors themselves. Spanning more than thirty hours of performance, it would be impossible to follow the piece in its entirety. Rather, what the audience observes is an almost endless series of marches, dances, and barely choreographed battle scenes in which it appears that no one ever really dies, though the actors are frequently injured. In the end, the Moors are defeated and convert to Christianity. They take on the blue garments of Christians, the king and newly converted queen are joined in Christian marriage, and all gather to cheer for the Cristo Aparecido.

Victoria Bricker's 1980 work *Indian Christ, Indian King* is distinguished by its effort to uncover the internal, historical logic of contemporary Maya rituals, including a version of the Moros y Cristianos pageant. Against Lévi-Strauss's notion of bricolage, in which myth is randomly constructed from "remains and debris" of historical events, Bricker proposes that the Maya transformed history into myth through the telescoping of time, by choosing to incorporate thematically analogous events from their own history. For Bricker, Mayan religion since the time of the conquest has served, in part, to narrate and ritualize their own history of ethnic conflict. For example, in the Cancuc Rebellion described in the preface of this book, the Spaniards were understood to be "Jews" in their persecution of the cult of the Virgin. The Bible itself was recast as a narrative of ethnic conflict.[10] Bricker pays particular attention to the Mayan version of the "Dance of the Conquest" to show how the Maya collapsed, layered, renarrated, and ritualized their history of ethnic conflict within it. In her interpretation, the dance ritually references simultaneously the reconquest of Spain, Spanish domination of the Indians throughout the colonial period, and the mistreatment of the Indians in the nineteenth century leading up to the Caste War.[11] In Max Harris's study, the Moros y Cristianos pageant is transformed in many communities in Mexico into a reenactment of the triumph of Spanish Catholicism over Aztec religion.

Though the people of Totolapan have a persistent memory of repeated waves of conquest, I did not find that this memory was rehearsed in their "Doce Pares" play. Rather, the successful performance of the work in its entirety in the context of the Cristo's fiesta seemed to predominate in importance over the content of the work itself, including any historical resonances with American themes. As I have said, spread out over three days and on four stages, the intricacies of the plot and storyline are inaccessible to all but the actors and directors. Even so, the performance is considered absolutely essential to the fiesta. One past director explained to another researcher, "I have always said that at the fiesta first of all we celebrate our Cristo, and in second place is the Danza, which many people come to see. On the few occasions that we have not presented the play, fewer people visited the pueblo and the festival was very sad."[12] Don Bruno, who now serves as director, has a similar perspective: "Without this work, the holiday falls apart: it is dead, the fiesta dies."

The Totolapan version of the play may also be unique for the danger that it represents to the actors, who engage in an endless series of battles with real machetes. Though occasional injuries do occur in other pueblos, one director explained to another researcher that the risk is intensified in the Totolapan performance:

> Each year some of the actors are hurt, as careful as we try to be, and even if they are skillful with the weapons. It's that there are times in the play that are general battles, where the two full groups, all the actors, participate. And really then there is no way to protect yourself. You see there is no way to restrict the actors, because the *cortes de machete* mark the beat of the music. But also this is what is beautiful. But when people come from other communities to participate they say "in Totolapan they send us into war." And one researcher said, "They are giving real blows, stop them! This is no longer a play." But still, in the end everything turns out well and no one holds any grudges.[13]

The Convergence of the Cristos: Pilgrimage and the Fiesta

The Quinto Viernes is not celebrated only by people from Totolapan; it is a supralocal festival and many visitors arrive as organized groups of pilgrims from surrounding communities. They are not simply spectators but are an integral part of the various events of the fiesta: sponsoring masses, paying for fireworks, and augmenting the prestige and grandeur of the event with their presence. Each group brings with them a small replica of their own beloved local image and in this way the Aparecido is kept company by his cristos hermanos, who converge upon the Totolapan iglesia to lend their sacred presence to the fiesta.

The fiesta weekend officially commences on Friday with the ceremonious welcome of groups of pilgrims to the iglesia. They adorn the church with their many banners and miniaturized versions of their own local saints, and join with the locals in observing every aspect of the fiesta, which concludes with their departure late on Sunday evening. In addition to groups representing the various pueblos in the municipality of Totolapan (Nepopualco, San Miguel, San Andres, Tepetlixtipa, Ahuatlan, and Santa Margarita), organized groups of pilgrims come from the neighboring pueblos of Atlatlaucan, Tepoztlán, and Ocotepec in the state of Morelos and from Juitepec, Cuecuecuhautita, Santa Rosa Xochiac (D.F.), and Tepetlixpa from the state of México. They come on foot, in cars, or in groups of cyclists. In addition to such formal pilgrimages, there are also more casual visitors who know little or nothing of the Cristo but come for the spectacle itself and the party atmosphere. At least two musical bands also arrive from out of state, usually from Guanajuato, Sinaloa, or Jalisco. The hiring of these bands, which come with large entourages that also need to be housed and fed, is the single greatest expense for the fiesta, sometimes constituting as much as a third to a half of the budget.

The most esteemed and anticipated pilgrims are those that arrive from Iztapalapa, a sprawl of poor and working-class neighborhoods in the southern part of Mexico City. Iztapalapa is renowned for its yearly reenactment of the passion of Christ during Holy Week. Epic in scale, the performance involves many thousands of actors and draws perhaps hundreds of thousands of observers each year. It claims to be the largest annual passion play of its sort in the world.[14] Nevertheless, the neighborhoods of Iztapalapa that come to honor the Cristo, the barrios of San Ignacio and San Miguel, claim no involvement in their hometown event. "That is not part of our tradition," they explain, "our part of Iztapalapa celebrates the Cristo Aparecido."

I was not able to determine the historical origins of the participation of the many other pueblos that come to the Quinto Viernes celebration. But the participants from Iztapalapa have oral traditions that narrate a familial relationship of three cristos hermanos: their own Cristo de la Cuevita, the Cristo Aparecido, and the Señor de Chalma. The religious life of their community is anchored by a devotion to this trinity of christs. The Cristo de la Cuevita, which resides in a chapel in the center of Iztapalapa, is particular to the barrio residents there, and is celebrated nearly universally by them. The biography of their Cristo resonates in many ways with that of Cristo Aparecido: in it emerge the familiar themes of miraculous appearance, discovery, and the resistance of an image to restorations. "Many years ago the image escaped a restoration and was hiding in a little cave in Iztapalapa. A man was wandering in search of his little lost burro and encountered the Cristo in the cave. Like the Cristo Aparecido, the Cristo de la Cuevita is very old and has been in Iztapalapa for many centuries." The Cristo de la Cuevita is not a crucifix, but rather a Cristo del Entierro, an image of Christ interred in a glass coffin. As a slightly drunken pilgrim from Iztapalapa explained to me, "It is an image of Jesus asleep in his bed." One woman, who had arrived with the group and immediately set about arranging the various banners and saints' images they had brought, added, "Well, though he is a Santo del Entierro (the Saint Entombed), we usually just call him Santo Tierra (Holy Earth) because it is from him that all life comes." Far from a funereal image, in the devotions of the people of Iztapalapa the Cristo del Entierro is transformed into a sleeping saint, the mother Earth, who is the source of life. The Cristo de la Cuevita therefore is as resistant to an association with suffering and death as is his hermano, the Aparecido.

Burdened by banners and heavy alcancías, large boxes filled with money that they have raised as an offering, the pilgrims from Iztapalapa make a two-day hike over the mountains. They stop to sleep in a pueblo along the way that offers them food and shelter for the night. They arrive in Totolapan bedraggled and dusty, and crowd into the bottom floor of the convento, where they sleep on bedrolls. Teenagers congregate in groups in the convento corridors, flirting and hanging out. A few of them are heavily pierced, with rings decorating their eyebrows, lips, and ears. Others wear the latest athletic fashions.

The journey is slowed substantially because in addition to the alcancías that take two people at a time to carry, the pilgrims carry several large and cumbersome nichos, which are packed in protective wooden crates. The nichos are miniaturized shrines, reliquaries ranging from two feet to three feet in height. Inside the elaborately adorned cases are small, finely worked reproductions of local virgins and christs. In addition to a nicho of their own Santo Cristo Tierra, the pilgrims from Iztapalapa have brought two nichos of the Cristo Aparecido. A prominent family of the community owns one of these, but the other belongs to their local mayordomía in honor of the Cristo Aparecido. Though the words *alcancía* and *nicho* are sometimes interchangeable, *alcancías* usually refer to the separate wooden boxes that contain the visiting pueblo's financial contribution to the fiesta, sometimes as much as $2,500 in loose change and small bills.

The Iztapalapa mayordomal nicho is particularly beautiful and very different from the many more recent versions one commonly sees, made of shiny tin and glass. Their nicho is dark and elegant, constructed of rich, dark wood and lined with deeply colored velvet, it is also covered with countless *milagros*, small, silver representations of body parts that each represent a miracle of physical healing. They explain that this was first nicho ever to make the pilgrimage from Iztapalapa, and a finely engraved silver plaque declares March 19, 1926, as the date of that event. The plaque refers both to the "Santuario del Señor de Totolapan" and to the peregrinación from Iztapalapa—the only instance I have encountered in which the location of the Cristo is described as a *santuario*, or shrine. The eighty-year-old nicho and its plaque indicates that there was a considerable devotion to the Cristo de Totolapan in Iztapalapa in the first decades of the twentieth century. The inscription of this plaque thus provides historical evidence for the local legend that the Cristo spent a period in Iztapalapa (probably from 1859 to 1861) before finally returning to Totolapan.

Though these nichos are only replicas, people explain they are nevertheless very powerful. Unpacked one by one from their crates, these are placed on tables inside the iglesia; by the end of the day there are eight or ten nichos in the church. These nichos are understood to have made the pilgrimage to their cristo hermano, just as the people themselves have. As the images emerge from their crates, people push me aside, urgently reaching forward to touch and rub their hands against the nichos, scooping up blessings onto themselves, and leaving behind a haze of fingerprints on the glass.

In addition to the cash contribution that the pilgrims offer to the mayordomos, the visitors from Iztapalapa have brought a *portada*, an elaborate and towering floral arrangement to decorate the large entryway to the church. The portada, made of artificial flowers attached to a wood frame, took two days to construct and more than half a dozen men to hoist, with pulleys and ropes, into place. With all these offerings, it is no wonder that the pilgrims are warmly welcomed and seen as lending much prestige to the festival.

Although the pilgrims mostly come on foot, some of their goods and supplies are brought by car. Don Pedro, an elderly resident of the pueblo, described how the peregrinos from Iztapalapa come walking such a long distance, and that they even transport in cars live pigs that they slaughter, cook, and eat while they are here. "I feel sorry for them, their fare is so humble, they have so little, but they always invite one to eat and you have to accept." In spite of his mournful pity for the impoverished pilgrims, his grandchildren, ages twelve and fourteen, who have come from Guerrero for the fiesta and know little about the Cristo, struggle to suppress their laughter at the image of pigs getting driven in cars like princes while people are compelled to walk.

The pilgrims from Iztapalapa are the only group that arrives accompanied by their parish priest. He tells me that has come out of curiosity and to see the fiesta; and he is interested to speak with me about popular religion.

Christ the Pilgrim

Though there are many pilgrims, visitors who come from other pueblos to participate in the fiesta, it is the Cristo himself who is the true "pilgrim" as he makes his annual sojourn through the pueblo, following the path that his children have created for him. The procession of the Cristo through town, which takes several hours, is the culminating event of almost two weeks of festivities. Much as the pilgrims from Iztapalapa stopped in a pueblo along the way for refreshment, so too the Cristo (and the friar who carries him) pauses to rest in each neighborhood, stopping at the decorative *descansos* erected by each barrio. He and his cristos hermanos are often identified as pilgrims in an additional sense. That is, they have often made long sojourns in search of a proper and suitable home. Recall, for example the Señor de Chalma. who passed through Totolapan in his search for an adequate resting place. And remember as well the poor Cristo de la Cuevita of Iztapalapa who, fleeing a restoration, sought shelter in a lowly cave. These christs are sojourners and survivors.

At four p.m. the procession is about to begin. One of the young friars gently removes the Cristo from his adorno to prepare the santo for the procession. Two mayordomos stand authoritatively, almost intimidating, at the front, *vigilando*, arms crossed, eyes focused on the Cristo. The friar brings the image behind the altar and faces it away from the congregation in order to protect the Cristo's modesty. For the first time I observe the Cristo's bare back, painted with blood and lashes. Ever so discreetly, the friar changes the Cristo's "skirt" for a new, processional vestment. Then the friar delicately removes the santo's hair, leaving him momentarily bald and exposed. But he quickly replaces it with a new hairpiece, recently donated locks, which he arranges meticulously so that the hair falls in soft, dark curls around the Cristo's pale shoulders. Each gesture is done slowly, with decorum and respect. The ritual transformation complete, and the image newly vested, the friar turns the Cristo around to present him to the congregation. It seems, at that moment, as if the entire room gently exhales. The friar glances at the mayordomos, searching for approval, and they nod their heads in assent: it has all been well done.

There is a moment of hushed excitement as the image then makes his way down the steps and into the aisle. The crowd pushes forward and the slow procession begins. We exit the church together, in silence. But outside the sisters are hawking candles in loud voices, thrusting them upon the procession. They seem only slightly embarrassed by yelling at the solemn moment, though there are few takers for their wares.

As each friar takes his turn with the Cristo, the crowd following him grows in size. And with each step, the friar destroys the delicate mosaics of flowers and sawdust with his sandaled feet. The beautiful, carpeted path is ephemeral and quickly erased. Some even comment: "All that work and so quickly ruined!" As soon as the procession passes, clean-up crews follow behind, sweeping up what remains of the tapetes. The image stops perhaps six or seven times throughout his two-hour pilgrimage.

Even during the "pilgrimage" itself, the focus of the fiesta remains diffuse: not everyone joins in the procession. Small groups gather to wait expectantly by the descanos, others rush to complete their tapete before the Cristo arrives, and still others clean up as the procession moves on. The actors from the Doce Pares pageant join the procession en masse, but at the halfway mark they split off and return to the atrio to continue their performance, though there will be no audience. Others observe the procession from their windows and doors, and still others remain inside, going about the ordinary business of running their households. The mood during the procession itself is subdued; somber but not mournful. Nobody weeps openly; and occasionally, when the Cristo draws near to the next descanso, there is jostling for space as the excitement mounts.

As the procession enters its final stretch, I fall back and join doña Luz, who is waiting at the descanso in her barrio, the last resting place before the image returns to the iglesia. Every year Luz helps to build the *casita del descanso* for her neighborhood. Weeks earlier, chatting in her home, she told me that during last year's procession she had become emotional when the santo came to rest at her descanso. She felt suddenly angry, and started to argue with the Cristo, to fight with him because he had recently "taken her parents." But even in her anger she felt that he offered her solace. She said that often when she sees him on these processions she argues and fights with him. Once she even discussed this with Padre Salvador, who reassured her that she can share with the Cristo anything that is in her heart.

Yet today the tone at the descanso is light-hearted; there is humor and joking, as a dozen women wait for the Cristo to arrive. One woman takes photographs and the others ask that she try to make sure they look beautiful in the photos. "Hace fotos, no milagros," she takes photographs, she doesn't work miracles, rejoins another. Everyone laughs heartily. They tell me to write about how their street was the most beautifully decorated of all, and they poke fun at others for being lazy in their decorations. But underlying the jocular playfulness is the sense that they are waiting: the mood is one of casual anticipation and camaraderie. This feeling of togetherness, of communitas, is part of the ritual. In the distance we can see the procession as it begins to approach, the Cristo leading them all.

A light rain shower begins to fall from a cloudless blue sky. I turn, eyebrows raised, to look at the other women in disbelief. They shrug their shoulders in nonchalance and smile, nonplussed by the apparent miracle: he always brings rain.

As the Cristo arrives at the descanso, a woman pushes me to the front of the crowd, close to the image. I am the nearest to him I have ever been, a privileged position. I am struck by the alabaster color of his skin, the serenity of his sleeping face. Beautiful, I think, as my heart catches in my throat.[15]

The Cristo Aparecido at the Border: Transnational Religion and the Mayordomía of the Immigrants

Today, as many as two hundred Totolapans have migrated to the United States. The largest percentage of these live in the mission community of San Juan Capistrano in southern California and surrounding communities, though others have settled in Atlanta, Georgia. From these locales, immigrants send financial contributions for the fiesta to the Cristo and continue to honor him in home altars even as they frequently embrace their new religious and cultural context. Religious Studies scholar, Manuel Vásquez, has observed, with others, that Latin American immigrants to the United States do not necessarily seek an expedited assimilation but rather "choose to live 'transnational lives,' experiencing simultaneous 'embeddedness' in their societies of origin and of settlement."[16] This is certainly the case for Totolapans in southern California, as I discovered in my research there in 2008.

The most salient feature of their religious practice is that the annual fiesta of the Cristo Aparecido is the occasion for a temporary return migration of Totolapans from all over the United States to the pueblo. Most of the immigrants from Totolapan are now middle-aged and many are U.S. citizens, though they come and go for the fiesta, they have no plans to return permanently to their pueblo of origin. One person I interviewed suggested that as many as 95 percent of all Totolapans in the United States return for the fiesta of the Cristo. Even many of those who are undocumented risk the return home, saying, "I am going to see my Cristo. He will help me return safely." So during the annual celebration, immigrants who may be too busy to visit one another in the United States embrace each other warmly on the decorated streets of Totolapan.

The Cristo extends his protection to his devotees across national borders. Immigrants' reflections seem to suggest that perhaps the Cristo has helped them weather the worst of the foreclosure crisis that hit their region of California particularly hard; this is not to say that Totolapans have not lost their homes—many have—but the Cristo watches over them and keeps their families safe in the midst of great difficulty. While others continue to lose their jobs in the economic downturn at the end of 2008, one immigrant reports that most still work at 70-80 percent capacity. Totolapans work in many industries—in the service industry, as gardeners, and in construction—but their relationship to the Cristo has helped them steer clear of the darker sides of the economy; no one from the pueblo is involved in drug trafficking.

Immigrants do find that due to the intensity of life in the United States, especially long hours of work, including evenings and weekends, that there is not as much time as they would like to practice their faith. Nevertheless, in the last three years the community of migrants from Totolapan has organized themselves into a transnational mayordomía of sorts, though they explain that they have not quite achieved the formality of organization and participation that would allow them to claim the title "mayordomía de los inmigrantes." This does seem to be the eventual goal. Thirteen immigrants from San Juan Capistrano and surrounds currently form the basis of this organization, and each donates $100.00 a year to sponsor a *misa de los migrantes*, a mass in honor of migrants, at the annual fiesta. Outside of this formal structure, the vast majority of immigrants make offerings of $50.00 or more to pay for flowers, cohetes, candles, and other offerings to the Cristo. The first misa de los migrantes was held around 2004, with just twenty people present. Now, in 2008, the iglesia is full; almost two hundred come to pray for the welfare of the migrants: "We pray to ask the Cristo Aparecido not to abandon us, the migrants," one explains. At the misa, family members pray for the continued health and safety of their families far away. For some undocumented immigrants, who deem the return journey too risky, their participation in the fiesta is virtual: DVD documentaries many hours long circulate after each fiesta, and after many repeated screenings, immigrant children are often as familiar with these films as they are with the Disney staples, The Little Mermaid and Finding Nemo.

One notes a general trend in the literature on transnational migrant communities from Mexico and beyond: that the ongoing financial contributions to community fiestas serves a self-interested material purpose, benefiting family members who remain in sending communities; "remittances from migration pay for increases in the social status of families in the village largely through the sponsorship of fiestas by these families."[17] Thus there seems to be a general consensus that remittances are either compulsory (by sending communities) or "status-driven."[18] These theories do little to explain the complex motivations of the people from Totolapan for continuing to engage in their local fiesta. In this instance, participation is completely voluntary, and the action is motivated by deep emotion, or sentiment: a deep love for their Cristo, whom they long for just as one longs for home.

Totolapan immigrants to San Juan Capistrano, California, by and large attend the famous Catholic mission church there. The Mission San Juan Capistrano, one of twenty-one in the California Mission system, is a favorite destination for school field trips. Each year almost every fourth grader in the state has to recreate a diorama of one of the missions, stimulating a micro-industry of arts and crafts products for this purpose. Students recreate idyllic scenes of mission life.[19] In the spring, groups of school children arrive to Mission San Juan almost every hour. The mission itself has an almost theme-park feel to it, and it is full of strange anachronisms and ahistorical inventions: including, most glaringly, a native Indian dwelling right in the middle of the grounds, as if the friars of yore would have invited such a structure. Unlike the conventos in Mexico that are currently guarded and administered by the state, the Mission San Juan Capistrano remains the property of the diocese, and is administered by a nonprofit organization. The state has no jurisdiction over the site as a national landmark.

Nevertheless, on Sunday mornings, the small capilla is full to capacity, with standing room only at both English and Spanish services. A Latino priest is in charge of the parish, of whom Totolapan immigrants are quite fond, for the most part. Immigrants make it clear that they have not attempted to shape Catholic practice in their new home parish, but rather immerse themselves fully in the preexisting communal life there. For example, many of their children have successfully completed the rigorous two-year preparation required for First Communion. They also participate enthusiastically in the celebration marking the famed annual return of the swallows to Capistrano, the Fiesta de los Golondrines. Totolapans show up en masse for this event, and even contribute a traditional *Brinco de Chinelo* band for the parade, made up of local Totolapan talent. At the same time, their inclination is to continue to formalize their ongoing participation in the annual celebration of the Cristo Aparecido in Totolapan, as time and money allow.

Conclusions

Here I have sought to uncover the spiritual and affective postures that devotees assume in their celebration of the Cristo Aparecido on both sides of the border. The tender regard and affection that devotees feel for the Cristo are not most importantly related to personal benefit. These feelings do not arise from his power to work miracles. In fact, when asked directly if the Cristo is miraculous, people tend to shy away from a straightforward affirmation. Rather, they almost always offer a qualification: "Well . . . sure, if one has faith." Or, "that depends on one's faith." Rather, people's affection for their santo stems simply from his very existence; the fact that he is, that he has been made manifest, and that he came to them.

As I have suggested, the themes of pity, compassion, sorrow, grief, are muted in devotion to the Cristo Aparecido. Instead, the spiritual posture in relation to the Cristo, as a beloved santo, is characterized by affection, warmth, tenderness, gentle care and concern. He is their Cristito, their "little Christ." Affection and tenderness for the divine are emotions that are alien to the spiritual vocabulary of mainstream U.S. Christians, and are especially curious or surprising when experienced in front of an image that some might find painful, garish, or distressing. These are the very emotions that, I argue in chapter 3, defined Nahua spiritual engagement with the *tlapialli*, indigenous sacred images, before the arrival of the Europeans. It is possible that more than any other feature of indigenous religious life these affective postures are what has survived centuries of colonial rule and Christian evangelization through to the present day.

I learned something about the role of affection in devotion to the image of Christ crucified when participating in the Posadas. On Christmas Eve throughout Mexico, people commonly celebrate the *acostamiento*, in which the niños Jesus are put to bed, that is, the infant Jesus is ceremoniously placed in his crèche. On the evening before Christmas, people bring their family statues of the infant Jesus to church, or hold private processions and celebrations in their homes. The infants are ceramic casts of various sizes, painted with fair skin, doe-eyes of the brightest blue, and endlessly long eyelashes and are available for sale in public markets throughout the season. Celebrations of the acostamiento differ slightly from community to community, but they often look like this: late at night, in the atrio the priests lead the community in singing lullabies to their niños, as they gently rock their infants to sleep. In the days immediately before and after Christmas, one can often see people toting these niños around, at the market, in the grocery store, always bundled securely in blankets, and tucked into the cradle of an arm. Men express this tenderness, warmth, care, and protectiveness as easily as women; both did their fair share of the rocking and cradling. Though it is not difficult to imagine these emotions arising in relationship to the infant Jesus, I believe they are not necessarily very different from the tenderness that is evoked for many believers toward the adult Christ on the cross.

I once observed a grandmother introducing her infant grandson to the saints' images at her neighborhood capilla. The capilla housed another miraculous crucifix, the Cristo de Ixcatapec, an image that is predictably graphic, bloody, and pained. The grandmother walked easily up behind the altar, carrying the boy in her arms and spoke quietly into the baby's ear as she gestured to the crucifix in his glass nicho. After gathering several flowers from large vases, she climbed the small, concealed stairs up to the Cristo. Talking gently all the while to the infant, the grandmother opened the glass door, pulled aside the lace curtain, and stroked the image with the flowers, smiling to the baby. I was struck by the warmth, sweetness, and intimacy of the act. Who could feel fear, sadness, or apprehension in front of a crucifix after such an introduction? One can hardly imagine a narrative more starkly opposed to the one that Roa wove around the Santo Cristo Aparecido.

9

Conclusion

The Gospel According to Totolapan

I conclude by way of a contrast, offering for the reader's consideration and contemplation two images of the Cristo Aparecido. Recall the Cristo as Fray Antonio de Roa first encountered him: gaunt, hungry, emaciated, and broken. This is the Cristo as captured in Lopez Beltrán's grainy black-and-white photo taken at the middle of the twentieth century and shown at the beginning of this book. Contrast this image of suffering with the santo as you have just left him at the close of his fiesta: he has been transfigured, literally transformed by the people's faith, as by the series of physical renovations that have been worked upon him during the last century (figure 9.1). The sharpnesses, the protruding ribs, of the earlier Cristo seem to have faded. His skin is now alabaster, the whitest of whites, and captures neither the pale pallor of death nor the flesh tones of a European conqueror. Instead, he emanates a numinous, unearthly glow.

Through the Cristo Aparecido I have sought to introduce the reader to a constellation of christs around which clusters a many-layered Christology: one in which the Gospel narrative of Jesus' suffering often fades into the background. The Aparecido is a *cristo vivo*, a living Christ, in both the religious and art historical sense of the phrase. Within fifty years of his creation he became for the Indians animate, infused with life and spirit, and expressing will, desire, agency, and power. He is also understood in the latter sense of *vivo*, in that he has been at the center of uninterrupted active devotion over the course of five centuries. Some might call the celebration of the Cristo Aparecido a form of animism or, less generously, a lingering "paganism" that points to the failure of Christian evangelization. However, this book was not driven by a theological quest for

FIGURE 9.I. Cristo Aparecido transfigured and transformed.

consistent or systematic meanings aimed to bring to light some universal, authoritative understanding of Christianity in which categories such as "success"
or "failure," "truth" or "error," might carry some weight. Instead, here I have
offered an exegesis of a specific, local Christian culture and, by extension, a
reflection on the diversity of Catholic engagements, none of which I am willing
to exclude as illegitimate. Roa's Christ and the Christ of the fiesta are both the
christs of a living, breathing, and evolving Christian faith.

The Cristo is a visual and material testament. Through telling and retell-
ing the story of his earthly sojourn, today the people of Totolapan narrate the
history of their own faith. I have said that frequently it is the life of the Cristo,
more than the life of Christ, that occupies their religious imagination. But
just as often this distinction is collapsed. There are moments when the biography of the image seems to parallel key moments in the life of the earthly
Jesus. The swaddled Cristo arrives to Totolapan in the sixteenth century in the
embrace of an Indian angel just as the infant Jesus appears swaddled in the
manger. In 1583 the Cristo was judged and condemned by the Inquisition as
an ordinary image, just as the earthly Jesus, examined, bound and scourged,
was declared only human, just a man, by Pontius Pilate in John's gospel. The
return of the image to Totolapan in the last half of the nineteenth century is
a resurrection of sorts for the Cristo, bringing new life and strength to the
faithful of the pueblo, who had waited in hope for the return of their Christ.
Here I have attempted to capture the depth and complexity of this local

expression of Christian faith: The gospel of our Lord Jesus Christ, according to Totolapan.

The motif of suffering is hardly absent in devotion to the Cristo, but it is sometimes muted and frequently appears in surprising or unlikely forms and expressions. In the colonial encounter, European missionaries presented a theological anthropology in which Christ's death on the cross was taken to be the ultimate expression of humanity: through Christ, human beings were defined, constituted, in part, by their liability to suffering. As the Indians came to see themselves as Christians, they were also meant to adopt this new notion of humanity in which they were to understand themselves first and foremost as sufferers. Within this new Christian imaginaire, outsiders should regard the indigenous people of the New World, these new Christians, not so much as noble savages but rather as noble sufferers. This continues to be one of the predominant and iconic representations of indigenous Americans today. Nonetheless, questions of theodicy are all but absent in the Cristo's long biography and the colonial period generally. That is, few have questioned or defended the benevolence or omnipotence of God, given the mass death and profound suffering of Indians.

I have suggested in this book that the fate of the Cristo and the fate of the Indian communities of Totolapan and Mexico City are somehow wedded together. Perhaps this relationship was foreseen in Bartolomé de las Casas's likening of the conquered and brutally exploited Indians of New Spain to "scourged christs." More likely this association began when the Indians decided to take Christ into their own hands, forming and shaping him from their own materials and media, and when they then transformed themselves into Christ-bearers, carrying him into monasteries and churches and departing quickly, before too many questions could be asked. Their fates were joined, as well, in a grim inversion, as the indigenous population threatened to disappear under the scourge of epidemic disease and, almost as if to replace them, hundreds of images of Christ, including our own Aparecido, came to populate the grieving land. Today the people of Totolapan are utterly identified with their Cristo: he has suffered as they have, but he has survived, as they have. Most of all, today he stands for their embattled faith; a faith vibrant, potent, and profound, but simultaneously, in their own self-perception, as fragile as their Cristo's delicate form. Through conquest, conversion, disruption, and migration, the people of Totolapan have a seamlessness experience of faith in which the Cristo stands as the living symbol of all they hold dear.

In her brilliant interpretive study of contemporary Chicana art, Laura Pérez explores the altar both as an artistic form and as a symbolic motif in diverse works in the last decades of the twentieth century. She explains that she therefore conceived her book itself as an "altar-like structure."[1] Similarly, my study of the Cristo has been an *ofrenda*, an offering: an unlikely altar upon which the Cristo Aparecido has rested, if only just for the time that these pages have focused the reader's attention upon the santo. Indeed, secular scholars occasionally find themselves seduced into assuming devotional postures vis-à-vis the objects of material religion that they study. This was true, for example, for the scholars that Harvard meso-Americanist, David Carrasco brought together to study the Mapa de Cuauhtinchan, a sixteenth-century indigenous codex recounting a local history of cosmic origins. As the esteemed group approached the image for the first time, they were invited to circumambulate the Mapa, as if paying homage and reverence.[2] Perhaps the scrutinizing, appreciative, interpretive gaze of the scholar can sometimes also be included among the diverse ritual uses of objects of material religion. Just as the many scholar-priests before me who were captivated by the story of Roa and his Cristo, I myself am now part of his biography.

I have traced the accumulation of meaning around the Cristo over centuries and charted the Cristo's extraordinary story of survival and repeated rescue. For the people of Totolapan, the Cristo Aparecido has become the material embodiment of religious and cultural collective identity. But just as much as I have focused on the multiplicity of meanings and understandings, and the varied ritual uses of the object, this book offers an example of an affective approach to the study of religion. That is, the goal has been not just to uncover how the Cristo has been understood but also to gather what feelings, what emotions, he has evoked. Religion is not only about belief and embodied practice but also about affect and emotion. Today the emotions of tenderness and affection for the Cristo predominate spiritual engagement. I hope this work has brought the reader to share, if even for a moment, these same sentiments for the imagen.

Notes

1. Juan Pedro Viqueira Albán, *María de la Candelaria.*
2. Ibid., 12. "Sí, en la ermita, detrás del petate, pusisteis al ídolo y subisteis a darle pleitesía, a vender vuestra alma al Demonio. Vertisteis los santos óleos sobre la faz monstruosa de Hicalahua. . . . Acordaos que os advertí de los embustes de María de la Candelaria, y no quisisteis oírme."
3. Ibid., 13.
4. See Juan Pedro Viqueira Albán, *Indios rebeldes e idólatras.*
5. Inga Clendinnen, "Ways to the Sacred," 109.
6. P. M. Jones writes, "Most historians would sum up popular religion as an unholy mixture of paganism, peasant magic and half-baked Christian doctrine," as cited in Eric Van Young, *The Other Rebellion,* 513.
7. Dipesh Chakrabarty, *Provincializing Europe,* 11. See also his *Habitations of Modernity.*
8. Chakrabarty, *Provincializing Europe,* 12.
9. Here Chakrabarty is summarizing the thinking of Ranajit Guha. See chapter 4 of Ranajit Guha, *Elementary Aspects of Peasant Insurgency in Colonial India.*
10. Latin American subaltern historian Florencia Mallon was recently compelled to make just such a move. In a foray into testimonial literature, she jointly authored a biography with the indigenous Chilean activist, Rosa Isolde Reuque Paillalef. Reuque's activism and feminism were deeply interwoven with her faith; in particular they were shaped by her participation in the *comunidades eclesiales de base.* In what became a profoundly personal and in some ways painful confrontation, Mallon was forced to examine her own particular ambivalence to religion in order to take seriously the

integrity of Reuque's religious beliefs and practice. Rosa Isolde Reuque Paillalef and Florencia E. Mallon, *When a Flower Is Reborn*. But see also here Gil Joseph's *Reclaiming the Political in Latin American History: Essays from the North (American Encounters/ Global Interactions)*.

11. Under the leadership of Argentine theologian Enrique Dussel, the self-described task of CEHILA (Comisión de Estudios de Historia de la Iglesia en América Latina), specifically its twelve-volume encyclopedic history of the church in Latin America, was to respond to this call to reinterpret history from the perspective of the poor.

CHAPTER 1

1. This approach is represented in a different geographical context in Richard H. Davis, *Lives of Indian Images*.

2. I employ the term "Indian" here and throughout advisedly, insofar as it was a meaningful social category and self-designation in the colonial period and sometimes in the present.

3. Fernando Cervantes, *The Devil in the New World*.

4. P. M. Jones as cited in Eric Van Young, *The Other Rebellion*, 513.

5. Historian William Taylor records that of 480 shrines with supralocal devotion, 219 have been to the Virgin Mary, while 261 are to images of Christ; two-thirds of the later were devoted to crucifixes. See "Two Shrines of the Cristo Renovado."

6. Recent scholarly works on Guadalupe include those by David Brading (2001), Louise Burkhart (2001), Ana Castillo (1996), Virgil Elizondo (1997), Stafford Poole (1995), and William Taylor (1987, 2002).

7. Marian devotion predominates in Spain, today as in the time of the conquest, while the inverse is true in Mesoamerica. This probably reflects the emphasis of the friars themselves.

8. Pál Kelemen, *Baroque and Rococo in Latin America*. Vol. 1, 50.

9. Most recently, Richard Trexler accepts this interpretation in his history of the passion play in Ixtapalapa: Richard C. Trexler, *Reliving Golgotha*. But see also David Batstone, *From Conquest to Struggle*; José Míguez Bonino, *Faces of Jesus*; and Jon Sobrino, *Jesus in Latin America*. These theologians conclude that Indians saw in the image of the suffering Christ a reflection of their own pain. See also art historians reiterating the theme of identification: Pál Kelemen, *Baroque and Rococo in Latin America, Vol. 1*; Elizabeth Weismann, *Mexico in Sculpture, 1521–1821*; and Paul Westheim, *La calavera*.

10. Bartolomé de las Casas, Helen Rand Parish, and Francis Sullivan, *The Only Way*; Gustavo Gutiérrez, *En busca de los pobres de Jesucristo*.

11. Gutiérrez, *En busca de los pobres*, 62 (orig: *Historia de Indias*, bk 3, ch. 138, and *Obras Escogidas* 2:511b).

12. Felipe Guamán Poma de Ayala and others, *El primer nueva corónica y buen gobierno*.

13. Anita Brenner, *Idols behind Altars*, 297.

14. See also those works published in the series of the same title (Lived Religions) by Johns Hopkins Press, including most of all Timothy Matovina's excellent

monograph, *Guadalupe and Her Faithful: Latino Catholics from Colonial Origins to the Present* (2005). For an argument in favor of this intellectual shift, see the recent book by Meredith McGuire, *Lived Religion: Faith and Practice in Everyday Life* (New York: Oxford University Press, 2008).

15. There are many others that have followed his, including the volume edited by Martin Austin Nesvig, *Local Religion in Colonial Mexico*.

16. As a point of fact, I trace my emphasis on experience to liberation theologians rather than to phenomenologists of other stripes.

17. See, for example, Bernardino de Sahagún, *Códice florentino*; and in English, Bernardino de Sahagún and others, *General History of the Things of New Spain*; Toribio Motolinía, *History of the Indians of New Spain*; and Gerónimo de Mendieta and Francisco Solano y Pérez-Lila, *Historia eclesiástica indiana*.

18. Guamán Poma de Ayala and others, *El primer nueva corónica y buen gobierno*.

19. The genre of object history has influenced both recent film and fiction. François Gerard's 1998 film "The Red Violin" follows an extraordinary instrument as it passes from the hands of musician to musician, traveling across five countries, over the course of more than three centuries. The instrument not only bears erotic and destructive power but also, as the viewer slowly realizes, is living out a long-ago predicted fate. It turns out that I share Gerard's curiosity for tracking the journey of an exceptional object over time and space. More recently, Pulitzer prize–winning author Geraldine Brooks's work of historical fiction, *People of the Book: A Novel* (New York: Viking, 2008), follows a rare illuminated Haggadah back through time to tell the story of the communities that preserved and protected the extraordinary text over six centuries.

CHAPTER 2

1. This account, including this final declaration, comes primarily from the testimony of Francisco de Tolentino at the Inquisition hearing investigating the Cristo's origins that took place in the convento of Totolapan in May of 1583. AGN Inquisición, vol. 133, exp. 29, fs. 244–294.

2. For a new consideration of the sacred bundle, see Guilhem Olivier, "Sacred Bundles, Arrows, and New Fire," in *Cave, City and Eagle's Nest*, 282–283.

3. I have culled biographical information about Roa from a handful of colonial sources. Antonio Osorio de San Román's *Consuelo de penitentes o mesa franca de espirituales manjares* (Seville, 1585) is the oldest published source. Alonso Fernández's *Historia eclesiástica de nuestros tiempos* (1611) draws extensively on Osorio de San Román's narrative, and may in turn have been a source for Juan de Grijalva and Federico Gómez de Orozco 's *Crónica de la orden de N.P.S. Augustin en las provincias de la nueva españa* (México, 1624). Grijalva's is the most thorough treatment of Roa's life and of the origins of devotion to the Cristo Aparecido, with several short chapters specifically dedicated to outlining the friar's life, ministry, and death. Grijalva's text also provides the basis for the eighteenth-century hagiographic account by Cabrera y Quintero, which is a self-described summary of Grijalva's more extensive treatment; see Cayetano Cabrera y Quintero and Víctor M. Ruiz Naufal, *Escudo de armas de México*. Grijalva's work also most likely forms the basis for Sebastian de Portillo y

Aguilar's *Chronica espiritual augustiniana: vidas de santos, beatos, y venerables religiosos del orden de su gran padre San Agustín, para todos los días del año* (Madrid: Alonso de Orozco, 1731–1732). The third volume in particular treats the life of Antonio de Roa, though this text was not available to the author. Finally, I consulted a late-colonial "revivalist" history, available only in manuscript form, written by an Augustinian friar named Manuel González de la Paz y del Campo. This, the lengthiest treatment, is in essence an emotional elaboration upon Grijalva's text. As these subsequent texts derive from Grijalva's work, the original source will be sufficient when the subsequent texts are unavailable.

4. Born in the Villa de Roa. His father was Hernán do Alvares de la Puebla, "camarero de la Duquesa de Alburquerque," and his mother was Inés López, a pious, innocent, and saintly woman. Grijalva and Gómez de Orozco, *Crónica de la orden*, 310.

5. Ibid., 311.

6. See, for example, John Leddy Phelan, *The Millennial Kingdom of the Franciscans in the New World*.

7. Grijalva and Gómez de Orozco, *Crónica de la orden*, 42.

8. "Ya V.S. sabe cómo la órden de San Agustín no es tan temida en la Nueva España como la de Santo Domingo é San Francisco: los religiosos de esta Orden . . . han aprobado y aprueban bien, y tenido gran cuidado en la conversión y doctrina de los indios, tanto como los demás, y en ellos no ha habido falta." See Mendoza, *Avisos*, page 306, cited in Joaquin García Icazbalceta, "Los Agustinos en México."

9. The fact that the Augustinians were perceived in their own time as less commanding (if only slightly) than the Franciscans and Dominicans has manifested itself in a related scholarly neglect in the present. The Franciscans have held particular fascination for scholars in the twentieth century. Not so the Augustinians. While Mexican scholars, Rubial García in particular, have in fact dedicated a few important volumes to the Augustinians, scholars outside of Mexico, and outside of the order itself, are for the most part indifferent to (and sometimes simply ignorant of) its rich history. A recent article by Mickey Abel-Turby published in the respected *Colonial Latin America Review* is a case in point. Abel-Turby sets out to contrast the missionary ideology of the Augustinians with the methods of the Franciscans. Apparently unaware of the existence of at least a dozen colonial self-histories and *crónicas* of the order, Abel-Turby cites none of these, not even Grijalva, oft-consulted on matters Augustinian. Abel-Turby bemoans the absence of internal reflection on Augustinian mission in the colonial period, calling the Augustinians "frustratingly mute" on the subject. Such is the paucity of written sources, he argues, that he must resort to visual images that they produced; Mickey Abel-Turby, "The New World Augustinians and Franciscans in Philosophical Opposition."

10. The year 1535 is given by Jesús Solís de la Torre, *Bárbaros y ermitaños*, 30. However, Grijalva offers a different year, 1536 (p. 313).

11. ". . . las tierras más ásperas, más tristes y estériles que entonces habían." Fray Antonio Osorio de San Román, *Consuelo de penitentes o mesa franca de espirutuales manjares*, 735. Cf. Alonso Fernández, *Historia eclesiástica de nuestros tiempos*, book 2, ch. 33, 125. Grijalva notes as well that the unpopulated regions of Mexico provided these friars with a figurative *desierto eremítico, Crónica de la orden*, 361.

12. *Bárbaros y ermitaños*, 31.

13. See Peter Gerhard's *A Guide to the Historical Geography of New Spain* (Norman: University of Oklahoma Press, 1993).

14. Grijalva and Gómez de Orozco, *Crónica de la orden*, 314.

15. Clara Bargellini, "Representations of Conversion."

16. Bernal Díaz del Castillo and J. M. Cohen, *The Conquest of New Spain*.

17. David Carrasco, *City of Sacrifice*.

18. "Con lo que mas illustraron el Reyno, y en lo que mostraron la grandeza, y generosidad de sus animos, fue en la fabrica de los templos y conventos, testigos a la posteridad de la opulencia del Reyno"; Grijalva and Gómez de Orozco, *Crónica de la orden*, 225.

19. Diego Valadés and Tarsicio Herrera Zapién, *Retórica cristiana*.

20. Robert Ricard, *The Spiritual Conquest of Mexico*, 285.

21. Alipio Ruiz Zavala, *Historia de la Provincia Agustiniana de Santisimo Nombre de Jesús de México*, vol. 2, 337. For a biography of doña Isabel Moctezuma that explains how she was in a position to make this endowment, see the essay by Donald Chipman in David G. Sweet and Gary B. Nash, eds., *Struggle and Survival in Colonial America*.

22. Guillermo Tovar de Teresa, José E. Iturriaga, and Enrique Krauze, *The City of Palaces*.

23. A. Neumeyer, "The Indian Contribution to Architectural Decoration in Spanish Colonial America."

24. This is the opinion expressed in Guillermo Bonfil Batalla and Philip Adams Dennis, *México Profundo: Reclaiming a Civilization* (Austin: University of Texas Press, 1996), 86.

25. Sabine MacCormack, *Religion in the Andes*, 377.

26. Regarding the descriptor "passional," I borrow this interesting and useful term from Timothy Mitchell, *Passional Culture*.

27. Grijalva and Gómez de Orozco, *Crónica de la orden*, 327.

28. David Freedberg, *The Power of Images*, 27.

29. "Alongside the repertory of private images were those created to adorn public or communal places of worship, such as cathedrals, parish churches, chapels, hermitages, monastic and conventual foundations, and colleges and seminaries. Larger in scale than devotional images, and usually more complex in significance, these decorations can be likened to symphonies of Catholic doctrine and devotion and must be interpreted by different strategies than those used for intimate devotional works." Isabella Stewart Gardner Museum, ed., *The Word Made Image*, 12.

30. For her discussion of the role of imagination, see MacCormack, *Religion in the Andes*, 16.

31. Inga Clendinnen, *Ambivalent Conquests*, 76.

32. For his description of it as a violent and terrifying sort of street theater, see Kenneth Mills, *Idolatry and Its Enemies*, 32.

33. MacCormack, *Religion in the Andes*, 389.

34. Paradoxically, these three destroyers of indigenous religious culture were also among its greatest and most meticulous and devoted recorders. Landa's *Relación de las cosas de Yucatán* (1566) is the single most important source for our current body of knowledge about the pre-Columbian culture of the Yucatan. Ramos Gavilán's *Historia del Santuario de Nuestra Señora de Copacabana* (1621) narrates the successful

replacement of indigenous sense of the sacred with the Christian holy in the arrival of the Virgin of Copacabana at Lake Titicaca. Thus even as Ramos Gavilán sought to eradicate indigenous cultural forms he also labored to memorialize and interpret them, though obviously within a Christian framework. Francisco de Ávila's *Hombres y Dioses de Huarochiri* (1621) is one of the most valuable extant sources on Peruvian Indian culture. The tone and language of Ávila's Quechua text reveal a surprising underlying affection for native Andean traditions: it is paradoxically a lovingly recorded description and a "formidable arsenal against idolatry." Pierre Duviols, *La destrucción de las religiones andinas*, 22.

35. Juan de Torquemada, *Monarquía indiana*, vol. 5, 44. Cortés's action did not go uncontested; some observers expressed concern about the ability of Indians to pay proper respect for these crosses: "'In my opinion,' Olmedo is said to have told Cortés, 'it is too early to leave a cross in these people's possession.'" Mills, *Idolatry and Its Enemies*, 280.

36. Torquemada, *Monarquía indiana*, vol. 1, 129.

37. Ibid., vol. 2, 365.

38. William F. Hanks, *Intertexts*, 252.

39. There are numerous accounts of this in Torquemada; see, for example, vol. 5, 303.

40. Torquemada, *Monarquía indiana*, vol. 1, 415.

41. Ibid., vol. 5, 298. Friars instructed Indians to raise crosses at crossroads in order to liberate themselves from harassment by devils.

42. The council declared that bishops "teach that images of Christ, the virgin mother of God, and the other saints should be set up and kept, particularly in churches, and that due honor and reverence is owed to them, not because anything is to be expected of them, or because confidence should be placed in images as was done by the pagans of old; but because the honor showed to them is referred to the original which they represent. Thus, through the images which we kiss and before which we uncover our heads and go down on our knees, we give adoration to Christ and veneration to the saints, whose likeness they bear" (1563). From *Decrees of the Ecumenical Councils*, edited by Norman Tanner, vol. 2, 774–776. Cited in Isabella Stewart Gardner Museum, ed., *Word Made Image*, ch. 1.

43. Note here the small marble and ivory crucifixes sculpted in the Philippines, perhaps by Japanese or Chinese tradesmen living there (*sangleys*), and shipped to the port of Acapulco; "there was hardly a church or home of a gentleman who prided himself upon his importance and dignity lacking one of these figures of Christ, in which the design of the body follows the natural curve of the ivory tusk." Sonia de la Roziére and Xavier Moyssén Echeverría, *México*, xxxvii.

An art exhibit in Lima in 1991 included many *crucificados* sculpted of marble. The catalogue of the exhibit attributes these to the sangleys and affirms that they were indeed the authors of many of the images that were imported to the New World; Fondo Pro Recuperación del Patrimonio Cultural de la Nación, ed., *Los Cristos de Lima*, 77. The possibilities for an Asian influence on indigenous (Mexican) religious sentiment are intriguing. These marble and ivory crucifixes are evidence of the existence of an international system of crucifix fabrication and distribution, in particular in response to this new market.

44. This is Estrada Jasso's argument.

45. Andrés Estrada Jasso, *Imágenes en caña de maíz*, 45. According to Estrada Jasso, Antonio Roa's crucifix of Totolapan is one of a handful representing the first series of crucifixes produced using caña technology in the New World, alongside the one given to Betanzos at the Dominican convento in 1538, and the Chalma crucifix that he dates to 1540. However, in my determination neither the Chalma, Totolapan, or Betanzo crucifixes are in fact constructed from the caña technology: they are sculpted, not molded, images.

46. Bonfil Batalla and Dennis, *México Profundo*, 12.

47. The artistic medium of the Cristo Aparecido was told to me by José Nao, restorer for INAH Morelos, who has worked on the Cristo Aparecido. The "quiote de maguey," the part used for sculptures, is the *tallo floral* of the plant. Antonio García-Abasolo, Gabriela García Lascurain, and Joaquín Sánchez Ruiz, eds., *Imaginería indígena mexicana*, 133. Indian artisans also carved crucifixes out of *tzompantle*. Like quiote de maguey, tzompantle is a particularly light wood, soft and easy to carve, and also native to Mexico. Roziére and Moyssén Echeverría, *México*, xxx.

48. William B. Taylor, "Cristos de Caña."

49. As evidence that these first cristos were most likely not the result of independent efforts of Indian artisans but were created in workshops under European supervision, Mendieta writes, "in completing these images they were brought to be shown to the guardian or the prior of the *convento* to determine if they were well made, used only with their approbation." As cited in García-Abasolo, García Lascurain, and Sánchez Ruiz, eds., *Imaginería indígena mexicana*, 83.

50. Quoted in Roziére and Moyssén Echeverría, *México*, xxix.

51. Other sources say this artist was from the Colegio of Tlatelolco. Torquemada writes, "There are many good sculptors of figures and I have in this town of Santiago an Indian, born here and known as Miguel Mauricio, who amongst the many good ones, far excels all others, and whose works are esteemed much more highly than those of certain Spanish sculptors"; as cited Ibid.

52. "The Indians are not comprehended within these Regulations, nor are the penalties to be imposed upon them, for they may freely exercise their crafts; but no Spaniard, whether he has been examined or not, may buy any work from one of them for resale within or without his shop, upon pain of penalty"; quoted Ibid.

53. See, for example, Matías de Escobar, *Americana thebaida*, 464–465.

54. Toribio Motolinía, *History of the Indians of New Spain*, 146–147. He goes on to explain how "These blankets and cloths are brought folded. Coming near the steps of the altar, the Indians kneel down and, having said a prayer, they unfold and spread out their offering. Then they take it at both ends and carry it in front of them, raising their hands two or three times and then laying it on the steps; whereupon they step back a little, make a genuflection like chaplains after giving the 'peace' to some great lord, and there pray awhile." I find this practice intriguingly reminiscent of the Guadalupe apparition story, echoing the ceremonial revelation of an image in front of an altar.

55. Juan Bautista Méndez and Justo Alberto Fernández, *Crónica de la Provincia de Santiago de México de la Orden de Predicadores, 1521–1564*, 92.

56. Alonso Ramos Gavilán, *Historia de Nuestra Señora de Copacabana.* This English translation of the passage is taken from Kenneth Mills, William B. Taylor, and Sandra Lauderdale Graham, *Colonial Latin America.*

57. Ramos Gavilán, *Historia de Nuestra Señora de Copacabana.*

58. "¡Oh prodigio de la Gracia y Omnipotencia Divina! La troza convertida en prodigiosa efigie de Cristo Crucificado"; José Velasco Toro, *Santuario y región,* 128. Though José Velasco Toro's interdisciplinary edited volume gathers several origin myths for the image, this one is taken from a 1746 text by Joseph de Villaseñor y Sánchez that claims to be based on mayordomal records.

59. Barbara Bode, *No Bells to Toll,* 375.

60. Torquemada, *Monarquía indiana,* vol. 5, 298.

61. Ibid., vol. 1, 392; vol. 5, 305.

62. I am not certain of what sources Méndez draws upon here, though he does cite the papers of one P. Pred. Fr. Alonso Franco, who had been "mozo" to the old religious who had known the first friars in whose time the image appeared. I do doubt the connection of this Cristo with Betanzos. Méndez and Fernández, *Crónica de la Provincia de Santiago de México,* 91.

63. Ibid., 90.

64. Juan de Magallanes, *Aparición de la milagrosa imagen del Santo Cristo.*

65. In the colonial context, caña images were not only simple representations of the crucifix but also sometimes composed entire scenes from the passion of Christ. In the late sixteenth century, Bishop Dávila Padillla tells of processional floats in which moveable images were manipulated by ropes strung under the carriages; with the use of these cords the images could be made to bow, and in one case Mary could be manipulated to repeatedly wipe the face of Christ on the road to Calvary. The full text of Dávila Padilla's letter is quoted in Estrada Jasso, *Imágenes en caña de maíz,* 65. One noteworthy aspect of this emphasis on the lightness of images for use in processions is the contrasting emphasis in Spain. There, in modern practice, the extreme weight of the ponderous *pasos* is central to the penitential aspect of the Holy Week processions. One such scene took forty men to carry, and still some men even died from heart attacks triggered by the tremendous burden. Mitchell, *Passional Culture,* 120.

66. Motolinía, *History of the Indians of New Spain,* 215.

67. A likely additional method for transporting religious images by foot within Mexico involved the adaptation of the same mode by which they were imported from Europe: the sculpted face and two hands of an image (those elements requiring the greatest degree of skill) were carried into to remote regions, and then local artisans completed the torso, legs, and a base.

68. Estrada Jasso, *Imágenes en caña de maíz,* 62.

69. Ibid.

70. Roy A. Harrisville, "Encounter with Grunewald," *Currents in Theology and Mission* 31, vol. 1 (February 1, 2004): 5–14.

71. Elizabeth Weismann, *Mexico in Sculpture, 1521–1821,* 9.

72. Ibid., 11.

73. The Cristo del Museo de San Luis Potosí displays a similar geometric pattern of lashings.

74. Roziére and Moyssén Echeverría, *México,* xxxi.

75. Nellie Sigaut, "La crucifixión en la pintura colonial."

76. Estrada Jasso, *Imágenes en caña de maíz*, 45. I am curious about the timing of and causes for the decline of this technology. Though two reliable scholars point to the end of the seventeenth century, Matías de Escobar's text completed in 1729 writes that "Las mismas Cañas que habían sido y dado materia para la idolatría, esas *mismas son hoy* materia de que se hacen devotos crucifijos," which would seem to indicate that the practice was still in common use almost to the middle of the eighteenth century. Escobar, *Americana thebaida*, 465. Elsewhere scholars have argued that the decline in such indigenous art forms coincides with the turning over of parishes to secular clergy.

77. Estrada Jasso, *Imágenes en caña de maíz*, 57.

78. Hanns Prem, "Disease Outbreaks in Central Mexico during the Sixteenth Century," 31.

CHAPTER 3

1. Lauro López Beltrán, *Fray Antonio de Roa: Taumaturgo penitente*, 87. Cited hereafter as López Beltrán, *Taumaturgo*.

2. Recently, Richard Trexler has described Roa's practices as a proto-passion play in the absence of any formal European tradition. See *Reliving Golgatha*, 26–33. It is noteworthy that the current residents of Totolapan have no passion play tradition.

3. James Lockhart, *The Nahuas after the Conquest*.

4. Serge Gruzinski, "Images and Cultural Mestizaje in Colonial Mexico," 54, argues that due to the obstacles posed by the diversity of indigenous languages, the image played a major role in the conquest and colonization of the New World.

5. "Estos humildes ermitaños son las piedras fundamentales de la magnifica obra augustiniana en el valle del Mezquital, las Huastecas, y la Sierra Alta." Solís de la Torre, *Bárbaros y ermitaños*, 31.

6. Serge Gruzinski, *The Conquest of Mexico*, 189–190.

7. These sources include Antonio Osorio de San Román's *Consuelo de Penitentes o Mesa Franca de spirituales manjares* (Seville, 1585), Alonso Fernández's *Historia eclesiástica de nuestros tiempos* (1611), and Juan de Grijalva's *Crónica de la orden de N.P.S. Augustin en las provincias de la nueva españa* (México, 1624). In addition to colonial material, a handful of contemporary secondary sources make brief mention of Roa (or of his crucifix), including Ricard, Gruzinski, and Rubial García, each of which is more helpful in providing tools for interpreting the social significance of Roa's life and practice than in yielding data additional to that which Grijalva or Fernández offers.

8. "Es tan admirable la vida del bendito Fr. Antonio de Roa, tan grandes sus penitencias . . . que puso en espanto estas naciones." Grijalva, *Crónica de la orden.*, 310.

9. Ibid., 317.

10. "Pues si eran los Indios testigos de la asperez y puridad de la vida de sus predicadores, que necesidad avia de mas milagros." Ibid., 136.

11. Grijalva uses this language in *Crónica de la orden*.

12. *Historia eclesiástica*, 127.

13. "Mios son los pecados (Dios mio) yo merecia essas penas, que vos no que sois la mesma inocencia." *Crónica de la orden*, 322.

14. AGN Inquisición, vol. 133, exp. 29, fs. 244–294.

15. *Crónica de la orden*, 312. See also Grijalva's description of Roa's physical mortifications as well as his concern for the poor in his discussion of Roa's youth in Spain, 311.

16. "Viendo que andaban los indios descalzos, quitóse el calzado; viendo que andaban desnudos, y que dormían por los suelos, cubrióse de un solo saco, y usaba de una tabla para dormir; viendo que comían raíces, y pasaban con extraña mendiguez, privóse de todo regalo de comida, y así ni pan, ni vino, ni carne, en muchos años lo quiso comer, haciéndose al talle de cada uno por ganarlos a todos a Dios." *Consuelo de penitentes*, 736. Cf. *Historia eclesiástica*, 126.

17. Burkhart, *Slippery Earth*, ch. 5.

18. ". . . considerando pues que los Indios estiman naturalmente poco el pecar, y derraman pocas lágrimas por sus culpas, determinó predicarles la sabiduria del misterio de la cruz . . . para moverles a penitencia, y ponerles temor de Dios, ofreció este santo sus carnes en sacrificio al Señor para el bien de sus ovejas."

19. *Crónica de la orden*, 131.

20. Osorio de San Román, *Consuelo de penitentes*, 737.

21. Juan de Torquemada, *Monarquía indiana*, vol. 5, 169.

22. Ibid., 56–57.

23. Ibid., 298.

24. "Un prision del huerto, un Cristo a la columna, un Ecce Homo; todas estas imagenes y las demas hacen milagros en los corazones. . . . ¿Quien no oye las voces y ve las lagrimas y contempla la sangre que representa una imagen de Cristo en el huerto? Que secretos dice un Cristo a la columna?" *Consuelo de penitentes*, 596.

25. Ibid.

26. I am attentive to the power of "seeing" images here in large part because of the work of Diana Eck. See her *Darsan, Seeing the Divine Image in India*.

27. *Crónica de la orden*, 327.

28. Magallanes writes of "la devoción, respeto, compunción y ternura que causa, creerá facilmente, que es obra de quien sólo puede causar en el alma estos efectos." Juan de Magallanes, *Aparición de la milagrosa imagen del santo cristo*, 67.

29. ". . . que es la innocéncia de Christo y la gravedad de nuestra culpa: la satisfacción de Christo, y la que nosotros devemos hazer." *Crónica de la orden*, 322.

30. Torquemada, *Monarquía indiana*, vol. 5, 71: "The idolatrous people that live a dead life without God . . . will be sought out by Jesus, as *hijos de dolores*, for which Jesus put himself on a cross and died to save them."

31. Art historian Ellen Ross similarly observes that the writing of late medieval women mystics does not linger over the various sufferings that "plague human beings," but rather the suffering that most concerns these women is "the physical and emotional (including mental and affective anguish) that emerges in their relationship to God." Ross also observes "the critical place of contrition and its associated suffering in the god-human relationship." Ellen M. Ross, *The Grief of God*, 34. Historian Maureen Flynn similarly observes that for sixteenth-century Spanish mystics, physical and emotional affliction were the primary human sensations permitted in spiritual practice. Maureen Flynn, "The Spiritual Uses of Pain in Spanish Mysticism," 271.

32. Jorge Klor de Alva, "Colonizing Souls," 12. See also his essays "Sahagún and the Birth of Modern Ethnography: Representing, Confessing, and Describing the Native Other," and "Contar vidas: La autobiografía confesional y la reconstrucción del ser nahua," *Arbor* 131 (1988), 49–78.

33. Torquemada, *Monarquía indiana*, vol. 5, 347, emphasis mine.

34. In contrast to the subtle persuasive methods of this friar stands the crude techniques of Diego de Landa's "inquisition." Landa was solely interested in the physical punishment of his "errant charges" and not in cultivating a desire for penance. See, for example, Inga Clendinnen, "Disciplining the Indians."

35. Toribio Motolinía, *History of the Indians of New Spain*, 149.

36. Torquemada, *Monarquía indiana*, vol. 5, 322.

37. Inga Clendinnen's extraordinary monograph *Ambivalent Conquests: Maya and Spaniard in the Yucatan* explores this theme. For Clendinnen, the friar Diego de Landa's torture of Mayan "backsliders" was intended to communicate this exclusivism to the Indians of the Yucatán.

38. Motolinía, *History of the Indians of New Spain*, 143–144.

39. López Beltrán, *Taumaturgo*, 89.

40. Ibid., 91. See also appendix.

41. "Para esto tenia este santo varon enseñados algunos Indios sus familiares, los quales tenia siempre consigo, y los llevava en su compañia donde quiera que iba. Los quales atormentavan su cuerpo, con hartas lagrimas y ternura: pero con tanta fiereza, como si fueran sus enemigos, por que les tenia ya persuadido este santo varon aque assi lo hiziessen." Grijalva and Gómez de Orozco, *Crónica de la orden*, 320, emphasis mine.

42. "El modo que tuvo este Apostólico varon fue tan raro, que hasta oy vemos espantados aquellos bárbaros." Grijalva and Gómez de Orozco, *Crónica de la orden*, 315.

43. Ibid., 321. "Se enternecían hasta las lágrimas . . . estavan tan admirados, y tan enternecidos que le dieran sus espaldas para ayudarle á llevar aquellos açotes."

44. "Las piedras de aquellas cierras hasta oy estan enternecidas, las mas elevadas cumbres oy se humillan a su nombre." Ibid., 315.

45. Louise Burkhart, *The Slippery Earth*, 144.

46. ". . . por todo el suelo no era otra cosa mas que un lago de sangre."

47. Grijalva's narrative suggests that European meanings of blood may not have been as limited as we might expect. Grijalva records that on his deathbed in 1563 Roa declared, "My soul is washed and purified in the blood of Christ, as fresh and hot as when it left his holy body": "mi alma es labada, y purificada, en la sangre de Cristo tan fresca, y caliente como quando salio de su sacratissimo cuerpo" (Grijalva and Gómez de Orozco, *Crónica de la orden*, 335). The graphic nature of this description of Christ's blood, fresh and hot, purifying Roa's soul suggests that he may actually have perceived his own blood as having purifying power for his Indian charges. Traditions asserting that Roa's blood sanctified the landscape of New Spain are noteworthy. Grijalva remarks that Roa's private disciplines in various small, scattered hermitages through-out the sierra left traces of blood that could still be seen (Ibid., 323). In some sense Roa's blood thus served to resanctify a landscape, which until then had been "silent with the memories of the ancient world" (Ibid., 193).

48. *Historia eclesiástica*, 127: "no le vian desmaya, ni flaqueza alguno, ni los Indios que le desnudavan, hallavan rastro de las ampollas que el fuego avia levantado."

49. López Beltrán, *Taumaturgo*, 99: ". . . su rostro siempre irradiaba una ilimitado alegría, y las palabras que hablan eran tan dulces, que se regocijaban en el Señor todos los que le veían y oían."

50. *Crónica de la orden*, 323.

51. Ibid., 127: "Todo esto tenía admirados a los Indios, y dezían que no era posible no fuese mas que hombre."

52. "Se descubren algunos carbones, los tomen, guardan, besan y veneran los Indios, como despojos de el Santo Roa, y tiene por cierto ser particulas de aquellas hogueras Manuel González de la Paz y del Campo," "Domicilio primera y solariega casa de el ssmo. dulcisimo Nombre de Jesús," 193.

53. Here I engage with the field of affect theory. See, for example, Sara Ahmed, *The Cultural Politics of Emotion*; Teresa Brennan, *The Transmission of Affect*; and Eve Kosofsky Sedgwick and Adam Frank, *Touching Feeling*.

54. Jonathan D. Spence, *The Memory Palace of Matteo Ricci*, 179.

55. Ibid., 246–247.

56. Ibid.

57. Karl Taube, "A Study of Classic Maya Scaffold Sacrifice."

58. See both Inga Clendinnen, *Ambivalent Conquests*, and Clendinnen, "Disciplining the Indians."

59. Carol H. Callaway, "Pre-Columbian and Colonial Mexican Images of the Cross," 226. Callaway's assumption that devotion to the Crucifix declined quickly is refuted by William Taylor's work; he points to the continuation of devotion to the Crucifix in dozens and dozens of supralocal shrines to Christ throughout Mexico that continue to form part of Mexican local identities today (Taylor, "Mexico's Virgin of Guadalupe in the Seventeenth Century"). Taylor also points to Mary's role as an intermediary for communication with Christ. William B. Taylor, *Magistrates of the Sacred*, 265.

60. Zelia Nuttall, "A Penitential Rite of the Ancient Mexicans." She argues that these were a common practice, and not limited to temple rituals and a religious and social elite.

61. For example, in pictographic depictions of human sacrifice, the images narrate historically specific events, and the focus is on the ritual and mythic quality of the episode rather than on the suffering of the individual victim.

62. David Stuart, "Blood Symbolism in Maya Iconography."

63. Inga Clendinnen explains that ritual prohibitions on bathing of the head and hair during periods of penitence or mourning help explain "the long, blood-matted hair of the priests that so horrified the Spaniards." Inga Clendinnen, *Aztecs: An Interpretation*, 52. See also Díaz del Castillo and Cohen, *The Conquest of New Spain*.

64. Elizabeth Hill Boone, *Stories in Red and Black*, 46.

65. Callaway, "Pre-Columbian and Colonial Mexican Images of the Cross," 213.

66. Torquemada, *Monarquía indiana*, vol. 5, 302.

67. Taylor, *Magistrates of the Sacred*, 61.

68. Brennan, *The Transmission of Affect*.

69. Taylor, *Magistrates of the Sacred*, 49.

70. Clendinnen, *Aztecs: An Interpretation*, 53.

71. As quoted Ibid.

72. Gruzinski, "Images and Cultural Mestizaje in Colonial Mexico."

73. Clendinnen, *Aztecs: An Interpretation*, 239.

74. "No es culto de Dios el dolor y sentimiento del pobre; no se hizo para la casa del Señor el que se labre con los sudores ajenos y miserables de los más desvalidos de la tierra. Sólo son para los altares los gemidos de un corazón arrepentido, no las lástimas y quejas de quien se mira despojado." Gregorio Antonio Pérez Cancio and Gonzalo Obregón, *Libro de fábrica del Templo Parroquial de la Santa Cruz y Soledad de Nuestra Señora*, 151–152.

75. See, for example, Louise Burkhart's conception of the "slippery earth."

76. Orlando Espín, a contemporary Hispanic theologian, looks at how miscommunication took place on a textual level, in the (mis)translation of key tenets of the Christian faith into a pictographic catechism. The Testerian manuscript, a collection of texts written by an indigenous convert to Christianity, translates God the Father as God the Friar, represented pictographically as a Franciscan brother. Failing to account for the transformation of understanding over time, Espín argues that errors such as these hindered the indigenous people from fully comprehending Trinitarian monotheism. Espín, *Faith of the People*, 44.

77. Instead, someone committed to the struggles of poor people and the eradication of their suffering, rather than of their ideas, must look at how communities of the poor forged new meanings in the colonial setting.

CHAPTER 4

1. Patrick J. Geary, *Furta Sacra*. William B. Taylor explores the phenomenon of furta sacra in a New World context in his "Two Shrines of the Cristo Renovado."

2. AGN Inquisición, vol. 133, exp. 23, fs. 244–294.

3. See here especially Pál Kelemen, *Baroque and Rococo in Latin America*, vols. 1 and 2.

4. P. J. Bakewell, *A History of Latin America*, 267.

5. Again, I am grateful and indebted to William Taylor, who through his teaching and writing has helping me to grasp the baroque aesthetic in Mexico.

6. William B. Taylor, *Magistrates of the Sacred*, 265–226.

7. Dates and locations of Roa's ministry are from Alipio Ruiz Zavala, *Historia de la Provincia Agustiniana de Santísimo Nombre de Jesús de México*, vol. 2, 342.

8. According to oral tradition, the friars removed the image from a window in the main sanctuary.

9. In his Inquisition testimony, Suárez de Escobar explained that the image was removed from its original green cross, which was left with the people of Totolapan as a relic, "as they had *always* held the crucifix in great veneration" (emphasis mine).

10. See here a discussion of *tiempo inmemorial* in Taylor, "Two Shrines of the Cristo Renovado."

11. Juan de Torquemada, *Monarquía indiana*, vol. 5, 203–204. The absence of nails at the feet of this crucifixion (Jesus is tied to the cross, rather) is noteworthy. This suggests the possibility of Indian authorship; a Spanish artist would never have made this iconographic error.

12. Ibid., vol. 5, 204. The same elderly man recalls that the image of Christ crucified had an angry face, *con rostro como enojado,* "And that is how they said that God ruled," he commented ("así decían ellos que reñia Dios").

13. Charles Gibson, *The Aztecs under Spanish Rule,* 135.

14. Fray Pedro Suárez de Escobar, provincial of the Augustinian order, observed that "other than these recent alterations, and other than being *slightly worn,* the image was much as had been when it was first brought by the Indian man," emphasis mine. "Dixo que en una cruz le trajo el yndio, y verde, y en ella a estado, y para traerle agora de Totolapa, un [___] le desencasavan los bracos y se lo dio un barniz por esta de la antiguedad. Algo gastado poca pero que es el mismo que el yndio entrego. Y la dicha cruz verde quedo en Totolapa. La tiene los yndios por relequia por aver tenido siempre al crucifixo en gran veneracion por la [___] y la cruz en que aora esta es otra." AGN Inquisición, vol. 133, exp. 23, fs. 244–294.

15. Moya de Contreras's permission is included in the Inquisición, vol. 133 materials.

16. In his testimony before the Inquisition hearing. he says, "of the relic of the santo crucifixo that we possess from the venturado Frai Antonio de Roa" and adds, "from the moment he was elected provincial, although unworthy [of the office], he had desired to make public this sovereign benefit."

17. Roa is *tenido en la horden por santo.* AGN Inquisición, vol. 133, exp. 23, fs. 244–294.

18. For a discussion of the many failed efforts to canonize Mexican saints, see Antonio Rubial García, *La santidad controvertida.*

19. Grijalva writes that Suárez rarely spoke, and "he lived in the conventos as if in solitude, rarely interacting at all with his brothers"; Grijalva and Gómez de Orozco, *Crónica de la orden,* 635.

20. The *definidor* was an administrative officer of the province, serving below the provincial. Periodic elections within the orders were major political events of note in Mexico City. See Antonio de Robles and Antonio Castro Leal, *Diario de sucesos notables (1665–1703).* Robles regularly notes when they were held. These elections were often contentious and full of politics; see Antonio Rubial García, "Votos pactados."

21. Grijalva and Gómez de Orozco, *Crónica de la orden,* appendix, liii.

22. "Apartir de 1578, el número de fundaciones en pueblos de indios disminuyó notablemente, pues en más de veinte años solamente se crearon siete nuevos conventos."Antonio Rubial García, *El convento agustino y la sociedad novohispana,* 129.

23. Grijalva writes that the illustrious Colegio de San Pablo was founded, "en virtud de una cedula Real en que su Magestad nos hazia merced de aquella Yglesia, y nos encargava el ministerio de los Indios de aquel barrio"; Grijalva and Gómez de Orozco, *Crónica de la orden,* 485.

24. Ibid., 483.

25. Eduardo Báez Macías, "El Convento de San Agustín de la Ciudad de México," 37. Báez Macias emphasizes the laborers and artists involved in the creation of the building—and not on the spiritual life contained within. His perspective is art historical.

26. Rubial García, *El convento agustino y la sociedad novohispana,* 129.

27. Museo Nacional de Arte, ed., *Pinceles de la historia*, 145, citing Pilar Gonzalbo, "Del tercero al cuarto concilio provincial mexicano . . . ," *Historia Mexicana* 34, no. 1 (July-September 1985): 7.

28. Hanns Prem, "Disease Outbreaks in Central Mexico."

29. ". . . con lo que mas illustraron el Reyno, y en lo que mostraron la grandeza, y generosidad de sus animos, fue en la fabrica de los templos y conventos, testigos a la posteridad de la opulencia del Reyno, y del gran numero de Indios, que entonces avia, pues auesdespues del cocoliztli, quedaron manos para tan sobervios edificios, tan fuertes, tan grandes, tan hermosos, y de tan perfecta architectura, que no nos dexo mas que dessar." Grijalva and Gómez de Orozco, *Crónica de la orden*, 225.

30. ". . . puso religiosos de asiento en muchos pueblos que habia sido Visitas. Quizá lo tuvo por conveniente para la mejor y más cómoda administración. Lo cierto es que en algunos pueblos era excusados religosos por tener pocos indios, y que cada día se menoscababan, por estar cerca de la cabecera; mas en otros fue muy necesario por estar apartados de los conventos y tener gente suficiente, y así, en el trienio siguiente algunos pueblos pequeños se redujeron a sus cabeceras y otros en otros trienios; en algunos quedaron religiosos, que hoy son casas de voto, aunque no todos, pues algunos son Vicarios que no tienen voto en los Capítulos." Esteban García, *Crónica de la provincia agustiniana del Santísimo nombre de Jesús de México*, 37. During this period the population of friars at the convento of Totolapan remained largely intact; Ibid., 7.

31. Ibid., 7.

32. At the cost of 150 pesos. I have not studied this document myself, but it is cited extensively in Báez Macías, "El Convento de San Agustín de la Ciudad de México," 39.

33. Grijalva and Gómez de Orozco, *Crónica de la orden*, 465.

34. The theft of that image and the resulting protests were captured in a subsequent painting; see Taylor, "Two Shrines of the Cristo Renovado."

35. Museo Nacional de Arte, ed., *Pinceles de la historia*, 152.

36. AGN Inquisición, vol. 133, exp. 23, fs. 244–294.

37. One witness says this miracle also occurred on Holy Thursday, but none of the friars present on that day mentions the event in his testimony. It must have been a separate event.

38. There is some inconsistency in the Inquisition testimony about precisely when this event, and the previous miracle, occurred. I have done my best to reconstruct the correct sequence and chronology.

39. "Y a este testigo le parescian muy blanca y muy resplandesiente y las carnes que casy eram umanas [___] que este testigo le paresica despues [___] le causo mucha admyracion y temor que no osaba pasar adelante y asy se quedo alli hyncado de rodillas por muchas [___]." AGN Inquisición, vol. 133, exp. 23, fs. 244–294.

40. ". . . tenya estatura mayor y . . . mas corpulento y muy blancas de suerte que le parescia a este testigo de carne umana." Ibid.

41. ". . . era tanta la gente hombres y mugeres y dellos [___] con la disiplina que boseaban y gritaban serraban biendo el [___] mylagro que era cosa espantosa y no se podia oyr [___] unos a los otros y los disiplinantes no querian pasar adelante [___] y se abrian las carnes con las disiplinas." Ibid.

42. ". . . y este testigo con mucho espiritu y ferbor empezo a predicar en alto bos el mylagro que hazia el santo crucifijo y que todos advirtiesen en ellos pues se mostrave mayor que nunca se avia mostrado y que era señal que entonces se mostraba mas manyfico y entonses hazerles mayors mersedes." Ibid.

43. I have encountered no evidence of the presence of moving images in the iconographically rich pre-Columbian religious belief and practice.

44. William A. Christian, *Moving Crucifixes in Modern Spain*, 6.

45. See his chapter on "live images" in David Freedberg, *The Power of Images*.

46. See Richard Trexler, "Dressing and Undressing Images."

47. "Dixo que viene a dezir y manifestar que como tal vicario a quien acuden los yndios de S. Juan S. Sebastian y Santa María a entendido de ellos algunos herrores que les a causado la publicación de milagros que se [___] de un crucifixo que esta en S. Pablo y de verle menear los braços. Porque unos piensan que esta bivo y que les echa su bendicion, y otros piensan que es el verdadero Jesucristo que murio en manos de los judios y otros piensan que es dios, y lo adoran como a dios y como es gente de poca capacidad que no se les levanta el entendimiento de los cavellos le parece que es cosa de grande advertia(?)." AGN Inquisición, vol. 133, exp. 23, fs. 244–294.

48. Gruzinski, *The Conquest of Mexico*, 193.

49. Taylor, *Magistrates of the Sacred*, 265–266.

50. The testimony of Samyn as well as other witnesses of this miracle form part of the documents included in AGN Inquisición, vol. 133, exp. 23, fs. 244–294.

51. The opening statements of the hearing mention the Council of Trent specifically.

52. "el publicar milagros sin fundamento y lo attribuyen a vanidad de los frailes y cudicia con el concurso de gente y limosnas para labrar su casas de S Pedro con los que por [___] le recogiesen." AGN Inquisición, vol. 133, exp. 23, fs. 244–294.

53. "Dixo q no lo avisto ni querido y alla mas de que le an dicho que alea los bracos y los baxa como que echa bendicion al pueblo y como esta bien barnizado y el barniz se derribe con el calor el Jueves Santo le enxugassen con una toalla y el pueblo dava gritos entendiendo que sudava y esto era publicado y notado y fray Pedro de Golegurto rector de S. Pedro dixo q este como avia crecido el dicho Jueves Santo y aquel noche los frailes pidieron a de [___] notado a [publicar] cura de la Cathedral [les diese] [___] como avia crecido y el les respondio q no le atten(dio) porque no le parecia q avia crecido." Ibid.

54. See note 47 above.

55. AGN Inquisición, vol. 133, exp. 23, fs. 244–294.

56. Ibid.

57. "Dieron permiso para ello con que el pasarlo sea sin publicidad y conmocion de pueblo y la parte donde le pusiera sea en lugar publico y decente, cubierto con su velo, como [___]estar y estan otras ymagenes de nuestro Senor Jesucristo de manera que todos los fieles christianos lo puedan veer y adorar sin que en esto por aora aya singularidad." Ibid.

58. Grijalva alludes only indirectly to the trial, mentioning certain "thorns" that Suárez suffered as provincial.

59. ". . . trajeron en procession la religion de san Agustín, de casa de Samacona, a nuestra Senora de la Paz, y fueron en casa del conde de Santiago, donde sacaron el

Santo Lignum Crucis y al Santo Cristo de Totolapa, y lo llevaron a la iglesia nueva con la capilla de la Catedral y cincuenta hachas." Robles and Castro Leal, *Diario de sucesos notables.*

60. Ibid., 223.

61. Ibid., vol. 1, 206.

62. A manuscript appearing in a copy of the Crónica de Nurenberg that had belonged to the Augustinian library recorded: "pues sólo dió lugar a que se sacase, los dos depósitos, i algunas himájenes y parte de algunos colaterales; y duró el fuego más de tres días en acabarse. Era Virrei el Señor Arzobispo don Fray Paio de Ribera y Correxido el Señor Conde de Santiago"; cited by Manuel Romero de Terreros, *La iglesia y convento de San Agustín,* 11.

63. "En medio del incendio, don Juan de Chavarría tuvo el valor de abrirse paso entre las llamas y rescatar la custodia, con el Santisimo Sacramento, que estaba expuesto en el altar mayor, accion cuyo recuerdo perpetuo, con autorizacion real, en la fachada de su casa, que existe hasta la fecha, y ostenta, dentro de un nichyo y esculpido en piedra, un brazo cuya mano sostiene un ostensorio." Ibid.

64. Báez Macías described the fire in his article on the convento but mourns, above all, that these objects of sentimental and spiritual value were salvaged while the "works by the genius of Pereyns, Zumaya, Suster, Arciniega, and perhaps Concha . . . were tragically reduced to ashes on the night of December 11 of 1676." Báez Macías, "El Convento de San Agustín de la Ciudad de México," 42.

65. Robles and Castro Leal, *Diario de sucesos notables,* vol. 1, 206.

66. It is mentioned specifically several times in the financial ledgers of the convento, a 156-page manuscript spanning the years from 1667 to 1692 housed today in the Archivo Judicial del Distrito Federal.

67. "Libro de gasto de la fábrica de la iglesia del convento de nuestro padre san Agustín de México." It mentions that in 1680 the order received 80 pesos "por la puerta de la capilla de Totolapan"; cited by Báez Macías, "El Convento de San Agustín de la Ciudad de México," 44. Báez Macías writes that "varias veces en la capilla del cristo de totolapan" is referenced in the manuscript; Ibid., 46.

68. "Procesión y dedicación de la iglesia de San Agustín. Este día, a la tarde, a las cuatro de ella, salió la procesión de la Catedral, y en ella todas las cofradías y estand-artes, y todas las religiosos con sus cruces, prestes, y los patriarcas de ellas aderezados ricamente de joyas . . . llevó el Santísimo Sacramento el señor arzobispo." Robles and Castro Leal, *Diario de sucesos notables,* vol. 2, 278.

69. Pamela Voekel, *Alone before God,* 27.

70. For a recent book-length treatment on these festivals, see Linda Ann Curcio, *The Great Festivals of Colonial Mexico City.*

71. Paul Ramírez, "Isolating Disease," 14.

72. Voekel, *Alone before God,* 18.

73. Brian Larkin, "Liturgy, Devotion, and Religious Reform in Eighteenth-Century Mexico City," 494.

74. John Chance and William B. Taylor, "Cofradias and Cargos," 8.

75. Nancy Farris, *Maya Society under Colonial Rule,* 265–266, as cited by Serge Gruzinski, "Indian Confraternities, Brotherhoods and Mayordomías in Central New Spain," 211.

76. Gruzinski, "Indian Confraternities," 211.

77. Ibid., 207. See also D. A. Brading, "Tridentine Catholicism and Enlightened Despotism in Bourbon Mexico," 12.

78. Brading, "Tridentine Catholicism and Enlightened Despotism in Bourbon Mexico," 12.

79. Chance and Taylor argue that before independence in the nineteenth century, mayordomías and cofradías were not connected to the civil hierarchy of cargos. That is, it was not until early in the twentieth century that costly individual sponsorship was more normative. See Chance and Taylor, "Cofradias and Cargos," 8.

80. Gruzinski, "Indian Confraternities," 206.

81. Gruzinski, *The Conquest of Mexico.*

82. Few contemporary sources explicitly engage the theme of religion in relation to epidemic disease in colonial Latin America. However, I found the following sources illuminating in terms of the social implications of disease in Latin America: Cabrera y Quintero and Ruiz Naufal, *Escudo de armas de México*; Noble David Cook, *Born to Die*; Donald B. Cooper, *Epidemic Disease in Mexico City, 1761–1813*; and Ramírez, "Isolating Disease."

83. Serge Gruzinski, "Images and Cultural Mestizaje in Colonial Mexico."

84. América Molina del Villar, *La Nueva España y el matlazahuatl, 1736–1739.* In my understanding of this particular epidemic I owe a tremendous debt of gratitude to Paul Ramírez, who generously shared with me his unpublished work on the subject. See Ramírez, "Isolating Disease."

85. Molina del Villar, *La Nueva España y el matlazahuatl.*

86. Ibid., 122.

87. Ibid., 135.

88. Ibid., 155–156.

89. Cabrera y Quintero as cited by Ramírez, 35. Ramírez and others remain uncertain about or contest these figures.

90. Cabrera y Quintero and Ruiz Naufal, *Escudo de armas de México*, 138.

91. Molina del Villar. *La Nueva España y el matlazahuatl*, 151.

92. Robert McCaa, "Spanish and Nahuatl Views on Smallpox and Demographic Catastrophe in Mexico," 405.

93. Molina del Villar, *La Nueva España y el matlazahuatl*, 147.

94. "Fuera de estas humanas providencias se ha solicitado también el Socorro espiritual de las divinas con plegarias, novenas, rogativas a Dios, su santísima Madre y santos especiales, abogados de esta ciudad y pueblo, procurando aplacar su justísima ira con procesiones y públicas penitencias; no ha bastado; mucho debe de ser el número y mucha la gravedad de nuestras culpas o poco eficaz el arrepentiemiento, cuando con todo esto se hace sorda su inmensa clemencia." This from "Carta del virrey Vizarrón Eguiarreta al Consejo General de Indias sobre la epidemia que ha cundido por toda la ciudad. 16 abril 1737" (AGI, Audiencia de México, leg. 504 ff. 3–3v. Quoted by Molina del Villar, *La Nueva España y el matlazahuatl*, 152).

95. Daniel T. Reff, *Plagues, Priests, and Demons*, 182.

96. Molina del Villar, *La Nueva España y el matlazahuatl*, 153.

97. "Para este, y otros asaltos se ha protejido de él, como de escudo, esta Augustini-ana Milicia." Cabrera y Quintero and Ruiz Naufal, *Escudo de armas de México*, 184 n. 373.

98. Ramírez, "Isolating Disease," 35.

99. Ibid., 41.

100. D. A. Brading, *Mexican Phoenix*, 125.

101. William B. Taylor, "Mexico's Virgin of Guadalupe in the Seventeenth Century," 289.

102. Ibid., 125.

103. William Taylor writes that the key years for development of devotion were 1731–1754. Allan Greer and Jodi Bilinkoff, *Colonial Saints*, 278.

CHAPTER 5

1. This is the argument of Pamela Voekel's groundbreaking book: see Voekel, *Alone before God*. See also William B. Taylor, *Magistrates of the Sacred*, 13.

2. Francisco de Solano and others, *Relaciones geográficas del Arzobispado de México, 1743*, 46–47.

3. José Antonio de Villaseñor y Sánchez and Ramón María Serrera Contreras, *Suplemento al Teatro americano: La ciudad de México en 1755*, 123.

4. Voekel, *Alone before God*, 52. See also Voekel, "Peeing on the Palace."

5. Voekel, *Alone before God*, 51.

6. Ibid., 55.

7. Brian Larkin, "Liturgy, Devotion, and Religious Reform in Eighteenth-Century Mexico City," 508.

8. Margaret Chowning, "Convent Reform, Catholic Reform, and Bourbon Reform in Eighteenth-Century New Spain," 14.

9. D. A. Brading, "Tridentine Catholicism and Enlightened Despotism in Bourbon Mexico," 7.

10. Ibid., 10.

11. Alipio Ruiz Zavala, *Historia de la Provincia Agustiniana de Santísimo Nombre de Jesús de México*, vol. 2, 378.

12. Chowning, "Convent Reform," 15.

13. Voekel, *Alone before God*.

14. A series of Augustinian biographies were published during those years that exalted friars as forgers of "a new Creole nation." Museo Nacional de Arte, ed., *Pinceles de la historia*, 169.

15. Ibid., 171.

16. Manuel González de la Paz y del Campo, "Domicilio primera y solariega casa de el ssmo. dulcisimo Nombre de Jesús."

17. Manuel Toussaint, *Colonial Art in Mexico*, 337–338.

18. Museo Nacional de Arte, ed., *Pinceles de la historia*, 172.

19. Grijalva's 1624 text identifies Bartolomé as the *fundador del yermo* at Chalma—the only mention of the location in his history.

20. José Sicardo, *Interrogatorio de la vida y virtues del venerable hermano fray Bartolomé de Jesús María*, 283.

21. Matías de Escobar, *Americana thebaida*, 371: "El mismo fenómeno se dio con los santones mestizos asimilados por los Agustinos, quienes encontraron en el 'retiro'

a un santuario la posibilidad de ejercer una influencia religiosa de la que estaban excluidos a causa de su origen étnico."

22. "Todo su empleo era pasar al corazon desde la vista las llagas y las espiras de aquel benditisimo y destrozado cadaver, misteriosos libro escrito por dentro y fuera." Joaquín Sardó, *Relación historica y moral*, 157.

23. Sicardo, Interrogatorio, 286.

24. Escobar, *Americana thebaida*, 371; "el mestizo Bartolomé cumplía . . . las funciones de intermediación que necesitaban los frailes para atraer a las comunidades indígenas: el 'chaman cristiano convertido en religioso no sólo aseguraba la ortodoxia de la preciación, sino que podía también suplantar con su "magia" a los hechiceros indios.'"

25. "Florencia imprimía su obra cuando los ermitaños indviduales ya habían desaparecido de Chalma, y seguramente de toda la Nueva España." They were marginalized and even sent to the Inquisition (i.e., Juan Bautist y Cardenas was four years in prison accused as an "iluso y alumbrado con grave sospecha de ser hereje sacramentario"). Ibid., 376. Rubial argues that they basically become literary fiction.

26. Ibid., 373.

27. José de Olivares, *Oracion panegyrica*.

28. Juan de Magallanes, *Aparición de la milagrosa imagen del Santo Cristo*, no page.

29. "Si la magestad del santo cristo de Totolapa por su hechura singular y devoción que causa, se discurre, que es obra de Angeles, lo mismo debiamos discurre de Chalma, y si nuestro venerable P. F. Antonio mereció por sus virtudes tan celestial prenda en Totolapan, eran menores las virtudes del P. F. Nicolas Perea." Ibid.

30. Sardó, *Relación historica y moral*, 72.

31. ". . . pero tan rara, tan singular, tan admirable, que dificulto, y aun no creo que haya otra en todo el órbe católico, que si le iguala." Ibid., 76.

32. Ibid., 81.

33. "[Primeramente considera] todo su sagrado bulto y nótense los tamaños, las proporciones, los vivos, con las demas circunstancias que representan un perfectísimo retrato del mismo Cristo muerto en la Cruz: y primeramente aquella postura tan natural de un cadáver pendiente de solas tres escarpias, y el ademan tan propio de la cabeza exánime y totalmente caida sobre el pecho hácia el lado diestro, no menos misteriosos que natural: aquella acción de los brazos, el siniestro recto y tirante hácia el cuerpo, y el diestro un poco algo curbo, denotando estar todo el cuerpo vencido hácia el lado diestro y como casi pendiente del brazo siniestro; y aun persuade mas esta accion el doblez de las rodillas que manifiesta aquel estado ó postura en que debió quedar despues de tres horas de clavado y pendiente en la cruz. . . . Nótese asimismo con el maciliento color de todo el cuerpo la figura cadavérica del rostro sacratísimo, los dispersos matices de la sangre, aquí purpúrea y rozgante, allí denegrida y coagulada, y el horrible destrozo que hizo en las espaldas la fiereza y crueldad de los azotes . . . se vendrá á ver que resulta forma, y compone un todo tan perfecto, tan natural, tan al vivo de un Dios hombre muerto y pendiente de una cruz . . . inspecionado con la debida reflexión todo este doloroso espectáculo." Ibid., 75–76.

34. Gonzalo Obregón, "El Real Convento y Santuario de San Miguel de Chalma," 119–120.

35. Ibid., 120.

36. An oil painting titled "Verdadero retrato de la milagrosa ymagen de Sto Christo de Chalma" hangs in the Museo Nacional de Arte in Mexico City. Done by the artist José de Mora in 1719, it antedates the fire and thus depicts the original image of the Señor de Chalma. Indeed, the painting is meant to be an exact copy, a *diapositiva*. Though by that time he would already have been moved to the new iglesia, it seems to me that he is represented there in his original cueva: light and shadow play across his face and body, and the cross itself is almost invisible, fading into the dark shadows of the cave.

37. María Rodríguez-Shadow and Robert Dennis Shadow, *El pueblo del Señor*, 41.

38. William H. Beezley, Cheryl English Martin, and William E. French, *Rituals of Rule, Rituals of Resistance*.

39. J. Lloyd Mecham, *Church and State in Latin America*, 443.

40. Ibid., 444.

41. This was true as of 1843; from data taken from Memoria de Justicias, 1844 and cited by Jan Bazant, *Alienation of Church Wealth in Mexico*, 9.

42. A petition sent to President Comonfort on February 17, 1857, requested (on sentimental grounds) that the monastery of St. Francis be reopened. The request met with an immediately positive response from Comonfort, who decreed the reopening of the monastery "as a special favor to the Franciscans." The monastery was in fact reopened a mere two days later.

43. Beezley, Martin, and French, *Rituals of Rule, Rituals of Resistance*, 129.

44. Ruiz Zavala, *Historia de la Provincia Agustiniana de Santisimo Nombre de Jesus de México*, vol. 2, 337.

45. Guillermo Tovar de Teresa, José E. Iturriaga, and Enrique Krauze, *The City of Palaces*.

46. Ibid., 13.

47. "La biblioteca quedó enteramente abandonada, las puertas abiertas y los libros y manuscritos a merced de quien quisiera llevárselos, multituud de libros destrozados y esparcidos por los claustros y celdas, otros tirados en el suelo de la biblioteca en el mas completo desorden . . . era como en el tiempo de los bárbaros." Manuel Rivera Cambas, *México pintoresco, artístico y monumental*, vol. 2, 219.

48. Tovar de Teresa, Iturriaga, and Krauze, *The City of Palaces*, 15.

49. "Destrucción continua del hermoso edificio de Seminario," *El Siglo Diez y Nueve*, May 15, 1861, 2.

50. "Sigue el despilfarro," Ibid.

51. Tovar de Teresa, Iturriaga, and Krauze, *The City of Palaces*, 14.

52. Oddly, the only santo he finds worthy of mention is an image of the virgin that did not merit mention in any other sources: "of all the *imágenes de vestir* that the convento had in its possession, the most noteworthy was the Nuestra Señora de la Paz, whose tunic . . . was embroidered with gold." Manuel Romero de Terreros, *La iglesia y convento de San Agustín*, 19.

53. Vol. 2, 219 mentions that "En la iglesia de San Agustín era venerado un crucifjo conocido por el 'santo cristo de Totolapam' que tenía una capilla especial; se le hicieron fiestas, deprecaciones y solemne procesión en la epidemia de 1736; la imagen fue acquirida de una indígena por el prior establecido en el pueblo de Totolpam."

54. ". . . destruyeronse los altares, y la sillería del coro se desarmó rudamente y se arrumbó sin orden ni concierto en una bodega. Quedó el templo abandonado y hasta inundado." Romero de Terreros, *La iglesia y convento de San Agustín*, 25.

55. "República mexicana. Distrito federal—Gefe de policía. Hace alungos días se había tenido noticia que un fraile Agustíno, asociado de otros individuos, pretendían seducir el escuadrón Guardia municipal sacándolo fuera de la capital para que se incorporara á las fuerzas revolucionarias. Para conseguir este objeto el mencionado fraile se valió de un oficial del relacionado escuadrón, a quien se le manifestó que si arreglaba la manera de sacarse la fuerza, recibiría una cantidad de dinero." *El Siglo diez y Nueve*, May 15, 1861, 3.

56. José Roberto Juárez, *Reclaiming Church Wealth*. The same investor had purchased another church for the same purpose of preservation. A legal document signed by Escandón specified that he was authorized to allow the use of the Augustinian convento as a place of worship. Bazant, *Alienation of Church Wealth in Mexico*, 416.

57. Ibid.

58. The need for a national library was first identified in 1833.

59. ". . . se ha gastado en ella una suma enorme á fin de convertirla en Biblioteca Nacional, para cuyo destino será siempre impropia." Joaquin García Icazbalceta, "Los Agustinos en México," vol. 1, 419.

60. "Procuraron los arquitectos ocultar, hasta donde les fué possible, el carácter religiosos del edificio." Romero de Terreros, *La iglesia y convento de San Agustín*, 28–29.

61. The rare books and manuscripts collection, the Fondo Reservado, remained at San Agustín until 1992, when it to was moved to UNAM.

62. From a pamphlet created in honor of the Cristo of Totolapan, March 1861, an invitation to celebrate the return of Roa's crucifix to Totolapan. López Beltrán, *Taumaturgo*, 23.

> La imagen de Jesuscristo, aparecida
> Al venerable Antonio Roa, su siervo amado,
> Más de doscientos años había estado
> En la opulenta capital como perdida.
> Ni esfuerzos mil, que la piedad inspira,
> Ni diligencia humana alguna se omitiera,
> Porque a su pueblo original volviera
> Pues por su adquisición gime y suspira.
> Y en medio de borrascosas tempestades
> A Totolapan, oh pueblo venturoso!
> Vuelve cual Padre tierno y bondadoso
> A predigarte su amparo y sus piedades,
> A desterrar horrores y calamidades,
> Si le rindes tu corazon, sencillo y candoroso.

63. Andrew Guilliford, "Curation and Repatriation of Sacred and Tribal Objects."

64. AGN Inquisición, vol. 133, exp. 29, fs. 244–294, for the idea that cruz was left as "consuelo."

65. "De una de las campanas que se colgaron en la torre se cuenta lo siguiente: En noviembre de 1655, se trajo del convento de San Agustín de Totolapa, una campana

grande que contra de los franciscanso, se subió a la torre de Catedral que estaba por terminarse, en presencia del virre; pero como 'estaba toda rajada,' ordenó el Duque de Alburquerque que se bajara, y entonces la recogieron los Agustínos y se la llevaron a su convento para fundirla de nuevo." Romero de Terreros, *La iglesia y convento de San Agustín*, 7.

66. López Beltrán, *Taumaturgo*, 76.

67. Ibid.

68. One resident, doña Bonifacia, does not hold to the "furta sacra" hypothesis. She surmised that because the Indian who had brought it was unknown, this had created anxiety among the locals who feared they themselves might be blamed for the theft. For this reason they sent him away: "No one recognized the man, and in a town like this we know everyone—we would have been able to say that it was the son of 'so-and-so' that left it. Those who would have been the mayordomos back then were worried that they might be blamed for this as a theft so they sent the Cristo away to Mexico. They worried that others would think the image was stolen because of its uncertain origins so they sent it away out of fear; they did not want to be blamed as thieves."

69. Another honors the Santísimo Sacramento, while the final one, named for San Nicolas Tolentino de Naturales, traces its origins not to a local image but rather to the church in neighboring Huastepec. Bishop Lanciego pastoral visitation, documentary source provided by William Taylor.

70. Solano and others, *Relaciones geográficas del Arzobispado de México*, 46–47.

71. Pastoral visit book of Archbishop Alonso Núñez de Haro y Peralta, 1779–1780. Archivo Histórico de la Mita, México, D.F., fol. 113ff.

72. González de la Paz y del Campo, "Domicilio primera y solariega casa de el ssmo. dulcisimo Nombre de Jesús. Historia de la imperial, augusta, religiosa casa de la orden de los ermitaños Augustinos de la ciudad de México. Chronica de su establecimiento, erección y continuación. Vidas y echos de sus religiosissimos prelados, y de muchos de sus mas singulares hijos," 193.

73. On destruction of Santa Muerte shrines see "Saint or Sinner? Mexico Debates a Cult's Status," by Jason Beaubien, *All Things Considered* on National Public Radio, April 13, 2009, and "Mexico's War on Saint Death" by Joseph Laycock (www.religiondispatches.org/archive/international/1428).

CHAPTER 6

1. As is held by the living memory of the old ones of Totolapan.

2. Adrian Bantjes, "Burning Saints, Molding Minds," 271.

3. Statements about the physical misery suffered by most Latin Americans and the political instability of Latin American governments introduce and frame the published Medellín statements. For example, in Guatemala note the military overthrow of the democratically elected Arbenz government in 1954, and in Chile the Allende government in 1973, and in Brazil the military coup in 1964, and so on.

4. Louis M. Colonnese and Catholic Church, Consejo Episcopal Latinoamericano, *The Church in the Present-day Transformation of Latin America in the Light of the Council.*

5. For a concise introduction to liberation theology, see my "The Catholic Church and Social Revolutionaries." I quote myself from this original article in full in the paragraph below.

6. For her excellent treatment of the emergence of a Bourbon spirituality, see Pamela Voekel, *Alone before God*.

7. Kristin Norget, "Progressive Theology and Popular Religiosity in Oaxaca, Mexico," 99–100.

8. Personal communication with Roger Nelson Lancaster.

9. Hugo Assman, "The Actuation of the Power of Christ in History: Notes on the Discernment of Christological Contradictions," 135.

10. See the many works on Christology written by liberation theologians, including especially Leonardo Boff's *Jesus Christ Liberator: A Critical Christology for Our Times* (Maryknoll, N.Y.: Orbis, 1978) and Jon Sobrino's *Jesus the Liberator: A Historical-Theological Reading of Jesus of Nazareth* (Maryknoll, N.Y.: Orbis, 1994). Gustavo Gutiérrez, *A Theology of Liberation: History, Politics, Salvation* (Maryknoll, N.Y.: Orbis, 1998) is always the best starting point for any serious engagement with liberation theology.

11. Carlos Salcedo Palacios, "Participación de don Sergio Méndez Arceo en el Concilio Vaticano II," in *Don Sergio Méndez Arceo, patriarca de la solidaridad liberadora*, edited by Leticia and Giulio Girardi Rentería Chávez (Mexico City: Ediciones Dabar, 2000). 145–156.

12. They were warehoused in a storage area of the chapel devoted to the Virgin of Guadalupe on the cathedral compound.

13. "Morelenses en peregrinación," *Correo del Sur*, May 21, 1961.

14. López Beltrán, *Taumaturgo*.

15. Lauro López Beltrán, "Consagración episcopal de don Sergio Méndez Arceo." This is an earlier piece that was republished posthumously as part of an edited volume paying tribute to Méndez Arceo's life.

16. Apparently the priest had embarked upon an unapproved "restoration" of the nave that involved whitewashing the sixteenth-century frescos. The priest was severely reprimanded by don Sergio. This information came from a personal interview conducted with Padre Julio Tinoco, who was parish priest in Totolapan from the late 1980s until 1993.

17. Thirty-three of these paintings were selected for restoration by an organization named Adopt a Work of Art, founded by engineer and cataloguer Juan Dubernard (among others). The Roa paintings were among these.

18. In the 1980s, as bishop, he also worked with other figures in the Catholic hierarchy to engineer a rapprochement with the Salinas government. For a discussion of this, see George W. Grayson, *The Church in Contemporary Mexico*.

19. Gabriela Videla, *Sergio Méndez Arceo*, 73.

20. J. Lloyd Mecham, *Church and State in Latin America*, 486–487.

21. Baltasar López Bucio, *Don Sergio Méndez Arceo*, 49.

22. Don Sergio himself described this first phase of his ministry as bishop as "la obra de las obras: la santificación del clero, la formación de los seminaristas y la promoción de las vocaciones." Ibid., 45.

23. These guidelines specified that priests should wear the tonsure, and dress in black and clerical collar in the street. They would not be admitted to Mass without it. They were not to go swimming with women outside of their immediate family, nor go to the movies, theatre, circus, cockfights, or boxing matches. Ibid., 48–49.

24. Baltasar López writes: "After the triumph of the Revolution, after the failure of 'la cristiada' the church organized catholic intellectuals in defense of what they called 'cultura católica.'" Ibid., 55.

25. Helen Delpar discusses the standardization of folk culture, and the 1920s in particular as the period of the creation of cultural nationalism in Mexico; Delpar, *The Enormous Vogue of Things Mexican*, 12–14. The observations of the secularizing effects of this process are my own.

26. López Bucio, *Don Sergio Méndez Arceo*, 55–56.

27. "En lo religioso, lo encontré alejado de las prácticas y casi altanero ante el sacerdote." Videla, *Sergio Méndez Arceo*, 51.

28. Ibid., 52.

29. Ibid..

30. "En esa catedral que desnudaste para que fuera canto y acogida, mariachis y pueblo, vida y Pascua . . . ," original Spanish of the epigraph, by Brazilian bishop Pedro Casaldáliga, as cited by López Bucio, *Don Sergio Méndez Arceo*, 16.

31. Personal communication with Baltasar López Bucio, who served for many years as don Sergio's personal secretary and who was himself sent to resolve this conflict.

32. Sergio Méndez Arceo, "Elogio del templo Catedral de Cuernavaca, que hace el Obispo en el décimo aniversario de la consagración, 1969," 1.

33. For Liberation theologians' fascination with the sixteenth century, see for example Gustavo Gutiérrez's decades-long engagement with the life and thinking of Bartolomé de las Casas (Gutiérrez, 1993), Orlando Espín's essay on sixteenth-century methods of evangelization (Espín, 1997), and Enrique Dussel's CEHILA project and his notion of "incomplete evangelization" (Comisión de Estudios de Historia de la Iglesia en Latinoamérica, 1981–).

34. Sergio Méndez Arceo, *Exhortación pastoral acerca del reacondicionamiento de la santa iglesia catedral de Cuernavaca*.

35. Ibid.

36. Sergio Méndez Arceo, "Instrucción sobre la devoción a los santos y sus imágenes," 37.

37. The word *retablo* obviously has many meanings. In this context it refers to the altarpiece.

38. Méndez Arceo, "Instrucción sobre la devoción a los santos y sus imágenes," 37. Don Sergio's negative evaluation of the santos as artistically inferior is not historically unique, but stands as only one example in a long tradition. David Brading records a conflict between priests and mayordomos that took place during Holy Week in 1793, in which the priests criticized the images that were to be processed, saying that they were "for the most part indecent in their construction and much more indecent in their adornment"; D. A. Brading, "Images and Prophets," 192.

39. Diana Serra Cary, "A Cathedral Comes into Focus," 487.

40. Local disregard for the first of these was made evident to the bishop by its haphazard placement in the church. Méndez Arceo, "Instrucción sobre la devoción a los santos y sus imágenes," 37. In the *Exhortación pastoral* published the previous year, he also writes of the merit of the Lady of the Asunción.

41. This story was repeated to me several times in interviews with local mayordomos and ex-párrocos of Totolapan.

42. Méndez Arceo, *Exhortación pastoral acerca del reacondicionamiento de la santa iglesia catedral de Cuernavaca*, 6–7.

43. Carlos Salcedo Palacios, "Participación de don Sergio Méndez Arceo en el Concilio Vaticano II," 150.

44. Reflecting don Sergio's own preference, the Vatican II document, *Sacrosanctum Concilium*'s section on Sacred Art and Sacred Furnishings, specifies: "The practice of placing sacred images in churches so that they may be venerated by the faithful is to be maintained. Nevertheless their number should be moderate and their relative positions should reflect right order. For otherwise they may create confusion among the Christian people and foster devotion of doubtful orthodoxy"; Pope Paul VI, *Constitution on the Sacred Liturgy: Sacrosanctum Concilium* (Vatican City: Roman Catholic Church, 1963), ch. 7, sec. 123.

45. Salcedo Palacios, "Participación de don Sergio Méndez Arceo en el Concilio Vaticano II," 150. See also don Sergio's own discussion of this in his statement in Sergio Méndez Arceo, "Reacondicionamiento de la Catedral de Cuernavaca," 254.

46. James Martin, "An Interview with Camille Paglia," 13–14.

47. Méndez Arceo, "Instrucción sobre la devoción a los santos y sus imágenes," 37.

48. A photo of the sanctuary taken immediately after the renovations were completed shows a more conventional image of the Crucifix, though still hung, suspended, as Méndez Arceo desired. The current image arrived some time later during Méndez Arceo's episcopacy. Don Sergio says of this: "Pero dos Imágines principales dominarán el recinto sagrado, el Cristo triunfal pendiente entre el Santuario y la Nave, del Arco triunfal, presentado ya en maqueta por Herbert Hoffman, y la Imagen de Nuestra Señora, la Virgen María, en su Misterio de la Asunción, en el lienzo del muro norte entre el crucero y el arco triunfal, a la vista del Pueblo fiel y del Celebrante," Méndez Arceo, "Reacondicionamiento de la Catedral de Cuernavaca," 254.

49. López Beltrán describes in detail don Sergio's episcopal shield; López Beltrán, "Consagración episcopal de don Sergio Méndez Arceo," 92. And Baltasar López describes his pectoral cross.

50. López Bucio, *Don Sergio Méndez Arceo*, 41.

51. Miguel Morayta describes a parish in Cuernavaca that followed a similar path—rejecting Vatican II reforms and finding a lefebrista priest to celebrate their mass for them. Those who follow the popular media may recognize that Mel Gibson, producer/director of the film *The Passion of the Christ*, counts himself as a follower of Lefebre.

52. José Moisés Hernández Zamora, *Recuperando la memoria de don Segio Méndez Arceo*, 35.

53. Methodist scholar Raul Macín Méndez Area writes: "Cuando Don Sergio sustituyó muchas de las imágenes que había en el interior de la Catedral de

Cuernavaca por versículos bíblicos y empezó a hacer hincapíe en la necesidad de que el pueblo católico de su diócesis leyera y estudiara la Biblia, sus enemigos empezaron a llamarle despectivamente el obispo protestante." Raul Macín Méndez Area, ¿*Político o cristiano?* 20.

54. *Correo del sur,* Morelos, Mexico. May 21, 1961, 6–7.

55. Brading, "Images and Prophets."

56. Miles Richardson, *Being-in-Christ and Putting Death in Its Place.*

57. Brading, "Images and Prophets," 202.

58. When the cathedral hosted a play titled "Murder in the Cathedral," one such journalist suggested that perhaps it should have been more aptly titled "Murder *of* the Cathedral." Personal communication with Baltasar López.

59. Miguel Morayta Mendoza and others, "Resolviendo conflictos entre pueblos de tradición nahua de Morelos," 41.

60. This event is mentioned in several texts but perhaps most interestingly in the illustrated "comic book" version of don Sergio's life, Leticia Rentería Chávez and Francisco Javier González Muñoz, *Don Sergio Méndez Arceo, VII Obispo de Cuernavaca,* 16.

61. The text of this handwritten note, dating to May 1961, is preserved in the Archivo Don Sergio, and is reproduced in Angel Sánchez Campos, "Don Sergio Méndez Arceo, Obispo de Cuernavca," 131.

62. See, for a discussion of this distinction, Robert Redfield, "Art and Icon." For a more recent engagement with the theme, see Joseba Zulaika, *Basque Violence.*

63. For a discussion of the "discovery" of the frescos, see Serra Cary, "A Cathedral Comes into Focus." Information about the people's reaction to this discovery is from a personal interview with Baltasar López.

64. López Bucio, *Don Sergio Méndez Arceo,* 41.

65. Even the political cartoonist/satirist RIUS, who often targeted the Church, recognized don Sergio's commitment. Rentería Chávez and Muñoz, *Don Sergio Méndez Arceo, VII Obispo de Cuernavaca,* 12.

66. "Santuario de Chalma," *Correo del Sur,* March 11, 1973. He begins by asking for the close attention of the congregation because of the movements of the pilgrims in the pews. The journalist records that the immediate silence and interest was noteworthy, even surprising. For centuries priests have stood beneath this image to expound their theology of the Señor de Chalma.

67. Morayta Mendoza and others, "Resolviendo conflictos entre pueblos de tradición nahua de Morelos," 40.

68. Personal interview with INAH restorer José Nao, who lived in the pueblo of Ocotopec while don Sergio was there. But see also Morayta Mendoza, Ibid.

69. Leonardo Boff quoted by Juan Luis Segundo, "The Shift within Latin American Theology," 19.

70. Ibid., 26.

71. Ibid., 24.

72. Hernández Zamora, *Recuperando la memoria de don Segio Méndez Arceo,* 104.

73. Videla, *Sergio Méndez Arceo,* 45.

74. Soledad Loaeza-Lajous, "Continuity and Change in the Mexican Catholic Church," which also discusses the Catholic Church's rapprochement with the state in the 1970s.

75. Michael W. Foley, "Organizing, Ideology and Moral Suasion."

76. "Mexico: Bishops Encourage Basic Communities," *LADOC* 20, no. 1 (1989): 12.

77. Gruzinski, "Indian Confraternities, Brotherhoods and Mayordomías in Central New Spain," 211.

78. John Chance and William Taylor exposed the deficiencies of this emphasis some twenty years ago. See John Chance and William B. Taylor, "Cofradias and Cargos." See also Jan Rus and Rob Wasserstrom, "Civil-Religious Hierarchies in Central Chiapas"; Nancy Farris, *Maya Society under Colonial Rule*, 268 and passim; and Charles Gibson, *The Aztecs under Spanish Rule*, 127–134. Finally, see Asunción Lavrin, "Rural Confraternities in the Local Economies of New Spain."

79. See especially Chance and Taylor, "Cofradias and Cargos," and Rus and Wasserstrom, "Civil-Religious Hierarchies in Central Chiapas."

80. Leah VanWey, Catherine Tucker, and Eileen Diaz McConnell, "Community Organization, Migration, and Remittances in Oaxaca."

81. María Rosas, *Tepoztlán*.

82. Roger N. Lancaster, *Thanks to God and the Revolution*, 51.

83. Morayta Mendoza and others, "Resolviendo conflictos entre pueblos de tradición nahua de Morelos," 41–42.

84. Xóchitl Levya Solano, "Catequistas, misioneros y tradiciones en Las Cañadas."

85. Ruth Judith Chojnacki, "Retrato de un catequista." See also her unpublished dissertation on the subject of the indigenous deacon program in Chiapas. "Indigenous Apostles: Maya Catholic Catechists Working the Word in Highland Chiapas," University of Chicago, 2004.

86. EGP, "Sebastián Guzmán, principal de principales," *Polémica* 10–11 (1983).

87. As summarized by Eric Wolf, "The Vicissitudes of the Closed Corporate Peasant Community," 327.

88. EGP, "Sebastián Guzmán, principal de principales," 91.

89. See also David Stoll, *Between Two Armies in the Ixil Towns of Guatemala*.

90. Lancaster, *Thanks to God and the Revolution*, 32.

91. Padre Julio explained to me, "Pues, el sacerdote que se va convirtiendo, se tiene que convertir en pueblo."

92. Here the padre was in error: the Cristo is not made of caña but of maguey, as INAH restorers subsequently determined.

93. Lancaster, *Thanks to God and the Revolution*, 51.

94. Harvey Gallagher Cox, *The Silencing of Leonardo Boff: The Vatican and the Future of World Christianity* (Oak Park, Ill.: Meyer-Stone Books, 1988).

95. Rentería Chávez and Muñoz, *Don Sergio Méndez Arceo, VII Obispo de Cuernavaca*, 29.

96. Personal communication with Rosemary Radford Ruether, who witnessed this event.

97. "Es imposible resaltar todos los casos en que vimos cómo se nublaba la cara de Don Sergio cuando él con mucha atención escuchaba ala gente humilde contando sus problemas." Hernández Zamora, *Recuperando la memoria de don Segio Méndez Arceo*, 50–51.

98. Ibid.

99. Morayta Mendoza and others, "Resolviendo conflictos entre pueblos de tradición nahua de Morelos," 43.

100. In 2006, the government of Mexico called for a massive process of cataloguing its colonial treasures. See Elisabeth Malkin, "Nothing is Sacred, as Looters Rob Mexican Churches of Colonial Treasures."

101. José María Vigil, "What Remains of the Option for the Poor?"

CHAPTER 7

1. A centuries-long process of secularization culminating in the 1860s transformed the dozens and dozens of monasteries that had served as the foundational institutions for the Christianization of New Spain into languishing "ex-conventos." While many of these buildings continue to be utilized for religious functions, they technically remain the property of the state, with the priests and bishops serving as "caretakers."

2. Brief stories about the conflict and interviews with the mayordomos and the priests aired on national radio.

3. Here the mayordomos of Totolapan rehearse a strategy common in the colonial period, where indigenous communities often embarked on a complex process of official appeal to outside authorities to intervene on their behalf against offending priests and civil authorities. See the *Códice Kingsborough*, for example—a pictographic plea for intervention in a local conflict with an abusive *encomendero*.

4. María del Rosío García Rodríguez, Alma Angélica Campos Valencia, and Mario Liévanos Ramos, *Totolapan: Raíces y testimonios*.

5. I borrow the biblical-historical term deliberately, to highlight the "flood" of illness and destruction brought by the conquest that wrought havoc on indigenous communities.

6. Totolapan sits about 1,900 meters above sea level.

7. See John W. F. Dulles, *Yesterday in Mexico*.

8. Miguel Morayta Mendoza and others, "Resolviendo conflictos entre pueblos de tradición nahua de Morelos," 44.

9. Coverage of don Sergio Méndez's funeral (no title), *Diario de Morelos*.

10. The neighboring ex-conventos of Tepoztlán and Tlaycapan are particularly fine examples of restorations within the diocese.

11. Anthropologist John Ingham notes the local sense of lay ownership over the ex-convento and parish church in nearby Tlayacapan. John M. Ingham, *Mary, Michael, and Lucifer*, 52.

12. Although the mayordomía has many community functions, it also requires a close working relationship and much contact with the clergy. The mayordomos are also in charge of ringing the church bells, policing the atrio at night, staffing the church bathrooms, and so on— all of which bring them into frequent contact with clergy.

13. This folk pageant reenacting the Spanish reconquista in which Christians "recovered" land from Islam is ubiquitous in communities of indigenous origin, rural and urban, throughout Meso-America. See Max Harris, *Aztecs, Moors, and Christians*.

14. See, for example, D. A. Brading, "Tridentine Catholicism and Enlightened Despotism in Bourbon Mexico," 17.

15. Ingham describes a similar situation in which a priest in the late 1950s kept a large dog in the convento to prevent the mayordomos from climbing the roof of the church to ring the bells during fiestas. Ingham, *Mary, Michael, and Lucifer,* 47.

16. At the same time, there was the altercation over use of the huerta. The mayordomos had given permission to a group of young men to play soccer there, while the priests had offered the space to a girls' group. The friars called the police, and in doing so any remaining *laso de amistad* with the friars was broken.

17. Sonia de la Roziére and Xavier Moyssén Echeverría, *México.*

18. Harvard Divinity School's Center for the Study of World Religions included a Religion and Art initiative that sought to explore precisely this issue. A conference hosted by the center in 2001 treated the theme of "Stewards of the Sacred: Sacred Artifacts, Religious Culture, and the Museum as Social Institution." Interest was largely motivated by the organizing efforts of Native American Nations to reclaim "artifacts" of spiritual and religious significance from museums (including Harvard University's Peabody Museum). Also see Martin Sullivan, "Sacred Objects and Sacred Knowledge in Museum Spaces," talk given in Harvard Divinity School Religion and Arts Initiative Lunch Series, 2003, also sponsored through the CSWR.

19. The next month, in May of 1998, the Cristo de la Columna was ceremoniously returned to Totolapan. In contrast to don Sergio's enthusiastic participation in celebrating the return of the Cristo Aparecido more than four decades previously, these friars refused to participate in welcoming the returning Señor de la Purisima Sangre, as was custom.

20. Redfield, "Art and Icon," 63.

21. Correo del Restaurador (www.conservacionyrestauracion.inha.gob.mx/html/publindice.html). In this sense INAH is following a global trend among museum directors.

22. In this capacity, INAH traces its genealogy back to the Commisión General de Monumentos, created in 1885 under Porfirio Díaz, and before that to the Sociedad Mexicana de Geografía y Estadística during the period of Benito Juárez's presidency. See Julio César Olivé Negrete and Augusto Urteaga Castro-Pozo, *INAH, una historia.*

23. The work of Manuel Toussaint and that of Dr. Atl (Gerard Murillo) are the most conspicuous examples of this interest. See also Clara Bargellini, "Representations of Conversion," 93.

24. Méndez Arceo, "Reacondicionamiento de la Catedral de Cuernavaca," 256.

25. The articles of the law clearly state that the designation *monumento histórico* extends to all churches and church buildings, the official residences of bishops, parish houses, seminaries, and convents (ch. 3, art. 36). Olivé Negrete and Urteaga Castro-Pozo, *INAH, una historia.*

26. For a more comprehensive analysis of the patrimonio nacional and INAH's role, see Enrique Florescano, ed., *El patrimonio nacional de México,* vol. 2.

27. But INAH's reach and influence extends even beyond this already broad and sweeping scope; an essay recently published on INAH's Web site asserts that INAH's concern for preservation extends beyond those structures and objects under its official

custody to encompasses as well any "patrimony" that is found in the hands of a cleric, in private hands, or in the possession of a specific community. Correo del Restaurador, "Los Proyectos."

28. INAH has been in Morelos only since 1983, and its jurisdiction over Church properties has been contested at several points over the years. There was, for example (in the early part of the 2000), an effort to have the cardinal's residence returned officially to the Church. But a national law passed in the fall of 2003 reiterates and restates INAH's authority, restorers assume optimistically once and for all. Teresita Loera, national director of restorations and preservation for INAH explains that technically now the churches and convents are really just under the "custody" of the Church—which are not owners.

29. As was said in the last chapter, don Sergio successfully convinced the people of Hueyapan to lend INAH their imagen for an exposition of colonial art. The image was never returned. The people perceived this as a premeditated theft of their image, and from that point on don Sergio was not permitted to enter the pueblo. It took over ten years for the santo to make its way home. Morayta Mendoza and others, "Resolviendo conflictos entre pueblos de tradición nahua de Morelos," 41.

30. Correo del Restaurador, "Los Proyectos."

31. Alicia Islas Jiménez, *Rescate y conservación de materiales orgánicos relacionados con una comunidad del sur de la ciudad de México*, 3.

32. Antonio García-Abasolo, Gabriela García Lascurain, and Joaquín Sánchez Ruiz, eds., *Imaginería indígena mexicana*, 233.

33. Juan Manuel and Alfredo Vega Cárdenas Rochas Reyes, *La iconografía Cristiana en la conservación y restauración de arte sacro virreinal*, Correo del Restaurador: Conservación y estudio del patrimonio, 4.

34. In her ethnography *No Bells to Toll*, Barbara Bode introduces the reader to an Andean santero named Pilatos and his workshop.

35. The power of the saints is infinitely transferable. That is, its power can be conferred to a subsequent generation or to multiple replicas. This was true, for example, with the Cristo of Chalma, which burned in the nineteenth century; a replica was fabricated incorporating some of its charred remains. In a community in the southernmost part of Morelos, several copies exist of the same image, reflecting internal divisions. At each local conflict, a newly separated faction would fabricate a likeness of the original image, and each of these is esteemed as an original, as the santo itself.

36. García-Abasolo, García Lascurain, and Sánchez Ruiz, eds., *Imaginería indígena mexicana*, 99, 141–142.

37. The notion that images experience damage as "injury" has roots deep in the colonial period. The *Escudo de Armas de México* tells of an image accidentally wounded in a melee—in which a stone damaged the right foot of a Cristo and the foot of the image became swollen and bruised, so that the people wrapped the foot in gauze. Cabrera y Quintero and Ruiz Naufal, *Escudo de armas de México*,150.

38. William B. Taylor, "Religion and Peasant Politics in Colonial Mexico," 8.

39. Andrew Guilliford, "Curation and Repatriation of Sacred and Tribal Objects," 26–27.

40. This aesthetic is not dissimilar from the Totolapan friars' preference for a modern renovation of the ex-convento rather than the careful preservation and restoration required by INAH. Islas Jiménez, *Rescate y conservación*, 3.

41. Don Otilio died a year before I arrived in Totolapan, but see his observations in García Rodríguez, Campos Valencia, and Liévanos Ramos, *Totolapan: Raíces y testimonios*, 152.

42. Islas Jiménez, *Rescate y conservación*, 3.

43. William B. Taylor, "Mexico's Virgin of Guadalupe in the Seventeenth Century," 289.

44. García-Abasolo, García Lascurain, and Sanchez Ruiz, eds., *Imagineria indígena mexicana*, 262.

45. Letter in the archives of the mayordomía parroquial of Totolapan.

46. Acta Constitutiva de la Honorable Jutna Vecinal de Totolapan, Morelos. Archive of the mayordomía parroquial of Totolapan.

47. In creating a junta vecinal that could support the agenda of the mayordomos, the citizens of Totolapan are appealing to a form of association with roots earlier in the century. The junta vecinal is a form of state-sanctioned local organization that emerged during the Cristero rebellion, and then within a few years the laws empowering these bodies were repealed. Knowingly or unknowingly, INAH has instilled them with a new sort of function and authority, quite distinct from their original purposes. Thus, when the peasants of Totolapan form the junta vecinal to gain authority, they are appealing to a structure with roots in the Cristero movement (according to the newspaper article). However, Padre Salvador then argues that it has no legitimacy because of a 1907 law. Teresa Loera explains that INAH works with all kinds of local structures and groups to marshal local support for INAH's mission. And they themselves have been transformed.

48. According to chapter 1, article 2 of this law, promulgated in 1972, INAH is in fact mandated to make precisely this sort of alliance. The law asserts INAH's authority to organize and authorize civil associations, including juntas vecinales and peasant unions, by designating them as auxiliary organs and thus empowering them to assist with the preservation of archeological monuments. See Olivé Negrete, César, and Urteaga Castro-Pozo, eds., *INAH, una historia*.

49. Correspondence from INAH, Dirección General, dated September 14, 1998. Oficio num 401-1-00370. Addressed to Sr. Otilio Adaya, president of the Junta Vecinal. Archive of the mayordomía parroquial of Totolapan.

50. "Los *mayordomos* no pueden intervenir en cuestiones internas de la Iglesia y menos en su gobierno interior." Letter from Bishop don Luis Reynoso, from the archive of the mayordomía parroquial of Totolapan. At the same time, the bishop's letter insists that all mayordomos must be approved by the parish priest according to guidelines established by each parish.

51. "Acta de la Reunión Sostenida con S.E. don Luis Reynoso Cervantes . . . ," from the Obispado de Cuernavaca, Gobierno Eclesiástico, dated October 12, 1998, archive of the mayordomía parroquial of Totolapan.

52. One commented, "We didn't want to be like Atlatlaucan, a community divided."

53. Taylor, *Magistrates of the Sacred*, 506.

54. Wolf, "The Vicissitudes of the Closed Corporate Peasant Community," 327.

55. The theme of the special propensity to resistance of Morelenses is explored in Jesús Sotelo Inclán's important book, *Raíz y razón de Zapata, Anenecuilco*.

56. Over the better part of last quarter of the eighteenth century, nearby Yautepec was plagued by disputes with an enterprising and capitalizing (secular) priest, Father Manuel de Agüero. In the case of Agüero, controversy centered around his business practices—he owned at least one hacienda and rented a piece of another property for the cultivation of indigo—and his unauthorized diversion of water from a collectively owned spring to irrigate his own crops. The people of Yautepec brought charges against Agüero for these transgressions, and even accused him of poisoning what water remained, making it unserviceable for rest of the pueblo. But the local community was not unanimous in its opposition to Agüero's practices. In the legal hearings in the case, indigenous locals testified both against him and on his behalf. Still, Father Agüero was so plagued by local opposition to his enterprise that though he himself had originally requested placement in Yautepec (perhaps largely due to its many opportunities for financial gain), he finally pleaded to be reassigned. He begged to be removed from the "horrible tormenta de aquel lugar." Cheryl English Martin, *Rural Society in Colonial Morelos*, 183.

57. Taylor, *Magistrates of the Sacred*, 509.

58. Ibid., 516.

59. Ingham, *Mary, Michael, and Lucifer*.

60. Letter from the mayordomía dated October 20, Archive of the mayordomía parroquial of Totolapan.

61. This critique is explored in the previous chapter and in the introduction, and is articulated variously by many of the contributing authors in José Míguez Bonino's edited volume, *Faces of Jesus*.

62. João Dias Araújo, "Images of Jesus in the Culture of the Brazilian People," 32.

63. Ibid., 37.

64. Taylor, *Magistrates of the Sacred*, 506.

65. In fact, in Mexico as throughout Latin America it may be debatable as to whether there is a correlation between the political mindset of a priest and whether he is a member of a religious order or not. In some instances, the most politically or even liturgically radical priests found some shelter within the religious orders. This is the case for Peruvian theologian Gustavo Gutiérrez, the so-called "father of liberation theology," who has only recently become a Dominican. This decision was motivated both by his sense of connection to the Dominican friar and original "defender of the Indians," Bartolomé de las Casas, and also by his search for some protection (a buffer) from his more conservative bishop and archbishop.

66. "Maltratan los santitos porque dicen que son piedras." It is doubtful that the friars called the saints "rocks"—but might this be the collective memory of their predecessors in the sixteenth century, who often disregarded local deities as *piedras*.

67. In her study of the rural Andes in the aftermath of the earthquake that struck Peru in May of 1970, Barbara Bode describes how indigenous communities struggled to understand and interpret the mass destruction of their saints' images in the earthquake. Barbara Bode, *No Bells to Toll*.

68. Oración Panegyrica, "Aqui, pues, donde la naturaleza con mejores trazos, que el arte, labró en el coraçon de el risco en varias grutas, y cuevas de peña viva hermosas bovedas de pedernal eterno, le adoraban estos miserables Gentiles en un Idolo, ó simulachro muerto, que ocupaba la principal de las cuevas, como Deidad suprema, y Numen primero entre otros muchos, que adoraban, tā Idolatras, como ciegos."

69. ". . . una obra . . . puede considerarse 'Viva,' por pertenecer de forma activa a un proceso social de culto. La obra de este sition presenta un claro ejemplo de las diferentes cargas culturales y valores universales contenidos en el patrimonio cultural que, además de ser obras de arte, fuente de información tecnológica, histórica e iconográfica, es principalmente objeto de culto, con diferentes significados y depositario de grandes valores," Francisco Javier Salazar Herrera, *El Santo Desierto de Tenancingo y la Escuela Nacional de Restauración*. Mexico City: INAH (www.conserva-cionyrestauracion.inha.gob.mx/html/publindice.html).

70. "Los brazos, por encontrarse en una cruz que no le correspondía, habían ido suf-riendo deformaciones, hastga haberse desprendido," in García-Abasolo, García Lascurain, and Sánchez Ruiz, eds., *Imaginería indígena mexicana*, 227. But see also p. 142 in the same text for use of the language of "suffering" to describe mistreatment of an image.

71. She writes: "un pueblo sin costumbres y sin tradiciones es un pueblo sin pasado y sin Istoria y sin Raices y sin leyenda."

72. The answer to the questionairre reads, "Mi propuesto es que lo resuelva el pueblo por que no es la Respuesta de uno es lares Puesta [sic] del pueblo."

CHAPTER 8

1. There is a vast literature on religious fiestas in Latin America, but for this discussion I have found most helpful works by contemporary scholars, especially Stanley H. Brandes, *Power and Persuasion*; Richard C. Trexler, *Reliving Golgotha*; Roberto Goizueta, "Fiesta: Life in the Subjunctive"; Max Harris, *Aztecs, Moors, and Christians*; and Kristin Norget, *Days of Death, Days of Life*.

2. "Ese día es para divertirse, estamos con el Cristo sí, lo veneramos, pero lo hacemos a nuestra manera, en forma alegre." This quote is from don Otilio Adaya, who (regrettably) I never met: I arrived in the pueblo shortly after he died. He is interviewed extensively in María del Rosío García Rodríguez, Alma Angélica Campos Valencia, and Mario Liévanos Ramos, *Totolapan* 151–152.

3. Religious Studies scholars have been particularly attentive to this phenom-enon, as I explores below. For an anthropological treatment of transnational religion see Stanley H. Brandes, *Skulls to the Living, Bread to the Dead*.

4. For an overview of the literature see William Taylor and John Chance, "Cofradias and Cargos." See especially, Evon Vogt, *Tortillas for the Gods*; Eric Wolf, *Sons of the Shaking Earth*; John Monaghan, "Reciprocity, Redistribution, and the Transaction of Value"; Jan Rus and Rob Wasserstrom, "Civil-religious Hierarchies in Central Chiapas"; among others.

5. See especially Roberto Goizueta, *Caminemos con Jesús*; Virgilio Elizondo, *Mother of the New Creation*; Orlando Espín, *Faith of the People*; Alex García-Rivera, *The Community of the Beautiful*; Ana Castillo, *Goddess of the Americas*.

6. Not only the quantity but also the clustering of diverse events under the general rubric of "fiesta" is noteworthy. For example, within this expansive list there are feast days that are universal in the Christian calendar, such as the feast of the Assumption celebrated on August 15—though in Totolapan it must be said that people celebrate the image of the Virgen de la Asunción more than the memory of Mary's assumption into heaven. Other celebrations are common to all of Mexico, for example the Day of the Dead and the Feast of the Virgin of Guadalupe.

7. A mid-colonial letter authored by an Augustinian priest and cited by D. A. Brading describes the cohetes as "music." Brading, "Images and Prophets." Also see George McClelland Foster, *Culture and Conquest*.

8. García Rodríguez, Campos Valencia, and Liévanos Ramos, *Totolapan*, 152.

9. Harris, *Aztecs, Moors, and Christians*.

10. Victoria Reifler Bricker, *The Indian Christ, the Indian King*, 62.

11. Ibid., 154.

12. García Rodríguez, Campos Valencia, and Liévanos Ramos, *Totolapan*, 153.

13. Ibid., 154.

14. This national spectacle is the subject of a recent book by Richard Trexler, *Reliving Golgotha*.

15. Estrada Jasso explains that images like the Cristo Aparecido are meant to be seen up close, and that their true beauty cannot be appreciated from a distance. Antonio García-Abasolo, Gabriela García Lascurain, and Joaquin Sanchez Ruiz, eds., *Imagineria indígena mexicana*, 198.

16. Manuel Vásquez, "Toward a New Agenda for the Study of Religion in the Americas," 11.

17. Leah VanWey, Catherine Tucker, and Eileen Diaz McConnell, "Community Organization, Migration, and Remittances in Oaxaca."

18. Jeffrey H. Cohen, "Transnational Migration in Rural Oaxaca, Mexico" Jeanine Kalver, *From the Land of the Sun to the City of Angels*; Alison Mountz and Richard Wright, "Daily Life in the Transnational Migration Community of San Agustin, Oaxaca and Poughkeepsie, New York."

19. As I helped my own fourth-grade son construct his, I insisted that the figurines of a native woman and a Spanish friar that he selected from the craft store stand squared against each other in a face-off.

CHAPTER 9

1. Laura Elisa Pérez, *Chicana Art*, 14.

2. David Carrasco and Scott Sessions, eds., *Cave, City and Eagle's Nest*.

Bibliography

Abel-Turby, Mickey. "The New World Augustinians and Franciscans in
    Philosophical Opposition: The Visual Statement." *Colonial Latin
    America Review* 5, no. 1 (1996): 7–23.
AGN Inquisición, vol. 133, exp. 29, fs. 244–294.
Ahmed, Sara. *The Cultural Politics of Emotion.* New York: Routledge, 2004.
Araújo, João Dias. "Images of Jesus in the Culture of the Brazilian People."
    In *Faces of Jesus: Latin American Christologies,* ed. José Míguez Bonino,
    30–38. Maryknoll, N.Y.: Orbis, 1984.
Ariés, Philippe. *The Hour of Our Death.* New York: A.A. Knopf, 1981.
Assman, Hugo. "The Actuation of the Power of Christ in History: Notes on
    the Discernment of Christological Contradictions." In *Faces of Jesus:
    Latin American Christologies,* ed. José Míguez Bonino, 125–136.
    Maryknoll, N.Y.: Orbis, 1984.
Báez-Jorge, Félix. *La parentela de María: Cultos marianos, sincretismo e
    identidades nacionales en Latinoamérica.* Xalapa: Biblioteca Universidad
    Veracruzana, 1999.
Báez Macías, Eduardo. "El Convento de San Agustín de la Ciudad de México.
    Noticias sobre la construcción de la iglesia." *Anales del Instituto de
    Investigaciones Estéticas* 16, no. 63 (1992): 35–56.
Bakewell, P.J. *A History of Latin America c. 1450 to the Present.* 2nd ed.
    Malden, Mass., Blackwell, 2004.
Bantjes, Adrian. "Burning Saints, Molding Minds: Iconoclasm, Civic Ritual,
    and the Failed Cultural Revolution." In *Rituals of Rule, Rituals of
    Resistance: Public Celebrations and Popular Culture in Mexico,* ed. William
    Beezley, Cheryl English Martin, and William French, 261–284.
    Wilmington, Del.: Scholarly Resources, 1994.
Bargellini, Clara. "Representations of Conversion: Sixteenth-Century Architecture
    in New Spain." In *The Word Made Image: Religion Art, and Architecture*

in Spain and Spanish America, ed. Isabella Stewart Gardner Museum, 91–126. Boston: Trustees of the Isabella Stewart Gardner Museum, c. 1998.

Batstone, David. *From Conquest to Struggle: Jesus of Nazareth in Latin America*. Albany: State University of New York Press, 1991.

Bazant, Jan. *Alienation of Church Wealth in Mexico; Social and Economic Aspects of the Liberal Revolution, 1856–1875*. Cambridge: Cambridge University Press, 1970.

Beezley, William H., Cheryl English Martin, and William E. French. *Rituals of Rule, Rituals of Resistance: Public Celebrations and Popular Culture in Mexico*. Wilmington, Del.: Scholarly Resources, 1994.

Belderrain, Josef. *Exhortacion instructiva que el r.p. fr. Josef Belderrain, provincial de la provincia del dulcisimo nombre de Jesus de Agustinos de Mexico, dirige á los prelados locales y demás religiosos de dicha provincia*. Mexico City: n.p., 1810.

Benuzzi, Silvia. *A Pilgrimage to Chalma: The Analysis of Religious Change*. Greeley: University of Northern Colorado, 1981.

Bode, Barbara. *No Bells to Toll: Destruction and Creation in the Andes*. New York: Scribner, 1989.

Bonfil Batalla, Guillermo, and Philip Adams Dennis. *México Profundo: Reclaiming a Civilization*. Austin: University of Texas Press, 1996.

Boone, Elizabeth Hill. *Stories in Red and Black: Pictorial Histories of the Aztecs and Mixtecs*. Austin: University of Texas Press, 2000.

Borhegyi, Stephen. "The Miraculous Shrine of Our Lord of Esquipulas in Guatemala and Chimayo, New Mexico." *El Palacio* 60 (1953): 83–111.

Boyd, E. "The Crucifix in Santero Art." *El Palacio* 60 (1953): 112–115.

Brading, D.A. *The First America: The Spanish Monarchy, Creole Patriots, and the Liberal State, 1492–1867*. Cambridge: Cambridge University Press, 1991.

———. "Images and Prophets: Indian Religion and the Spanish Conquest." In *The Indian Community of Colonial Mexico: Fifteen Essays on Land Tenure, Corporate Organizations, Ideology and Village Politics*, ed. Airj Ouweneel and Simon Miller, 184–204. Amsterdam: CEDLA, 1990.

———. *Mexican Phoenix: Our Lady of Guadalupe: Image and Tradition across Five Centuries*. Cambridge: Cambridge University Press, 2001.

———. "Tridentine Catholicism and Enlightened Despotism in Bourbon Mexico." *Journal of Latin American Studies* 15, no. 1 (1983): 1–22.

Brandes, Stanley H. *Power and Persuasion: Fiestas and Social Control in Rural Mexico*. Philadelphia: University of Pennsylvania Press, 1988.

———. *Skulls to the Living, Bread to the Dead: [The Day of the Dead in Mexico and Beyond]*. Malden, Mass.: Blackwell, 2006.

Bravo Pérez, Benjamín. *Procesos de conversión a partir de la religiosidad popular*. Mexico City: Parroquia del Inmaculado Corazón de María, n.d.

Brennan, Teresa. *The Transmission of Affect*. Ithaca: Cornell University Press, 2004.

Brenner, Anita. *Idols behind Altars*. New York: Payson and Clarke, 1929.

Bricker, Victoria Reifler. *The Indian Christ, the Indian King: The Historical Substrate of Maya Myth and Ritual*. Austin: University of Texas Press, 1981.

Bucher, Bernadette, Rolena Adorno, and Mercedes López-Baralt. *La Iconografía política del Nuevo Mundo*. Río Piedras: Editorial de la Universidad de Puerto Rico, 1990.

Burdick, John. *Blessed Anastacia: Women, Race, and Popular Christianity in Brazil.* New York: Routledge, 1998.

Burkhart, Louise M. *Before Guadalupe: The Virgin Mary in Early Colonial Nahuatl Literature.* Albany: Institute for Mesoamerican Studies, State University of New York at Albany, 2001.

———. *The Slippery Earth: Nahua-Christian Moral Dialogue in Sixteenth-century Mexico.* Tucson: University of Arizona Press, 1989.

Bynum, Caroline Walker. *Holy Feast and Holy Fast: The Religious Significance of Food to Medieval Women.* Berkeley: University of California Press, 1987.

Cabrera y Quintero, Cayetano, and Víctor M. Ruiz Naufal. *Escudo de armas de México.* Ed. facsimilar / con un estudio histórico y una cronología de Víctor M. Ruiz Naufal. Mexico City: Instituto Mexicano del Seguro Social, 1981.

Calancha, Antonio de la, and Ignacio Prado Pastor. *Crónica moralizada de Antonio de la Calancha.* 6 vols. N.p., 1974.

Callaway, Carol H. "Pre-Columbian and Colonial Mexican Images of the Cross: Christ's Sacrifice and the Fertile Earth." *Journal of Latin American Lore* 16 (1990): 199–231.

Carrasco, David. *City of Sacrifice: The Aztec Empire and the Role of Violence in Civilization.* Boston: Beacon, 1999.

Carrasco, David, and Scott Sessions, eds. *Cave, City, and Eagle's Nest: An Interpretive Journey through the Mapa de Cuauhtinchan no. 2.* Albuquerque: University of New Mexico Press; published in collaboration with the David Rockefeller Center for Latin American Studies and the Peabody Museum of Archaeology and Ethnology, Harvard University, 2007.

Carrillo Cázares, Alberto, and Agustín Francisco Esquivel y Vargas. *La primera historia de La Piedad, "El fénix del amor": estudio literario e histórico con facsímil de la edición original y notas.* Zamora, Mich.: Colegio de Michoacán; La Piedad, Mich.: Foro Cultural Piedadense, 1990.

Casas, Bartolomé de las. *The Only Way.* Edited by Helen Rand Parish, translated by Francis Sullivan. New York: Paulist Press, 1991.

Castañeda, Quetzil E. *In the Museum of Maya Culture: Touring Chichén Itzá.* Minneapolis: University of Minnesota Press, 1996.

Castillo, Ana. *Goddess of the Americas,* New York: Riverhead, 1996.

Cervantes, Fernando. *The Devil in the New World: The Impact of Diabolism in New Spain.* New Haven: Yale University Press, 1994.

Chakrabarty, Dipesh. *Habitations of Modernity: Essays in the Wake of Subaltern Studies.* Chicago: University of Chicago Press, 2002.

———. *Provincializing Europe: Postcolonial Thought and Historical Difference.* Princeton: Princeton University Press, 2000.

Chance, John, and William B. Taylor. "Cofradias and Cargos: An Historical Perspective on the Mesoamerican Civil-Religious Hierarchy." *American Ethnologist* 12, no. 1 (1985): 1–26.

Chávez, Angélico. "The Penitentes of New Mexico." *New Mexico Historical Review* 29, no. 2 (1954): 97–123.

Chojnacki, Ruth Judith. "Indigenous Apostles: Maya Catholic Catechists Working the Word in Highland Chiapas." Ph.D. Dissertation, University of Chicago, 2004.

"Retrato de un catequista: La religión liberadora y la comunistas en los Altos de Chiapas." *Nueva Antropología: Revista de ciencias sociales 56, no.* Etnicidad y política: 43–62.

Chowning, Margaret. "Convent Reform, Catholic Reform, and Bourbon Reform in Eighteenth-century New Spain: The View from the Nunnery." *Hispanic American Historical Review* 85, no. 1 (2005): 1–37.

Christian, William A. *Local Religion in Sixteenth-century Spain.* Princeton: Princeton University Press, 1981.

———. *Moving Crucifixes in Modern Spain.* Princeton: Princeton University Press, 1992.

Clendinnen, Inga. *Ambivalent Conquests: Maya and Spaniard in the Yucatan, 1517–1570.* Cambridge: Cambridge University Press, 1987.

———. *Aztecs: An Interpretation.* New York: Cambridge University Press, 1991.

———. "Disciplining the Indians: Franciscan Ideology and Missionary Violence in Sixteenth-century Yucatán." *Past and Present* 94 (1982): 27–48.

———. "Ways to the Sacred: Reconstructing 'Religion' in Sixteenth-Century Mexico." *History and Anthropology* 5 (1990): 105–141.

Cohen, Jeffrey H. "Transnational Migration in Rural Oaxaca, Mexico: Dependency, Development, and the Household." *American Anthropologist* 103, no. 4 (2001): 954–967.

Colonnese, Louis M., and Catholic Church, Consejo Episcopal Latinoamericano. *The Church in the Present-day Transformation of Latin America in the Light of the Council: Second General Conference of Latin American Bishops, Bogotá, 24 August, Medellin, 26 August-6 September, Colombia, 1968.* 2 vols. Bogota: General Secretariat of CELAM, 1970.

Comisión de Estudios de Historia de la Iglesia en Latinoamérica and Enrique D. Dussel. *Historia general de la Iglesia en América Latina.* Salamanca: CEHILA, Ediciones Sígueme, 1981.

Constable, Giles. "Attitudes toward Self-inflicted Suffering in the Middle Ages." In *Ninth Stephen J. Brademas, Sr., Lecture.* Brookline, Mass.: Hellenic College Press, 1982.

Cook, Garrett W. *Renewing the Maya World: Expressive Culture in a Highland Town.* Austin: University of Texas Press, 2000.

Cook, Noble David. *Born to Die: Disease and New World Conquest, 1492–1650.* Cambridge: Cambridge University Press, 1998.

Cook, Noble David, and W. George Lovell. *Secret Judgments of God: Old World Disease in Colonial Spanish America.* Norman: University of Oklahoma Press, 1991.

Cooper, Donald B. *Epidemic Disease in Mexico City, 1761–1813; An Administrative, Social, and Medical Study.* Austin: Published for the Institute of Latin American Studies by the University of Texas Press, 1965.

Correo del Restaurador, www.conservacionyrestauracion.inha.gob.mx/html/publindice.htm.

[Coverage of don Sergio Méndez's funeral] (no title). *Diario de Morelos,* February 9, 1992, 1–4.

"Cristos metropolitanos." *La Reforma,* April 6, 1996.

Crumrine, N. Ross. In *Pilgrimage in Latin America*, ed. Alan Morinis. Westport, Conn.: Greenwood, 1991, 71–90.

Curcio, Linda Ann. *The Great Festivals of Colonial Mexico City: Performing Power and Identity*. Albuquerque: University of New Mexico Press, 2004.

Davis, Richard H. *Lives of Indian Images*. Princeton: Princeton University Press, 1997.

Dean, Carolyn. *Inka Bodies and the Body of Christ: Corpus Christi in Colonial Cuzco, Peru*. Durham: Duke University Press, 1999.

Delpar, Helen. *The Enormous Vogue of Things Mexican: Cultural Relations between the United States and Mexico, 1920–1935*. Tuscaloosa: University of Alabama Press, 1992.

"Destrucción continua del hermoso edificio de Seminario." *El Siglo Diez y Nueve*, May 15, 1861.

Díaz del Castillo, Bernal, and J.M. Cohen. *The Conquest of New Spain*. Baltimore: Penguin, 1963.

Díaz del Castillo, Bernal, and David Carrasco, *The History of the Conquest of New Spain*. Albuquerque: University of New Mexico Press, 2008.

Dulles, John W.F. *Yesterday in Mexico: A Chronicle of the Revolution, 1919–1936*. Austin: University of Texas Press, 1961.

Dussel, Enrique D. *El episcopado latinoamericano y la liberación de los pobres, 1504–1620*. Mexico City: Centro de Reflexión Teológica, 1979.

Dussel, Enrique D., and Michael D. Barber. *The Invention of the Americas: Eclipse of "the Other" and the Myth of Modernity*. New York: Continuum, 1995.

Duviols, Pierre. *La destrucción de las religiones andinas*. Mexico City: Universidad Nacional Autónoma de México, 1977.

Eck, Diana L. *Darsan, Seeing the Divine Image in India*. 3rd ed. New York: Columbia University Press, 1998.

EGP. "Sebastián Guzmán, principal de principales." *Polémica* 10–11 (1983): 87–92.

Elizondo, Virgilio. *Guadalupe, Mother of the New Creation*. Maryknoll, NY: Orbis Books, 1997.

Escobar, Matías de. *Americana thebaida: Crónica de la Provincia Agustiniana de Michoacán* [1729], ed. Nicolás Navarrete. Morelia, Mich.: Balsal Editores, 1970.

Escobedo, Helen, Paolo Gori, and Néstor García Canclini. *Mexican Monuments: Strange Encounters*. New York: Abbeville, 1989.

Espín, Orlando. *Faith of the People: Theological Reflections on Popular Catholicism*. Maryknoll, N.Y.: Orbis Books, 1997.

———. "Popular Religion as an Epistemology of Suffering." *Journal of Hispanic/Latino Theology* 2, no. 2 (1994): 55–78.

Espín, Orlando, and Miguel H. Díaz. *From the Heart of Our People: Latino/a Explorations in Catholic Systematic Theology*. Maryknoll, N.Y.: Orbis, 1999.

Estrada Jasso, Andrés. *Imágenes en caña de maíz*. San Luis Potosi: Universidad Autónoma de San Luis Potosí, 1996.

Farris, Nancy. *Maya Society under Colonial Rule: The Collective Enterprise of Survival*. Princeton: Princeton University Press, 1984.

Fergusson, Erna. *Fiesta in Mexico*. New York: A. A. Knopf, 1934.

Fernández, Alonso. *Historia eclesiástica de nuestros tiempos, que es compendio de los excelentes frutos que en ellos el estado Eclesiástico y sagradas religiones han hecho y hazen, en la conversión de idólatras y reducción de hereges. Y de los ilustres martirios de varones Apostólicos, que en estas heroicas empresas han padecido.* Toledo, Spain, 1611.

Fernández, Eduardo C. *La Cosecha: Harvesting Contemporary United States Hispanic Theology (1972–1998).* Collegeville, Minn.: Liturgical Press, 2000.

Florescano, Enrique, ed. *El patrimonio nacional de México.* Mexico City: Consejo Nacional Para la Cultura y las Artes, 1997.

Flynn, Maureen. "The Spiritual Uses of Pain in Spanish Mysticism." *Journal of the American Academy of Religion* 64, no. 2 (1996): 257–278.

Foley, Michael W. "Organizing, Ideology and Moral Suasion: Political Discourse and Action in a Mexican Town." *Comparative Studies in Society and History* 32, no. 3 (1990): 455–487.

Fondo Pro Recuperación del Patrimonio Cultural de la Nación, ed. *Los Cristos de Lima: Esculturas en madera y marfil, s. XVI–XVII.* Lima: Banco de Crédito del Perú, 1991.

Foster, George McClelland. *Culture and Conquest: America's Spanish Heritage.* New York: Wenner-Gren Foundation for Anthropological Research, 1960.

Freedberg, David. *The Power of Images: Studies in the History and Theory of Response.* Chicago: University of Chicago Press, 1989.

Galeano, Eduardo H. *Open Veins of Latin America: Five Centuries of the Pillage of a Continent.* New York: Monthly Review Press, 1973.

García, Esteban. *Crónica de la provincia agustiniana del Santísimo nombre de Jesús de México.* Book 5. Madrid: Impr. de G. López del Horno, 1918.

García-Abasolo, Antonio, Gabriela García Lascurain, and Joaquin Sanchez Ruiz, eds. *Imaginería indígena mexicana: Una catequesis en caña de maíz.* Córdoba: Publicaciones Obra Social y Cultural Caja Sur, 2001.

García Ayluardo, Clara. "A World of Images: Cult, Ritual, and Society in Colonial Mexico City." In *Rituals of Rule, Rituals of Resistance: Public Celebrations and Popular Culture in Mexico,* ed. William H. Beezley, Chery English Martin, and William E. French, 95–114. Wilmington, Del.: Scholarly Resources, 1994.

García Canclini, Néstor. *Hybrid Cultures: Strategies for Entering and Leaving Modernity.* Minneapolis: University of Minnesota Press, 1995.

García Icazbalceta, Joaquín. "Los Agustinos en México." In *Obras de J. Garcia Icazbalceta,* vol. 1, 415–419. Mexico City, 1905.

García-Rivera, Alex. *The Community of the Beautiful: A Theological Aesthetics.* Collegeville, Minn.: Liturgical Press, 1999.

———. "The Sense of Beauty and the Talk of God." Graduate Theological Union Distinguished Faculty Lecture. Berkeley, Cal., 2002.

———. *A Wounded Innocence: Sketches for a Theology of Art.* Collegeville, Minn.: Liturgical Press, 2003.

García Rodríguez, María del Rosío, Alma Angélica Campos Valencia, and Mario Liévanos Ramos. *Totolapan: Raíces y testimonios.* Cuernavaca: Universidad Autónoma del Estado de Morelos, Unidad Central de Estudios para el Desarrollo Social, Ayuntamiento de Totolapan 1997–2000, 2000.

Geary, Patrick J. *Furta Sacra: Thefts of Relics in the Central Middle Ages.* Rev. ed. Princeton: Princeton University Press, 1990.

Gerhard, Peter. *A Guide to the Historical Geography of New Spain.* Norman: University of Oklahoma Press, 1993.

Gibson, Charles. *The Aztecs under Spanish Rule: A History of the Indians of the Valley of Mexico, 1519–1810.* Stanford: Stanford University Press, 1964.

Girard, François, Samuel L. Jackson, Greta Scacchi, Jason Flemyng, Don McKellar, Lion's Gate Films, Rhombus Media (Firm), and Mikado Film. *The Red Violin.* Videorecording. Universal City, Cal.: Universal Studios, 1999.

Gledhill, John. "The Indigenous Past in the Mexican Present." In *The Archeology of Mesoamerica: Mexican and European Perspectives,* ed. Warwick Bray and Linda Manzanilla. London: British Museum Press, 1998.

Glucklich, Ariel. *Sacred Pain: Hurting the Body for the Sake of the Soul.* Oxford: Oxford University Press, 2001.

Goizueta, Roberto S. *Caminemos con Jesús: Toward a Hispanic/Latino Theology of Accompaniment.* Maryknoll, N.Y.: Orbis, 1995.

———. "Fiesta: Life in the Subjunctive." In *From the Heart of Our People: Latino/a Explorations in Catholic Systematic Theology,* ed. Orlando Espín, 84–99. Maryknoll, N.Y.: Orbis, 1999.

González de la Paz y del Campo, Manuel. "Domicilio primera y solariega casa de el ssmo. dulcisimo Nombre de Jesus. Historia de la imperial, augusta, religiosa casa de la orden de los ermitaños Augustinos de la ciudad de Mexico. Chronica de su establecimiento, erección y continuación. Vidas y echos de sus religiosissimos prelados, y de muchos de sus mas singulares hijos." Manuscript, Biblioteca Melchor Ocampo de la Universidad de Morelia, Morelia, Mich.

González Leyva, Alejandra. *Chalma, una devoción agustina.* Toluca: Instituto Mexiquense de Cultura, Universidad Autónoma del Estado de México, 1991.

González Martínez, José Luis. *Fuerza y sentido: El catolicismo popular al comienzo del siglo XXI.* Mexico City: Ediciones Dabar, 2002.

Gow, David D. "The Roles of Christ and Inkarrí in Andean Religion." *Journal of Latin American Lore* 6, no. 2 (1980): 279–298.

Grayson, George W. *The Church in Contemporary Mexico.* Washington, D.C.: Center for Strategic and International Studies, 1992.

Graziano, Frank. *Cultures of Devotion: Folk Saints of Spanish America.* New York: Oxford University Press, 2006.

Greer, Allan, and Jodi Bilinkoff. *Colonial Saints: Discovering the Holy in the Americas, 1500–1800.* New York: Routledge, 2003.

Grijalva, Juan de, and Federico Gómez de Orozco. *Crónica de la orden de N.P.S. Augustín en las prouincias de la Nueua España, en quatro edades desde el año de 1533 hasta el de 1592* [1624]. Mexico City: Imprenta Victoria, 1924.

Gruzinski, Serge. *The Conquest of Mexico: The Incorporation of Indian Societies into the Western World, 16th–18th Centuries.* Cambridge: Polity Press, 1993.

———. "Images and Cultural Mestizaje in Colonial Mexico." *Poetics Today* 16, no. 1 (1995): 53–77.

———. "Indian Confraternities, Brotherhoods and Mayordomías in Central New Spain. A List of Questions for the Historian and the Anthropologist." In *The Indian Community of Colonial Mexico: Fifteen Essays on Land Tenure, Corporate Organizations, Ideology and Village Politics,* ed. Arij Ouweneel and Simon Miller, 205–223. Amsterdam: CEDLA, 1990.

————. *Man-Gods in the Mexican Highlands: Indian Power and Colonial Society,*
1550–1800. Stanford: Stanford University Press, 1989.

Guamán Poma de Ayala, Felipe, John V. Murra, Rolena Adorno, and Jorge Urioste.
El primer nueva corónica y buen gobierno. Mexico City: Siglo Veintiuno, 1980.

Guha, Ranajit. *Elementary Aspects of Peasant Insurgency in Colonial India.* Delhi: Oxford
University Press, 1983.

Guidieri, Remo. "Statue and Mask. Presence and Representation in Belief." *Res* 5
(1983): 15–22.

Guilliford, Andrew. "Curation and Repatriation of Sacred and Tribal Objects." *Public
Historian* 14, no. 3 (1992): 23–38.

Gutiérrez, Gustavo. *Las Casas: In Search of the Poor of Jesus Christ.* Maryknoll, N.Y.:
Orbis, 1993.

————. *En busca de los pobres de Jesucristo: El pensamiento de Bartolome de las Casas.*
Lima: Instituto Bartolomé de las Casas, 1992.

Hanks, William F. *Intertexts: Writings on Language, Utterance, and Context.* Lanham,
Md.: Rowman and Littlefield, 2000.

Harris, Max. *Aztecs, Moors, and Christians: Festivals of Reconquest in Mexico and Spain.*
Austin: University of Texas Press, 2000.

Hernández Zamora, José Moisés. *Recuperando la memoria de don Sergio Méndez Arceo.*
Cuernavaca: Fundación don Sergio Méndez Arceo, 2000.

Herrera, Tomás de, Fernando Rojo Martínez, and Balbino Rano Gundín. *Alphabetum
Augustinianum: Matriti 1644.* 2 vols. Rome: Publicazioni Agostiniane, 1990.

Hughes, Jennifer Scheper. "The Catholic Church and Social Revolutionaries." In
*Religion and Society in Latin America: Interpretive Essays from the Conquest
to the Present.*, ed. Lee Penyak and Waltar Petry. Maryknoll, N.Y.: Orbis,
forthcoming.

————. "The Iconography of Suffering: Indigenous Perspectives on Christian
Self-inflicted Violence and the Brutality of the Crucifix in Colonial Mexico." Paper
presented at the annual meting of the American Academy of Religion, Atlanta,
2003.

————. "Spiritual Practice versus Art in a Mexican Cult." Paper presented at the
annual meeting of the American Academy of Religion, San Antonio, 2004.

Ingham, John M. *Mary, Michael, and Lucifer: Folk Catholicism in Central Mexico.*
Austin: University of Texas Press, 1986.

Isabella Stewart Gardner Museum, ed. *The Word Made Image: Religion, Art, and
Architecture in Spain and Spanish America, 1500–1600.* Boston: Trustees of the
Isabella Stewart Garner Museum, 1998.

Islas Jiménez, Alicia. Una comunidad del sur de la ciudad de México, afirma sus lazos
de identidad a través de la restauración de una escultural religiosa. Correo del
Restaurador. Número 1. Conservación y restauración del patrimonio religioso.
INAH, www.conservacionrestauracion.inah.gob.mx/html/publindice.html.

Jiménez Limón, Javier. "Suffering, Death, Cross and Martyrdom." In *Mysterium
Liberationis: Fundamental Concepts in liberation Theology,* ed. Ignacio Ellacuría,
702–715. Maryknoll, N.Y.: Orbis, 1993.

Joseph, Gilbert M. *Reclaiming the Political in Latin American History: Essays from the
North.* Durham, NC: Duke University Press, 2001.

Juárez, José Roberto. *Reclaiming Church Wealth: The Recovery of Church Property after Expropriation in the Archdiocese of Guadalajara, 1860–1911.* Albuquerque: University of New Mexico Press, 2004.

Kalver, Jeanine. *From the Land of the Sun to the City of Angels: The Migration Process of Zapotec Indians from Oaxaca, Mexico to Los Angeles, California.* Amsterdam: University of Amsterdam, 1997.

Kelemen, Pál. *Baroque and Rococo in Latin America.* Vol. 1. New York: Macmillan, 1951.

———. *Baroque and Rococo in Latin America.* Vol. 2. 2nd ed. New York: Dover, 1967.

Klor de Alva, Jorge. "Colonizing Souls: The Failure of the Indian Inquisition and the Rise of Penitential Discipline." In *Cultural Encounters: The Impact of the Inquisition in Spain and the New World,* ed. Mary Elizabeth Perry and Anne J. Cruz, 3–22. Berkeley: University of California Press, 1991.

Kubler, George. "Pre-Columbian Pilgrimages in Mesoamerica." In *Fourth Palenque Round Table, 1980,* ed. Merle Greene Robertson and Elizabeth P. Benson, 11–23. San Francisco: Pre-Columbian Art Research Institute, 1985.

Lancaster, Roger N. *Thanks to God and the Revolution: Popular Religion and Class Consciousness in the New Nicaragua.* New York: Columbia University Press, 1988.

Larkin, Brian. "Liturgy, Devotion, and Religious Reform in Eighteenth-Century Mexico City." *The Americas* 60, no. 4 (2004): 493–518.

Lavrin, Asunción. "Rural Confraternities in the Local Economies of New Spain: The Bishopric of Oaxaca in the Context of Colonial Mexico." In *The Indian Community of Colonial Mexico: Fifteen Essays on Land Tenure, Corporate Organizations, Ideology and Village Politics,* ed. Arij Ouweneel and Simon Miller, 224–249. Amsterdam: CEDLA, 1990.

Levya Solano, Xóchitl. "Catequistas, misioneros y tradiciones en Las Cañadas." In *Chiapas: Los rumbos de otra historia,* ed. Juan Pedro and Mario Humberto Ruz Viquiera, 375–405. Guadalajara: Universidad de Guadalajara, 1995.

Lewis, Oscar. *Life in a Mexican Village: Tepoztlan Re-studied.* Urbana: University of Illinois Press, 1963.

León-Portilla, Miguel. *Native Mesoamerican Spirituality: Ancient Myths, Discourses, Stories, Doctrines, Hymns, Poems from the Aztec, Yucatec, Quiche-Maya and Other Sacred Traditions.* New York: Paulist Press, 1980.

Loaeza-Lajous, Soledad. "Continuity and Change in the Mexican Catholic Church." In *Church and Politics in Latin America,* ed. Dermot Keogh, 272–298. New York: St. Martin's, 1990.

Lockhart, James. *The Nahuas after the Conquest: A Social and Cultural History of the Indians of Central Mexico, Sixteenth through Eighteenth Centuries.* Stanford: Stanford University Press, 1992.

López Beltrán, Lauro. "Consagración episcopal de don Sergio Méndez Arceo." In *Don Sergio Méndez Arceo, patriarca de la solidaridad liberadora: Testigo, teólogo y profeta de América Latina,* ed. Leticia and Giulio Girardi Rentería Chávez, 91–104. Mexico City: Ediciones Dabar, 2000.

———. *Fray Antonio de Roa: Taumaturgo penitente.* 2nd ed, Mexico City: Editorial Jus, 1969.

López Bucio, Baltasar. *Don Sergio Méndez Arceo: Profeta para nuestro tiempo. Semblanza de su vida sacerdotal, primera parte: 1907–1956.* Mexico City: Ediciones Dabar, 1993.

López Rodríguez de Figueredo, Tomás Francisco. *Sermon panegirico que en celebridad de la Santisima Virgen María en su expresiva advocacion de la luz, dijo en la Iglesia del Santuario de Chalma, el dia 11 de mayo de 1842 el br. d. Tomas Francisco Lopez Rodriguez de Figueredo, examinador sinodal de este arzobispado, cura propio y juez eclesiástico de la parroquia de Santa Maria de la Asuncion Jalatlaco. Dalo a luz el r.p. prior del convento de religiosos agustinos, del expresado santuario.* Mexico City: Impr. del Aguila dirigida por J. Ximeno, 1842.

MacCormack, Sabine. ""The Heart Has Its Reasons": Predicaments of Missionary Christianity in Early Colonial Peru." *Hispanic American Historical Review* 65, no. 3 (1985): 443–466.

———. *Religion in the Andes: Vision and Imagination in Early Colonial Peru.* Princeton: Princeton University Press, 1991.

Macín, Raúl, Méndez Arceo. *¿Político o cristiano? Una revolución en la iglesia.* Mexico City: Editorial Posada, 1973.

Mackay, John Alexander. *The Other Spanish Christ: A Study in the Spiritual History of Spain and South America.* New York: Macmillan, 1932.

Magallanes, Juan de. *Aparicion de la milagrosa imagen del Santo Cristo que se venera en el religioso convento y santuario de religioso hermitaños del Orden de N.P.S. Augustin, de S. Miguel de Chalma.* [1731] Mexico City: Impreso por J. Ojeda, 1839.

Malkin, Elisabeth. "Nothing Is Sacred, as Looters Rob Mexican Churches of Colonial Treasures." *New York Times,* October 4, 2006.

Martin, Cheryl English. *Rural Society in Colonial Morelos.* Albuquerque: University of New Mexico Press, 1985.

Martin, James. "An Interview with Camille Paglia." *America* 171, no. 15 (1994): 10–17.

Mathews, Holly F. "'We Are Mayordomo'": A Reinterpretation of Women's Roles in the Mexican Cargo System." *American Ethnologist* 12, no. 2 (1985): 285–301.

Matovina, Timothy M. *Guadalupe and Her Faithful: Latino Catholics in San Antonio, from Colonial Origins to the Present.* Baltimore: Johns Hopkins University Press, 2005.

McCaa, Robert. "Spanish and Nahuatl Views on Smallpox and Demographic Catastrophe in Mexico." *Journal of Interdisciplinary History* 25, no. 3 (1995): 397–431.

McGuire, Meredith. *Lived Religion: Faith and Practice in Everyday Life.* New York: Oxford University Press, 2008.

Mecham, J. Lloyd. *Church and State in Latin America: A History of Politico-Ecclesiastical Relations.* Chapel Hill: University of North Carolina Press, 1934.

Megged, Amos. *Exporting the Catholic Reformation: Local Religion in Early-Colonial Mexico.* Leiden: E.J. Brill, 1996.

Mejido, Manuel. "A Critique of the 'Aesthetic Turn' in U.S. Hispanic Theology: A Dialogue with Roberto Goizueta and the Positioning of a New Paradigm." *Journal for Hispanic and Latino Theology* 8, no. 3 (2001): 18–48.

Méndez, Juan Bautista, and Justo Alberto Fernández. *Crónica de la Provincia de Santiago de México de la Orden de Predicadores, 1521–1564.* Mexico City: Porrúa, 1993.

Méndez Arceo, Sergio. *Compromiso cristiano y liberación,* vol. 2. Mexico City: Centro de Estudios Ecuménicos, 1988.

———. "Elogio del templo Catedral de Cuernavaca, que hace el Obispo en el decimo aniversario de la consagración, 1969." Cuernavaca, 1969. Unpublished sermon, from personal archive of Pbro. Angel Sánchez Campos.

————. *Exhortación pastoral acerca del reacondicionamiento de la santa iglesia catedral de Cuernavaca*. Cuernavaca, 1959.

————. "Instrucción sobre la devoción a los santos y sus imágenes." In *Cuernavaca: Fuentes para el estudio de una diócesis*. *CIDOC Dossier No. 31*, ed. Baltasar López Bucio, 1, 4/37–38. Cuernavaca: CIDOC, 1960.

————. "Reacondicionamiento de la Catedral de Cuernavaca." In *Cuernavaca: Fuentes para el estudio de una diócesis*. *CIDOC Dossier No. 31*, ed. Baltazar López, 1, 4/250–4/256. Cuernavaca CIDOC, 1960.

Mendieta, Gerónimo de, and Francisco Solano y Pérez-Lila. *Historia eclesiástica indiana*. [1585]. Madrid: Atlas, 1973.

"Mexico: Bishops Encourage Basic Communities." *LADOC* 20, no. 1 (1989): 10–14.

Míguez Bonino, José, ed. *Faces of Jesus: Latin American Christologies*. Maryknoll, N.Y.: Orbis, 1984.

Mills, Kenneth. *Idolatry and Its Enemies: Colonial Andean Religion and Extirpation, 1640–1750*. Princeton: Princeton University Press, 1997.

Mills, Kenneth, William B. Taylor, and Sandra Lauderdale Graham. *Colonial Latin America: A Documentary History*. Wilmington, Del.: Scholarly Resources, 2002.

Mitchell, Timothy. *Passional Culture: Emotion, Religion, and Society in Southern Spain*. Philadelphia: University of Pennsylvania Press, 1990.

Molina del Villar, América. *La Nueva España y el matlazahuatl, 1736–1739*. Mexico City: Colegio de Michoacán, Centro de Investigaciones y Estudios Superiores en Antropología Social, 2001.

Monaghan, John. "Reciprocity, Redistribution, and the Transaction of Value in the Mesoamerican Fiesta." *American Ethnologist* 1, no. 4. (Nov. 1990): 758–774.

Montejano y Aguiñaga, Rafael. *El Señor del Saucito y su templo*. 4th ed. San Luis Potosi, Mexico: n.p., 1983.

Morayta Mendoza, Miguel, Catherine Good, Alfredo Paulo, and Cristina Saldaña. "Resolviendo conflictos entre pueblos de tradición nahua de Morelos: Una ruta por la costumbre, [A1] ley y la diversidad religiosa." Unpublished manuscript, n.d.

"Morelenses en peregrinación." *Correo del Sur*, May 21, 1961, 6–7.

Motolinía, Toribio. *History of the Indians of New Spain*. Washington, D.C.: Academy of American Franciscan History, 1951.

Mountz, Alison, and Richard Wright. "Daily Life in the Transnational Migration Community of San Agustin, Oaxaca and Poughkeepsie, New York." *Diáspora* 5, no. 3 (1996): 403–428.

Murillo Rodríguez, Silvia. *La vida a través de la muerte:Eestudio biocultural de las costumbres funerarias en el Temazcaltepec prehispánico*. Mexico City: INAH, 2002.

Museo Nacional de Arte, ed. *Pinceles de la historia: El origen del reino de la Nueva España, 1680–1750*. Mexico City: Museo Nacional de Arte, Universidad Nacional Autónoma de México, Instituto de Investigaciones Estéticas, 1999.

Nesvig, Martin Austin. *Local Religion in Colonial Mexico*. Albuquerque: University of New Mexico, 2006.

Neumeyer, A. "The Indian Contribution to Architectural Decoration in Spanish Colonial America." *Art Bulletin* 30 (1974): 104–121.

Norget, Kristin. *Days of Death, Days of Life: Ritual in the Popular Culture of Oaxaca.* New York: Columbia University Press, 2006.

———. "Progressive Theology and Popular Religiosity in Oaxaca, Mexico." In *Latin American Religion in Motion*, ed. Christian Smith and Joshua Prokopy, 91–110. New York: Routledge, 1999.

Novak, Kinga. "A Social History of the Imagery of Christ's Suffering in Colonial Mexico." M.A. Thesis, New York University, 1997.

Nuttall, Zelia. "A Penitential Rite of the Ancient Mexicans." *Archeological and Ethnographic Papers of the Peabody Museum* (1904): 26.

Obregón, Gonzalo. "El Real Convento y Santuario de San Miguel de Chalma." In *Estudios históricos americanos: Homenaje a Silvio Zavala*, ed. Julio Le Riverend. Mexico City: Colegio de México, 1953.

Oktavec, Eileen. *Answered Prayers: Miracles and Milagros along the Border.* Tucson: University of Arizona Press, 1995.

Olivares, José de. *Oracion panegyrica, que a la festiva solemnidad de la nueva capilla, que se consagró á N. Seänora de Gvadalvpe, y translacion de la peregrina, y milagrosa efigie de Christo Crucificado, que por tiempo immemorial se adora, y venera en las cuebas, y santuario de s. Miguel de Chalma, del orden de n.p. san Augustin.* Mexico City: Viuda de B. Calderon, 1683.

Olivé Negrete, Julio César, and Augusto Urteaga Castro-Pozo, eds. *INAH, una historia.* Mexico City: INAH, 1988.

Olivier, Guilhem. "Sacred Bundles, Arrows, and New Fire." In *Cave, City and Eagle's Nest: A Interpretive Journey through the Mapa de Cuauhtinchan No. 2*, ed. Davíd Carrasco et al., 281–316. Albuquerque: University of New Mexico Press, 2007.

Orozco, Luis Enrique. *Los Cristos de caña d maíz y otras venerables imágenes de Nuestro Señor Jesucristo.* Guadalajara, 1970.

Orsi, Robert A. *The Madonna of 115th Street: Faith and Community in Italian Harlem.* 2nd ed. New Haven: Yale University Press, 2002.

Osorio de San Román, Antonio. *Consuelo de penitentes o mesa franca de espirituales manjares.* [Seville, 1583] Madrid: Fundación Universitaria Española, Universidad Pontificia de Salamanca, 1999.

Otten, Charlotte M., and American Museum of Natural History, eds. *Anthropology and Art; Readings in Cross-cultural Aesthetics.* Garden City, N.Y.: Published for the American Museum of Natural History by the Natural History Press, 1971.

Ouweneel, Arij, and S. Miller, eds. *The Indian Community of Colonial Mexico: Fifteen Essays on Land Tenure, Corporate Organizations, Ideology, and Village Politics.* Amsterdam: CEDLA, 1990.

Parker, Cristián. *Popular Religion and Modernization in Latin America: A Different Logic.* Maryknoll, N.Y.: Orbis, 1996.

Paso y Troncoso, Francisco del, and Edward King Kingsborough. *Códice Kingsborough. Memorial de los indios de Tepetlaoztoc al monarca español contra los encomenderos del pueblo.* Madrid: Fototipía de Hauser y Menet, 1912.

Pelikan, Jaroslav Jan. *Jesus through the Centuries: His Place in the History of Culture.* New Haven: Yale University Press, 1985.

Pérez, Laura Elisa. *Chicana Art: The Politics of Spiritual and Aesthetic Altarities*. Durham: Duke University Press, 2007.

Pérez Cancio, Gregorio Antonio, and Gonzalo Obregón. *Libro de fábrica del Templo Parroquial de la Santa Cruz y Soledad de Nuestra Señora: Años de 1773 a 1784*. Mexico City: Instituto Nacional de Antropología e Historia, 1970.

Perkins, Judith. *The Suffering Self: Pain and Narrative Representation in Early Christianity*. London: Routledge, 1995.

Phelan, John Leddy. *The Millennial Kingdom of the Franciscans in the New World*. 2nd ed. Berkeley: University of California Press, 1970.

Poole, Stafford. *Our Lady of Guadalupe: The Origins and Sources of a Mexican National Symbol*. Tucson: University of Arizona Press, 1995.

Prem, Hanns. "Disease Outbreaks in Central Mexico during the Sixteenth Century." In *"Secret Judgments of God": Old World Disease in Colonial Spanish America*, ed. Noble David Cook and W. George Lovell, 20–48. Norman: University of Oklahoma Press, 1991.

Rabasa, José. "Thinking Europe in Indian Categories; or, Tell Me the Story of How I Conquered You." Paper presented at the annual meting of the Modern Language Association, 2001.

———. *Writing Violence on the Northern Frontier: The Historiography of Sixteenth-Century New Mexico and Florida and the Legacy of Conquest*. Durham: Duke University Press, 2000.

Ramírez, Paul. "Isolating Disease: Cayetano Cabrera y Quintero's Escudo de Armas de México and the Matlazahuatl Epidemic of Mexico City, 1736–1737." Unpublished manuscript, University of California, Berkeley, 2005.

Ramos Gavilán, Alonso. *Historia de Nuestra Señora de Copacabana*. [1621] 2nd ed. La Paz: Academia Boliviana de la Historia, 1976.

Ramos Sosa, Rafael. "La fiesta barroca en ciudad de México y Lima." *Historia* 30 (1997): 263–286.

Redfield, Robert. "Art and Icon." In *Anthropology and Art: Readings in Cross-Cultural Aesthetics*, ed. Charlotte M. Otten. Garden City, N.Y.: Natural History Press, 1971.

———. *Tepoztlan, a Mexican Village: A Study of Folk Life*. Chicago: University of Chicago Press, 1930.

Reff, Daniel T. *Plagues, Priests, and Demons: Sacred Narratives and the Rise of Christianity in the Old World and the New*. Cambridge: Cambridge University Press, 2005.

Rentería Chávez, Leticia, ed. *Va por ti el compromiso: testimonios sobre Don Sergio Méndez Arceo*. Mexico City, 2002.

Rentería Chávez, Leticia, and Francisco Javier González Muñoz. *Don Sergio Méndez Arceo, VII Obispo de Cuernavaca*. Cuernavaca: Equipo! Celebrando a don Sergio!, 2000.

Reuque Paillalef, Rosa Isolde, and Florencia E. Mallon. *When a Flower Is Reborn: The Life and Times of a Mapuche Feminist*. Durham: Duke University Press, 2002.

Ricard, Robert. *The Spiritual Conquest of Mexico: An Essay on the Apostolate and the Evangelizing Methods of the Mendicant Orders in New Spain, 1523–1572*. Berkeley: University of California Press, 1982.

Richardson, Miles. *Being-in-Christ and Putting Death in Its Place: An Anthropologist's Account of Christian Performance in Spanish America and the American South*. Baton Rouge: Louisiana State University Press, 2003.

————. "The Image of Christ in Spanish America as a Model for Suffering." *Journal of Inter-American Studies and World Affairs* 13, no. 2 (1971): 248–257.

Rivera Cambas, Manuel. *México pintoresco, aríistico y monumental. Las descripciones contienen datos científicos, históricos y estadísticos.* Mexico City: Impr. de la Reforma, 1880.

Robles, Antonio de, and Antonio Castro Leal. *Diario de sucesos notables (1665–1703).* 2nd ed. Mexico City: Editorial Porrua, 1972.

Rochas Reyes, Juan Manuel, and Alfredo Vega Cárdenas. *La iconografía Cristiana en la conservación y restauración de arte sacro virreinal.* Mexico City: INAH, www.conservacionyrestauracion.inha.gob.mx/html/publindice.htm.

Rodríguez-Shadow, María, and Robert Dennis Shadow. *El pueblo del Señor: Las fiestas y peregrinaciones de Chalma.* Toluca: Universidad Autónoma del Estado de México, 2000.

Romero de Terreros, Manuel. *Atlatlauhcan.* Mexico City: Instituto Nacional de Antropología e Historia, 1956.

————. *La iglesia y convento de San Agustín.* [1950] Mexico City: Universidad Nacional Autónoma de México, Instituto de Investigaciones Estéticas, 1985.

Rosas, María. *Tepoztlán: Crónica de desacatos y resistencia.* Mexico City: Ediciones Era, 1997.

Ross, Ellen M. *The Grief of God: Images of the Suffering Jesus in Late Medieval England.* New York: Oxford University Press, 1997.

Roziére, Sonia de la, and Xavier Moyssén Echeverría. *México: Angustia de sus Cristos.* Mexico City: Instituto Nacional de Antropología e Historia, 1967.

Rubial García, Antonio. *El convento agustino y la sociedad novohispana: 1533–1630.* Mexico City: Universidad Nacional Autónoma de México, 1989.

————. *Una monarquía criolla: La provincia agustina de México en el siglo XVII.* Mexico City: Consejo Nacional para la Cultura y las Artes Dirección General de Publicaciones, 1990.

————. *La plaza, el palacio y el convento: La ciudad de México en el siglo XVII.* Mexico City: Consejo Nacional para la Cultura y las Artes, 1998.

————. *La santidad controvertida: Hagiografía y conciencia criolla alrededor de los Venerables no canonizados de Nueva España.* Mexico City: Universidad Nacional Autónoma de México Facultad de Filosofía y Letras: Fondo de Cultura Económica, 1999.

————. "Votos pactados. Las prácticas políticas entre los mendicantes novohispanos." *EHN* 26 (January-June 2002): 51–83.

Rubial García, Antonio, Francisco Jiménez, and Pedro Angeles Jiménez. *La hermana pobreza: El franciscanismo de la Edad Media a la evangelización novohispana.* Mexico City: Facultad de Filosofía y Letras Universidad Nacional Autónoma de México, 1996.

Ruether, Rosemary Radford. *Introducing Redemption in Christian Feminism.* Sheffield: Sheffield Academic Press, 1998.

————. "Two Spiritualities of Violence: Mesoamerican and Christian." *National Catholic Reporter* 2002.

Ruíz Baía, Larissa. "Rethinking Transnationalism: National Identities among Peruvian Catholics in New Jersey." In *Christianity, Social Change, and Globalization in the Americas*, ed. Anna Peterson, Manuel A. Vásquez, and Philip J. Williams, 147–164. New Brunswick: Rutgers University Press, 2001.

Ruiz Zavala, Alipio. *Historia de la Provincia Agustiniana de Santisimo Nombre de Jesús de México*. 2 vols. Mexico City: Editorial Porrúa, 1984.

Rus, Jan, and Rob Wasserstrom. "Civil-Religious Hierarchies in Central Chiapas: A Critical Perspective." *American Ethnologist* 7, no. 3 (1980): 466–478.

Sahagún, Bernardino de. *Códice florentino*. 3 vols. Mexico City: Secretaría de Gobernación, 1979.

Sahagún, Bernardino de, Arthur J.O. Anderson, Charles E. Dibble, and Jay I. Kislak. *General History of the Things of New Spain: Florentine Codex*. Monograph no. 14, pt. 1–13. Santa Fe: School of American Research; Salt Lake City: University of Utah, 1950.

Salazar Herrera, Francisco Javier. *El Santo Desierto de Tenancingo y la Escuela Nacional de Restauración*. Mexico City: INAH, www.conservacionyrestauracion.inha.gob. mx/html/publindice.html.

Salcedo Palacios, Carlos. "Participación de don Sergio Méndez Arceo en el Concilio Vaticano II." In *Don Sergio Méndez Arceo, patriarca de la solidaridad liberadora*, ed. Leticia and Giulio Girardi Rentería Chávez, 145–156. Mexico City: Ediciones Dabar, 2000.

Sallnow, M.J. "A Trinity of Christs: Cultic Processes in Andean Catholicism." *American Ethnologist* 9, no. 4 (1982): 730–749.

Sánchez Campos, Angel. "Don Sergio Méndez Arceo, Obispo de Cuernavca." In *Don Sergio Méndez Arceo, patriarca de la solidaridad liberadora: Testigo, teólogo y profeta de América Latina*, ed. Leticia and Giulio Girardi Rentería Chávez, 105–144. Mexico City: Ediciones Dabar, 2000.

Santacruz Vargas, Julia. "De la cruz que domina, manipular y persuade." In *Iconografia Mexicana IV: iconografía del poder*, ed. Beatriz Barba Piña Chán, 185–198. Mexico: INAH, 2002.

———. "Santuario de Chalma." *Correo del Sur*, March 11, 1973, 5–8.

Saravia, Javier. *La religiosidad popular, extranjera en su propia tierra*. Mexico City: Obra Nacional de la Buena Prensa, 2003.

Sardó, Joaquín. *Relación histórica y moral de la portentosa imagen de N. Sr. Jesucristo crucificado aparecida en una de las cuevas de S. Miguel de Chalma, hoy real convento y santuario de este nombre. Con los compendios de las vidas de los dos venerables religiosos legos y primeros anacoretas de este santo desierto, F. Bartolomé de Jesús María, y F. Juan de San Josef*. Mexico City: Impresa en casa de Arizpe, 1810.

Scarry, Elaine. *The Body in Pain: The Making and Unmaking of the World*. New York: Oxford University Press, 1985.

Schele, Linda, Mary Ellen Miller, and Justin Kerr. *The Blood of Kings: Dynasty and Ritual in Maya Art*. New York: G. Braziller; Fort Worth: Kimbell Art Museum, 1986.

Schiller, Gertrud. *Iconography of Christian Art*. Translated by Janet Seligman. Greenwich, Conn.: New York Graphic Society, 1971.

Schneider, Robert A. "Mortification on Parade: Penitential Processions in Sixteenth- and Seventeenth-Century France." *Renaissance and Reformation* 10, no. 1 (1986): 123–146.

Sedgwick, Eve Kosofsky, and Adam Frank. *Touching Feeling: Affect, Pedagogy, Performativity* Durham: Duke University Press, 2003.

Segundo, Juan Luis. "The Shift within Latin American Theology." *Journal of Theology for Southern Africa* 52 (1985): 17–29.

Serra Cary, Diana. "A Cathedral Comes into Focus. An Important Discovery and Restorations of Artistic Treasures in Cuernavaca." In *Cuernavaca: Fuentes para el estudio de una diócesis. CIDOC Dossier No. 31*, ed. Baltazar López, 1, 4/484–489. Cuernavaca: CIDOC, 1962.

Sicardo, José. *Interrogatorio de la vida y virtudes del venerable hermano fray Bartolomé de Jes'us María. . . . Formado para las informaciones, qve por comission del ilustrissimo señor doctor don Francisco de Aguiar, y Zeijas, arçobispo de la Santa Iglesia Metropolitana de Mexico; pasan ante el señor doctor don Diego de la Sierra, canonigo doctoral de dicha Iglesia.* Mexico City: Juan de Ribert, 1683.

Sigaut, Nellie. "La crucifixión en la pintura colonial." *Relaciones* (Zamora) 51 (1992): 101–140.

———. "Sigue el despilfarro." *El Siglo Diez y Nueve*, May 15, 1861.

Sobrino, Jon. *Jesus in Latin America.* Maryknoll, N.Y.: Orbis, 1987.

Solano, Francisco de; Catalina Romero; Catholic Church, Archdiocese of Mexico City; and Centro de Estudios Históricos (Spain), Departamento de Historia de América. *Relaciones geográficas del Arzobispado de México, 1743.* Madrid: Consejo Superior de Investigaciones Científicas, Centro de Estudios Históricos, Departamento de Historia de América, 1988.

Solís de la Torre, Jesús. *Bárbaros y ermitaños: Chichimecas y Agustinos en la Sierra Gorda, siglos XVI, XVII, XVIII.* Queretaro, Mex.: 1983.

Sotelo Inclán, Jesús. *Raíz y razón de Zapata, Anenecuilco.* Mexico City: Editorial Etnos, 1943.

Spence, Jonathan D. *The Memory Palace of Matteo Ricci.* New York: Penguin Books, 1985.

Stoll, David. *Between Two Armies in the Ixil Towns of Guatemala.* New York: Columbia University Press, 1993.

Stuart, David. "Blood Symbolism in Maya Iconography." In *Maya Iconography*, ed. Elizabeth P. Benson and Gillett G. Griffin, 175–221. Princeton: Princeton University Press, 1988.

Sullivan, Martin. "Sacred Objects and Sacred Knowledge in Museum Spaces." Presentation at the Harvard Divinity School Religion and Arts Initiative lunch series. Harvard Divinity School Center for the Study of World Religions, 2003.

Sweet, David G., and Gary B. Nash, eds. *Struggle and Survival in Colonial America.* Berkeley: University of California Press, 1981.

Tamez, Elsa. "Reliving Our Histories: Racial and Cultural Revelations of God." In *New Visions for the Americas: Religious Engagement and Social Transformation*, ed. David B. Batstone, 33–56. Minneapolis: Fortress, 1993.

Taube, Karl. "A Study of Classic Maya Scaffold Sacrifice." In *Maya Iconography*, ed. Elizabeth P. Benson and Gillett G. Griffin, 331–351. Princeton: Princeton University Press, 1988.

Taylor, William B. "Cristos de Caña." In *Oxford Encyclopedia of Mesoamerican Cultures*, ed. Davíd Carrasco, 286–287. New York: Oxford University Press, 2001.

———. "La iglesia entre la jerarquía y la religión popular: Messages from the Contact Zone." Unpublished manuscript, Berkeley, CA, 2003.

———. *Magistrates of the Sacred: Priests and Parishioners in Eighteenth-century Mexico.* Stanford: Stanford University Press, 1996.

————. "Mexico's Virgin of Guadalupe in the Seventeenth Century: Hagiography and Beyond." In *Colonial Saints: Discovering the Holy in the Americas, 1500–1800*, ed. Allan Greer and Jodi Blinkoff. New York: Routledge, 2002.

————. "Religion and Peasant Politics in Colonial Mexico: The Cristo Renovado of Ixmiquilpan and Santa Teresa." Unpublished manuscript, Berkeley, Cal., 2005.

————. "Shrines without Pilgrims? Miraculous Images and Sacred Places in Colonial Mexico and Beyond." Paper given at CASBS Seminar, University of California, Berkeley, 2002.

————. "Two Shrines of the Cristo Renovado: Religion and Peasant Politics in Late Colonial Mexico." *American Historical Review* 110, no. 4 (2005): 945–974.

————. "The Virgin of Guadalupe in New Spain: An Inquiry into the Social History of Marian Devotion." *American Ethnologist* 14, no. 1 (1987): 9–33.

Torquemada, Juan de. *Monarquía indiana: De los veinte y un libros rituales y monarquía indiana, con el origen y guerras de los indios occidentales, de sus poblazones, descubrimiento, conquista, conversión y otras cosas maravillosas de la mesma tierra.* [1615] 7 v. Mexico City: Universidad Nacional Autónoma de México, Instituto de Investigaciones Históricas, 1975.

Toussaint, Manuel. *Colonial Art in Mexico*. Trans. and ed. Elizabeth Weismann, [1949] Austin: University of Texas Press, 1967.

Tovar de Teresa, Guillermo, José E. Iturriaga, and Enrique Krauze. *The City of Palaces: Chronicle of a Lost Heritage.* 2 vols. Mexico City: Vuelta, 1990.

Trexler, Richard C. "Dressing and Undressing Images: An Analytical Sketch." In *Religion in Social Context in Europe and America, 1200–1700*, ed. Richard Trexler, 374–408. Tempe: Arizona Center for Medieval and Renaissance Studies, 2002.

————. *Reliving Golgotha: The Passion Play of Iztapalapa.* Cambridge: Harvard University Press, 2003.

Tweed, Thomas. *Our Lady of the Exile: Diasporic Religion at a Cuban Catholic Shrine in Miami.* New York: Oxford University Press, 2002.

Turner, Victor Witter, and Edith L.B. Turner. *Image and Pilgrimage in Christian Culture: Anthropological Perspectives.* New York: Columbia University Press, 1978.

Unamuno, Miguel de. "El Cristo yacente de Santa Clara de Palencia." In Unamumo, *Andanzas y visiones españoles*, 297–300. Madrid: Renacimiento, 1929.

Valadés, Diego, and Tarsicio Herrera Zapién. *Retórica cristiana.* Mexico City: Universidad Nacional Autónoma de México, Fondo de Cultura Económica, 1989.

Van Young, Eric. *The Other Rebellion: Popular Violence, Ideology, and the Mexican Struggle for Independence, 1810–1821.* Stanford: Stanford University Press, 2001.

VanWey, Leah, Catherine Tucker, and Eileen Diaz McConnell. "Community Organization, Migration, and Remittances in Oaxaca." *Latin American Research Review* 40, no. 1 (2005): 83–107.

Vargas Lugo, Elisa, Elena Isabel Estrada de Gerlero, and María del Consuelo Maquívar, eds. *Parábola Novohispana: Cristo en el arte Virreinal.* Mexico City: Fomento Cultural Banamex; Comisión de Arte Sacro, Arquidiócesis Primada de México, 2000.

Vásquez, Manuel. "Toward a New Agenda for the Study of Religion in the Americas." *Journal of Interamerican Studies and World Affairs* 41, no. 4 (1999): 1–20.

Vásquez, Manuel A., and Marie F. Marquardt. *Globalizing the Sacred: Religion across the Americas*. New Brunswick: Rutgers University Press, 2003.

Vázquez Santa Ana, Higinio. *Cristos célebres de México*. N.p., 1950.

Velasco Toro, José. *Santuario y región: Imágenes del Cristo Negro de Otatitlán*. Xalapa: Universidad Veracruzana, 1997.

Vetancurt, Augustín de, Juan Manuel de San Vicente, Juan de Viera, Antonio Rubial García, and Gonzalo Obregón. *La Ciudad de México en el siglo XVIII (1690–1780): Tres crónicas*. Mexico City: Consejo Nacional para la Cultura y las Artes, Dirección General de Publicaciones, 1990.

Videla, Gabriela. *Sergio Méndez Arceo: Un Señor Obispo*. Cuernavaca: Correo del Sur, 1982.

Vigil, José María. "What Remains of the Option for the Poor?" *TEP Update: South-South Dialogue and Exchange* (Cape Town) 7, no. 1 (1994).

Villaseñor y Sánchez, José Antonio de, and Ramón María Serrera Contreras. *Suplemento al Teatro americano: La ciudad de México en 1755*. Seville: Escuela de Estudios Hispanoamericanos del Consejo Superior de Investigaciones Científicas; Mexico City: Instituto de Investigaciones Históricas de la Universidad Nacional Autónoma de México, 1980.

Viqueira Albán, Juan Pedro. *Indios rebeldes e idólatras. Dos ensayos históricos sobre la rebelión india de Cancuc, Chiapas, acaecida en el año de 1712*. Mexico City: CIESAS, 1997.

———. *María de la Candelaria: India natural de Cancuc*. Mexico City: Fondo de Cultura Económica, 1993.

Virreinato, Museo Nacional del, and INAH. *Pintura Novohispana*, vol. 3, *Siglos XVII–XX*, part 2. Tepotzotlán: Asociación deAmigos del Museo del Museo Nacional del Virreinato, 1996.

Voekel, Pamela. *Alone before God: The Religious Origins of Modernity in Mexico*. Durham: Duke University Press, 2002.

———. "Peeing on the Palace: Bodily Resistance to Bourbon Reforms in Mexico City." *Journal of Historical Sociology* 5, no. 2 (1992): 183–208.

Vogt, Evan. *Tortillas for the Gods*. Cambridge, MA: Harvard University Press, 1976.

Wedig, Mark E. "The Visual Hermeneutics of Hispanic/Latino Popular Religion and the Recovery of the Image in Christian Praxis." *Journal of Hispanic and Latino Theology* 8, no. 3 (2001): 6–17.

Weismann, Elizabeth. *Mexico in Sculpture, 1521–1821*. Westport, Conn.: Greenwood, 1971.

Westheim, Paul. *La calavera*. 2nd ed. Mexico City: Era, 1971.

Wiethaus, Ulrike. *Maps of Flesh and Light: The Religious Experience of Medieval Women Mystics*. Syracuse: Syracuse University Press, 1993.

Wolf, Eric. *Sons of the Shaking Earth*. Chicago: University of Chicago Press, 1979.

———. "The Vicissitudes of the Closed Corporate Peasant Community." *American Ethnologist* 13, no. 2 (1986): 325–329.

Wood, Stephanie. "Adopted Saints: Christian Images in Nahua Testaments of Late Colonial Toluca." *The Americas* 47 (1991): 259–293.

———. "The Cosmic Conquest: Late Colonial Views of the Sword and Cross in Central Mexican Titulos." *Ethnohistory* 38 (1991): 176–195.

Wroth, William. *Images of Penance, Images of Mercy: Southwestern Santos in the Late Nineteenth Century*. Norman: Published for Taylor Museum for Southwestern Studies, Colorado Springs Fine Arts Center, by University of Oklahoma Press, 1991.

Zulaika, Joseba. *Basque Violence: Metaphor and Sacrament*. Reno: University of Nevada Press, 1988.

Index

LaVergne, TN USA
08 April 2010
178517LV00002B/3/P